PUBLIC PERSONNEL MANAGEMENT

CONTEXTS

AND

STRATEGIES

Third Edition

DONALD E. KLINGNER

Florida International University

JOHN NALBANDIAN

University of Kansas

PRENTICE HALL

Englewood Cliffs, New Jersey 07632

Library of Congress Cataloging-in-Publication Data

Klingner, Donald E.
    Public personnel management : contexts and strategies / Donald E.
Klingner, John Nalbandian. -- 3rd ed.
        p.   cm.
    Includes bibliographical references and index.
    ISBN 0-13-735259-X
    1. Civil service--Personnel management. 2. Personnel management.
3. Public administration.   I. Nalbandian, John, 1944-
II. Title.
JF1601.K56 1993
350.1--dc20
                                                        92-29018
                                                            CIP

Editorial/production supervision and
  interior design: Marielle Reiter
Cover design: Joe DiDomenico
Manufacturing buyer: Mary Ann Gloriande
Prepress buyer: Kelly Behr
Acquisitions editor: Julie Berrisford
Editorial assistant: Nicole Signoretti
Copy editor: Jeannine Ciliotta

© 1993, 1985, 1980 by Prentice-Hall, Inc.
A Simon & Schuster Company
Englewood Cliffs, New Jersey 07632

ISBN 0-13-735259-X

90000

Printed in the United States of America
10 9 8 7 6 5 4 3 2 1

ISBN 0-13-735259-X

9 780137 352593

Prentice-Hall International (UK) Limited, *London*
Prentice-Hall of Australia Pty. Limited, *Sydney*
Prentice-Hall Canada Inc., *Toronto*
Prentice-Hall Hispanoamericana, S.A., *Mexico*
Prentice-Hall of India Private Limited, *New Delhi*
Prentice-Hall of Japan, Inc., *Tokyo*
Simon & Schuster Asia Pte. Ltd., *Singapore*
Editora Prentice-Hall do Brasil, Ltda., *Rio de Janeiro*

CONTENTS

PART IV   DEVELOPMENT

Chapter 8   Improving Employee Performance through Leadership

Chapter 9   Training, Education, and Staff Development

Chapter 10   Performance Appraisal

PREFACE

Public personnel administration has always fascinated us as a field where values, politics, and techniques are joined in debates that fundamentally affect the planning, acquisition, development, and sanction (PADS) functions of a personnel system. The third edition builds on this perspective in three ways.

First, we have tried to acknowledge the tremendous pressures public employers face to increase productivity. To that end, after two new introductory chapters, Chapter 3 deals with the personnel activities that constitute the planning and evaluation function in human resources management, covering subjects like planning, budgeting, and productivity. Resource constraints and agency mission(s) are fundamental issues that must be decided by the larger budgetary and policy-making process before hiring can begin. While the issue of who gets jobs dominates the acquisition of human resources, the issue of overall size of public employment and the relative priorities of alternative programs are primary.

In addition, we have tried to extend the productivity discussion by asking how the demands for productivity interact with issues of workforce diversity and individual rights. We struggled with this discussion because the relationships are just emerging, and they are not clear enough to write about definitively. But that caution did not seem important enough to preclude raising the issues.

Second, we have reemphasized the legal aspects of human resources management and have included a new chapter on organizational justice. There are more references to legal cases throughout the new edition and more detailed explanation of those cases as a way of conveying the value conflicts that arise in organizations. The same value questions we tried to raise in the second edition are often rigorously debated in the Supreme Court opinions we describe in this edition. And just as the Court sometimes balances interests to achieve justice, we have accepted the premise that organizational justice is the product of agreement among stakeholders about the expectations and obligations of employees and employer.

Third, we have tried to break out of the mold that equates public personnel systems with merit systems. We acknowledge that merit systems—those that use knowledge, skills, abilities, and job performance as the basic criteria of decision making—are the most comprehensive and pervasive personnel systems in the public sector. This is because, over time, they have shown themselves to be the most effective at dealing with the range of functions required of personnel systems, as well as capable of incorporating competing values. But we realize that civil service systems exist side by side with, or interact with, competing personnel systems that have strong claims to legitimacy despite the fact that they do not deal with the complete range of personnel functions and represent values that may conflict with those supported by civil service systems. By identifying these different systems, we suggest that some or all of the core personnel functions—planning, acquisition, development, and sanction—are carried out differently in different personnel systems. Further, we try to show in this edition how different personnel systems or partial systems reflect different values.

In addition to these three major changes, we have placed less emphasis on a systems approach to understanding personnel administration. We have put aside the functional labels "procurement" and "allocation" in favor of more accepted and commonly used terminology, and as a means of emphasizing the primary importance of planning and budgeting in human resources management. We now speak of the "acquisition" of human resources rather than "procurement," and we discuss "planning" instead of "allocation."

We hope the changes in this edition reflect the challenges human resources managers face as well as our own understanding of the field. We have tested this edition in our own undergraduate and graduate classrooms, and we think it presents the field in a way that advanced undergraduate and graduate students can understand.

We would like to acknowledge the helpful and critical comments made by our students, who tested the clarity of the text and the validity of the exercises and case studies in class. We extend our appreciation to the reviewers who made a variety of suggestions about the manuscript: Sandra Biloon of the Barney School of Business and Public Administration; Tom Lewinsohn of the Department of Personnel of the City of Kansas City, Missouri; and Neil Reichenberg of the International Personnel Management Association of Alexandria, Virginia. We would like to thank Tom McFee and the staff at ASPER (DHHS), who contributed many ideas about developing a corporate human resource capability in public agencies, and John Palguta of the U.S. Merit Systems Protections Board for his guidance and the reports he shared with us. We would like to thank Sally Kraus Marshall, Donna Beecher, Barbara Wamsley, and Gary Brumback for assistance in clarifying the transition from job evaluation to evaluation of work and people. And we would like to thank the members and staff of the National Academy of Public Administration for exemplifying the ideals to which this book is dedicated—public service and good government.

Donald E. Klingner
John Nalbandian

I would like especially to thank my wife Janette and my children Amy, Heidi, and John. After all, our work and children are the only things that live beyond our life, and of these, children are the most rewarding.

Donald E. Klingner

I remind myself that I am fortunate that Don invited me to join him on the second edition after he alone had successfully authored the initial version. It speaks to his generosity, and I have benefited from it as I have from our long friendship. I would also like to recognize a few other special people. Tom Lewinsohn has been the personnel director in Kansas City, Missouri, for several years. He has shown me by example that frankness and personal integrity are essential to earning the respect of elected officials, administrative staff, and employees. Also, I would like especially to recognize my son and wife. John's ambition and Carol's modesty bring out the best in me.

John Nalbandian

CHAPTER

1

WELCOME TO THE WORLD
OF PUBLIC
PERSONNEL MANAGEMENT

INTRODUCTION

Public personnel management incorporates the policies and techniques
used to manage those who work in the public sector, the 17.5 million
Americans employed by some 80,000 units of government like cities, school
districts, states, and the federal government.

The fundamental political decisions about public personnel management influence who gets and who keeps public jobs. These jobs are scarce
resources in our society and there is intense competition for them not just
among individuals, but more broadly among advocates of competing public
personnel values and systems—political, civil service, collective bargaining,
and affirmative action. Therefore, the world of public personnel management is often characterized more by conflict and compromise than by cooperation and harmony.

By the end of this chapter, you will be able to:

1. Define the functions needed to manage human resources in public
   agencies (planning, acquisition, development, and sanction—PADS).

2. Explain why public jobs are scarce resources, and how scarcity adds dynamism and competition to the process of deciding who gets government jobs, and how they are allocated.
3. Describe the four values that underlie the conflict over public jobs in the United States (responsiveness, efficiency, individual rights, and social equity).
4. Define a personnel system as the set of laws, policies, and practices used to fulfill the four public personnel functions (PADS), and give examples of the four public personnel systems now operating in the United States (political, civil service, collective bargaining, and affirmative action).
5. Describe the history of public personnel management in the United States as a conflict among competing personnel systems and values.

PUBLIC PERSONNEL MANAGEMENT FUNCTIONS

Public personnel management consists of four fundamental functions through which elected officials, administrators, personnel specialists, and supervisors manage human resources. These functions, designated by the acronym PADS, are listed in Table 1-1, along with the activities that comprise them.

Budgeting and human resource planning are necessary to plan the work of public agencies. Describing, classifying, and evaluating jobs is necessary to allocate tasks to employees (also known as "position management"). The purpose of recruitment and selection is to acquire employees. Orienting, training, motivating, and evaluating employees helps develop their knowledge, skills, and abilities. Finally, the sanction function serves to establish and maintain expectations and obligations that employees and employers have toward one another, realized daily through discipline and grievance procedures.

TABLE 1-1 Public Personnel Management Functions

FUNCTION	PURPOSE
Planning	Budget and human resource planning; dividing tasks among employees; deciding how much jobs are worth; position management
Acquisition	Recruitment and selection of employees
Development	Orienting, training, motivating, and evaluating employees to increase their knowledge, skills, and abilities
Sanction	Establishing and maintaining expectations and obligations that employees and the employer have toward one another

PUBLIC JOBS AS SCARCE RESOURCES

Basic decisions about public personnel management are important because jobs are the most visible way we measure economic and social status for individuals and groups in the United States. Public jobs are scarce resources because they are limited by tax revenues, and they have enormous significance for the course of public policy making generally. Because public jobs are scarce and important, there is intense competition for them among individuals and more broadly among advocates of competing public personnel values and systems. Each system is supported by specific values and beliefs that have played important roles in the history of public personnel management in the United States. These systems often compete and interact within public agencies to influence the process by which individual employees are hired, paid, developed, and controlled. The allocation of public jobs, both in broad public policy terms and in specific cases involving a single individual, is the issue that shapes the way the four functions are carried out and focuses conflict among the four competing values.

COMPETING VALUES

Public personnel management may be seen as the continuous interaction among four fundamental societal values that often conflict. The goal of much public policy making is to develop compromises among two or more of the values. The goal of those who must actually carry out the policies is to develop and implement rules, regulations, procedures, and practices that will effectively fulfill the four functions within a spirit of compromise.

1.   *Responsiveness* is the belief that government answers to the will of the people expressed through elected officials. Political and personal loyalty to elected officials are best ensured through an appointment process that considers political loyalty, along with education and experience, as indicators of merit. Often, in order to promote responsive government, the filling of a number of public jobs is made the prerogative of authorized elected officials.

The decision to contract out for goods or services is often made on two levels—an explicit level based on the objective of obtaining goods or services more efficiently, and an implicit level based on the desire to reward the prospective contractor for support of a candidate or elected official. Examples of contracts awarded on the basis of both explicit and implicit criteria include procurement of weapons by the military from private defense contractors, state highway construction and maintenance, or the privatization of solid waste or transportation services by local governments.

2. *Efficiency* is the desire to maximize the ratio of inputs to outputs in any management process. This value is captured in the phrase "the biggest bang for the buck." In the personnel world, efficiency means that decisions about who to hire, reassign, or promote should be based on the knowledge, skills, and abilities (KSAs) of applicants and employees. Merit is defined traditionally in terms of KSAs and performance rather than political loyalty.

Efficient service is often best achieved through privatization and contracting out, rather than through public agencies and employees, because of the belief that the private sector's profit motive and emphasis on the bottom line (reduction of unnecessary personnel costs) enables it to provide services more cheaply.

3. *Individual rights* emphasize that individual citizens will be protected from unfair actions of government officials. These rights are protected by the Bill of Rights as well as the Fourteenth Amendment to the Constitution. In addition to these legal protections, public employees' rights are maintained through job security and due process (civil service), and through merit system rules and regulations that protect public employees from inappropriate partisan political pressure (such as requiring them to campaign for elected officials or contribute a portion of their salary toward election campaigns, or run the risk of losing their jobs if they refuse), and provide job security and due process. In a parallel fashion, public employees who are union members will have recourse to work rules, contained in collective bargaining agreements, that protect them from arbitrary management decisions.

4. *Social equity* is the belief that individuals should be accorded preference in selection and promotion in public positions based on previous sacrifices (veterans) or discrimination (minorities and women) that prevent them from competing fairly for jobs. Like individual rights, social equity is concerned with fairness. But unlike individual rights, it is the social aspect of equity that provides its group orientation. Social equity emphasizes fairness to groups like women, racial minorities, the disabled, and veterans, groups that would otherwise be disadvantaged by a market economy that accepts the legitimacy of discrimination in hiring and in pay scales.

COMPETING PERSONNEL SYSTEMS

Personnel systems consist of the laws, policies, rules, regulations and practices through which personnel functions (PADS) are fulfilled. There are several basic public personnel systems: political systems, civil service, collective bargaining, and affirmative action. Civil service is the predominant system, and the only complete system (because it includes all four functions and can incorporate all four competing values).

Political Systems

Political systems are those where personnel functions and decisions are carried out with political motives and objectives uppermost. They are characterized by legislative or executive approval of individual hiring decisions, particularly for policy-making positions. In federal and state governments, for example, cabinet members and other directors of administrative agencies are political appointees. Their appointments are called political appointments, or excepted appointments. Political appointees serve at the discretion of those who appoint them; they may be fired at any time, particularly if successful job performance depends on political philosophy or loyalty.

Contracting out for public services may fall into the political system because the decision to contract out, and the choice of contractor, both are at least partly motivated by politics as well as concerns for efficiency. And even if the contract bid and selection process is run fairly (with sealed bids and an objective analysis of contractors' qualifications), contracting out is still political because private sector personnel policies and practices differ in many respects from those of civil service systems based on merit. For example, hiring and promotion decisions in the private sector are more likely to be determined by a manager's preference rather than the applicant's KSAs. It is usually simpler to dismiss or transfer private sector employees. Pay equity is less likely in the private sector, compared with the public. And a more elaborate set of employee rights is likely to accompany public employment compared with that in the private sector, except where union contracts are in place.

The contracting out system is supported by legislators, elected officials, and many private sector interest groups who compete to decide what services shall be contracted out, how many jobs will be involved, and who will receive the contracts—political supporters or those who have not made any contributions.

Civil Service System

Civil service systems are designed with two objectives: the enhancement of administrative efficiency and the maintenance of employee rights. Proponents of civil service systems think that staffing public agencies rationally (based on jobs needed to carry out specific programs and the KSAs needed to accomplish these goals), and treating employees fairly are the best ways to maintain an efficient and professional public service. This means giving them good pensions and health benefits; giving them equal pay for work of comparable worth; hiring and promoting them on the basis of KSAs; treating them impartially once on the job; and protecting them from partisan political influences.

Overall policy objectives of civil service systems are controlled by elected officials, who often appoint agency heads responsible for managing the bureaucracy. The legislature (Congress, a state legislature, or a local governing body) maintains control over resources by limiting the total number of employees an agency can hire, staffing levels in particular agencies or programs, and the personnel budget (money allocated for wages, salaries, and benefits).

Civil service systems are supported by citizens and groups who want to keep "politics" out of public personnel decisions and run government like a business, by employees holding civil service jobs, by job applicants seeking fair consideration for public jobs, and by federal court decisions that uphold the job security rights of civil service employees. Together, these outcomes are considered desirable by those who support the notion of a professional public service as the best way to achieve the values of efficiency and individual rights and a bureaucracy responsive to political direction.

Collective Bargaining Systems

Collective bargaining is a specialized personnel system that exists within civil service systems. Under collective bargaining, employees negotiate with management over such items as wages, benefits, and conditions of employment. In all cases, contracts negotiated between an agency's managers and leaders of the union representing its employees are subject to the approval of the appropriate legislative body (Congress, a state legislature, a county or city commission, or a school board), because these political bodies are the only ones who can legally make a policy decision. Contracts may also provide for additional protections for individual employees against disciplinary action or discharge, an obvious indication of the intermingling of civil service and collective bargaining systems. Because some overlap exists in the grievance procedures available under civil service and collective bargaining systems, employees are usually required to select one procedure, but not both.

Collective bargaining systems are supported by employee organizations (unions or professional associations). They reflect the values of individual rights (of union members). Even though collective bargaining is commonly associated with negotiation over wages, the primary motive is to ensure equitable treatment by management.

Affirmative Action Systems

Affirmative action is a specialized personnel system that usually exists within civil service systems. For the affirmative action system to operate, the governmental jurisdiction must have acknowledged an imbalance in the percentage of minorities in its workforce and those qualified minorities in a relevant labor force. Alternatively, members of a group protected against discrimination may have sued the public employer, resulting in a judicial ruling requiring the agency to give special consideration to members of the "protected class" in various personnel decisions, especially hiring and promotion.

Affirmative action is supported by female, minority, and handicapped job applicants and employees; and by the interest groups supporting them. It is also supported by social equity advocates who contend that the efficacy of representative democracy depends upon the existence of a representative bureaucracy.

SYSTEMS IN COLLISION: A CONCEPTUAL ANALYSIS OF THE HISTORY OF PUBLIC PERSONNEL MANAGEMENT

We have seen that public personnel management consists of the four human resource management functions (planning, acquisition, development, and sanction) carried out within public agencies. These functions are carried out differently in different personnel systems. The personnel systems themselves are influenced by the values of those contending for public jobs. Figure 1-1 shows this relationship: While civil service systems predominate, several basic systems (including political systems, civil service, collective bargaining, and affirmative action) might be present in any public organization, and in theory each system would shape some personnel activities in a different way. Each system proposes alternative processes for deciding who gets public jobs, and is supported by at least one of four competing values (responsiveness, efficiency, individual rights, and social equity).

When the governing body consists primarily of advocates of one personnel system and the values it enhances, personnel systems tend to have a clear and recognizable influence on the entire range of personnel functions. For example, a governing body dominated by union supporters would be expected to protect union jobs and resist privatization, contracting out, and political appointments. A governing body dominated by partisan political interests could be expected to attempt to fill public jobs or award contracts for political gain. A governing body influenced by racially or ethnically dominated neighborhood groups might advocate political influence over hiring practices and affirmative action. Finally, a municipal governing body elected to achieve "good government" would probably favor civil service systems for the city.

FIGURE 1-1 Values, Systems and Functions in Public Personnel Management

Values $\longrightarrow$ Personnel Systems $\longrightarrow$ PADS

When the governing body consists of advocates of each of these alternative personnel systems and values, the actual practice of personnel management in government agencies may be weak, unstable, or poorly articulated—that is, different systems may have a differential impact on different personnel functions. Disagreements over individual selection and promotion decisions reflect more basic disagreements over the criteria (decision rules) by which scarce public jobs should be allocated. Or personnel policies and practices may operate at two levels—an ideal level of desirable law, rules, and practice; and actual practices that may not be supported by law and regulations, but are widely used by personnel specialists and line managers to get the job done. For example, an agency may maintain an elaborate affirmative action system to give the appearance of complying with affirmative action law, but its actual selections may reflect the biases of managers who make the hiring decisions. Or an agency may engage in collective bargaining, but do so in bad faith because it is really more interested in undercutting the union by privatizing the service (and laying off the employees who are union members). In these circumstances, public personnel management becomes highly politicized.

Over time, personnel systems will reflect the dominant values in a particular jurisdiction. The more stable the values, the more permanent the personnel system and practices will become. The history of public personnel management can be understood as the dynamics of competition among these four systems and their underlying values. Although several alternative systems—or all four—can be present in an agency simultaneously, in reality one or two systems are dominant within society—and the culture of the organization—at any one time. What follows is a historical analysis of public personnel management in the United States, based on the dynamism of competing systems.

Political Systems

President Andrew Jackson articulated a philosophy of patronage following his election in 1828. It was his view that public jobs in the federal sector were quite simple to master, and that they belonged to the common people. Jackson's election roughly coincided with the development of political parties, and signaled the birth of the spoils system, which rewarded party members and campaign workers with jobs once their candidate was elected.

The spoils system expanded as the functions of government and the number of government employees grew after the Civil War (1861–1865). Political "machines" developed in big cities, supported by newly arrived immigrants. These systems were designed from the street level up, with precinct workers, district committees, assembly districts, and county committees arranged in a sort of political hierarchy whose mission was to nominate candidates and win elections. With electoral victory of candidates who had been nominated in conventions of loyalist delegates came the opportunity and obligation to dispense patronage or public jobs to those who had worked hardest for the party. Party loyalty would be verified, a political clearance might be issued, and in return the new jobholder would pay (often monthly) a "voluntary" assessment to the party. This went to pay the party officials who had provided the job, and to finance future election campaigns.

The political patronage system had many virtues. While it did not result in the selection of highly qualified employees or efficient government services, it did help millions of immigrants make the transition from rural areas of countries like Germany, Italy, Poland, and Ireland to life in cities like New York, Boston, Philadelphia, and Chicago. Effective party machines, partisan political leaders (often serving as role models because they were of the same culture and language as the immigrants they represented), and local precinct workers brought government to these people. In some cases, "government" was the help they needed to survive—baskets of food when they had none, buckets of coal in the winter, help in paying for weddings and funerals, help filling out immigration and voter registration forms, and sometimes a job with the city gas company or street repair department when one became available. The patron also showed more recent immigrants that assimilation into the alien American culture was the key to economic, social, and political power. In return, the party asked only for each person's vote, for loyalty, and for a small percentage (say 2%) of salary from patronage jobs.

Reaction against political patronage systems focused at the federal level in 1883 when the assassination of newly elected President Garfield by a disappointed job seeker caused an outpouring of criticism against the inefficiencies of the spoils system. But patronage remained a powerful force at the state and local levels.[1] In 1888, when New York City comprised only Manhattan and a slice of the Bronx, the Tweed Ring (a political machine) controlled some 12,000 jobs and a $6 million payroll. During the 1960s, many county sheriff's deputies throughout the East and Midwest were political appointees. The county sheriff is an elected position. Newly elected sheriffs routinely discharged the patronage employees appointed by their predecessors and replaced them with their own appointees, who received their jobs on the basis of having supported the sheriff's candidacy—and sometimes because of an informal commitment to "voluntarily" return a percentage of their salaries to the sheriff as a direct political contribution, or as a disguised contribution through the purchase of tickets to political dinners or other fundraising events. The same system prevailed for appointments in many state agencies, such as transportation, public works, and corrections.

Although elected officials and other supporters of patronage systems defended the contributions as voluntary, in reality employees who quit making contributions risked losing their jobs, because local party leaders declined to give them the political clearance they needed to certify their loyalty for the patronage position.[2]

There are several good reasons why political patronage systems have been popular throughout most of our nation's history. First, both elected officials and scholars have defended the need for elected officials to achieve partisan political objectives by placing loyal supporters in key confidential and policy-making positions within administrative agencies. Otherwise, there is no way that these agencies or their actions will be responsive to the mandates of the electorate. Second, elected officials have always viewed public jobs as one of the rewards they have available to encourage financial contributions and other forms of political support. And there is often no clear distinction between legitimate and illegitimate rewards. For example, if the director of a state human service agency calls a subordinate and brings to his attention the job application of the wife of a contributor to the governor's upcoming campaign, is this unacceptable political meddling, or a harmless effort to maintain political responsiveness by ensuring that a qualified yet politically connected applicant receives an opportunity to be considered for the job? Or if a county commissioner calls the director of the county planning department to ask that favorable consideration be given to an upcoming request for a zoning variance by a developer who is also a major campaign contributor, is this corruption, or a sign of accessible government decisions? Or is it something in between, something Plunkett of Tammany Hall would have called "honest graft?"

Elected officials get elected—and reelected—by providing voters with access to bureaucrats who often seem not to understand that rules must sometimes be bent, or broken, for voters to feel that justice has been done. Elected officials have always defended patronage jobs as necessary to the survival of a strong political party system: Without jobs to distribute as rewards, how can parties earn the loyalty and financial support they need to run campaigns and win elections? Unless they get many smaller contributions from grateful patronage employees, candidates are forced to rely on larger contributions from fewer interest groups, making them more indebted to lobbyists or interest groups with narrow objectives.

It is often hard to draw a clear distinction between political appointments and those resulting from civil service or affirmative action systems. For example, is a civil service employee who buys a ticket to a political fundraising dinner making a voluntary contribution reflecting a constitutional right to political expression and association, or a coerced decision reflecting the belief that the cost of the ticket is less than the risk of negative job consequences? And what about appeals by United Way local board members—who also happen to be CEOs of major public and private employers—for pledges by employees, with considerable pressure from supervisors to have all the employees in a work unit contribute? Are these pledges voluntary, or are they implicitly coerced by prominent administrators who have been invited to become board members—and to enjoy the social status and recognition this brings—in return for their ability to generate support from their agencies' employees?

The boundary between political appointments and affirmative action is equally difficult to draw in some cases. For example, in a city characterized by ethnic or racial tensions, the choice of a black or Hispanic police chief may be widely perceived as affecting not only the political strength of various groups, but also the policies of the police department with respect to patrol techniques, citizen complaints, and so on.

Although patronage systems have always been a part of public personnel management, they enjoyed a resurgence in the 1980s at all levels of government due to increasing emphasis on political control of bureaucracies, contracting out, and privatization. Contracting out is simply the purchase of goods or services (such as cars, office supplies, military weapons systems, or computers) from private sector firms. Public agencies can also contract to purchase services (such as police, fire, and rescue service) from other public agencies. Privatization, on the other hand, is the management and operation of historically public functions by private contractors. A municipal parks department may decide it is more efficient to divest itself of a municipal golf course by selling it to a private contractor. Or a municipal solid waste department may be abolished and the collection and recycling activities taken over by a private waste disposal company with its own management, trucks, and employees. Privatization experiments are being conducted for many traditional public services—for example, Texas and Tennessee are experimenting with privatized prison systems.

It is important to remember that whatever the merits of contracting out or privatization in terms of productivity or efficiency, they always allocate jobs from the public sector to the private sector, or to quasi-public grant-funded agencies that are hybrids of civil service and patronage systems. So these contracts can easily become political currency. While the rhetoric of privatizing or contracting out may be to provide services more efficiently, the underlying reason may be to provide a contract to political supporters of one or more elected officials, or to break a powerful union by sending a message to its negotiators that the governing body may react to pressure for wage or benefit increases by deciding to privatize the activity and lay off the workers instead. A decision not to privatize or contract out may signal the strength of employee unions or professional groups.

Nor is the boundary between politics and efficient administration easy to determine. Privatization and contracting out raise larger questions about the professionalism of government. They result in a shift in the focus of performance evaluation from the work unit and its individual employees by management, to the legislative evaluation of a contractor's compliance with contract provisions. Granted, contracting out may be a more efficient means of performing a public service. But if a county commissioner resigns in order to bid successfully on a contract (which happened recently with a handicapped transportation services contract in Broward County, Florida), is this an example of greater efficiency or merely political corruption and conflict of interest?

Legal guidelines do not necessarily provide clear answers to these questions. The Supreme Court has clearly decided that individual employees in state or local government administrative agencies may not be removed from positions for patronage reasons, with the exception of positions where political affiliation can make a difference in job performance. But it has also refused to review state court decisions upholding the exclusion of many employees from administrative agency designation. For example, county sheriff's deputies in Broward County, Florida (Fort Lauderdale) are hired and fired "at will" because they are considered judicial employees. Their Dade County (Miami) counterparts, fifteen miles to the south, are given civil service protection because they are classified as administrative employees within a unified city-county (charter) form of government. Civil service employees have no legal basis (under civil service laws or collective bargaining agreements) to protest job privatization or contracting out through the courts. Though these decisions result in job loss for groups of employees in the affected areas, this job loss is related to overall issues of funding and government structure, not to individual disciplinary action for cause.

Civil Service Systems

Civil service or "merit" systems arose out of public outrage at the waste and inefficiency of political patronage systems. By the 1880s, the federal government had grown larger and more complex as additional cabinet-level departments were added to acknowledge the importance of agriculture, interstate commerce, and protection of natural resources (Interior). Along with this increased size and complexity of federal activities came a growing public recognition that public jobs were not simply the spoils of office. Rather, they were technically or professionally demanding positions of public trust. They should therefore be allocated and rewarded on the basis of the knowledge, skills, and abilities of jobholders and applicants, rather than on the basis of political loyalty or party affiliation. Civil service systems were initiated in major eastern states such as New York and Pennsylvania during the 1880s, but the event that galvanized public attention was the assassination of President Garfield by a disgruntled office seeker in 1883, which led immediately to the passage of the Pendleton Act by Congress.

A civil service system consists of a body of impersonal rules that grow out of the principles listed in Table 1-2.

TABLE 1–2 Civil Service System Principles

1. Recruitment should be from qualified individuals from appropriate sources in an endeavor to achieve a workforce from all segments of society, and selection and advancement should be determined solely on the basis of relative ability, knowledge, and skills, after fair and open competition which assures that all receive equal opportunity.

2. All employees and applicants for employment should receive fair and equitable treatment in all aspects of personnel management without regard to political affiliation, race, color, religion, national origin, sex, marital status, age, or handicapping condition, and with proper regard for their privacy and constitutional rights.

3. Equal pay should be provided for work of equal value with appropriate consideration of both national and local rates paid by employers in the private sector, and appropriate incentives and recognition should be provided for excellence in performance.

4. All employees should maintain high standards of integrity, conduct and concern for the public interest.

5. The work force should be used efficiently and effectively.

6. Employees should be retained on the basis of the adequacy of their performance, inadequate performance should be corrected, and employees should be separated who cannot or will not improve their performance to meet required standards.

7. Employees should be provided effective education and training in cases in which such education and training would result in better organizational and individual performance.

8. Employees should be:
(a) protected against arbitrary action, personal favoritism, or coercion for partisan political purposes.
(b) prohibited from using their official authority or influence for the purpose of interfering with or affecting the result on an election or a nomination for election.

9. Employees should be protected against reprisal for the lawful disclosure of information which the employees reasonably believe evidences:
(a) a violation of any law, rule, or regulation,
(b) mismanagement, a gross waste of funds, an abuse of authority, or a substantial and specific danger to public health or safety.

Source: Civil Service Reform Act of 1978.

The period between 1883 and 1937 is important in the development of public personnel administration based on merit principles. These principles of merit and political neutrality reflect what Hugh Heclo has identified as the civil service ideal—the principle that a competent, committed workforce of career civil servants is essential to the professional conduct of the public's business.[3] While the Pendleton Act of 1883 espoused efficiency as well as the elimination of politics from personnel decisions, efficient methods of recruiting, selecting, and paying employees were not available then. The application of science to administration in the twentieth century began to provide the tools, for example, in the areas of selection and position classification. The U.S. Army's experience with selecting officer candidates during World War I gave birth to the field of personnel measurement and testing. Because of the need to select candidates with the necessary skills and abilities to become officers, and to not waste training resources (or to allow those lacking these critical skills and abilities to make risky battlefield decisions), psychologists developed aptitude, ability, and performance tests that were carried over into the private industrial sector during the 1920s.

Position classification is often cited as the cornerstone of public personnel management not only because of its centrality among personnel functions, but also because it epitomizes the connection between efficiency and the elimination of politics from administration. It suggests that public personnel management can be conducted in a routine and politically neutral fashion. This provides merit systems with their philosophical attraction, even if the precept is less than accurate in practice.

For management, position classification offers a uniform basis for grouping jobs by occupational type and skill level, an equitable and logical pay plan based on the KSAs (knowledge, skills, and abilities) needed to perform the job, translates labor costs (for pay and benefits) into impersonal grades that can be added, subtracted, averaged, and moved about to create organizational charts; it clarifies career ladders, and it aids in the recruitment, selection, training, and assessment processes through its specification of duties and qualifications for each position.

At the same time, it can be used to minimize political or administrative abuse and to protect individual rights with regard to personnel functions. Pay rates are tied to positions, so individual favorites cannot be paid more than others. The work to be performed is specified in a job description. Thus, hiring people at a high salary and asking them to assume few responsibilities—which occurs frequently in political patronage positions—is minimized. Budgets are allocated in terms of positions, so ceilings can be established to preclude hiring. Units may be assigned an average allowable position grade, thus ensuring that they will not become top heavy.

The relationship between political patronage systems and civil service systems is intermittently marked by intense conflict, for both systems represent powerful and equally legitimate values—responsiveness and efficiency. Further, the relationship between politics and administration centers around the enduring question of how governments can bring expertise to bear on the development of public policy while retaining the supremacy of political values.

For example, the tremendous economic, military, and social problems confronting the United States during the New Deal and World War II (1933–1945) brought about the emergence of administrative effectiveness, which combines the scientific principle of efficiency with the political principle of accomplishing objectives demanded by events. This combination of efficiency and effectiveness required that most positions be covered by the civil service system, but that sensitive or policy-making positions be filled by political appointees who were either personally or politically responsive to the elected officials who appointed them. This represented a new kind of patronage, one made to foster program goals in addition to maintenance of party strength and executive-legislative relationships. It resulted in programs consistent with elected officials' philosophy and vision of government, and with administrators' ability to make operational plans and manage resources efficiently (including human resources).

Inevitably, the predominance of administrative effectiveness as a hybrid of politics and efficiency created strains in the civil service reform model of public personnel management, which had been based on the fundamental distinction between politics and administration. The civil service model viewed personnel management as a neutral administrative function; the effectiveness model viewed it as a management-oriented function under the direction of the executive branch. Administrators saw the need for effectiveness, but were loathe to return to the politics of the patronage system as the only alternative to civil service systems.[4]

Given the obvious need for politically responsive agency management, one might wonder why civil service systems pay so much attention to protection from political influence. The reason is that incidents which occur frequently indicate that elected officials consider political loyalty the most important criterion for selection to administrative positions, regardless of the applicants' KSAs. Two examples should suffice.

The National Endowment for the Arts came under heavy attack in 1990 from conservative Republican Senator Jesse Helms because of its sponsorship of art exhibitions containing works some observers considered pornographic or supportive of homosexuality. The director of the NEA found himself under fire from conservatives (who objected to public support of "unacceptable" art), and from artists (who considered this censorship). Under these circumstances, the director's qualifications were less important than his ability to walk a political tightrope between the two positions.

A more prosaic incident involved Jewell V. "Buck" Pleake, employed in a patronage position as a shop foreman for the Indiana State Highway Commission (department). Mr. Pleake was fired in 1974 because he quit making "voluntary" political contributions to the Republican party, which had given him political clearance for the job. He contacted the head of the Indiana State Employees Association, who asked Governor Otis Bowen to clarify his ambiguous role as chief administrative officer of the state and symbolic head of the political party that had elected him governor.

Much of the history of public personnel management can be viewed as efforts to reconcile civil service and patronage systems at an operational level. The Pendleton Act (1883) created the civil service system at the federal level, leading eventually to the development and implementation of civil service systems for a majority of professional and technical positions.

The Civil Service Reform Act (CSRA) of 1978, passed almost a century later, was designed to maintain bureaucratic responsiveness but still protect the career civil service from political interference. It created a Senior Executive Service (SES) of supergrade (GS-16 to GS-18) administrators who voluntarily elected to leave their civil service positions in return for multiyear performance contracts, in exchange for the possibility of higher salaries and greater career challenge and flexibility. As might have been expected, the results of the CSRA are mixed. Some administrators successfully made the transition to SES appointments and received performance bonuses. Other administrators, and impartial observers, felt that the system was flawed from the beginning because of inadequate rewards, unclear performance standards, political pressure on career civil servants to join the SES, and inadequate training for new SES members to teach them how to function in an environment where productivity and control over expenses were more important than they had been in traditional civil service positions.

The CSRA did establish that public personnel management agencies had at least two contradictory objectives—protecting employee rights and making agencies politically responsive—which required that the old federal Civil Service Commission be split into two agencies, the Merit Systems Protection Board (MSPB) and the Office of Personnel Management (OPM). The MSPB is responsible for hearing appeals from employees alleging that their rights under civil service system laws and rules have been violated; the OPM is responsible for developing and implementing personnel policies within federal agencies.

Collective Bargaining Systems

Public personnel management began with political patronage systems, developed greater efficiency and protection from partisanship as civil service (merit) systems emerged, and then moved to a hybrid of these opposing systems (administrative effectiveness). During the 1960s and 1970s a third personnel system came to the fore in the public sector—collective bargaining. While all public employees covered by collective bargaining agreements are also covered by civil service systems, under collective bargaining the terms and conditions of employment are set by direct contract negotiations between agency management and unions (or employee organizations). This is in contrast to the patronage system, where they are set and operationally influenced by elected officials, or the civil service system, where they are set by law and regulations issued by management and administered by management or an outside authority (such as a civil service board).

Collective bargaining in the public sector has many of the same procedures as its private sector counterpart, such as contract negotiations and grievance procedures. But fundamental differences in law and power outweigh these similarities. Public-sector unions never have the right to negotiate binding contracts with respect to wages, benefits, or other economic issues. The right to approve (or disapprove) negotiated contracts is reserved to the appropriate legislative body (city council, school board, state legislature) because only legislatures are policy-making bodies with the authority to appropriate money to fund contracts. This means that both labor and management realize that ratification of negotiated contracts is more critical than negotiation of them, and set their political strategies accordingly. Second, the closed shop, where employees have to join a union to be eligible for employment, is common in private sector trade and craft unions throughout the United States. But federal and state laws have uniformly considered this an illegal abridgement of an employee's constitutional rights to join (or not join) an organization as a condition of employment. So many public employees are "free riders"—they are covered by the terms of a collective bargaining agreement, but they are not dues-paying union members.

Collective bargaining systems emphasize the protection of individual employee rights through emphasis on seniority as the sole criterion governing layoffs, eligibility for overtime, eligibility for training or apprenticeship programs, and even promotions. Naturally, collective bargaining systems in their extreme manifestations are opposed by both patronage and civil service proponents because collective bargaining poses an alternative model for the allocation and retention of jobs.

Affirmative Action Systems

Affirmative action systems arose in the public sector as a direct result of the civil rights movement of the 1960s and the women's rights movement of the 1970s. They were based on the observation that public- and private-sector personnel systems frequently discriminated against minorities and women (sometimes deliberately, and at other times inadvertently). They were supported by the fundamental beliefs that a representative bureaucracy was essential for our government to function as a democracy; and that other personnel systems had not been effective at ensuring proportional representation.[5] In fact, all these systems had worked (albeit for different reasons) to perpetuate the dominance of white males. Because patronage systems are based on personal and political loyalty, and since most elected officials are white males, appointments of white males to patronage jobs are the rule. Civil service systems favor education and experience, which traditionally have been a strength of white males who have access to higher education and managerial positions. And the seniority systems favored by collective bargaining tend to perpetuate the racist or sexist bias toward the selection of white males that was so frequent until the civil rights movement of the 1960s.

Affirmative action systems are controlled by state and federal administrative agencies, which are responsible for monitoring compliance with affirmative action laws by public agencies or contractors. This system takes effect when a gross disparity exists between the percentage of minority or female employees in an agency and their percentage in a relevant labor pool (such as the community served by that agency, or the percentage of applicants qualified for the position), and when the agency has resisted the voluntary adoption of techniques (such as recruitment, selection, training, or promotion) that would reduce this disparity. In such a case, members of the affected class may sue the agency to force it to take affirmative action in the selection or retention of women or minority group members. If success-ful, these court efforts may result in considerable judicial control of the agency's personnel system. The court can require an agency to hire or promote specific numbers or percentages of underutilized groups (qualified females or minority group members) until their representation in the agency work force is more proportionate with their representation in the community. Thus, state and federal courts are also responsible for implementation and enforcement of affirmative action laws.

Speaking realistically, there are some legal and political limits to this control. Given the current composition of the Supreme Court, and the fact that most Justices consider quotas to be a violation of the individual rights of applicants who are not members of a protected class, the federal court system is not likely to compel federal or state agencies to observe hiring quotas. The Court cannot compel affirmative action compliance for legisla-tive or judicial positions. It cannot require an agency to hire minority or women employees if agency managers elect not to fill any vacancies, or to retain minority and women employees in civil service positions if funds are not available to do so. But because courts have the ultimate authority to adjudicate conflicts within our political system, they can effectively influ-ence the manner in which the other three public personnel systems oper-ate. They can discourage avoidance of affirmative action compliance by requiring agencies to justify the transfer of positions to political patronage systems; they can order the abandonment of civil service rules or tech-niques that have a disparate effect on women and minorities; and they can abrogate collective bargaining agreements that use seniority rules to per-petuate previous patterns of racism or sexism.

Table 1-3 illustrates the history of public personnel management as the conflict and compromise among four competing public personnel sys-tems (and one hybrid), each championing one or more underlying values. Like all conceptual analyses of history, it oversimplifies reality for the sake of intellectual clarity. And it is important to remember that civil service systems are the dominant system because they perform all the personnel functions (PADS) and can incorporate all the values.

Conflict among values and public personnel systems is limited and regulated by the dynamic realities of the competition itself. Because jobs

TABLE 1-3 The Interplay of Systems, Values, and History

PUBLIC PERSONNEL SYSTEM	UNDERLYING VALUE	ERA OF DOMINANCE
Patronage	Responsiveness	1828–1882
Civil service	Efficiency, individual rights	1883–1933
Administrative effectiveness (hybrid)	Responsiveness, efficiency	1934–present
Collective bargaining	Individual rights	1970–1980
Affirmative action	Social equity	1964–1980

and resources are finite, jobs allocated through one system cannot be allocated through others. This means that the ultimate conflict among values and systems may require resolution at a micro level with each specific selection decision.

Each value, carried to its extreme, creates distortions that limit the effectiveness of human resources management because other values are artificially suppressed. This means that attempts by each system or value to dominate lead inevitably to stabilizing reactions and value compromises. For example, responsiveness carried to extremes results in the hiring of employees solely on the basis of patronage, without regard for other qualifications; or in the awarding of contracts based solely on political considerations (graft and corruption). Efficiency, carried to extremes, results in overrationalized personnel procedures—for example, going to decimal points on test scores to make selection or promotion decisions, or making the selection process rigid in the belief that systematic procedures will produce the "best" candidate. Individual rights, carried to extremes, results in overemphasis on seniority, or overemphasis on due process and rigid disciplinary procedures (as opposed to the rights of the public, managers, and other employees to have employees who are competent, diligent, and not liability risks). And social equity, carried to extremes, results in personnel decisions being made solely on the basis of group membership, disregarding individual merit or the need for efficient and responsive government.

SUMMARY

Public personnel management can be viewed from several perspectives. First, it is the functions (planning, acquisition, development, and sanction) needed to manage human resources in public agencies. Second, it is the process by which a scarce resource (public jobs) is allocated. Third, it reflects the influence of four competing values (political responsiveness, efficiency, individual rights, and social equity) over how public jobs should be allocated. Fourth, it is the laws, rules, and regulations used to express these abstract values—personnel systems (political appointments, civil service, collective bargaining, and affirmative action). The history of public personnel management in the United States can be understood conceptually as the conflict among competing personnel systems and values.

KEY TERMS

administrative effectiveness
affirmative action
Civil Service Reform Act (1978)
civil service (merit) system
collective bargaining
contracting out
efficiency
individual rights
KSAs (knowledge, skills and abilities)
merit system
Merit Systems Protection Board (MSPB)
PADS (planning, acquisition, development, sanction)
Pendleton Act (1883)
personnel management
political patronage
position management
privatization
public personnel system
representative bureaucracy
responsiveness
scientific management
Senior Executive Service (SES)
social equity
spoils system
U.S. Office of Personnel Management (OPM)
values

DISCUSSION QUESTIONS

1. What are the four public personnel management functions (PADS)?
2. Why are public jobs scarce resources?
3. What are the four competing values that affect the allocation of public jobs?
4. What is a public personnel system?
5. What are the four competing public personnel systems?

CASE STUDY: VALUES AND FUNCTIONS IN PUBLIC PERSONNEL MANAGEMENT

Identify the appropriate value(s) and the personnel functions in the following examples.

1. A state is going to fill a vacancy in its community development agency. The state representative who controls the appropriations committee for all legislation involving the agency has suggested the position be filled by an applicant from her district. A major contributor to the governor's reelection campaign contends that the job ought to be filled by a prominent real estate developer. Neither candidate has the education or experience specified as desirable in the job description.

2. A federal agency is considering a layoff. It anticipates a budget shortfall that is going to require cutbacks in personnel. The agency director has suggested that a layoff score be computed for each employee, based primarily on the person's performance appraisal. The Federation of Federal Employees, which is the recognized bargaining agent for the agency's employees, strongly objects and proposes that the layoffs be based on seniority.

3. A county anticipates a request by surrounding cities to provide water services for all county residents. This will require upgrading the skills of a substantial number of county employees and will provide those employees with opportunities for advancement. The union insists that the training slots be allocated to current employees on a seniority basis. The affirmative action officer, seeing this as an opportunity to increase the number of minorities in higher paying positions, proposes that several of the openings be set aside for current minority employees.

NOTES

[1]William L. Riordan, *Plunkett of Tammany Hall* (New York: Dutton, 1963).

[2]Donald Klingner, *Public Personnel Management: Contexts and Strategies* (Englewood Cliffs, NJ: Prentice-Hall, 1980), Chap. 1.

[3]Hugh A. Heclo, *A Government of Strangers* (Washington, DC: The Brookings Institution, 1977), p. 20.

[4]Wallace S. Sayre, "The Triumph of Techniques over Purpose," *Public Administration Review 8* (1948), 134–37; and John Fischer, "Let's Go Back to the Spoils System," *Harper's 191* (October 1945), 362–68.

[5]Frederick Mosher, *Democracy and the Public Service*, 2nd ed. (New York: Oxford University Press, 1982).

CHAPTER

2

THE JOB OF THE PUBLIC
PERSONNEL MANAGER

INTRODUCTION

Public personnel management is, among other things, a set of functions required to manage human resources in public organizations. At a more individual level, it is the work that public personnel managers share with supervisors, other administrators, and political leaders. Because the context of public personnel management influences the way in which personnel managers and personnel departments perform their roles, we must examine how the functions of personnel management are shared among agencies and individuals, and how personnel systems influence role performance.

By the end of this chapter, you will be able to:

1. Discuss the size and scope of public employment.
2. Explain how the functions of personnel management are shared among political leaders, line managers and supervisors, and the personnel department.
3. Explain why civil service systems are the only complete public personnel system.

4. Explain how the structure and function of personnel management differ in different personnel systems.
5. Describe what it means to be a professional public personnel manager.
6. Discuss how public personnel managers can begin to resolve the ethical dilemmas posed by competing personnel systems.

THE SIZE AND SCOPE OF PUBLIC EMPLOYMENT

While in the public's view federal employees often symbolize government bureaucracy, in reality they constitute only about 17 percent of all public employees. The number of public employees has generally risen over the past two decades, with most of the increase being at the state and local level. Table 2-1 shows these historical trends.

TABLE 2-1 Government Employment, 1940–1988

Year	EMPLOYEES (IN MILLIONS)			
	Total	Federal	State	Local
1940	4.4	1.1	3.3	
1950	6.4	2.1	1.1	3.2
1960	8.8	2.4	1.5	4.9
1970	13.0	2.9	2.8	7.4
1980	16.2	2.9	3.8	9.6
1988	17.5	3.1	4.2	10.2

Source: U.S. Bureau of the Census, *Public Employment in 1988*, Series GE-88-1 (Washington, DC: U.S. Government Printing Office, 1989).

The table shows that most government growth (at least since World War II) has occurred at the state and local levels. Of the 10.2 million local government employees, 2 million are employed by counties, 3.0 million by cities and towns, 4.7 million by school districts, and .5 million by other special districts (such as airports).

In 1988, the latest year for which data are available, these 17.5 million public employees were employed in a variety of functions, as shown in Table 2-2. The primary federal functions were national defense, postal service, and financial management; the primary state and local functions were education, police protection, highways, corrections, welfare, and utilities—with the emphasis on education.[1]

TABLE 2-2 Government Employment by Function, 1988

	NUMBER OF EMPLOYEES (IN THOUSANDS)					
Function	Total	%	Federal	%	State and Local	%
Total	15,341	100.0	2,937	100.0	12,404	100.0
Education	6,138	40.0	13	0.5	6,125	49.4
Health	1,577	10.3	240	8.1	1,336	10.7
Defense	1,043	6.8	1,043	6.8	—	—
Police	749	4.9	77	2.6	672	5.4
Postal service	744	4.9	744	4.9	—	—
Highways	544	3.5	4	0.1	540	4.3
Corrections	449	2.9	14	0.5	435	3.5
Financial admin.	448	2.9	139	4.7	310	2.5
Welfare	442	2.9	13	0.5	429	3.5
Utilities	425	2.8	—	—	425	3.4
Nat. resources	390	2.5	216	7.4	174	1.4
Judicial/legal	299	2.0	37	1.3	263	2.1
Fire prot.	251	1.6	—	—	251	2.0
Parks & rec.	241	1.6	23	0.8	218	1.8
Housing & CD	129	0.8	28	0.9	101	0.8
Sewerage	111	0.7	—	—	111	0.9
Solid waste	109	0.7	—	—	109	0.9
All other	1,252	8.2	347	10.4	905	7.8

Source: U.S. Bureau of the Census; *Public Employment in 1988,* Series GE-88-1 (Washington, DC: U.S. Government Printing Office, 1989).

SHARED RESPONSIBILITY

Responsibility for the design and implementation of personnel systems is shared among three general groups: political leaders, personnel directors and specialists, and line managers and supervisors. Political leaders (legislators, executives, and their political appointees) are responsible for establishing the objectives and constraints for personnel systems. Agencies must be created, program priorities established, and funds allocated to meet program objectives before jobs can be designed or positions filled. This is true regardless of which system (political appointment, civil service, collective bargaining, or affirmative action) dominates the way personnel functions are performed.

Personnel directors and specialists are responsible for designing and implementing personnel systems, or for supervising those who do so. In civil service systems, they usually work within a personnel department that functions as a staff support service for line managers and supervisors. Personnel directors and specialists both help line managers use human resources effectively, and constrain their personnel actions within the limits imposed by political leaders, laws, and regulations.

Most public personnel management functions (PADS) are performed by the managers and supervisors who operate personnel systems, rather than by the personnel departments that design them. Supervisors are responsible for the day-to-day activities that, in the end, determine the nature of the relationship between employees and the organization which is the most important factor in personnel management. Supervisors tell employees what is expected of them, train employees, provide feedback to let them know how they are doing, and recommend pay increases and promotion, or disciplinary action and dismissal, based on their assessment of the employee's job performance. Line managers and supervisors are responsible for "street-level" implementation of personnel systems. Their behavior is critical because the relationship between individual employees and supervisors is the most important factor influencing the effectiveness with which employees are developed and utilized. In short, supervisors set the tone of the relationship between employee and employer.

TABLE 2-3 Shared Responsibility for Personnel Functions

| | LEVEL | | |
	Political Officials	Line Managers, Supervisors	Personnel Directors & Specialists
		Function	
Planning	Estimate revenues, set program priorities	Manage within a budget	Develop job descriptions, implement pay and benefit plans
Acquisition	Influence values that guide selection processes	Hire and fire employees	Develop hiring rules and procedures
Development	Define agency and program goals and priorities	Make sure employees have clear goals, skills, feedback, rewards	Develop training & evaluation systems
Sanction	Determine appropriate personnel system	Counsel and discipline employees	Develop rules and procedures for grievance and discipline

Table 2-3 illustrates how responsibility for personnel functions is shared among these three groups.

COMPETITION AND INTERDEPENDENCE AMONG SYSTEMS

It would be easier to understand the impact of systems and values on the performance of personnel functions if we could distinguish which personnel system controlled each public position. That way, we could understand which system of laws, rules, and procedures influenced the fulfillment of personnel functions with respect to that position. But this is not possible because public personnel systems both compete with and depend upon each other. The discussion about conflicting values and systems has already clarified the ways in which these systems compete. But they are also symbiotic, because all personnel systems except the civil service system are incomplete systems. That is, only the civil service system is concerned with the entire range of personnel management functions. Other systems are concerned primarily with deciding who gets jobs (acquisition issues). Collective bargaining systems are really a hybrid of collective bargaining and civil service, with collective bargaining being concerned with pay and benefits (an aspect of the planning function), and with discipline and grievances (the sanctions function). Civil service systems continue to determine how other functions (acquisition and development) are performed.

Table 2-4 shows how civil service systems compete with, and supplement, the other personnel systems. It is important to note here that, in the history of public personnel management theory, civil service systems have traditionally been regarded not only as the only complete system, but as the only legitimate one. Mosher, for example, considers political appointments, collective bargaining and affirmative action to be threats to civil service

TABLE 2-4   Competition and Interdependence among Public Personnel Systems

	CIVIL SERVICE	POLITICAL APPOINTMENT	AFFIRMATIVE ACTION	COLLECTIVE BARGAINING
		Functional Emphasis		
Planning	yes	yes	no	yes
Acquisition	yes	yes	yes	no
Development	yes	no	no	no
Sanction	yes	no	yes	yes
		System Functionality		
	complete	incomplete	incomplete	incomplete

systems.[2] Yet regardless of the moral superiority with which civil service reformers would like to clothe the civil service system, the validity of these alternative systems is irrefutable: Each system is supported by legitimate competing values.

However, it is equally significant that civil service systems are predominant because they alone can perform the entire range of personnel functions. Civil service systems have also remained predominant because they can subsume and incorporate conflicts among alternative values and systems. This is an ability no other system has demonstrated. For example, we frequently find that political appointees manage agencies comprised of civil service employees. These employees may also be members of unions covered by collective bargaining agreements, and vacancies may be filled by affirmative action compliance procedures.

The existence and legitimacy of civil service systems and their three competitors do much to complicate the role of the public personnel manager, and the ways in which the personnel department performs its functions. The following sections describe how the role of the public personnel manager differs in each of the four personnel systems, and how patterns of law and historical practice have led alternative systems to emphasize different functions and to perform them differently.

Civil Service

In a civil service system, the personnel director usually directs a personnel department or office that functions as an administrative support service to the city manager, school superintendent, hospital administrator, or other agency administrator. The personnel department develops policies and procedures for managing the agency's human resources.

In the area of planning (classification and compensation), the personnel department is responsible for managing the civil service system. This means maintaining the system of positions that have been categorized into a plan according to criteria like degree of difficulty or type of work. The pay system is usually tied to the classification system, with jobs involving similar degrees of difficulty being compensated equally. Periodic checks are conducted to compare the actual work a person is doing with the duties outlined in a job description for the position. Yearly updates of the pay plan are also performed in anticipation of collective bargaining and budget planning within a civil service system.

The personnel department is also responsible for developing and updating the agency's retirement and benefits programs. It is responsible for maintaining records like eligibility and use of sick leave and vacation time, enrollment and maintenance in various health insurance programs, and life insurance or savings bond purchases. It also handles eligibility and processing of personnel action requests (retirements and other related changes in job status), including calculation of authorized retirement benefits, disability retirement determinations, and monitoring of compensation claims for job-related injuries.

In the area of acquisition (recruitment, testing, and selection), the personnel department might be responsible for developing schedules of tests for jobs that are frequently available, like secretary, clerk, and maintenance worker. It advertises vacant or new positions, conducts an initial review of job applications, and administers written tests. It might arrange interviews with applicants, conduct them, and evaluate test results. The personnel department compiles a list of those eligible for employment, maintains the list to ensure it is up to date as job applicants secure other employment, and provides a list of eligibles to managers in units where vacancies actually exist. The managers conduct interviews and select applicants. The personnel department then processes the paperwork required to employ and pay the person.

The personnel department must also keep track of and process all personnel actions—promotions, transfers, and dismissals. It also has a section that establishes and staffs an employee grievance and appeals procedure. People who work in this section are responsible for advising supervisors throughout the organization of appropriate codes of conduct for employees, the procedures and paperwork necessary to discipline an employee for violations of these rules, and the procedures to follow in the event the employee appeals this disciplinary action or files a grievance.

With respect to training, the personnel department might be responsible for orienting new employees to the organization, its work rules, and the benefits it provides. It might also keep track of and distribute notices of training or transfer opportunities. It might be responsible for conducting training to familiarize supervisors with the technical aspects of a newly developed performance appraisal system.

Political Appointment

In a political appointment system, the personnel director functions primarily as a staffing specialist and political adviser. His or her title is usually not even that of personnel director. But regardless of title, it is this person's responsibility to identify individuals who deserve or require a top-level political position working for an elected official, and to make recommendations to that official as to who should be hired in which position. The official then makes the appointment (or nominates the individual, if legislative confirmation is required) based upon the candidate's objective KSAs, financial or campaign support for the elected official, or support by an influential interest group seeking access to the policy-making process.

Once hired, political appointees are subject to the whims of the elected official. Few rules govern their job duties, pay, or rights, and they are usually fired "at will." To the extent that development functions are performed at all, they are performed within civil service systems.

TABLE 2-5   Collective Bargaining Systems in State and Local Government, 1980

	NUMBER	PERCENT
Total	5,030,564	48.8%
State	1,162,878	40.5
Local	3,867,686	52.0
Counties	547,169	34.9
Cities	1,247,748	54.4
Special districts	143,787	37.8
School districts	1,928,982	60.2

Source: U.S. Bureau of the Census, *Labor Management Relations in State and Local Governments: 1980*, Series SS No. 102 (Washington, DC: U.S. Government Printing Office, 1980), p. 1.

Collective Bargaining

If any employees in the agency are covered by a collective bargaining agreement, the personnel department is usually responsible for negotiating the agreement (or hiring an outside negotiator who performs this function), bringing pay and benefit provisions into accord with contract provisions, orienting supervisors on how to comply with the contract, and representing the agency in internal grievance resolution or outside arbitration procedures.

In 1980, the latest year for which statistics are available, about half of state and local government employees were covered by collective bargaining agreements. Table 2-5 shows these relationships. Because collective bargaining is a partial personnel system, civil service systems continue to provide most of the rules and procedures relating to acquisition and development.

Affirmative Action

The affirmative action department is responsible primarily for implementing human resource acquisition decision rules emphasizing social equity for protected classes (minorities, women, persons with disabilities). Thus, it most heavily affects recruitment, selection, and promotion policies and procedures. The affirmative action director shares responsibility with the personnel director in this area. Once members of protected classes are hired, other personnel systems (civil service or collective bargaining) influence the way in which planning, development, and sanction functions are performed.

Some Conclusions

The primary conclusion to be drawn from this discussion is that while public personnel directors perform the same functions regardless of the system in which they operate, the system has profound effects on the relative importance of these functions, their organizational location, and their method of implementation. The authority of personnel managers varies widely. Those working in predominantly political systems have little authority beyond that given to them by political leaders, and are concerned mainly with acquisition. Those working in civil service systems are more constrained by laws, and have responsibilities for a wider range of functions. Those working with collective bargaining systems are responsible for negotiating and administering collective bargaining agreements with unionized employees, who are also members of civil service systems. Those working in affirmative action systems are usually affirmative action officers, with predominant responsibilities for acquisition.

It is overly simplistic to say that public personnel directors work within one system or another. It is much more likely that an individual director will be in charge of the personnel function in an agency that includes several personnel systems. Thus, while someone might be in charge of labor relations, that person might report to the personnel director; the same would be true for the affirmative action officer in many public agencies. The role of the personnel director involves significant elements of role conflict because the director is responsible not only for supervising all the personnel functions, but for resolving conflicts in how they are performed, based on alternative values and decision rules. This leads directly to the issues of professionalism and ethics.

ARE PUBLIC PERSONNEL MANAGERS PROFESSIONALS?

The issue of whether public personnel managers are professionals has been debated for years. In many practical ways, the issue seems to boil down to the extent to which personnel managers can engage in the conflicts among public personnel systems and values, and yet keep from being captured by any one of them. Conceptually, the issue seems to focus on the extent to which there is an identifiable body of KSAs that define the occupation of the human resources manager, an accepted process of education and training for acquiring these KSAs, and a standard of ethics that guides their application. For academics who develop theory in the field, the issue of professionalism seems to focus on the extent to which there is an underlying body of theory that forms the basis for developing and implementing alternative approaches to the personnel functions; setting these approaches theoretically within the governmental context; and then describing the extent to which role strain or role conflict among the conflicting expectations of alternative personnel systems are an aberration, or "come with the territory."

Answers to practitioners' and academicians' questions seem to hinge upon how the public personnel manager's role is defined. Initially, civil service reformers sought to establish the credibility of personnel management by emphasizing its political neutrality and focusing on administrative efficiency. This emphasis served to establish public personnel management as a technical field with a body of techniques used to perform human resource management functions, and it separated public personnel administration from politics. Ironically, however, this emphasis on political neutrality and insistence on discovering the "one best way" to manage human resources had an opposite effect on the field as well. It isolated public personnel managers from the value conflicts that characterized the world of other professionals (such as law and medicine), and minimized the ethical dilemmas that constantly confronted them—dilemmas that grew out of the political context in which all public employees operate. This created the illusion among public officials (and among personnel directors and specialists themselves) that the field was value-free. It focused personnel management on administrative techniques instead of broad human resource policy questions. This devalued the status of the profession, and downgraded the importance accorded the study of personnel systems and values.

A Historical Overview: Yesterday and Today

A look at the history of testing and selection will emphasize this dilemma and its consequences. Beginning in the 1920s, public personnel directors began to develop testing and selection techniques that emphasized selection of the best candidate through the use of objective hiring standards. But necessary as these techniques were to move past the previous focus on political responsiveness and a spoils system which dictated appointments to technical and professional jobs, it distracted the focus of personnel professionals from the value conflicts inherent in the acquisition function.

In the "real world" of contemporary public personnel management, political leaders often disagree about which personnel system should predominate in determining how personnel functions are performed. In those instances where competing systems have developed and implemented contradictory rules for performing a function, it is usually the public personnel director who responds to, mediates among, or initiates conflict among competing systems. For example, the creation of a vacant position by the retirement or transfer of the incumbent will require the personnel manager to respond to, propose, or attempt to mediate among competing decision rules for filling the position:

1. **Civil service:** Fill the position with one of the applicants who placed highest on the civil service test for the position.
2. **Civil service/political appointment:** Revise the minimum qualifications for the position to include the candidate with the most political

support, and then pick that candidate from among the most qualified applicants for the position.

3. **Civil service/affirmative action appointment:** Conduct targeted recruitment efforts, making sure the applicant pool has a sufficient representation of women and minorities who also meet the minimum qualifications for the position. Then pick either the most qualified applicant or the most qualified minority applicant, depending on the extent of pressure and legal authority to appoint a minority group member.

4. **Civil service/collective bargaining appointment:** See if the position can be filled from within through a bidding process that emphasizes seniority.

Seen in this light, it is evident that the practice of public personnel management may require managers to resolve ethical dilemmas in seeking compromise among competing personnel systems, and among the values and interest groups these systems represent. Effective job performance requires that they not only be adept at using a range of techniques, but sensitive to the competing values and systems that influence technical choices. To the extent that they operate as mediators among these competing systems and values, public personnel managers function as professionals, and academicians see them as such. To the extent that they act as if they function in an environment devoid of value conflicts, public personnel managers are likely to function as technical specialists, and to be viewed as such by academicians.

A Field in Transition

It is evident from this analysis that the field of public personnel management is turbulent and transitional. Some traditional public personnel departments continue to function as technical staff agencies within an environment characterized by agreement on values. This role is most common for personnel departments or civil service boards operating within civil service systems in homogeneous political environments. More progressive departments might be called upon to take a more active role in designing, implementing, or evaluating human resource management systems within an agency that operates in an environment characterized by disagreement on personnel systems and values.

These activities usually require the use of analytical human resource management information systems. For example, they might conduct analyses like the cost of absenteeism, sick leave abuse, and fringe benefits for the agency. They might distribute and evaluate ratings on employee performance evaluation systems to measure their effect on productivity. They might experiment with new techniques for selecting employees (such as assessment centers), or new techniques of job design intended to meet employee needs and increase employee productivity (such as job sharing or flextime). They might be responsible for developing policies and procedures for substance abuse testing; for developing proposals for establishing EAPs (employee assistance programs) to help employees maintain productivity while resolving personal problems; or for encouraging QCs (quality circles), groups of employees responsible for proposing and implementing changes in procedures to make the organization more productive. They might be called upon to monitor the frequency of turnover in various departments, "cost out" proposed changes in pay and benefits, and monitor the compliance of benefits contractors with previously negotiated contracts.

Some Conclusions

What conclusions can be drawn from this variety of activities? First, traditional management emphasizes the technical side of personnel management, with less emphasis on policy-related analytical work, relationships with outside organizations, and conflicting values. In addition, both employees and line management are seen as clients, and are perceived as being served through the merit system. The traditional department's work includes recordkeeping and the processing of personnel transactions, especially in smaller government agencies or units.

A more contemporary view emphasizes different activities and relationships. While the traditional functions continue to be important, they are relatively less important than the "brokering" or mediating of conflicts among competing personnel systems. For example, the modern personnel director might be called upon to prepare cost-benefit analyses of alternative pay and benefit proposals related to collective bargaining with employees in the solid waste department. At the same time, he or she might also be asked to evaluate the comparative feasibility, productivity, and cost of privatizing or contracting this entire function out (thus making the collective bargaining analysis obsolete). Or, since the majority of employees in the department are minorities, the director might be asked to assess the impact of contracting out on the city's overall level of affirmative action compliance. Modern personnel directors do not work in isolation; rather, they work closely with other officials within their own agency (budget directors, attorneys, collective bargaining negotiators, affirmative action compliance officers, and supervisors) and outside it (legislative staff, union officials, affirmative action agencies, civil service boards, health and life insurance benefit representatives, pension boards, ethics commissions, and employee assistance programs dealing with substance abuse and other personal problems).

Most public personnel departments have moved cautiously into the modern era because of their traditional reluctance to be identified with or become involved in "politics." Yet as their function is increasingly viewed as the development and management of human resource systems involving the reconciliation of value conflicts, they are overcoming this reluctance and working outside the confining environment of the civil service system. And they are finding that this expanded role brings benefits as well as risks. They are able to bring their expertise to bear on a range of critical human resource issues in a variety of contexts—issues traditional personnel managers might define as falling outside their area of responsibility. For example, they can work with legislators on privatization and benefits issues, with labor negotiators on alternative pay and grievance procedures, and with affirmative action compliance agencies on affirmative action proposals or minority business contracting procedures. By continuing to assert their central role in the most critical issues of agency management, they are developing not only their own professional status, but the status of their profession.[3]

WHAT KSAs DOES THE PUBLIC PERSONNEL MANAGER NEED?

Traditional public personnel management requires that personnel directors know the laws and regulations that control practices within a particular system, as well as the techniques used to perform personnel functions within that system. For example, traditional civil-service-oriented personnel management requires knowledge of civil service rules and regulations (such as competitive examination procedures, or how to select from a list of eligible applicants), as well as how to develop and administer examinations, write job descriptions, administer pay and benefit programs, and process personnel actions.

Contemporary public personnel management requires these skills and more. It requires a knowledge of public personnel management techniques, an understanding of historical developments in the field, and the ability to resolve ethical dilemmas among competing values under conditions of change and uncertainty. Personnel rules and procedures are not value-neutral; rather, they are the implicit or explicit implementation of a particular public personnel system (or compromises among several such systems). This means that each selection or promotion decision must be viewed not merely as a technical exercise, but as a case that reflects and exemplifies this historical conflict over alternative values, power, and personnel systems.

Public personnel directors must be sensitive to the need for administrative systems to be responsive to legitimate political values and public participation in governance, especially in local government. These kinds of changes inevitably challenge the shield that the rhetoric of "merit" has provided the traditional manager. Now there is no escaping the political pressure personnel managers must face. They work under consent decrees and with unions that traditionally have set barriers to hiring women and minorities. At the same time, they are expected to respond to their political leaders while maintaining the integrity of the civil service system they oversee. Yet they have no guidance from within the traditional civil service system for how to integrate these increasingly insistent and conflicting demands.

Modern public personnel managers tend to view their world as a conflict- and change-oriented environment, rather than as a stable one. First, theirs is a world in which trends such as privatization and contracting out have blurred distinctions between public and private. Second, their world is controlled by a myriad of complex and conflicting laws involving affirmative action, labor relations, personal/professional liability, employee privacy, due process, and pay equity. Third, their world is characterized by constant technological innovations in areas such as data security, teleconferencing, computerized data bases and report generation,[4] and applications of interactive video to training and orientation.[5] Fourth, their world is characterized by changes in workforce composition (demographics). For example, robotics and automation have led to the creation and absorption of many middle management and clerical positions; the workforce is aging, and the number of women and minorities is increasing—by 1980, over half the workforce employed outside the home in the United States was female. And the number of Blacks and Hispanics is increasing as well (they will constitute 50 percent of the births in the United States by 2076).[6] Fifth, this leads to changes in organization such as real-time problem solving, decentralization, and networking.[7]

These changes in the context of public administration have led public personnel managers to adopt a changing definition of the field. In general, there is increased awareness of the impact of environmental factors— among them technology, economics, politics, and social conditions. There is also continued awareness of the importance of human resources to organizational productivity. Within the field of human resources management, this means an increased number and diversity of personnel management professionals. It means increased responsibilities in the general area of environmental mediation and adaptation, including interpretation and compliance with government regulations, predicting the effects of changes in technology and workforce composition on jobs,[8] and developing programs and systems to help line managers increase productivity. Examples are job humanization, flexible work schedules and benefits, training and education, and performance-oriented evaluation systems.

Potentially, the power of public personnel managers in public organizations is increasing. This is a *potential* consequence resulting from their successful ability to move from a traditional view of the field (involving primarily technical skills) to a modern view (involving primarily professional skills as an interpreter of conflicting interests and mediator among them). At the same time, they will be called upon to protect the integrity of merit systems.

The modern public personnel manager needs several general types of KSAs to perform well in this enhanced role. Public personnel managers must exhibit continued concern for productivity and effectiveness. They must become and remain competent in law, technology, and quantitative/analytic skills. They must have a humanistic orientation toward employees, a positive orientation to managerial objectives, and close working relationships with other personnel professionals inside and outside the organization. No one manager can possess expertise in all these areas, but no complex personnel department can overlook them in their complement of KSAs.

This also means changes in the teaching of public personnel management. Among these are greater reliance on comparative and contextual models, and closer ties to the real world of public personnel management through internships and cooperative programs; continued development of the field through research, training, and technical assistance; and deliberate attempts to attract and hold the best and brightest students. Fortunately for the public personnel professional, there are a variety of professional organizations dedicated to easing the sometimes painful transition between traditional and contemporary roles.[9] And many government agencies also can provide research and reference materials valuable to both students and practitioners of public personnel management.[10]

RESOLVING ETHICAL DILEMMAS

Traditional public personnel managers are usually impatient or complacent with ethical choices. In their view of public personnel administration, ethical dilemmas are easily resolved because this system is based entirely upon the civil service system as a moral ideal, with the political patronage system as its arch-enemy and moral opposite (or at best something to be continually wary of). The competing claims of alternative public personnel management systems (politics, collective bargaining, and affirmative action) are considered challenges to the morally superior civil service system.[11] Public personnel managers operating under these beliefs function either as "true believers" or as pragmatists. They are inclined to consider ethics unnecessary, because it is easier to think of administrative actions as purely technical and rational and infused with moral superiority, or impractical because competing claims require pragmatic compromise.

But modern public personnel managers are more likely to find that ethical dilemmas are challenging and inevitable because they arise directly out of the role conflicts implicit in the public personnel manager's job. They "come with the territory." To succeed, public personnel managers must not only do things right, they must do the right things.[12] It is the fate of the public personnel manager to wrestle with choices imposed by external conflicts among competing systems, and to derive from these choices the existential satisfaction of each day coming closer to unattainable objectives under conditions of ethical uncertainty.

The inevitability of political and ethical dilemmas for the modern public personnel administrator is the dominant theme of this book, in that these dilemmas are based upon conflict among personnel systems, values, and power centers for the right to allocate scarce public jobs. Not only does resource scarcity prohibit maximum achievement of all values simultaneously, but each of them can be maximized only at the expense of the others. In addition, the use of management information for evaluative purposes presupposes some purpose for evaluation. The evaluator collects and interprets information for the purpose of changing organizational behavior. Just as value-free administration is impossible, so value-free evaluation is a contradiction in terms.

The problem of ethical administration, then, is neither illusory nor easily resolved. It arises inevitably out of legitimate but conflicting role expectations. How can ethical dilemmas be resolved? Six steps are worthy of discussion:

1. Assume that administrative acts have ethical content.
2. Determine in advance whom they affect.
3. Visualize the effect of alternative actions on the people or groups involved.
4. Make a choice consistent with your own moral standards, drawing on other guidelines such as applicable laws, the advice of friends, or the expectations of co-workers.
5. Understand that you may have to explain this choice later to outsiders unfamiliar with your job, and prepare yourself to do so.
6. Forget this choice—put it behind you so you can face the next one clearly.

SUMMARY

Public employees constitute about 20 percent of the total workforce in the United States, or 17.5 million employees. Most of these people work for state and local governments, primarily in education.

Public personnel management consists of the functions needed to manage human resources in public agencies. These functions are shared among political leaders, line managers and supervisors, and the personnel department. Civil service systems are the predominant public personnel system because they have articulated rules and procedures for performing the whole range of personnel functions. Other systems, though incomplete, are nonetheless legitimate and effective influences over one or more personnel functions. While personnel functions remain the same across different systems, their organizational location and method of performance differ depending upon the system.

Public personnel management may be viewed as a technical specialty or as a profession. Traditional personnel managers (those who operate within a consensus on one system and its underlying values) tend to define themselves, and to be defined by others, as technical specialists working within a staff agency. Contemporary personnel managers (those who operate as interpreters or mediators among competing systems and values) tend to define themselves, and to be defined by others, as professionals whose role involves a blend of technical skills and ethical decision making.

KEY TERMS

administrative effectiveness
efficiency
ethics
individual rights
line manager
personnel director
personnel specialist
position management
privatization
profession
public personnel management
representative bureaucracy
role
staff function
technical specialist

DISCUSSION QUESTIONS

1. How many public employees are there? Which functional areas predominate for each level of government?
2. What are the shared roles of political officials, managers, and personnel directors for fulfilling public personnel functions?
3. Describe similarities and differences in the way personnel managers perform their functions in different systems.

4. What are the factors that distinguish public personnel managers as professionals or as technicians?

5. What knowledge, skills, and abilities does the public personnel manager need?

6. How can public personnel managers resolve the ethical dilemmas they face?

CASE STUDY: JOB DESCRIPTION FOR A PUBLIC PERSONNEL MANAGER

Review the following job description, and then answer these questions about it:

1. What are the primary duties and responsibilities of the position?

2. What KSAs are required to perform these duties satisfactorily?

3. What minimum qualifications are required to ensure that the incumbent (the person occupying the position) has these KSAs?

4. How can a job description like this help ensure that government is run efficiently and employees treated equitably?

PERSONNEL OFFICER 1

00-05-1-001

Definition of Work

This is technical and administrative personnel management work in a small or moderate-sized institution within an agency, or in an assigned phase of a larger personnel program.

Work involves planning, organizing, and directing a personnel program in a smaller institution within a central agency such as Social and Rehabilitation Services and the Department of Corrections; or administering a specialized phase such as training, recruiting, or classification in a large personnel program; or assisting in administering the total personnel program in a large state agency. Work may include responsibility for employee benefits, safety, labor relations, and transactions. Work usually includes providing guidance and advice to organizational officials in developing and adopting internal personnel policies, procedures, and practices, and maintaining effective liaison with central personnel officials. Supervision may be exercised over clerical and other employees. Work is performed independently under administrative supervision and is reviewed through records, reports, and conferences for adherence to Civil Service and internal policies and regulations.

Examples of Work Performed

Plans, organizes, and directs a personnel program; performs work associated with classifications, labor relations, workmen's compensation, benefits, affirmative action, transactions, and recruitment; directs the preparation of transaction or position description forms.

Directs a limited training program in a large agency; designs and maintains an orientation program for employees; develops and maintains supervisory and other functional training programs in such areas as personnel, payroll, and budget; exercises functional supervision over technical and professional employees involved in training programs.

Directs a comprehensive recruitment program; supervises clerical and other employees in interviewing, screening, and selecting applicants, as well as contacting vocational schools, placement agencies, universities, and other sources to secure the services of qualified personnel to fill agency vacancies.

Interviews job applicants; reviews their qualifications for employment; informs applicants of civil service examination and certification procedures and provides them with information on agency personnel needs; refers promising applicants to agency supervisors.

Assists in a classification program; maintains a position inventory and current position descriptions; classifies or reclassifies positions to lower-level classes; prepares organizational charts; counsels employees and departmental employees concerning procedures in classification.

Supervises a small group of clerical employees engaged in nontechnical personnel activities.

Interprets civil service laws, rules, and procedures to departmental officers and employees, and interprets departmental and employee needs to the central personnel division.

Performs related work as required.

Required Abilities, Skills, Knowledge

Knowledge of public personnel administration theory and practice including position classification, salary administration, employee performance evaluation, employment and placement methods, management-employee relations, affirmative action-equal employment opportunity, recruitment, employee benefits, and staff training and development.

Knowledge of supervisory methods and techniques.

Knowledge of English usage and written communication format.

Ability to communicate information concisely and accurately.

Ability to read, interpret, and apply written information to daily work.

Ability to interact with employees, supervisors, management officials, representatives from other state agencies, and the general public in order to establish and maintain effective working relationships with them.

Ability to carry out work with only general administrative guidelines and policy direction.

Ability to use arithmetic (addition, subtraction, multiplication, division, percentages).

Education and Experience

Graduation from an accredited four-year college or university with 20 semester hours of coursework in personnel, public, or business administration, counseling or guidance or psychology. Technical or professional experience in personnel work may be substituted for the required college study on a year-for-year basis.

NOTES

[1]A comparison of Tables 2-1 and 2-2 will show that the number of full-time employees differs because Table 2-1 includes all employees, and Table 2-2 includes full-time equivalent employees (combining part-time employees into full-time positions).

[2]Frederick Mosher, *Democracy and the Public Service*, 2nd ed. (New York: Oxford University Press, 1982).

[3]Donald Klingner, "The Changing Role of Public Personnel Management in the 1980s," *The Personnel Administrator 24*, 9 (September 1979), 41–48; and John Nalbandian, "From Compliance to Consultation: The Role of the Public Personnel Manager," *Review of Public Personnel Administration 1*, 2 (Spring 1981), 37–51.

[4]Michael Dertouzos and Joel Moses (eds.), *The Computer Age: A Twenty-Year View* (Cambridge, MA: MIT Press, 1980).

[5]U.S. Congress, House Committee on Science, Space and Technology, *The Power of Video Teleconferencing: Changing the Way We Do Business: Hearings of November 6, 1991* (Washington, DC: U.S. Government Printing Office, 1992).

[6]Anthony Downs, *2076—A Look at the Third Century*. Conference Presentation, University of Chicago Policy Studies Symposium. (Washington, DC: The Brookings Institution, 1982).

[7]Marilyn Ferguson, *The Aquarian Conspiracy* (Los Angeles, CA: J.P. Tarcher, 1980); and John Naisbitt, *Megatrends*, 2nd ed. (New York: Warner, 1980).

[8]Adele Goldberg (ed.), *A History of Personal Workstations* (Reading, MA: Addison-Wesley, 1988).

[9]Chief among these are the International Personnel Management Association (IPMA), 1617 Duke Street, Alexandria, Virginia 22314, (703) 549-7100; the American Society for Public Administration (ASPA), Section on Personnel Administration and Labor Relations (SPALR), 1120 G Street, N.W., Suite 700, Washington, DC 20005, (202) 393-7878; and the National Academy of Public Administration, 1120 G Street, N.W., Suite 850, Washington, DC 20005-3801, (202) 347-3190.

[10]For example, the U.S. Office of Personnel Management (OPM), Office of Systems Innovation and Simplification, Room 7638, 1900 E Street, N.W., Washington, DC 20415-0001, (202) 653-2511; the U.S. Merit Systems Protection Board (MSPB), Office of Policy and Evaluation, 1120 Vermont Avenue, N.W., Washington, DC 20419, (202) 653-7208; and the U.S. Equal Employment Opportunity Commission (EEOC), Office of Communications and Legislative Affairs, 1801 L Street, N.W., Washington, DC 20507, 1 (800) 669-EEOC.

[11]Frederick Mosher, *Democracy and the Public Service*, 2nd ed. (New York: Oxford University Press, 1982).

[12]Warren Bennis and Bert Nanus, *Leaders: The Strategies for Taking Charge* (Harper & Row, 1985).

CHAPTER

3

BUDGETING, PLANNING, AND PRODUCTIVITY

Through the budget process, political differences are debated and transformed into concrete government programs. The budget preparation and approval process is the primary means by which the field of public personnel management is related to the larger political context; it is central to the human resources planning function. Because pay and benefits can constitute some 70 percent of an agency's budget, the most vital budgetary items often are the number of personnel and the costs associated with their employment.

Human resource planning is that aspect of public personnel management which mediates between the external political environment and core activities such as job analysis, job classification, job evaluation, and compensation. In brief, human resource planning matches "wish lists" proposed by agency managers with political realities often generated by projected revenue shortfalls. The process begins with a request to line managers from the budget office: "How many positions and what kind of positions do you need in order to meet program objectives?" It ends with a legislative authorization of programs and funds connected to these requests.

Refusals to allocate requested funds focuses attention on doing more with less. This call for enhanced productivity has stimulated innovations in service delivery, technology, and personnel practices, but in many cases it also has resulted in decreased quality and quantity of public services.

By the end of this chapter you will be able to:

1. Discuss the relationship between budgeting, human resources planning, and productivity.
2. Identify the essential steps in the budget process and how human resources management and budgetary decisions are connected.
3. Describe various methods of human resources forecasting.
4. Discuss the values involved in cutback management.
5. Describe the differences between responsiveness, effectiveness, and efficiency.
6. Discuss the pros and cons of contracting with private firms for public services.
7. Identify the personnel manager's role in productivity programs.

BUDGETING AND FINANCIAL MANAGEMENT

A *budget* is a document that attempts to reconcile program priorities with projected revenues. It combines a statement of organizational activities or objectives for a given time period with information about the funds required to engage in these activities or reach these objectives. A budget has many purposes: information, control, planning, evaluation.[1]

Historically, the most important purpose of a public sector budget has been external control—that is, limiting the total resources available to an agency and preventing expenditure for activities or items not allowed by law. This control has applied to both money and jobs. The type of budget used for control purposes is called a *ceiling budget:* It controls an agency directly by specifying limits to expenditures through appropriations legislation, or indirectly by limiting agency revenues.

Other types of budgets have been developed for different purposes. A line-item budget, which classifies expenditures by type, is useful for controlling types of expenditures as well as their total amount. Performance and program budgets are useful for specifying the activities or programs on which funds are spent, and thereby assist in their evaluation. By separating expenditures by function (such as health or public safety) or by type of expenditure (such as personnel and equipment) or by source of revenue (such as property tax or user fees), administrators and legislators can keep accurate records of an agency's financial transactions for the maintenance of internal efficiency or external control.

Budgeting is like a game in that its participants, rules, and time limits usually are known in advance by all players.[2] The primary participants are interest groups (including employees), public agency administrators, the chief executive, and legislative committees.

Although each participant's game plan will differ with circumstances, each participant has a generally accepted role to play. Interest groups exert pressure on administrators to propose or expand favorable programs. Department administrators use these pressures and their own sense of their department's goals and capabilities to develop proposals and specify the resources (money, time, and people) needed to accomplish them. Chief executives coordinate and balance the requests of various departments. After all, resources are limited and departmental objectives should be congruent with the overall objectives of the city, state, or national government. In many cases, the chief executive has a staff agency responsible for informing departments or agencies of planning limitations, objectives, and resource limits. The chief executive presents the combined budget request of all departments within the executive branch to a legislature or board (city council, county commission, state legislature, or Congress).

Legislative action on appropriations requests varies, depending on the legislature's size and the staff's capabilities. At the national and state levels, committees consider funding requests from various agencies. These committees examine funding requests in the light of prior expenditures, testimony from department heads and lobbyists, and the committee members' own feelings about the comparative importance of the agency's programs and objectives. Appropriations requests are approved (reported out of committee) when the committee agrees on which programs should be funded, and on the overall level of funding.

The entire legislature usually approves committee proposals, unless the funding relates to programs that affect the interests of groups that have not expressed their opinions adequately during committee hearings. Legislation authorizing new programs is usually considered separately from bills that appropriate funds for those programs.

In an elementary view, after new programs are authorized and funded, the executive branch is responsible for executing them. The chief executive is responsible for administering the expenditure of funds to accomplish the objectives intended by the legislature; department administrators are responsible for managing their budgets and programs accordingly. *Financial management* is the process of developing and using systems to ensure that funds are spent for the purposes for which they have been appropriated. Through an accounting system, each agency keeps records of financial transactions and compares budgets with actual expenditures. Agency managers engage in financial management when they take steps to limit expenditures, or transfer funds from one budget category to another to meet program priorities, or when they borrow or invest idle funds.

The process of budget preparation, approval, and management is shown in Figure 3-1. This process is a recurrent ritual whose frequency depends on the length of the appropriations cycle. Most governments budget annually, although the problems associated with continually developing

Stages   **Actors**

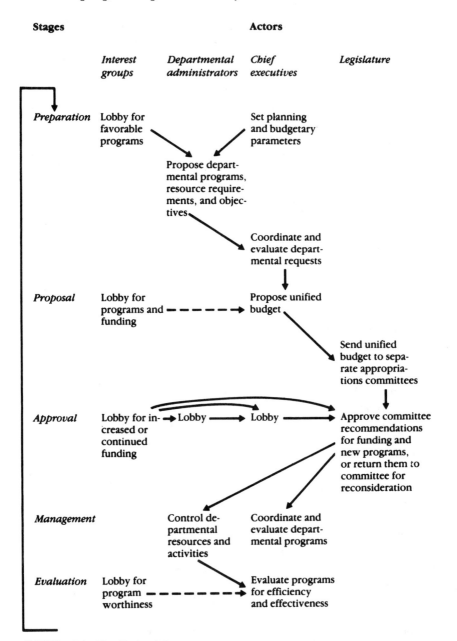

FIGURE 3-1 The Budget Process

and evaluating programs have led many state legislatures to develop biennial budgets (every two years). In the typical annual budget cycle, however, an agency or a department normally is developing the next year's budget a year in advance of the period for which it is requesting funds. At the same time, it is also evaluating programs from the prior year. Figure 3-2 represents the time frame within which annual budgets occur. Although most governments follow an annual cycle, their budget years begin and end on different dates. Most state governments use a fiscal year beginning July 1 and ending June 30, while the federal government's fiscal year begins October 1 and ends September 30. Other governments use a calendar year, January 1 to December 31.

Budgeting, then, is the process by which general policy objectives are translated into specific programs, with funds allocated for their accomplishment. Financial management and *auditing* are the means by which expenditures are limited to those purposes. These practices are therefore at the heart of the resource allocation process, and they constitute the key financial relationship between politics and public administration. The budget preparation and approval process is complex. It can be viewed politically as a contest among opposing agencies for scarce resources; organizationally as the formal set of policies and procedures that govern the approval process; or informally as a ritualized interaction among the conflicting expectations of program managers, chief executives, legislators, and lobbyists.

The role public personnel managers play in the budget preparation and approval process combines their staff responsibility of assisting other department heads, and their line responsibility of directing their own de-

FIGURE   3-2   The Budget Cycle

Source: Klingner, Donald E., *Public Administration: A Management Approach.* Copyright © 1983 by Houghton Mifflin Company. Used with permission.

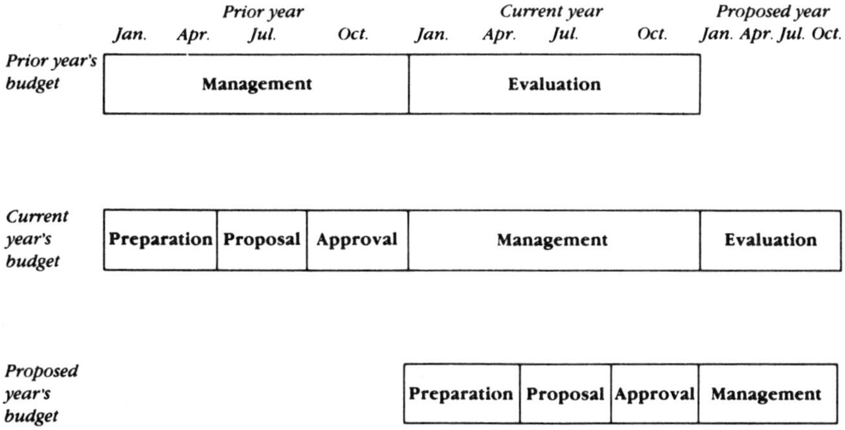

partments. Their staff responsibility is to work with department heads so that the budget proposals of these departments will conform to personnel policy and practices and will include sufficient funds to hire the employees needed to meet agency objectives. For example, a city police chief may have received a mandate from the city council to "put a hold on crime." Translated into budget terms, this may mean that the council is willing to allocate additional money to hire more police officers. Working with the chief executive officer, and the personnel and budget departments, the police department will analyze staffing, examine the classification scheme to determine the salary associated with each new position, and determine total costs including wages, benefits, uniform allowances, recruitment and training. Then the department will develop a request reflecting the combined analysis and possibly the political realities of the budget process in order to anticipate the city council's reaction. The police chief will submit the request to the city manager (or mayor), who then reviews it against other council priorities and revenue projections, and forwards it to the council as part of a total proposed budget.

The second major budget preparation function of a personnel director is to develop and defend the budget needed to provide support services to other departments: human resource planning, recruitment and selection, job analysis and classification, operation of the payroll and benefits system, training and orientation, performance evaluation, grievances and disciplinary action, and collective bargaining. For example, in a metropolitan area comprised of many local governments, personnel managers will commonly conduct an annual or biennial wage and salary survey to determine the pay scales for certain positions common to all jurisdictions. These data will then be used to make recommendations to the city manager concerning whether or not pay rates should be changed, or to support the government's position in salary negotiations with a union. Or the city may need to develop new job descriptions or testing procedures as a result of affirmative action pressure. The cost of these activities, including the rationale for them, is presented by the personnel director to the city manager. In this respect, the personnel director functions as a line manager.

Because pay and benefits constitute such a large proportion of an agency's budget, human resource managers as well as budget officers are heavily involved in budget management throughout the year. In this instance, agency managers and supervisors play the primary role because they are responsible for controlling and reallocating human resources to meet program priorities within budget constraints. Agency personnel managers respond to the priorities set by managers by filling positions, paying employees, and otherwise implementing their decisions.

In a cutback situation, however, agency personnel managers may have to prepare plans to reduce personnel expenditures. These plans commonly include freezes on hiring and promotions and cutbacks on hours worked, proposed reductions in benefits, and contracting out for services previously provided by government.

HUMAN RESOURCE PLANNING

The budget preparation and approval process is, in effect, the "engine" that forces legislative and executive decisions on programs and expenditures. While the budget is a central policy-making and control mechanism, human resource planning would be incomplete if it did not include a concern for the interaction among goals, budget, position allocations, workforce skills and competencies and final products or services.[3]

Given the extent to which public agency expenditures are comprised of pay and benefits, and the use of personnel ceilings to control agency activity, human resource planning is the means by which public officials use the budget to allocate resources among competing priorities and programs.

In addition, human resource planning relates to two other important allocation and planning activities: job analysis and classification, and compensation and benefits. By establishing the duties and qualifications for positions, job analysis allows positions to be classified by type of occupation and level of difficulty. This, in turn, enables uniform and equitable pay and benefit programs to be established for each position. Without these two additional steps, it would not be possible for human resource planners to use forecasts to estimate human resource costs.

Forecasting

The primary goal of human resource planning is to match the demand for employees with the supply. In budgetary crises this requires cutbacks; in times of growth, obviously, a government must plan for new employees. The larger the government unit, the more important it is to anticipate not only personnel needs, but the supply of labor that will be available. Will the knowledge, skills, and abilities be available in the market when the public employer needs them? Again, in larger government units the public personnel manager could work with department heads and the budget office to forecast future human resource needs and then use these combined estimates to develop a coordinated staffing program for the agency or government.

Incrementalism (or *decrementalism*) is a forecasting method that projects straight-line changes in personnel needs based on various factors that influence the quality and quantity of service delivery. The defining characteristic of incrementalism in human resources forecasting and planning is its assumption that goals and purposes remain the same or will change only marginally. For example, an incremental human resource plan might call for a 5 percent increase in the number of positions allocated to each organizational unit for each 5 percent increase in population served. Similarly, a 5 percent increase in revenues might trigger requests for more personnel, incrementally. A decremental plan might call for a 5 percent reduction in personnel for a 5 percent reduction in population served or revenue shortfall. Neither one is very effective as a comprehensively rational forecasting technique because both assume no changes in policy goals and purposes, and therefore project no changes in the kinds of people that may need to be hired or laid off.[4]

The most widely used forecasting technique is *collective opinion.* It involves first gathering information from a variety of sources inside and outside the agency and then reaching a group consensus about the interpretation of these data. Some information sources are shown in Table 3-1.

This information could relate to such external factors as enabling legislation, budgetary and personnel ceilings, changes in agency structure or objectives, affirmative action goals, collective bargaining, or pressures for political responsiveness. Internal factors might include current human resource utilization, projected staffing needs, or shifts in program priorities. For example, a group of agency personnel directors might conclude that a new state law requiring the issuance of environmental impact permits for beachfront developers, and the funding of the program for a certain dollar figure, would require a 20 percent increase in employees for the state environmental management agency over the next three years.

Usually this human resource "planning" process is not a rational one.[5] That is, new positions are created and abolished as a reaction to legislative funding priorities influenced by agency plans, interest group pressures, political tradeoffs, and anticipated revenue, rather than to meet a systematic and multiyear analysis of agency needs and labor market supply.

Two rational approaches to human resource planning are available. First, macro-level forecasting techniques such as categorical and cluster

TABLE 3-1   Sources of Information

LOCATION OF SOURCE	RELATIONSHIP	SOURCES OF INFORMATION
Outside agency	Personal	Clients, legislators, lobbyists, other agency administrators
	Impersonal	Newspapers, budget hearings, professional conferences, polls
Inside agency	Personal	Subordinates, supervisors, coworkers
	Impersonal	Meetings, conferences

Source: Reprinted from Donald E. Klingner, *Public Administration: A Management Approach.* © 1983 by Houghton Mifflin, Boston, MA. All rights reserved.

forecasting may be used. *Categorical forecasting* estimates further needs for separate occupational groups, such as doctors, lawyers, and personnel managers. *Cluster forecasting* groups those occupations with common skill requirements and those that are required for other positions to function. It is a technique most often used by larger organizations. For example, a personnel manager may estimate that he or she needs to add one job analyst to the personnel department for every 1000 new employees in the organization, because this is the ratio of analysts to employees needed to handle routine requests for reclassification.

Modeling, or *simulation*, is a second forecasting technique. Some applications require the use of mathematics and computers, others do not.[6] The simulation process requires developing a model that duplicates reality with respect to the crucial environmental, organizational, or interpersonal factors affecting a particular agency goal. A model specifies the conditions that affect the relative feasibility of procuring alternative personnel levels and skills. It requires that guidelines be established, current programs identified, and outputs determined. Next, it requires that possible alternative combinations of human resources be substituted to determine their effect on outputs.

For example, a personnel director seeking to estimate future personnel costs for a department might review the turnover date for secretarial positions. If the rate was 33 percent annually, he or she would conclude that if the number of positions in the agency were to remain constant, one-third of the secretarial positions would need to be filled annually. Anticipated costs for this activity could then be projected by computing the cost of recruitment, selection, orientation, and training for new employees, minus any salary dollars saved for the time positions were vacant.

The personnel director might assist a county welfare administrator by using modeling to predict how many employees will be needed. The model might be stated in this way:

1. Currently, with unemployment at about 6 percent, welfare applications can be processed within time standards by three full-time employees, using a manual index card system.
2. If unemployment increases to 8 percent, the office will need to add one more employee to handle the additional workload, or change to a computer system in order to process welfare applications more efficiently.

Which forecasting technique should be used? Although most organizations will continue to use nonrational, incremental approaches largely geared to revenue forecasts, rational techniques may be adopted fairly easily by many agencies, particularly those that have adequate and competent staff, sufficient data on current programs and resource requirements, receptive management, and access to computer facilities.[7] The administrator's skill and commitment to seeking the best solution determines the technique used and its effectiveness in forecasting.[8]

Having used a variety of techniques to forecast the *demand* for human resources within the agency, managers may use similar techniques to forecast the *supply* of qualified applicants—the potential labor market from which the agency can recruit. This is influenced by a number of factors inside and outside the agency, among them the state of the economy, the level of technology, the educational system, competing employers, the nature of the labor market, the agency's compensation system, the number of vacancies, the agency's recruitment practices, affirmative action considerations, and any collective bargaining working rules regarding staffing procedures.

In theory, by subtracting the aggregate *supply* of human resources from the aggregate *demand* for these resources within the organization, human resource planners can compute the *need*. This figure is then used to set up programs for acquiring, developing, and utilizing human resources.

Other Planning Activities

Human resource planning provides external legislative control over resources and program priorities through activities like job analysis, classification, and evaluation. But managers must also relate forecasts to other personnel activities—recruitment, performance evaluation, training, selection and promotion, affirmative action, compensation, labor-management relations, and career development.[9]

If governmental goals and community needs are to be anticipated effectively, recruitment must occur far enough in advance to be completed by the time a program needs to be operational. Given the nature of the labor market for the particular position, this may require that recruiters be given several fiscal years of lead time.

If the labor market is a difficult one to recruit in, test-validation specialists may need to assist in developing selection or promotion criteria that screen out unqualified applicants or employees but do not screen out qualified ones as well. If anticipated needs are to be met from within the agency, the personnel department must develop a performance evaluation system to identify qualified employees, and possibly training programs to qualify people for them.

If career development is important, the personnel department can assist employees by identifying model career patterns that employees can use to plan their future in the organization. Having identified these patterns, it is then up to the agency to follow through by utilizing its performance evaluation, training, and affirmative action programs to see that employees have a substantial and equitable opportunity to achieve their objectives.

The level of compensation for a position determines the size and quality of the applicant pool. A position characterized by both low salary and benefits in relation to market conditions will be hard to fill with qualified employees, or it will show high turnover as employees become sufficiently qualified to compete for jobs in the private-sector market. The personnel manager can often justify higher salaries by showing that the cost of replacing and training new employees is greater than the cost of a boost in pay and benefits. Compensation and benefits have to be adjusted to meet conditions in the external labor market or the terms of a negotiated collective bargaining agreement. This is particularly true if the employer bargains collectively with multiple employee associations, or if the union representing a group of employees also represents similar employees in nearby competing organizations.

If certain groups are underutilized, and this is reflected in the affirmative action objectives of the agency, human resource supply forecasts will have to consider not just the aggregate supply of employees in a particular type of job, but the similarities and differences between this general labor market and the specific market for female or minority-group employees and applicants.

Cutback Management

With cuts in federal spending, demands on state and local governments escalate. At the same time, taxpayers may resist increases in state and local taxes to pay for services. The problem is worsened by the regressive nature of sales and property taxes, which do not rise proportionately with income.

Such losses in funds often mean that public agencies are required to practice cutback management. This means that agencies will hire fewer employees, because such a large portion of a government's budget goes for salaries and benefits. This is especially true in school districts and local governments. Obviously, this creates problems. Cuts in the school district's budget means fewer teachers and larger classes; cuts in the public works department can mean unpatched streets and less frequent trash pickup; cuts in the police department mean slower responses to nonessential calls for service and less attention to minor crimes, and more time in police cars than in mixing with the community face to face.

At the agency level, the cutback process also has ramifications. First, it is difficult to cut an agency's programs equitably. Both the contributions of each program to agency goals and the comparative effects of alternative cuts on public services are difficult to measure without resolving the problems related to productivity measurement and program evaluation. A second problem, one closely related to the responsibilities of the public personnel manager, is that the easiest methods of reducing agency expenditures are seldom the most appropriate from a productivity or effectiveness standpoint.[10] Such methods involve across-the-board cuts, hiring freezes, a reduction in force, or attrition. Across-the-board cuts, like the incremental or decremental methods discussed earlier in the chapter, are an irrational method of reducing expenditures in the absence of more definitive program evaluation information.

Hiring freezes prohibit an agency from filling vacated positions and authorizing new ones. Though this may result in a reduction of costs in pay and benefits, the long-term consequences are harmful. Jobs with high turnover rates (clerical, service delivery, or technical positions) go unfilled because of hiring prohibitions, while career administrators tend to stay with their jobs. Unless the agency can subvert the intent of a freeze by more contracting out—and this is likely to attract strong opposition from unions and other employee groups—attrition is likely to trigger productivity decreases.

A reduction in force has disadvantages as well. A RIF, as it is called, is the laying off of employees within those occupational groups and organizational units determined to be of lowest priority to the agency's mission. This is usually done on the basis of seniority, but it may also be based on other factors such as social equity or productivity. As might be expected, the threat of a RIF causes a drop in agency morale, coupled with intense internal politicking to have one's own organizational unit or job category exempted from the reduction. In addition, a RIF has hidden costs that tend to offset the immediate benefits of a reduction in personnel expenses. These are the costs of lump-sum leave and retirement payouts, counseling, maintenance of a callback system for employees affected by a RIF, increases in unemployment compensation charge-backs, and other hidden costs.[11]

In addition to the convulsive effects of large-scale cutbacks, these allocational decisions spotlight value conflicts. Advocates of fiscal responsiveness and administrative efficiency often advance the cutback idea, with consequences sharply felt not only in reduced service levels generally, but also by proponents of social equity and individual rights. If the agency has been hiring a high percentage of minorities and/or women to redress previous patterns of discrimination, reductions in force will mean that they are the first to be dismissed, because they have, on the whole, less seniority than their white male counterparts. As the seniority of the average employee increases, this has consequences for compensation and retirement benefits. Since most employees laid off are at the bottom on the organization, the average grade level of employees also tends to rise.

Given the problems brought by any "solution" to cutback management, it can only be expected that public personnel managers will find it difficult to find appropriate answers. However, it is necessary that they recognize their mediating role in arranging compromises among the competing values in this situation. The pressure for cutbacks can be resisted by encouraging the agency to maintain and broaden its base of support from influential users of its services. If cuts are inevitable, their impact can be minimized by examining the organizational mission and limiting activities to those programs required by law; or by using the results of rational mechanisms such as cost benefit analysis or program evaluation. Often, however, cutbacks occur in programs that serve a deserved but politically isolated or unpopular clientele.

Perhaps more vital than these strategies, however, is maintaining communication with users, clients, and employees. At some point they should be informed fully and frequently about anticipated actions. When clients and employees need to discover for themselves cutback plans, the secrecy will produce distrust of virtually all administrative officials.

PRODUCTIVITY AND ADMINISTRATIVE EFFICIENCY

The governmental response to revenue shortfalls has focused attention on the productivity of public employees. For example, the Civil Service Reform Act of 1978 included a pay-for-performance provision designed to motivate and reward superior performance. In addition, experiments with alternative work schedules, assistance programs for employees with drug and alcohol problems, and the innovative design of work to capture the motivation of employees all represent the impact of the efficiency value of employee development.

In times of economic hardship or in response to political corruption, the demand for administrative efficiency in government increases to the point that it seems to contain virtue beyond dispute. But in the field of public personnel administration, competing value claims frequently weaken initial enthusiasm for productivity. Administrative efficiency suffers as legislators seek to protect favored programs or projects. Efficiency also clashes with claims to social equity and employee rights as seen in the area of cutback management.

Administrative efficiency may represent a threat to employee rights in other ways as well. For example, with the majority of employees at the local level working for school districts, it makes sense for major public sector productivity advances to focus on the teaching profession. This is exactly what was advanced in the 1980s with an endorsement of salary increases based on merit rather than seniority or advanced educational credits. As might be expected, these initiatives met with resistance from both the National Educational Association and the American Federation of Teachers, who claimed that effective teaching is difficult to measure, and that attempts to differentiate teaching performance would inevitably result in arbitrary salary allocations.

With these competing value claims, why has productivity in government received so much attention in the last two decades? Contemporary economic conditions are one answer. Where citizens want or need government services but money is not available to provide them at existing levels, public employers are forced to hold the line in the provision of services with reduced resources. The other answer is that the search for administrative efficiency has become a political issue as well as an economic one. In other words, for government to respond to public demands it must become efficient, or at least appear to be moving in that direction. Recall that both efficiency and responsiveness are among the central values that drive the world of public personnel management. In the 1980s and early 1990s, in order to be politically responsive, government leaders endorsed the value of administrative efficiency even if the cost is reduced emphasis on social equity and employee rights. To be efficient is to be responsive. In the 1970s Proposition 13 placed limits on property tax levies in California and led the way to the politicization of productivity in the public sector. Proposed constitutional restrictions on deficit spending also reflect this trend toward the merging of efficiency and responsiveness.

In sum, stimulated by adverse economic conditions, productivity has become a major interest in the public sector, reflected in the merger of efficiency with the value of political responsiveness.

What Is Productivity?

Various terms like output, performance, efficiency, effectiveness, and "bang for the buck" are commonly associated with productivity. Technically, productivity concerns two specific assessments of performance. First, *efficiency* is measured as a ratio of outputs to inputs. In other words, measuring efficiency requires identification of a performance outcome, such as the number of school lunches served in the cafeteria or the number of arrests made by a police officer or police department, and identification of the resources used to produce the outcome, such as employee hours worked or funds allocated to meal service or wages in the police department. The efficiency ratio then becomes:

$$\frac{\text{number of meals served}}{\text{number of cafeteria employee hours worked}}$$

The resultant ratio measures number of meals served per hour worked. Efficiency will increase in either of two ways: by increasing the number of meals served with the same number of employees, or by serving the same number of meals with fewer employees.

In the private sector and in many public-sector cases, efficiency and productivity are synonymous. But what if, in our example, efficiency were increased by serving more meals and making more arrests—yet the meals were unappetizing and not fully consumed and the arrests failed to lead to convictions and crowded the courts? Could we say that productivity had improved? Probably not.

Productivity also implies *effectiveness*, a concern with the quality of the output measured against some standard. Thus, a more valid productivity measure would be:

$$\frac{\text{number of meals consumed}}{\text{number of cafeteria hours worked}}$$

where consumption is distinguished from meal preparation. Similarly,

$$\frac{\text{number of arrests leading to convictions}}{\text{salary and wages of police officers}}$$

attempts to incorporate a quality measure for the original output, number of arrests.

Concerns for efficiency focus attention on input-output ratios and answer the question "Are we getting the most for our money?" Implied in this question is another, "Are we accomplishing the goal we set out to accomplish?" On top of this pyramid of questions is a third, "Is the goal we set out to accomplish worthwhile in light of the other goals we might have chosen?" Question 1 looks at efficiency, question 2 at effectiveness, and question 3 at responsiveness.

Thus, in the cafeteria example, the responsiveness question might have been, "Do we want to invest public money in school lunches or library books?" Once this question is answered, the school district can attend to the effectiveness and efficiency questions. Because the responsiveness question requires explicit value judgments resulting in allocational winners and losers, governments frequently focus on efficiency questions—saving money. It is a lot easier and more popular to ask why the superintendent of schools is making $80,000 a year than it is to determine whether the school district should be hiring more teachers or buying more computers. Critical responsiveness questions are often avoided until losses in service become so obvious that explicit discussions of political priorities cannot be avoided.

Examples of Productivity Improvement

Productivity programs seem to cluster into three areas. The first includes changes in organizational structure, processes, and operating procedures:

- Privatization
- Flexibility in civil service procedures

- Centralization of management support services like typing, payroll, purchasing
- Pooling fiscal accounts to increase interest revenue
- Selective decentralization or reorganization into homogeneous units
- Increased use of performance measures and work standards to monitor productivity
- Consolidation of services
- Use of economic-rational decision models for scheduling and other problems
- Energy conservation
- Recycling projects

A second set of projects and innovations involve increased use of technology:

- Labor-saving capital equipment—shifting from three-and two-person sanitation crews to a one-person side-loaded truck
- Automation in areas like recordkeeping, payroll, and billing
- Electronic data processing for scheduling, tracking of projects, and early warning of problems

The last area includes personnel-related activities:

- Job simplification
- Incentive awards
- Increased sophistication in training
- Job-related performance appraisal methods
- Specification of work standards
- Increased office communication, team building, and organizational development
- Total quality management
- Alternative work schedules

These represent the kinds of activities undertaken to increase productivity in the public sector. A significant number relate directly to managing personnel and the performance of individual employees and work units. Another important focus for productivity involves proposals to contract with private firms to provide public services.

Productivity and Privatization

Why should a city government collect trash when a private vendor could do the same? Why should the government manage lodging and concessions in public parks when private businesses could do the same?

These examples highlight the most popular form of privatization—contracting with private business to deliver services governments have been providing. Governments have contracted with private business for services like street construction and repair, tree trimming and planting, ambulance service, vehicle towing and storage, building and grounds maintenance, data processing, legal services, and tax bill processing.[12] Chandler and Feuille identify four characteristics of the services most frequently contracted for by local governments.[13] First, there is no compelling reason that government deliver the service. Second, there are usually a number of private sector firms that could supply the service. Third, the service usually requires low levels of skilled labor. Fourth, outputs are usually easy to monitor.

Sharp's literature review shows that contracting out frequently saves public dollars.[14] Advocates claim that firms competing in the marketplace are likely to provide services more efficiently than government monopolies. They also highlight the savings that can be achieved through economies of scale. For example, while one city may be unable to purchase an expensive piece of equipment to repave streets, a private company with contracts to several cities could. Advocates also point out that private companies have more flexible personnel practices, allowing them to hire and lay off employees easily and save money with less generous wages and benefit packages.

According to Sharp, critics assert that privatization may result in cutting corners to maximize profits, provide incentives to deal only with clients who are easy to serve, increase the risk of graft and corruption, and reduce the capacity to deliver the service if privatization does not work. Another concern is that the flexibility which accompanies privatization may release the private firm from obligations to follow open meetings laws and open records acts. Further, privatization confuses questions of accountability. Who do citizens hold accountable when they are dissatisfied with a service provided by a private firm but contracted for by the government?

Goodman and Loveman claim that the issue of public versus private gets caught up in symbolic and philosophical arguments when the real issue is "under what conditions will managers [whether public or private] be more likely to act in the public's interest. . . . Managerial accountability to the public's interest is what counts most, not the form of ownership."[15] They continue: "Takeover artists like Carl Icahn saw the same excesses in corporations that many people see in governmental entities: high wages, excess staffing, poor quality, and an agenda at odds with the goals of shareholders. Monitoring of managerial performance needs to occur in both public and private enterprises, and the failure to do so can cause problems whether the employer is public or private."[16]

Contracting out for public services is often a rational way to increase government productivity. It holds the promise of saving tax dollars and providing a reasonable level of service. But in many circles it remains a controversial avenue to productivity enhancement because it involves the reallocation of jobs. Reallocation of jobs from the public to the private sector brings values and personnel systems into conflict and points out the inherently political underpinnings of public personnel policy and administration. For example, those responsible for finances may favor contracting out as a way of averting a costly union contract and work rules. But the loss of public jobs invites the political displeasure of employee unions. Even though many public employees would be hired by the private contractor, unions object strenuously to contracting out because their members will usually find themselves with lower wages and benefits even if they do not lose their jobs.[17]

Social equity may suffer as women and minorities who benefit from gains in government employment find themselves at a disadvantage with employers who might show less commitment to affirmative action and merit. On the other hand, as the Supreme Court has closed the door on opportunities for patronage in government jobs, contracting out provides an opportunity for rewarding political supporters. In large urban areas this may work to the advantage of minority contractors who are politically favored by an administration in power.[18]

While those who favor contracting out point to "inflexibility" and "red tape" in government personnel systems, merit system protections for the individual rights of public employees suffer with private personnel systems, where grievance procedures are less developed. And, of course, private employers are under no obligation to provide constitutional protections to their employees or to the clients they serve.[19]

While the beginnings of an initiative to contract out a public service may simply reflect a concern to save public dollars, it is worthwhile to remember that jobs are scarce resources in our society. Any attempt to manage their allocation is likely to invite strong reactions from those invested in the current distribution. As we have seen throughout this book, those investments reflect fundamental differences in the values that shape public personnel management.

EXPANDING THE PERSONNEL MANAGER'S ROLE IN PRODUCTIVITY PROGRAMS

The enthusiasm for productivity improvement in government opens opportunities for an expanded role for the personnel manager. Activities aimed at productivity improvement affect core personnel functions but do not necessarily fall within the formal responsibilities of the personnel department. In the productivity area line managers and budget analysts consistently play a larger role than personnel specialists. In a way, this role assignment is understandable, since line managers are most familiar with daily operations and because in reality the primary motive of productivity enhancement in the public sector is saving money. In addition, the line manager and the budget analyst are familiar with numbers and ratios and tracking production figures and budgetary accounts throughout the year. Thus, it is very easy for the personnel department to be shut out of the productivity action.

The price for entering this field is expertise that those initially involved in productivity projects will value and subsequently search out. The personnel department has an opportunity to contribute in at least three areas. First, many projects involve some kind of management by objectives and the writing of job standards that specify minimally acceptable work performance. When performance appraisal systems measure what employees actually do rather than the kinds of people they are (dependable, reliable, trustworthy, and so on), there is probably no one more competent to advise on the writing of these performance objectives or standards than the personnel department. The use of the results-oriented job descriptions described in Chapter 6 clearly shows this kind of connection between the formal aspects of personnel administration and productivity improvement. Along similar lines, the personnel department is in a unique position to compare and suggest adjustments in performance standards from different departments within a government jurisdiction. There is nothing that lowers morale more than an employee's perception that two people who are doing the same kind of work and who are paid the same wages are operating under different job standards.

The second area focuses on productivity improvements directly relating to the motivation of employees. In grouping productivity projects, one cluster centers around issues like work incentives, job design, job-related performance assessments, realistic training goals and workable designs, and alternative work schedules. These kinds of projects are aimed directly at enhancing both the employee's motivation and his or her ability to work. To develop programs in these areas and to anticipate their consequences requires sophisticated understanding of employee motivation, the factors contributing to job satisfaction, equity theory, how people learn, and how organizations and work units change as well as how they resist change. In the vast majority of organizations, public and private, this knowledge does not exist in a way that is readily accessible to the line managers and planners who might need it. Academically, this knowledge is found in other disciplines: psychology, sociology, anthropology, social psychology, communication studies, and political science. The application of social science knowledge to real-life problems is often referred to as *applied behavioral science* (ABS). In the federal government, the extensive research by the Office of Personnel Management and the Merit Systems Protection Board into federal employee attitudes and the effectiveness of pay for performance fall into this category of expertise.

The third area of expertise extends the personnel administrator's knowledge into the fiscal area. Most prominent is an understanding of health insurance and health benefits, and worker's compensation and disability insurance. In addition, successful programs designed to boost the motivation of employees must develop out of expert knowledge of motivation, and expertise in the fiscal assessment of program results. Thus, anyone who can develop models that include the fiscal implications of projects that apply behavioral science knowledge will be valued. For example, knowing the cost of hiring and training a new employee and the time it takes before that employee is performing satisfactorily can lead to dollar savings. The sooner that employee leaves the organization, the less time the organization has to recover its costs. Given that the greatest turnover occurs among employees with a short time on the job, knowledge of how to retain good employees, for example through realistic job interviews,[20] can translate into cost savings. As another example, it is commonly known that dissatisfied employees are more likely to quit.[21] Once one can establish the cost of turnover, it is statistically possible through regression analysis to determine the fiscal implications of variations in the morale of a workforce. The design of such an evaluation is complex, but the point here is that knowledge of the applied behavioral sciences allows one to develop models that assess the costs of productivity projects which will affect employees.

SUMMARY

There is a close relationship between budgeting, planning, and productivity in human resource administration, which involves both political and technical decisions. Often, the human resource manager is centrally involved in both. Because government budgets are largely personnel budgets, personnel managers unfamiliar with budgeting, human resource planning, and productivity enhancement are likely to influence only peripherally critical organizational and governmental issues.

A budget represents compromises over political and technical issues concerning governmental programs and objectives. In part, these decisions are influenced by the demand and supply of labor connected to the achievement of government objectives. Productivity concerns focus on how to implement government programs and services with as few resources as possible. Frequently, the focus is on how to scale back on programs and service levels without damaging the quality of public services unacceptably.

One area that continues to attract advocates of administrative efficiency is the privatization of public services. But the hope that the private sector can deliver public services at lower cost is tempered by concerns that employee and client rights will be eroded, that social equity claims will receive less attention, and that accountability mechanisms like open meeting laws and open records requirements will be diminished.

The claim that government spending is beset by waste and inefficiency is wearing thin, and citizens are beginning to realize that cutting government costs means cutting the number of public employees. This in turn means reducing government services: longer lines, more children in classrooms, dirtier streets, more errors and, overall, less attention to the concerns and quality of life of individual citizens.

KEY TERMS

Applied behavioral sciences
Auditing
Budget
Categorical Forecasting
Ceiling budget
Cluster Forecasting
Collective opinion
Cutback management
Effectiveness
Efficiency
Financial management
Human resource forecasting
Human resource planning
Incrementalism (decrementalism)
Modeling (simulation)
Productivity
Responsiveness

DISCUSSION QUESTIONS

1. Why does budgeting epitomize the impact of the value of political responsiveness on public personnel management?
2. How is human resource planning and forecasting in public agencies related to the budget process?

3. Describe the relationship between human resources planning and other personnel management activities.

4. What are the effects of cutback management on a workforce, and how should the human resource manager respond to them?

5. Define each term and then describe the relationship between responsiveness, effectiveness, and efficiency.

6. What are the pros and cons of contracting out?

7. Describe the public personnel manager's expanded role in seeking productivity improvements.

CASE STUDY

One year ago, in April, Cityville (pop. 80,000), a suburban city, hired you, Arlene Mayberry, as the new city manager. You brought a reputation for sound financial management and were chosen unanimously by the council. Cityville has experienced revenue shortfalls in the past two years due to a decline in sales tax revenue. The shortfall resulted in modest increases in the mill levy during these two years. The school board's mill levy increased substantially a year ago due to a cutback in state aid to school districts. The county's levy is scheduled to rise modestly for the next three years due to commitments previous commissions made to a significant capital improvements program.

In April Save Our City, a group dedicated to holding the line on taxes, surprised everyone, including you, by electing two of its slate of three candidates to the city council. The council now consists of these two members, Robert Pipes and Caroline Nixon, both elected to four-year terms; Jane Scott, a very politically astute middle-of-the-road council member who has two years remaining on the council; Max Laney, an ex-police officer supported by the Fraternal Order of Police. Laney also has two years remaining on the council. Ron Reaume, who ran on a platform expressing concern for rebuilding a sense of community and respect for diversity, was elected to a two-year term. Reaume has already said he will not run for reelection. Scott and Laney have not indicated their plans.

You view this group as very diverse politically and potentially difficult to work with. You expect that a number of issues will be decided on 3–2 votes. In the summer following the election, after considerable debate and political maneuvering, the new council accepted the budget you had proposed on one of those 3–2 votes. The fiscal year runs from January 1 to December 31. None of the council members wanted to raise taxes, and the two-mill increase you reluctantly proposed was reduced to one mill with the two Save Our City council members voting against adoption; they favored no tax increase under anything other than financial exigency.

After adoption, Pipes and Nixon jointly issued a press release calling for tightening the belt, increased productivity, and sacrifices just like those made by private-sector small businesses and ordinary citizens. The newspaper carried a front-page story without editorial comment, even though the publisher is known to be sympathetic to their cause.

After the budget was adopted, during the fall and winter it became obvious that police-community relations were showing signs of strain. A self-appointed task force representing a coalition of culturally diverse groups met and held a number of forums to gather information about how citizens felt they were being treated by the police. Every opinion imaginable was expressed during these forums, which were not well attended. It was clear that individual members of minority populations in Cityville felt they had been treated inequitably by the police. For example, one African-American youth said he was walking home from a late-night job carrying a bag of groceries when he was stopped by the police and told to empty the contents of the bag.

In the spring, responding to a 911 family disturbance call, the police shot and killed an Asian wielding a knife. The police claimed self-defense; the family, speaking little English, was distraught and suggested that the police had acted too quickly and more out of concern for their own safety than for the victim or family.

The event heightened tension in the community, even though the vast majority of Cityville supported the police. The council was aware of this majority, but Reaume in particular believed something ought to be done and urged city staff to make some suggestions. He became an occasional visitor to the meetings of the task force on police-community relations and pledged to introduce their anticipated report to the council. Laney defended the police at the next council meeting, noting that police work had become more dangerous in Cityville, and that these events, tragic as they are, happen in today's violent world.

The next week, Pipes and Nixon declared that it might be worthwhile to look into a possible contract with the sheriff's department for law enforcement. They contended that the sheriff's department was larger, had better training, and could provide law enforcement more cheaply than Cityville could on its own. Laney went through the roof. The leadership of the police union quickly set up appointments with each of the council members. Reaume backtracked a bit, suggesting that rebuilding the sense of community in Cityville practically required maintaining an independent police force.

As this political maneuvering was going on, the budget process was beginning. The police chief, Jack "Buck" Fischbach, requested a meeting with you. Buck was a no-nonsense cop, professionally trained and tolerant of city managers at best. He had been one of the original founders of the Fraternal Order of Police in Cityville when he was just a corporal, years ago. He reminded the city manager that ten years ago the city had passed a half-cent sales tax to hire new police officers. You knew this. The chief added that since that time, in order to show fiscal restraint, the city had not hired a single officer, despite the addition of some 10,000 citizens. This was news to you, and you kicked yourself for not knowing it already. Further, the chief claimed that the police had become exasperated and very angry because lack of staffing had required them to cut back on the very community-oriented activities they were now being criticized for not having performed. He said he was going to develop and present to you a budget proposal designed to augment staff over a five-year period. You knew that the only way to hire more police would be to raise the mill levy.

After the chief leaves, you get a call from the newspaper publisher wanting to know how things are going.

Questions:

1. What are you going to tell the publisher?
2. How are you going to approach the budget?
3. How are you going to deal with the chief of police?
4. How are you going to deal with the council?
5. Why did you want to become a city manager in the first place?

NOTES

[1]Richard W. Lindholm, et al., "The Budgetary Process," in J. Richard Aronson and Eli Schwartz (eds.), *Management Policies in Local Government Finance* (Washington, DC: International City Management Association, 1975), pp. 63–64.

[2]Aaron Wildavsky, *The Politics of the Budgetary Process* (Boston: Little, Brown, 1974).

[3]Eugene B. McGregor, Jr., "The Public Sector Human Resource Puzzle: Strategic Management of a Strategic Resource," *Public Administration Review 48* (November–December 1988), 945.

[4]Albert C. Hyde and Torrey Whitman, "Workforce Planning—the State of the Art," in Jay M. Shafritz (ed.), *The Public Personnel World: Readings in the Professional Practice* (Chicago: International Personnel Management Association, 1978), pp. 65–73.

[5]Cynthia A. Lengnick-Hall and Mark L. Lengnick-Hall, "Strategic Human Resources Management: A Review of Literature and a Proposed Typology," *Academy of Management Review 13*, 3 (1988), 457.

[6]Milton Drandell, "A Composite Forecasting Methodology for Manpower Planning Utilizing Objective and Subjective Criteria," *Academy of Management Journal 16*, 3 (September 1975), 512.

[7]Ibid., 512–18.

[8]Steven C. Wheelwright and Darral G. Clark, "Corporate Forecasting: Promise and Reality," *Harvard Business Review 54* (November–December 1976), 64–70.

[9]Ernest C. Miller, "The Human Resource Executive and Corporate Planning: A Personnel Symposium," *Personnel 54*, 5 (September–October 1977), 12–22.

[10]Stephen K. Doig, "Federal Budget Cuts Appear Not So Deep," *The Miami Herald*, September 6, 1981, p. D6.

[11]Leonard Greenhalgh and Robert McKersie, "Cost-Effectiveness of Alternative Strategies for Cutback Management," *Public Administration Review 41*, 6 (November–December 1980), 575–84.

[12]Elaine B. Sharp, *Urban Politics and Administration* (New York: Longman, 1990).

[13]Timothy Chandler and Peter Feuille, "Municipal Unions and Privatization," *Public Administration Review 51* (January–February 1991), 15–22.

[14]Sharp, *Urban Politics.*

[15]John B. Goodman and Gary W. Loveman, "Does Privatization Serve the Public Interest?" *Harvard Business Review 69* (November–December 1991), 28.

[16]Ibid., 35.

[17]Chandler and Feuille, "Municipal Unions and Privatization."

[18]Ibid.

[19]Donald F. Kettl, "Privatization: Implications for the Public Work Force," in Carolyn Ban and Norma Riccucci (eds.), *Public Personnel Management: Current Concerns—Future Challenges* (New York: Longman, 1991).

[20]John P. Wanous, *Organizational Entry: Recruitment, Selection and Socialization of Newcomers* (Reading, MA: Addison-Wesley, 1982).

[21]William H. Mobley, *Employee Turnover: Causes, Consequences, and Control* (Reading, MA: Addison-Wesley, 1982).

CHAPTER
4

Analysis, Classification, and Evaluation

The first edition of this book emphasized the key role of job analysis and classification in personnel management. This is equally true today. But the function and orientation of public personnel management have changed so dramatically over time that even the appropriate name of these activities is now in doubt. Scholars and managers are not sure whether the focus of analysis and classification is on positions, on work, or on human resources.

This chapter will explore why the history and competing objectives of public personnel management have led us to this watershed.

By the end of this chapter, you will be able to:

1. Relate the historical development of analysis and classification to the differing objectives of position management, work management, and human resource management.
2. Describe how traditional job descriptions (those oriented toward position management) are unsuitable for supporting public personnel management as its focus has changed to work management and employee management.
3. Analyze work using a results-oriented description (ROD) which incor-

porates the objectives and philosophy of work management and employee management into the traditional process of job analysis.

4. Show how the objectives and techniques of classification are also influenced by its changing historical focus on position management, work management, and employee management.
5. Learn how to evaluate a job, using the point-factor method.
6. Critique traditional job evaluation, and discuss alternatives to it.
7. Discuss the implications of job evaluation for pay equity as a public policy issue.
8. Discuss the relationship between evaluation and other personnel activities.

HISTORY AND FOCUS OF ANALYSIS AND CLASSIFICATION

One way of looking at the history of public personnel management is to see it as a conflict among different values and personnel systems. While the objective of all these systems is the accomplishment of work, each relies on a different set of values and structures to organize public jobs. Thus, the locus and method of external control has frequently been as important as managerial accomplishment of the agency's mission.

Initially, under political patronage systems, jobs were not analyzed or classified at all. They were simply awarded to political supporters in return for contributions to successful campaigns. In this sense, the primary purpose of public jobs was their function as "spoils," along with some minimally acceptable levels of performance. Indeed, many advocates of the spoils system felt that any individual could perform any public job, without the necessity of setting minimum qualifications. Not only were minimum qualifications considered unnecessary, they tended to interfere with the freedom of an elected official to allocate jobs as rewards for campaign support. In this sense, administration and politics were inseparable.

Position Management

Traditionally, legislators and top administrators have sought to implement legislative intent and to maintain control over political and civil service systems by limiting the number of persons an agency can hire and limiting the total amount that can be spent on salaries and benefits. The underlying assumption of position management is that bureaucratic agencies tend to resist policy direction from elected officials. The way for these officials to control agencies is by limiting the amount of money they can spend, through a budget, and limiting the number and type of personnel they can employ, through position management. Frequently, position and budgetary controls are combined through the imposition of average grade-level restrictions, which in effect limit the number of positions that can be created and filled at each level of the agency hierarchy. A low average grade level means that most positions are low-level positions. Theoretically, at least, these mechanisms are successful at forcing bureaucratic compliance, efficiency, and accountability.

Work Management

Public managers have policy objectives to accomplish and limited resources with which to accomplish them. These resources and policy objectives are set by the legislature and top administrators through a strategic management process. The most critical resources an agency has are its human resources. For the work to get done with the most efficient use of human resources, the agency must hire the right number of people, with the right qualifications, for the right jobs, in the right locations. It must pay people enough money to be competitive with other employers, but not more. This is true regardless of which type of public personnel system predominates. But it is especially true for agencies that focus on mission and consider themselves bound to clear performance standards and clear paths of political accountability.

Job analysis and position classification arose from a heritage of civil service reform which reflected growing support for the application of scientific principles to administration (scientific management), and growing acceptance of the need for insulating public agencies from political pressure in order to promote efficiency and protect employee rights (politics-administration dichotomy).

Personnel management, as a branch of administrative science, is based on the bureaucratic model described by the German sociologist Max Weber. According to this model, bureaucratic organizations are the most efficient form of organization. They are characterized by a division of labor, a hierarchy of authority, reliance on rational rules as the basis for decision making, and selection and promotion on the basis of merit. Organizational applications of the bureaucratic model were developed during the early 1900s by "scientific managers" such as Frederick W. Taylor and his adherents. Taylor was an industrial engineer who believed there was "one best way" to do a job or run an organization. Given this rationale, engineering-oriented approach to management, it followed that the manager's primary function was to plan and organize work in the most technically efficient manner.

With respect to jobs, this involves the first principle of any science—organizing and classifying phenomena. In the case of work, jobs are classified into distinct groups on the basis of characteristics and level of responsibility. This was first embodied in the Classification Act of 1923, which provided for job analysis and classification for some federal positions. It is important to realize that classification developed and thrived in personnel administration because it was based on a scientific principle augmented by morality. That is, classification was considered beneficial not only because it carried the principle of description over from the natural sciences, but also because it supported the twin values of agency efficiency and individual equity. On the one hand, classification helps the line manager and the personnel manager to divide labor more efficiently. On the other, it provides for the equitable compensation of employees according to the true worth of their jobs. Last, it decreased the opportunity for political favoritism by providing that pay be based on a realistic assessment of duties and qualifications, rather than as a reward for political responsiveness.

Employee Management

Employees have a different perspective—*employee management.* They want their individual skills and abilities to be fully utilized in ways that contribute to a productive agency and to their own personal career development. They want to be managed as individuals, through a continual process of supervision, feedback, and reward. Most supervisors share this perception. They want to be able to match employees with work needs, flexibly and creatively, so that they can get their jobs done. They want to be able to use and reward employees based on their contributions to a work unit. At heart, they see job descriptions and job classification systems as "administrivia," needed to justify budget requests and to keep the folks in personnel happy, but not related to agency mission or day-to-day supervision.

The chapters of this book on productivity and performance management represent a combination of work focus and employee focus for analysis and classification. This is based on the assumption that people work most productively when they have adequate skills, clear objectives, adequate resources and organizational conditions to do their jobs, and clear feedback and consequences. They work as individuals, but also as members of work groups that collectively shape the culture of the agency and the ways in which employees work together to meet objectives.

These three different perspectives on job analysis, classification, and evaluation frequently come in conflict. Employees emphasize human resources management; managers emphasize work management; and personnel specialists have traditionally emphasized position management. Much of the trend toward professional (rather than technical) personnel management can be seen as the transition of public personnel managers from a policing role (control over employees and managers through position management) to an enabling role (facilitation of employee productivity and satisfaction, or of managerial autonomy and responsibility) through more enlightened job analysis, classification, and evaluation techniques.

TRADITIONAL JOB ANALYSIS

Traditional analysis focuses on the job as the unit of analysis. *Job analysis* is the process of recording information about the tasks (job elements) performed by an employee. It is done by observing or interviewing the worker, with the corroboration of the supervisor. It results in a *job description* (a written statement of the employee's responsibilities, duties, and qualifications). It may also include a *qualifications standard*, which specifies the minimum KSAs or qualifications (education, experience, or others) an employee needs to perform the position's duties at a satisfactory level.

Figure 4-1 is an example of a traditional job description. Note that it is useful primarily for external control and internal payroll management purposes (because it specifies job title, occupational classification, salary,

FIGURE   4-1 Traditional Job Description

Job Title: Secretary
Position No: 827301-2
Pay Grade: GS-322-4

Responsibilities: Works under the direction of the Supervisor, Operations Support Division

Duties: Performs a variety of clerical functions in support of the Supervisor and the mission of the Division:
    types correspondence and reports
    compiles reports
    maintains inventory of supplies
    arranges meetings and conferences
    answers the phone
    handles routine correspondence
    performs other duties as assigned

Qualifications:
    high school degree or equivalent
    typing speed of 40 wpm
    at least six months experience as a Secretary at grade GS-322-3, or
    equivalent

and location of the job in the hierarchy). Thus, each job (or position) can be identified as one of a number of identical positions in the agency, and its grade level serves to fix its salary and relationship to other positions above and below it in the agency's bureaucratic hierarchy.

A Critique of Traditional Job Analysis

But if the goal of the personnel system is to promote rational management of work or employees, this analysis is deficient because it views the job as separate from the mission of the organization or the person who performs it. It does not specify the performance expected of the employee, nor does it specify the linking or enabling relationship among KSAs, performance standards, and minimum qualifications, which in reality is needed by both supervisors and employees for employees to work productively in an organization. What do these deficiencies mean?

This job description lists the general duties performed by any number of secretaries. Because it applies to a range of positions, it is necessarily vague concerning the nature of the tasks (job elements) involved. The employee may be working in a foundry, a personnel office, or a chemical supply house. In each case, specific duties will differ. The entry "other duties as assigned" leaves the job description open to any additions the supervisor may assign, but does not leave room for changes in the work caused by the employee's particular skills or abilities. Thus, this traditional job description is flexible, but only unilaterally, and in a way that assumes hierarchical and downward control over work performance by the agency.

Employees and supervisors both know that a general statement of job duties must at some point be augmented by more specific information about the conditions under which the job is performed. For example, is typing done on a typewriter or a word processor? That fact, in combination with the skills and motivation of a range of applicants, will make a real difference in the level of productivity that can be expected. Is the filing system a database or a manual system using paper documents? What types of correspondence are considered "routine"? Do all duties occur continuously, or do some require more work at certain times? Are all duties equally important, or are some more important than others? What written guidelines or supervisory instructions are available to aid the employee? What conditions make task performance easier or harder?

Thus, from the applicant or employee's point of view—and the supervisor's—there is not enough useful information for orientation purposes. The employee's or applicant's query, "What is expected of me in this job?" is not answered very well. And the supervisor must use orientation or an initial on-the-job adjustment period to teach employees how the work they do *really* fits into the mission of the agency.

More critically, at least in the eyes of managers and supervisors who are interested in employee performance as it relates to the accomplishment of agency objectives, there are no standards for minimally acceptable employee performance of each of the duties. This omission causes basic problems for the supervisor, who is the person responsible for arranging the conditions of work so as to make the employee productive. How can this be done if the quantity, quality, or timeliness of service required is not specified? Moreover, it is hard to establish or evaluate performance standards unless these take into account fluctuating conditions. For example, it is easier for a salesperson to increase sales 10 percent annually in an industry growing by 20 percent annually than to achieve the same rate of increase in a declining market.

Moreover, traditional job descriptions specify a general set of minimum qualifications for each position. If jobs have been classified according to the type of skill required, these minimum qualifications may also be based on the KSAs needed to perform duties. In general, however, traditional methods blur the following logical sequence of relationships among tasks, standards, KSAs, and minimum qualifications:

1. Each task must be performed at a certain minimum standard for the organization to function well.
2. Certain KSAs are required to perform each task up to standard.
3. Certain minimum qualifications ensure that the employee will have the requisite KSAs.

Thus, even though position descriptions are traditionally seen as the cornerstone of personnel management, it is evident that they serve a dual role. The use of standardized job descriptions for a range of positions, with each one identified by a different position number and organizational location, is useful for reducing paperwork and providing position management (external control over the total number of positions and their salary level). But these advantages work against their usefulness as a work management or employee management tool. For these purposes, individual jobs should each have a separate job description, in recognition of the variability of tasks, conditions, standards, and KSAs they require. They should help the manager and the employee by serving as links among personnel functions such as selection, orientation, training, and performance appraisal. These two problems—the lack of clear relationship among tasks, standards, KSAs, and qualifications, and the lack of clear information about the nature of the job—reduce the usefulness of such job descriptions for executives, managers, and employees.

Executives are handicapped because such traditional job descriptions describe only the personnel inputs into a job and not the resultant outputs in terms of organizational productivity. That is, they do not specify how many employees would be needed to produce outputs at a given level of quantity, quality or timeliness. Because traditional job descriptions do not lend themselves to output analysis, they are not a useful part of the human resource planning, management, or evaluation process. They most closely resemble the line-item budget, which has long been recognized as more useful for controlling resource inputs than program outputs.

Managers are handicapped because they cannot readily use such job descriptions for recruitment, orientation, goal setting, or performance evaluation. If new employees are recruited on the basis of the brief description of duties and qualifications given in the traditional job description, extensive interviewing by managers may be needed to select the applicants most qualified for a particular job. Orientation will require clarification of the job description to fit the particular organizational context, and it may be incomplete because of other demands on the manager's time. If the organization uses MBO goal setting and evaluation procedures, these will occur independently of the job description. This means that job descriptions will be used only by the personnel department for position management, recruitment, and other external control-oriented activities. Managers will seek to manage work by an unrelated set of MBO and performance appraisal procedures.

Employees are generally unable to use traditional job descriptions for orientation, performance improvement, or career development. Because job descriptions give only a brief outline of duties, employees must wait to find out about working conditions and performance standards until after they have been hired. Yet this may be too late; unclear or inequitable psychological contracts are a cause of much unrest between employees and organizations. Evaluating employees without giving them clear performance standards is a sure way to increase anxiety and frustration.

Moreover, employees cannot use traditional job descriptions for career development because they do not specify how increases in minimum qualifications are related to increases in skills required for satisfactory task performance. It is easiest for employees to accept the qualifications for a position and to strive to meet them through upward mobility programs if these linkages are more apparent.

But personnel managers, and the personnel management function itself, are most seriously affected by the focus of traditional job descriptions on cataloguing and managing positions, rather than managing work. Because traditional job descriptions are not very suitable to work management, they are regarded as irrelevant by executives, managers, and employees. Inevitably, job descriptions tend to be regarded in the same light as inventories of office equipment or the updating of workplace safety regulations—something that must be done to satisfy the requirements of outside agencies, but that tends to detract from the agency's ability to meet its objectives. If personnel managers consider job descriptions to be one of the most important personnel tools, and if job descriptions are perceived by managers and employees as useless for their purposes, then the impression may be created that other personnel activities are equally unimportant. This logic is frequently used to belittle performance evaluation, job analysis, training needs surveys, and other items from the personnel manager's stock in trade.

Consequently, the primary result of the traditional job description's focus on external control objectives is to divorce personnel management from work management and employee management. This traditional view of job descriptions has in large part been responsible for the traditional view of personnel management as a series of low-level operational techniques used mainly for external control or system maintenance purposes.

How to Improve Traditional Job Descriptions

Job descriptions would be more useful if they clarified the organization's expectations of employees and the links among tasks, standards, KSAs, and minimum qualifications. These improved job descriptions would contain the following information:

1. **Tasks**: What work duties are important to the job?
2. **Conditions**: What things make the job easy (such as close supervision or written guidelines explaining how to do the work) or hard (such as angry clients or difficult physical conditions)?
3. **Standards**: What objective performance levels (related to organizational objectives) can reasonably be set for each task, measured in terms of objectives such as quantity, quality, or timeliness of service?
4. **KSAs**: What knowledge, skills, and abilities are required to perform each task at the minimum standard, under the above conditions?
5. **Qualifications**: What education, experience, and other qualifications are needed to ensure that employees have the necessary KSAs?

Two examples of results-oriented job descriptions (RODs) are shown in Figure 4-2. These results-oriented descriptions provide clearer organizational expectations to employees. They encourage supervisors and employees to recognize that both standards and KSAs can be contingent upon conditions. For example, a secretary can type neater copy more quickly with a word processor than with a manual typewriter, and different skills are required. In the second example, an increase in each probation officer's caseload from 60 to 100 clients would inevitably affect the quantity, quality, or timeliness of visits with probationers. A probation officer preparing PSIs for a new judge might be expected to have a lower level of accepted recommendations.

Thus, job descriptions can do more than just establish a link between tasks, conditions, and standards that is useful to employees and super-

---

Word Processor/Receptionist
  Operations Support Division
  Position No: 827301-2
  Pay Grade: GS-322-4

Responsibilities: Works under the direction of the Supervisor, Operations Support Division

TASKS	CONDITIONS	STANDARDS
Type letters	Use IBM PC, Word Perfect and agency style manual	Letters completed in 2 hours, error-free
Greet visitors	Use appointment log provided by Supervisor	No complaints from scheduled visitors about waiting, provided Supervisor is on time
Maintain files	Use DBM software and instructions provided by Supervisor	Update files weekly, with accuracy and completeness

KNOWLEDGE, SKILLS, AND ABILITIES REQUIRED

Able to type 40 wpm
Courtesy
Word Perfect, Lotus 1-2-3

MINIMUM QUALIFICATIONS

High school degree or equivalent
Two years word processing, especially Word Perfect
One year database management, especially Lotus 1-2-3

FIGURE   4-2   Results-Oriented Descriptions (RODs)

visors. This link is the logical connection between duties and qualifications that is required for content validation of qualifications standards under affirmative action programs or civil service systems. Chapter 8 on workplace productivity improvement, will describe how results-oriented descriptions (RODs) can be used to help supervisors improve performance.

Juvenile Probation Officer
State Department of Corrections

TASKS	**CONDITIONS**	**STANDARDS**
Meet clients to record their behavior	Caseload of not more than 60; supervisor will help with hard cases; use departmental rules and regulations	See each probationer weekly; keep accurate and complete records per DOC rules & regulations
Report criminal activity to supervisor		
Prepare presentence investigation reports	Average of 5 per week, per court instructions; supervisor will review	Reports complete & accurate, per Judge; Judge will accept recommendations in 75% of cases

KNOWLEDGE, SKILLS, AND ABILITIES REQUIRED

Knowledge of the factors contributing to criminal behavior
Ability to counsel probationers
Ability to write clear and concise probation reports
Knowledge of different judges' sentencing preferences for particular types of offenders and offenses
Knowledge of law and DOC regulations concerning presentencing investigations and probation

MINIMUM QUALIFICATIONS

High school degree or equivalent plus four years of experience working with juvenile offenders, or a BS degree in criminal justice, psychology, or counseling
Possess a valid driver's license

THE HISTORY OF CLASSIFICATION

The history of personnel management can be seen as the history of classification. Initially, the dual objectives of external political control and mechanistic internal management practices derived from the application of administrative science and hierarchical control meant that positions were what was classified, and the name of the field was position classification. Viewed in this context, position classification is the process of categorizing positions according to occupation or *level of responsibility*. That is, all positions are grouped within a matrix, or classified, based on the type of work performed and the level of responsibility required.

Position classification follows logically from job analysis, for it assumes that each position can be logically placed both vertically and horizontally within a lattice (the *table of organization*, or *organizational chart*). Traditional position classification simplifies job analysis and position management, for it means that a standardized description can be written for an entire group of positions (those requiring the same qualifications because they comprise the same tasks, conditions, and standards).

Position classification simplifies external control of agencies because it is possible for legislators or elected officials to control the personnel inputs to an agency by specifying (and limiting) the number, occupational type, and grade levels of all positions in the agency. It is useful to managers because it limits and specifies the ways in which employees can be moved from position to position. Two types of position classification are commonly used: type of work and level of responsibility.

On the other hand, those who emphasize the relation of analysis to work management or employee management generally consider position classification irrelevant or counterproductive. That is, the focus of traditional classification is on inputs: How many positions, at what grade level and in which occupations, are allocated to a particular work unit? This focus is largely irrelevant to output or to employee needs, which tend to direct attention to an entirely different set of questions. For the manager who wishes to focus on work performance, the classification system is an impediment that prevents flexible reassignment of people based on their relative skills and abilities and the work needs of the agency. For employees, the classification system is an artificial and infuriating barrier that prohibits advancement and fails to recognize the impact of the individual on the job. It also reinforces outdated hierarchical and mechanistic views of work by confining performance to a rigid set of externally imposed tasks, without any focus on the more important issues, such as the flexible use of human resources to accomplish agency objectives, or the development of employees through creative personnel management processes set up by personnel directors and implemented by supervisors.

The incompatibility of traditional position classification with the ascendant objectives of work management and employee management has given rise to a number of "nether world" personnel practices. Such practices are activities carried on by personnel directors and supervisors to achieve agency objectives and manage employees within the confines of an inflexible and unresponsive position classification system. They include:

gaining approval for individual changes in classification based on the impact of the person on the job; and escaping from the confines of a classification system by making positions *exempt* (unclassified political appointments). Two examples will illustrate.

A major reorganization of the federal government's classification system occurred with the passage of the Civil Service Reform Act of 1978. One of the provisions of this reform was the reclassification of senior administrative positions (grades GS-16 to GS-18) into a Senior Executive Service (SES). Employees in these positions were offered the option of continuing in civil service positions or transferring into exempt positions where individual performance contracts provided more opportunity for merit pay for productive performance, and more flexibility for supervisors to use topnotch executives regardless of their specific occupational skills.

As a second example, a major county government recently centralized fire and rescue service by consolidating all municipal fire departments into one central county agency. One of the major obstacles to this reorganization was the differences in duties and pay of various fire and rescue personnel in different municipal governments.

POINT-FACTOR JOB EVALUATION

The data used in analyzing a job for purposes of developing a job description also form the basis for a *job evaluation*. The purpose of job evaluation is to determine the worth of the job or position (rather than the value of the work or quality of the person's performance. Although several methods of job evaluation have been used, the most prominent today is the *point-factor* method. It compares jobs on an absolute scale of difficulty, using several predetermined job worth factors which are quantified to make numerical comparisons easier. This is how it is done:

1. Analyze all jobs in the organization.
2. Select factors that measure job worth across all positions. Common factors include supervisory responsibility, difficulty of duties, working conditions, and budgetary discretion. It may be necessary to break jobs into broad occupational classes first, and to develop separate compensable factors for each class.)
3. Weight job factors so that the maximum possible value is 100. (For example, there could be five factors worth 20 points each, or two worth 20 each and one worth 60).
4. Develop and define quality levels for each job worth factor, and apportion points within that factor to each quality level. (For example, if "working conditions" is selected as a job worth factor with a total value

of 20 points out of 100, then the following quality levels might be established for this job worth factor:

(a) 0 points: office work
(b) 10 points: occasional outside work, some walking or standing required
(c) 20 points: constant outside work in bad weather; heavy lifting required.

5. Evaluate each job along each job worth factor, and compute the point total.
6. Establish realistic pay ranges for benchmark positions based on market comparisons with similar jobs elsewhere.
7. Pay benchmark jobs the market rate, and pay other jobs in proportion to their comparative point totals.

Table 4-1 shows how a simplified example of the point-factor method might work in practice. It can immediately be seen that this initial attempt to create an equitable pay system has resulted in some apparent inequities: police lieutenants would make more than the police chief, and police officers would make more than the sergeants who supervise them. Note, however, that this is entirely due to the choice of job worth factors, their

TABLE 4-1 Example of Point-Factor Job Evaluation

JOB WORTH FACTORS skill (30 points), working conditions (30 points), and responsibility (40 points) = 100 points total

QUALITY LEVELS

Skill:	30—professional knowledge and independent judgment
	20—technical knowledge under supervision
	10—some technical skill under close supervision
Working conditions:	30—constantly unpleasant and dangerous
	20—occasionally unpleasant or dangerous
	0—office work
Responsibility:	40—makes decisions affecting a major program area
	25—makes decisions affecting a department
	10—makes decisions affecting a service to individual clients

COMPENSABLE FACTORS

Position	Skill	Conditions	Responsibility	Total	Salary
Mayor	30	0	40	70	$35,000
Police chief	30	0	25	55	27,500
Lieutenant	30	10	25	65	32,500
Sergeant	20	10	10	40	20,000
Police officer	10	30	10	50	25,000

TABLE 4-2   Revised Example of Point-Factor Job Evaluation

JOB WORTH FACTORS skill (20 points), working conditions (20 points), and responsibility (60 points) = 100 points total

QUALITY LEVELS
Skill:	20—exercises professional judgment independently
	14—exercises judgment with some supervision
	7—exercises technical skill under supervision
Working conditions:	20—constant danger and discomfort
	10—occasional danger or discomfort
	0—office work
Responsibility:	60—in charge of a large organization
	45—in charge of a major department
	30—supervises more than ten employees
	15—supervises less than ten employees
	0—no supervisory responsibilities

POINT-FACTOR EVALUATION

Position	Skill	Conditions	Responsibility	Total	Salary
Mayor	20	0	60	80	$60,000
Police chief	20	0	45	65	48,750
Lieutenant	20	10	30	60	45,000
Sergeant	14	20	15	49	36,750
Police officer	7	20	0	27	20,250

relative weights, the choice of quality levels, and their relative weight. Each of these four choices is based on the professional judgment of the job analyst. When the results appear to defy reality or common sense, the job analyst will usually alter the choice or relative weight of the job worth factors, or the definition and relative weight of the quality levels for each factor.

These changes would probably result in alterations of the method to the example shown in Table 4-2. In this case, the relative value of the five jobs has been altered by changing the value of the job worth factor "responsibility" from 40 to 60 points, and by reducing the value of the other two factors to 20 points each. And the quality factors' point values have been readjusted based on the change in point allocation to the three job worth factors.

Once ratings have been established by the job analyst, they should be reviewed for objectivity and "reality testing" by a committee representing the major divisions of the agency. The committee should be chaired by an objective facilitator who will get the group to reach consensus on adjustments to the point values and relative salaries for the various positions.

A CRITIQUE OF JOB EVALUATION, AND ALTERNATIVES TO IT

Point-factor methods of job evaluation are extremely popular because of their objectivity, stability, and reliability for pay-setting purposes. Despite their complexity and high development costs, they have largely supplanted other evaluation methods because of their perceived internal validity (within the agency) and the ease with which objective factors can be used to validate the system in the face of attacks by employees, unions, and affirmative action compliance agencies.

But all job evaluation methods have a fundamental weakness—they focus on the relative worth of jobs or positions, rather than the relative importance of the work to the mission of the agency or the relative quality of employee's performance. Thus, in an era where the focus of human resource management is shifting from inputs to outputs, and where work is allocated flexibly rather than hierarchically, job evaluation has increasingly come under attack as outmoded and off target.[1] Critics charge that it reinforces bureaucratic hierarchy and lack of initiative and discourages innovation, development of internal and external relationships, and mission orientation among employees. Employees tend to focus on internal competition for upward classification and pay increases rather than on customers and mission. And classification and evaluation systems tend to stifle organizational change by tying any alteration in work duties or relationships to potential changes in internal status and pay. Creative managers soon learn that jobs can be "upgraded" by rewriting job descriptions to gain more job evaluation points. Thus, job evaluation creates incentives to create additional supervisory positions and waste resources, because supervisors can gain higher grades based on the number of resources they use and the number of employees they supervise.

There are at least two alternatives to traditional job evaluation: rank-in-person systems and market models.

Rank-in-Person Systems

Rank-in-person systems are traditionally found in the military, in paramilitary organizations such as police and fire departments and the U.S. Public Health service, in the U.S. Foreign Service, and in university faculties. *Rank-in-person* systems differ from traditional job classification and evaluation (*rank-in-job* systems) because their focus is not on the duties of a particular position, but on the KSAs of the employee. Under a rank-in-job system, all employees are classified by type of occupation and level of responsibility, and these factors are tied to a job analysis, classification, and evaluation system. Under a rank-in-person system, employees qualify for promotion from one rank to another based on skills, knowledge, experience, and education (assuming promotional opportunities are available).

Since the rank attaches to the person rather than to the position, employees can be freely assigned or reassigned within the organization without its affecting pay or status. This has the advantage of reducing the immobility and status concerns generated by traditional job evaluation. It also enables the matching of employees to work based on the specific skills or abilities required. This feature offers organizations that use rank-in-person systems tremendous flexibility, and it is much more effective at utilizing workforce diversity to match employee talents with agency needs. For example, assume the U.S. Public Health Service needs to respond to an increased incidence of hepatitis among hospital workers in Phoenix. Since the USPHS uses a rank-in-person system, it can search its employee data banks to come up with a list of specialists who are experienced in hepatitis-B research and education, bilingual, and living in or able to relocate to Phoenix. Once identified, individuals can quickly be put to work without worrying about whether they are in the "right" grade level or occupational specialty.

Market Models

An even less formal option is also available—abandoning job classification and evaluation altogether, and relying on managerial flexibility, performance appraisals, and the market mechanism to set salaries. Under this model, which is mostly followed in small, entrepreneurial private businesses, managers are given the authority to *manage to budget*. This means they can hire as many employees as they need, at whatever salary they choose, in order to accomplish their mission. Employees (and the manager) are hired under short-term performance contracts. Successful managers are those who hire the right employees, pay them appropriate salaries, and utilize them effectively to meet mission requirements. Successful employees are those who can negotiate mission-oriented performance contracts, price themselves realistically in the job market, and sell themselves to a succession of managers and employers. The validity of the system is based on the financial survival of the employer. If you get a paycheck, you are being paid fairly and doing well; if not, you aren't!

There are obviously major disadvantages to both alternatives. Rank-in-person systems still must control total budget allocations for personnel by personnel ceilings and average grade levels. And employees will continue to focus on assignments perceived as developmental or as required for advancement to the next highest rank ("ticket punching"). The agency must develop relatively sophisticated human resource management information systems if it is to effectively match work with employees. A traditional rank-in-job system requires only a match of the occupational code and grade level of the vacant position with a roster of employees who meet the minimum qualifications for that grade level. A rank-in-person system requires cataloguing (and confidentiality) of a range of employee data, detailed analysis of the KSAs required by an agency, and rapid matching of skills with needs through a real-time, user-accessible information system.

Market models are often used in the private sector. They are frequently used in conjunction with job evaluation systems to validate them. But they do not allow for the external (executive and legislative) control of inputs that characterizes the public sector. However, both political and contract positions are filled on this basis, in that pay or contract provisions can be set politically through the approval of individual political appointments or the contract approval process. And they raise profound questions of equity, such as those addressed in the following discussion.

JOB EVALUATION AND PAY EQUITY

The relationship between job evaluation and pay equity is perhaps the clearest example of the way in which competing values and systems affect pay in public agencies.

Market models are clearly the most efficient method of setting pay rates. They are flexible, mission-oriented, and externally valid. They have traditionally been followed in the private sector (except for collective bargaining). And several public-sector personnel systems (political and contracting out) use them as well.

But market models frequently conflict with two other values: individual rights and social equity. The conflict between individual rights and efficiency is exemplified by collective bargaining, which will be discussed as a partial personnel system in Chapter 13. Under collective bargaining, pay rates are set by bilateral or multilateral negotiations between labor and management. From an employee's viewpoint, collective bargaining is necessary because of the power of large employers to depress wages below the rate considered fair or necessary.

The conflict between efficiency and social equity is epitomized by the civil rights and affirmative action movements. The private sector can legitimately save money by paying lower wages to youth, the elderly, women, minorities, and disabled employees. This is considered good business practice, and is justified by the resultant cost savings. But public agencies are required to treat employees equitably based on merit factors. Clearly, a public agency that is required to provide equal protection to all employees as persons, and that is required to follow due process in setting pay, could not justify paying lower wages to these groups simply because market factors would justify it.

It is this conflict which has given rise to demands for *pay equity* among women and minorities (equal pay for work requiring equivalent skill, effort and responsibility); and to conflicting demands for acceptance of market economics by private sector employers.

EVALUATION AND OTHER PERSONNEL ACTIVITIES

Analysis, classification, and evaluation are clearly the heart of personnel management, and the key to an effective match between the individual employee and the organization. It helps the employee know when duties are being assigned equitably or not. And by viewing the hierarchy of job descriptions within a particular occupational cluster, an employee can develop ideas about the direction of possible career advancement and the KSAs necessary for advancement. From the manager's perspective, they connect human resource planning to the budgetary and legislative process. They improve employee relations by clarifying the terms of work in a manner that is equitable and flexible. And they achieve external political responsiveness through control over inputs and accountability for results.

SUMMARY

Many current controversies in public personnel management center around the appropriateness of a focus on jobs, work, or employees. Traditional job analysis defines the position as the unit of analysis, and develops classification and evaluation systems based on type and level of work. More contemporary approaches focus on flexible use of human resources to accomplish the mission of the agency. Examples of the differences in these two approaches are the transition from traditional job descriptions to newer results-oriented descriptions, and the use of rank-in-person or market models in favor of traditional rank-in-job evaluation systems. Political and contract systems already use these newer approaches. Civil service systems, for the most part, do not. One of the key points of conflict within public personnel management is the extent to which the system should be driven by market models (which are more efficient), or by broader concerns of social equity and individual rights.

KEY TERMS

employee management
exempt (unclassified) position
grade level
job analysis
job classification
job description
job evaluation
job worth factor
level of responsibility

management by objectives

management to budget
market model

organization chart (table of organization)
pay equity

point-factor evaluation
position management

qualifications standard ("qual standard")
rank-in-job
rank-in-person

results-oriented description (ROD)
standards
tasks

work management

DISCUSSION QUESTIONS

1. How does the historical development of analysis and classification relate to the differing objectives of position management, work management, and employee management?

2. Why are traditional job descriptions unsuitable for supporting personnel management as its focus has changed to work management and employee management?

3. How do results-oriented descriptions (RODs) differ from traditional job descriptions? Why are they more effective?

4. Why are jobs classified, and how?

5. What is the point-factor method of job evaluation? What steps does it involve?

6. How does traditional job evaluation limit agency effectiveness? What alternatives are there to it? What are the disadvantages of these alternatives?

7. How does job evaluation relate to alternative personnel systems (collective bargaining and affirmative action) and values (individual rights and social equity)?

8. How do analysis, classification and evaluation relate to other personnel activities?

CASE STUDY: PICKING A MINORITY RECRUITMENT DIRECTOR FOR A STATE POLICE DEPARTMENT

You have recently been appointed by the governor of your state as personnel director of the state police. This organization consists of about 1,000 officers and 200 civilian employees. Its primary mission is to promote highway safety through enforcement of traffic laws and assistance to motorists.

In recent years, the state police organizatoin has come under increasing public criticism. The major grievance is that too much attention is being paid to writing traffic tickets and enforcing the 55 MPH speed limit; a more proper focus would be on organized crime and drug trafficking, which law enforcement officials privately admit is both growing and impossible to stop through the efforts of local law enforcement agencies. In addition, many people believe that the state police discriminates against women and minorities in both employment and enforcement of traffic laws.

Morale is low among younger officers, who see themselves as victims of societal conflicts. Turnover among recruits, those who have completed a three-month training course at the State Police Training Center, averages 25 percent during the first year. Reasons most often given for leaving the organization are working conditions, lack of immediate promotion opportunities, and the feeling that promotion is based on politics or personality rather than performance.

Many observers consider the state police to be a highly political organization because its top administrative positions are gubernatorial appointments. Some observers believe that, as a result, top management lacks experience in law enforcement or management, and that this reduces the morale and effectiveness of the organization.

As director of personnel for the state police, your task is to select an assistant who will be solely responsible for developing, administering, and evaluating a minority-recruitment program for the agency. The three resumés shown are those that you and your screening committee have picked as being the most qualified of several hundred applicants who responded to nationwide advertising for the position. You have scheduled each applicant to report for an interview; you have completed the interview process; and it is now time to rank the three applicants.

Divide into work groups with four or five people in each group (groups A, B, C, and so on). Within 25 minutes, place all three candidates in rank order, based on their qualifications for the position. Before you do so, be prepared to defend your selection by developing answers to these questions:

1. What job duties are most important to the position? (*example:* planning a recruitment program)

TABLE 4-3 Minority Recruitment Director

CANDIDATE	GROUP A	GROUP B	GROUP C	GROUP D	GROUP E
Harold Murphy					
Willie Jones					
Norma Sikorsky					

2. What skills, knowledge, and abilities will successful applicants need? (*example:* be able to communicate with people from different backgrounds)

3. What minimum qualifications will successful applicants need? (*example:* education, experience, credentials or licenses, other qualifications)

4. In what rank order should the candidates be placed, on the basis of your answers to questions 1 through 3? (see Table 4-3)

5. Why is the applicant you chose the most qualified of the three?

6. What selection criteria were most important in making the choice? (see Table 4-4)

7. Which value (political responsiveness, agency efficiency, or social equity) is most enhanced by your selection decision and criteria? Is this an appropriate definition of "merit" in this situation?

8. How confident are you that the selection criteria you used are job-related?

9. How would you validate the criteria if asked to do so by a federal court or an affirmative action compliance agency?

TABLE 4-4 Selection Criteria

CRITERION	GROUP A	GROUP B	GROUP C	GROUP D	GROUP E
Education					
Experience					
Credentials					
Race/sex					
Politics					
Other (specify)					

Willie Jones
1327 W. Addison St.
Minneapolis, Minn.

Employment History:

1986–present: Assistant Dean of Admissions at Northern Minnesota State Teachers College. Responsible for minority recruitment, minority financial aid, and internship programs for a 25,000 student state university offering a range of undergraduate programs. Since 1986, the percentage of minority students has increased from 3 percent to 13 percent of the student body.

1984–1986: Administrative assistant to the Dean of Admissions, Texas Technical Institute. Responsible for review of applicants for admission, counseling of minority students, and administration of minority financial aid programs.

1970–1984: 1st Lieutenant to Major, U.S. Army. Responsible for a variety of combat and staff assignments in the U.S. and overseas. Rifle Platoon Leader responsible for the health, morale, welfare, and safety of 43 men (1970–1971). Company Executive Office (1972–1973). Battalion Air Operations Officer responsible for scheduling aircraft and helicopters to support personnel and units of the battalion in South Vietnam (1974–1975)., Battalion Advisor 11th Airborne Division, ARVN: one of twenty officers selected to advise in combat 10 ARVN Airborne Battalions in the use of U.S. weapons and tactics.
Awards and Decorations:
Silver Star, Bronze Star Medal with "V" Device for Valor (2 Oak Leaf Clusters), Air Medal, Army Commendation Medal with "V" Device for Valor, and Purple Heart (2 Oak Leaf Clusters).

Education:

B.A. in History, Jackson State University, Mississippi, 1984

Personal Data:

5'11"
180 pounds
married, two children
excellent health

Harold Murphy
3732 18th Street
Arlington, Va.

Employment History:

1989–present: Personnel Director for Northern Virginia Community College. Responsible for management of labor relations, staff recruitment and selection, training, and affirmative action compliance. Responsible for representing NVCC in first collective bargaining session with staff union.

1987–1989: Assistant to the Personnel Director, Tennessee Industrial-Technical College, Nashville. Responsible for position classification, grievances and appeals, and labor-management relations for 300 staff employees.

Education:

M.S. in Government (Personnel Management), The George Washington University, Washington, D.C. Wrote master's thesis on "Minority Recruitment Problems and Prospects in Virginia State Government." 3.87 GPA. (1986)

B.A. in Business Administration (Personnel Management), The George Washington University (1983). Senior honors thesis on "Conflicts Between Seniority and Affirmative Action Guidelines in Public Labor Management Relations." Phi Beta Kappa, Pi Sigma Alpha, Woodrow Wilson Fellowship, cum laude.

Professional Activities:

"Managing Labor Relations in State University Systems," American Association of University Personnel Administrators Conference, New Orleans, March 1974.

Personal Information:

married
good health

References:

upon request

Norma Sikorsky
P.O. Box 6597
Salem, Oregon

Employment History:

1987–present: Assistant to the Governor of Oregon, responsible for the development of statewide affirmative action plans for state agencies. Supervised three employees with a staff budget of $100,000. Made recommendations on affirmative action to state agency heads. Responsible for extensive coordination and public relations work with state and local minority representatives and groups. Represented the state at numerous affirmative action conferences.

1983–1985: Deputy Assistant Director for Education, State of Oregon. Responsible for advising the Assistant Director on secondary curriculum matters throughout the state. Developed and implemented the first race relations program used in Oregon high schools (1985). Developed and implemented statewide curriculum changes in women's athletic programs.

1975–1982: High school teacher, Clackamas High School, Coos Bay, Oregon. Responsible for teaching social studies, civics, and athletics.

Education:

M.A. in Education, University of Oregon, Eugene (1983)

B.A. in Education, University of Oregon, Eugene (1975)

References:

Governor Tom McCall, Oregon

Simon Merkle, Ed. D.
Director for Education
State Office Building
Salem, Oregon

William Jackson, Director
Equal Employment Opportunity Comission
Salem, Oregon

NOTES

[1]E. Lawler III, "What's Wrong with Point-Factor Job Evaluation," *Management Review* 75, 11 (November 1986), 44–48.

CHAPTER

5

PAY AND BENEFITS

Pay and economic benefits are important to employees because they provide for economic well-being and offer an objective, economic measure of the individual's worth to the organization. They serve as a measure of comparison for internal equity (compared to other employees in the agency) and external equity (compared with other employers in the job market). Both measures are important, for they affect satisfaction, performance, and turnover.

To be effective, pay and benefit systems must be equitable, flexible, and easy to administer. Flexibility is important because different employees have different needs. For example, family health care benefits are more useful in a situation where there is one wage earner with children; they are less important to single wage earners, or to families where dependents are already covered by another insurance policy. Yet flexibility and ease of administration are contradictory. Some benefits (such as Social Security) are required by law; others are optional (depending on the type of personnel system and the conditions of employment).

The high and increasing cost of employee benefits (up from about 10 percent of salary in 1960 to over 40 percent today), the importance and expense of health care, and the need to combine flexibility and ease of administration within a package that meets employer productivity needs and employee equity concerns means that compensation and benefits managers enjoy an increasingly important role in human resource management today.

By the end of this chapter, you will be able to:

1. Discuss the methods of setting pay under alternative public personnel systems.
2. Discuss merit pay and its relationship to performance evaluation, seniority, and cost-of-living allowances.
3. Describe the statutory benefits to which employees are entitled by law (Social Security, worker's compensation, and unemployment compensation).
4. Discuss public employee pension systems and the public policy issues associated with pension fund management.
5. Discuss health insurance plans, and the managerial and public policy issues associated with the increasing cost of health care.
6. Discuss other emergent benefit issues (sick leave and holiday pay, parental leave, and child care), and their impact on employer productivity and workforce diversity.
7. Discuss the relationship between pay and benefit systems and the conflict among public personnel systems and values.

SETTING PAY UNDER ALTERNATIVE PERSONNEL SYSTEMS

Pay setting in public agencies is governed by legal constraints, historical practice, and the relative power of stakeholders. Four primary laws apply: The Fair Labor Standards Act of 1938, the Equal Pay Act of 1963, the 1964 Civil Rights Act (Title VII), and the Age Discrimination in Employment Act of 1967. In this section we discuss the provisions of the laws that apply to public agencies, the outcome of these laws' interaction with historical practice, and the impact of these outcomes on the pay-setting process under alternative personnel systems.

Laws

The Fair Labor Standards Act (FLSA) was originally passed in 1938 to regulate minimum wages, overtime pay, and recordkeeping requirements for private employers. In 1985, the U.S. Supreme Court's decision in *Garcia v. San Antonio Metropolitan Transit Authority* made state and local governments subject to its wage, hour, and recordkeeping requirements. This court case has had a profound effect on public personnel practices in state and local government. Employees must be paid the minimum wage ($4.25 per hour as of April 1, 1991). All civil service employees (with the exception of executives, administrative employees, and professionals) must be paid time-and-a-half for overtime, defined as more than 40 hours per work week (or given "comp time" during the same pay period). Employers are required to keep records going back two to three years of *all* employees' wages and hours, and to provide these records to the Department of Labor upon request.

Because it is not always clear whether employees are exempt from or covered by the FLSA, and because covered employees require more complex staffing patterns or considerably higher personnel costs, keeping up with FLSA provisions is critical to state and local governments. Many local government employees (particularly police officers and firefighters) have irregular work schedules that pose particular problems for compensation specialists.[1]

The Equal Pay Act of 1963 requires employers to provide men and women with equal pay for equal work. In order to win relief under this law, the plaintiff must demonstrate that jobs requiring equal skill, effort, and responsibility, and performed under similar working conditions, are paid differentially on the basis of sex. But "equal work" is narrowly defined under the terms of this act—it does not include dissimilar jobs, and it exempts pay differentials resulting from the impact of seniority or merit systems.

The Civil Rights Act of 1964 (Title VII) forbids discrimination with respect to pay and benefits on the basis of non-merit factors. While it does not prohibit any sex-based pay differentials that are legal under the Equal Pay Act of 1963, subsequent court cases have held that it goes beyond the equal pay provisions of the EPA by in some cases allowing equal pay for comparable jobs—those not identical, but requiring equivalent skill, effort, responsibility, and performed under similar working conditions.

The Age Discrimination in Employment Act prohibits employers from paying older workers less than younger ones for equal work. And as the work force gets grayer, it has another important provision—prohibiting employers from using pension plan provisions to force older employees to take early retirement.

The Interplay of Laws and Historical Practice

Judging by its laws related to pay equity, the United States is an egalitarian society—discrimination in pay and benefits on the basis of age, sex, race, or other non-merit factors is prohibited. But judging by its history of personnel practice with respect to pay equity, there is ample evidence to justify the conclusion that our society is profoundly racist and sexist. In fairness, however, there are two sides to this question, and one should not reach even tentative conclusions on so important an issue without examining both.

Proponents of labor market mechanisms for pay setting will usually admit that women and minorities earn less than men, and that pay rates for male-dominated jobs are higher than those for female-dominated jobs. But they deny that these differences are based on sex or race discrimination as such. They attribute the difference in men's and women's salaries to traditional labor market explanations: Women have lower seniority than men because they leave the labor market to have babies or move from one job to another to accompany their husbands (without commensurate increases in pay or status). Minorities tend to cluster in low-paying, low-status service jobs.

Proponents of pay equity, on the other hand, charge that women and minorities have been concentrated in these occupations and employment situations precisely because of social values and conditions. As justification for this view, they compare salaries for different groups in the public and private sectors. In the private sector, where antidiscrimination laws apply but "employment at will" laws limit the power of women and minorities to protest employment conditions, the disparity between salaries of white males and other groups is about 40 percent, *and has remained essentially unchanged since comparative statistics were kept in the 1930s!* In the public sector, where similar laws apply but are more enforceable because of civil service systems and collective bargaining rights, the pay differential between white males and other groups is almost nil at entry level and only 5 to 10 percent thereafter.

At the heart of this controversy is a fundamental dilemma that must be recognized and addressed, but can never be resolved as long as the two values of social equity and agency efficiency compete across the range of personnel systems and activities. For advocates of agency efficiency, it simply makes no sense to pay women and minorities more than one would have to pay them under a market model (unless required to by specific laws such as minimum wage provisions of the FLSA). The fact that women and minorities receive lower wages may be socially and ethically unfortunate, but it is the primary responsibility of the employer to provide services while meeting a payroll at the lowest possible cost, not to be an instrument for solving social problems. Advocates of comparable worth hold exactly the opposite view. For them, balancing the budgets of public agencies by maintaining lower salaries for women and minorities is morally indefensible. It violates Title VII for private employees;, and denies public employees the rights to equal protection and due process they are guaranteed under the Fourteenth Amendment. At present, the judicial status of comparable work is unclear, but the decisions of the Supreme Court in the 1990s suggest that this issue is more likely to be dealt with in legislatures and through labor relations than in the courts.

The Politics of Setting Pay

The manner in which pay is set under alternative public personnel systems reflects the conflict among these two values, and the historical practice within which these values and systems have evolved.

Pay for political appointments is set by the appointing executive, though always within general limits established legislatively. Adjustments to pay are set the same way, based both on statutory limits and external and internal market comparisons. In local governments, frequent tradeoffs occur between salaries and benefits, so that it is (some would say this is deliberate) hard to determine the actual rate of pay increase or to compare it meaningfully with pay paid for similar work in other jurisdictions.

Pay for civil service employees is authorized by the legislature and approved by the chief executive. While civil service pay increases are usually justified or opposed on the basis of market comparisons, market factors are only indirectly used as the basis of setting pay. And the greater job security of civil service employees represents an intangible financial benefit that is difficult to factor into the market equation. This model applies most directly to federal civilian employees, whose pay and benefits are set directly by Congress rather than through collective bargaining (as is the case in most state and local governments).

Almost 60 percent of public employees have their pay and benefits set through collective bargaining. Under this process (which is described more completely in Chapter 13), pay, benefits, and working conditions are set by direct negotiations between agency management and employee union representatives. But there are critical differences between collective bargaining in the public and private sectors. Public employees are usually prohibited from using the strike as a weapon to influence the outcome of salary negotiations; and economic issues (such as pay and benefit increases) must be ratified by the appropriate legislative body prior to taking effect. This is because state and local governments are prohibited from deficit financing of operating budgets, and because state legislatures may not legally delegate their appropriations authority to management negotiators in the collective bargaining process.

In practice, this means that collective bargaining systems set wages by a combination of direct negotiations and indirect political influence on the legislature. For example, teachers' and police officers' unions (or their auxiliaries) frequently support local candidates to the school board or city council in exchange for implicit promises of support for pay and benefit increases when negotiated agreements are up for legislative ratification.

The increase in privatization and contracting out in the past ten years is a powerful alternative to union political influence over the contract negotiation and ratification process. Some union supporters would even call it a threat. It offers managers and elected officials the option of approving a negotiated contract, or of deciding to provide the same services by privatizing the entire function or by discharging civil service employees and hiring contract workers instead. As we will see, contract employees have much lower pay and benefits than their unionized or civil service counterparts (because these salaries and benefits are set by a market model rather than through legislative deliberations and collective bargaining). To be blunt, elected officials regard employees as voters, constituents, and possibly as a public human resource; private employers tend to regard them as primarily a production cost. And the interplay of these two systems and values has provided much of the ferment in public personnel management over the past decade.

Affirmative action initially developed because of concerns by minorities and women over *access* to jobs. But inevitably, as these groups' access to jobs increased, they have altered their focus to the *allocation* of pay and benefits. The primary target of affirmative action proponents has been the impact of seniority systems on minority access to promotions, and the resultant impact of this access on salaries. In most cases, courts have held that seniority systems developed with a race- (or sex-) neutral intent are legitimate, even if their effect is to give preference to white males. In some cases, however, courts have ordered modification of seniority systems, primarily by establishing dual seniority lists and requiring quota-based promotions until workforce comparability is achieved. This extreme solution is invoked only in cases where there are historical patterns of racism or sexism, where voluntary affirmative action compliance is ineffective, and where the resultant quota system is a temporary expedient that does not entirely bar qualified white males from consideration.

Setting Civil Service Pay through a Wage Survey

The discussion above should lead the reader to conclude that wages and salaries in public agencies are set by a variety of processes (job evaluation, individual negotiations, collective bargaining, and court order), depending on the type of personnel system and the interplay of law and historical practice. For the majority of positions filled through civil service systems, wages are set by salary surveys that establish external equity. These are then used as the basis for proposing and gaining legislative approval of pay structures. Here's how the process works.[2]

Jobs are first analyzed, classified, and evaluated according to the guidelines presented in the previous chapter. A typical classification and evaluation process will place jobs into four major categories (professional, administrative, technical, and clerical—the PATC breakdown). *Benchmark positions* are identified; they can be found in a number of comparable agencies to enable comparisons. They are likely to include positions for which the employer hires many applicants, or those which present recruitment or retention problems. Second, the relevant labor market is defined for different types of positions. It is usually national or regional for professional and administrative occupations, and local for technical and clerical jobs. Third, the employer obtains information about prevailing salaries for previously identified benchmark positions. This information is available from newspaper ads, job descriptions, or wage surveys conducted by professional organizations.

The selection of equivalent positions against which to compare benchmarks is important. Usually, this requires a detailed analysis of the salary level, job title, qualifications, and duties. By conducting such a survey, the employer will be able to compare the midpoint and range of wages or salaries offered for positions with those offered for identical positions in the relevant labor market.

After the labor market survey is completed, the employer uses the results to set tentative wage or salary levels. For jobs that have relatively few positions at the same level of responsibility, a single pay grade may suffice. For jobs that have a range of responsibilities and pay levels (such as engineer or manager), it will be necessary to establish a series of pay grades. The compensation specialist faces a dilemma in setting pay grades and rates. On the one hand, it is desirable to have a large number of *pay grades* so that jobs may be adequately defined based on market conditions and the agency's needs. On the other hand, a large number of pay grades within one occupation makes it difficult for managers to reassign employees easily, or for employees to move around based on the relationship of their skills to the agency's needs. One solution that has been proposed to both problems is *pay comparability* (based on market surveys) and *broad banding* (establishing relatively few pay levels within an occupation, and allowing managers considerable discretion in setting individual salaries within these levels). At the heart of this controversy is the argument about whether the purpose of a job classification and evaluation system is external control or internal equity and flexibility.

Once the pay structure is established, it may be necessary to adjust pay rates to fit local labor markets. For example, the federal government recently conducted a wage and salary survey that led to the establishment of higher pay rates (*locality pay*) for general civil service employees in New York and San Francisco than for identical jobs in other parts of the country.[3]

MERIT PAY AND ITS RELATIONSHIP TO PERFORMANCE EVALUATION, SENIORITY, AND COST-OF-LIVING ALLOWANCES

In theory, pay systems maintain a separation between these concepts so that individuals are compensated in three separate ways for three separate compensable factors. First, *merit pay* is given to reward superior performance, on the assumption that such rewards make it more likely that this performance will be continued. Second, seniority pay increments (also known as *time-in-grade* increases) are given on the assumption that seniority increases an employee's skills, and hence value to the agency. Third, *cost-of-living allowances* (COLA) are given to all employees in the agency to maintain external pay equity in the face of inflation.

But in reality, there is no clearer example of the confusion between intent and effect of pay systems than the relationships that exist among these three factors. First, the total amount of payroll budget allocated to merit increases is usually quite small (1 to 2% at most) because of budget constraints and uneasiness among elected officials about voter reactions to "paying employees bonuses to do what they ought to be doing anyway," or unwillingness to trust managers to allocate bonuses fairly. This means that personnel managers and supervisors are faced with the unpalatable alternative of allocating relative small bonuses to a few employees (thereby heightening conflict over the distribution of relatively large increments), or spreading the merit money in small symbolic increments among a larger group of employees. Second, merit pay is usually permanent, in that it becomes part of the base pay upon which future increments are computed. Third, despite the impact of work groups on organizational performance, merit pay is usually allocated to individuals. Thus, it tends to undermine the organizational climate regardless of how it is allocated. Under these circumstances, it is easy to see why many employees, supervisors, and managers consider merit pay to be not worth the trouble. Last, *seniority pay* has also been named as a culprit in discouraging performance, turnover, and risk-taking in agencies. Just because employees have done things longer is no guarantee they now do them better. Indeed, given the need for innovation in the face of technological change, it is equally likely that experience is an impediment to efficiency.

Taken together, these three types of adjustments have a negative impact on agency efficiency and employee performance in civil service systems. If (as is sometimes the case) legislative pay increases fail to keep pace with inflation, managers and personnel directors out of necessity seek to retain competent employees by using combinations of COLA, time-in-grade increments, and merit increases. In the end, the distinctions between the purposes of these systems, and their effects, tends to disappear.

Clearly, one of the problems faced by civil service systems is their tendency to blur the distinction between cost-of-living increases and merit increases. Traditionally, merit increases become part of an employee's base salary from which future increments are calculated. Since the total amount of payroll allocated to merit pay is generally slight (1 to 2%), this guarantees that merit awards will be perceived as either insignificant or unrelated to performance. One innovative solution is to (1) make performance awards on an annual basis rather than building those awards into the employee's base salary, and (2) lump a range of financial awards together to increase their economic and symbolic value.

Let's look at how these features can complement one another. For an employer with a 2 percent merit pay pool, the first year of system operation would result in 2 percent merit pay increases. If these were allocated annually rather than in perpetuity, the merit pay pool would increase arithmetically (2%, 4%, 6%) annually until it held enough money to pay significant performance bonuses and motivate significant performance increases. Of course, the viability of this system assumes that external pay equity is maintained through COLA, and that retained merit pay funds are used for this purpose rather than diverted to other purposes.

Other public personnel systems do not have this problem, though they avoid it by different strategies. Political systems (and contracting out) use a market model; the salaries paid to individuals are set on the basis of personal qualifications and value. While this method is subjective and open to inequities, the individual has one response that always brings results— get a higher job offer elsewhere, show it to your employer, and be prepared to get a pay increase (if the negotiations are successful) or move (if they are not). Under collective bargaining, merit pay for individual employees does not exist. Employees as a group may receive salary increments based on increased productivity (*benefit sharing*); negotiated contracts may provide for seniority increments; and the periodic renegotiation of economic issues compensates for changes in the cost of living. Provisions for employees under affirmative action systems are the same as those for civil service employees.

STATUTORY ENTITLEMENT BENEFITS

Employee benefit programs may be separated for analytical purposes into two categories: entitlement benefits and discretionary benefits. *Entitlement benefits* are those to which employees are entitled by law (Social Security, worker's compensation, and unemployment insurance). *Discretionary benefits* are those which are not mandated by law, but which may be provided by the employer as part of a benefit package to attract or retain employees. As we will see, there is considerable range in the discretionary benefits offered to employees, depending not only upon the employer's budget but upon the type of personnel system within which the jobs are placed.

Social Security

Beginning in 1983, all state and local governments were required to deduct employee contributions to the Social Security system, a federally administered *defined contribution* plan intended to supplement employer-sponsored discretionary retirement systems. Currently (1990), employees pay 7.65 percent of their wage income up to a maximum of $50,400. Employers are required to match this contribution. The Social Security system also provides disability, death, survivor, and senior citizens' health benefits (Medicare). Federal employees do not belong to the Social Security system; they have their own defined-contribution pension system or the optional federal employee retirement system (FERS).

Worker's Compensation

Worker's compensation is an employer-financed program that provides a percentage of lost wages and some medical and rehabilitation benefits to employees who are unable to work because of job-related injury or illness. Employers pay a percentage of payroll into a state-operated insurance pool. Because the percentage paid is based on the history of claims against the fund, employers seek to avoid payment of benefits for claims they consider fraudulent, and to adopt workforce health and safety policies to reduce the incidence of job-related injuries and accidents.[4]

Unemployment Compensation

Beginning in 1976, state and local government employees have been eligible for *unemployment compensation*. This benefit provides a portion of regular wages to employees who have been laid off without cause, and who are actively looking for work and unable to find it. There is wide variation from state to state concerning waiting periods for eligibility, length of time benefits are paid, and level of benefits provided. States establish unemployment compensation funds through enabling legislation and employer contributions; the federal government funds and administers the program through the U.S. Employment Service in the Department of Labor.

DISCRETIONARY BENEFITS: PENSIONS

Retirement benefits are one of the key discretionary elements of an employee benefit system. There are over 3500 separate public employee retirement systems covering almost 30 million public employees and retirees (although 120 large municipal and state systems include over 90 percent of those employees covered). They receive over $50 billion annually, and have net assets of over $250 billion.

Obviously, the magnitude of public pension funds, and the value of their benefits to the individual employee, means that there are many managerial and policy issues associated with their development and administration. From the viewpoint of the individual employee, some primary issues are vesting, portability, defined benefit versus defined contribution plans, disability retirement, and the relationship between pension plan requirements and age discrimination. From the viewpoint of pension fund management policy, key issues are disclosure requirements, actuarial standards, and strategic investment potential.

Vesting and Portability

Normally, employers require employees to have worked a minimum number of years (usually 10) prior to vesting. *Vesting* simply means that an employee is entitled to that portion of accrued retirement benefits contributed by the employer (naturally, any employee contributions can be reclaimed by the employee upon withdrawal from the system when employment is terminated). Vesting discourages turnover. This may be an advantage or a disadvantage to the agency. Employees and some employers favor *portability*, which means that benefits earned in one agency may be transferred to another. Many state systems are already portable, in that employees working in one state agency or local government are eligible to transfer benefits if they work for any other agency that is a member of that state system. True portability involves giving employees the option of having their employer's contribution to retirement benefits go to a public pension fund, or to a private retirement annuity account (such as the TIAA-CREF system).

Defined Benefit versus Defined Contribution

State and local systems have traditionally been *defined benefit* systems. That is, employees and employers contribute a portion of salary, but the benefits are predictable based on number of years' service and salary level. Private annuity funds are more likely to work on a *defined contribution* basis. That is, employees or employers contribute a fixed percentage of salary, and benefits will vary depending on the success of investments by the fund. Increasingly, given the dangers of unfunded liabilities and pay-as-you-go funding options for retirement systems, defined contribution plans are supplanting their defined benefit counterparts.

Disability Retirement

At its best, disability retirement allows employees who are unable to work because of illness or injury and not normally eligible to retire (in terms of age or years of service) to retire with benefits. At its worst, it is a device used by employees to retire early at the employer's expense, or by employers to induce an unwanted employee to retire early. Personnel directors can fulfill the intent of disability retirement programs, and minimize fraud, by considering alternatives such as light duty positions or early retirement programs.[5]

Age Discrimination

One additional issue faced by public pension systems is the relationship between benefit accrual provisions and age discrimination in employment. Traditionally, pension systems interlocked with mandatory retirement policies in that employees were forced to retire by a certain age (65 or 70) because the employer stopped paying benefits into the pension plan when the employee reached that age. However, recent court decisions have held that such provisions represent disparate treatment of older workers, and thereby violate the Age Discrimination in Employment Act of 1967.[6]

This logic was enacted into law by the Older Workers Benefit Protection Act (PL 101–43), which became law in 1990. This law permits early retirement programs provided that they do not result in age discrimination. Early retirement incentives that provide a flat dollar amount, service-based benefits, a percentage of salary to all employees above a certain age, or give employees who retire credit for additional years of service will be lawful. In addition, many agency managers favor the flexibility that such programs offer, as opposed to involuntary layoffs based on reduction-in-force criteria.

This law was applied to state and local governments beginning in 1992. In those states where state law denies disability retirement to an individual after a certain age, modifications have to be made in the plan.[7]

Standards of Disclosure

In the private sector, pension systems are regulated by ERISA (the Employee Retirement Income Security Act of 1974). There is no public sector counterpart to this law. This means that public sector pension plans, like collective bargaining activities, are regulated by a hodgepodge of state laws. There are no uniform standards for informing beneficiaries, taxpayers, or elected officials concerning their financial condition. In some cases, public pension funds have been managed by private investment firms whose speculative investments during the junk bond era of the 1980s have placed public pension funds at risk and given rise to issues of disclosure and accountability for fund management.[8]

Actuarial Standards

Much confusion also exists about the actuarial standards to which public pension systems should conform. These standards are assumptions about the rates of employment, death, inflation, and so on that are used to calculate the relationship between payments into the system and benefits drawn from it. Two types of systems are used—*fully funded* and *pay-as-you-go*. In a fully funded system, contributions of current employees are adjusted to meet the demands on the system by retirees, so that the system always remains solvent. Under a pay-as-you-go plan, employee contributions bear no necessary relation to payments, and funds are appropriated from general revenues to pay retirees' pensions. However, there is no federal requirement that public pension funds be operated in conjunction with generally accepted accounting principles applicable to private pension plans as set forth in ERISA. This lack of uniform accounting, auditing, and actuarial standards led the General Accounting Office (GAO) to report recently that about 56 percent of the 72 pension plans it reviewed were not actuarially sound.[9]

Strategic Investment Potential

Perhaps the most neglected aspect of public pensions is their strategic investment effect. Traditionally, the administration of state and local pension systems restricted pension fund investments to low-interest, low-risk assets. During the 1980s, some pension fund managers were able to obtain higher rates of return by investing more speculatively (unsecured government bonds, real estate). While the excesses of the 1980s have called a halt to much of this activity, it is still necessary for states to establish some reasonable balance between security and rate of return. This is particularly true given the potential of public pension funds, because of the sheer size of their investment activity, for stimulating and directing economic growth in specified geographic areas or industries. For example, in Minnesota the Minneapolis Employee Retirement Fund (MERF) has formed an investment corporation that lends money to high-tech industries wishing to relocate to the area.

DISCRETIONARY BENEFITS: HEALTH INSURANCE

There is widespread agreement today that there are serious problems with the system of health care delivery in the United States. Growing at twice the rate of inflation, medical costs have climbed from $248 billion in 1980 to $600 billion in 1990 (this is 12% of our gross national product).[10] Despite this high cost, there are tremendous inequities in the distribution of health care benefits. Many Americans are denied health care because they cannot afford it. In 1984, 34.7 million Americans (17.4%) had neither private nor public health insurance coverage.[11]

The increased cost of medical technology and increased longevity are primarily responsible for the increase in health costs. Our present system is geared toward the development of high-technology advances that provide a longer life span for the elderly at a high price; it is driven by a third-party reimbursement system that discourages cost control or cost-benefit analysis. As a result, retirees are creating a staggering liability for employers. Today, it is estimated that total employer liabilities for health-care coverage for current employees are $85 billion for those Americans who are covered by employer-financed plans.[12]

In the absence of sweeping public-policy reforms needed to overhaul our health system, employers have adopted what for them are reasonable strategies to contain health-care costs. These are: (1) providing "permanent" employees (those with job security through civil service or collective bargaining systems) with education, early detection, and treatment programs, (2) using temporary or contract employees to meet fluctuating employment needs, and (3) excluding high-risk applicants (for example, those who abuse drugs or carry the AIDS virus) from "permanent" employment through civil service systems.[13]

Benefits (primarily employer-financed health benefits, pensions, sick leave, and paid holidays and vacation) constitute a large and increasing share of personnel costs.[14] Health care costs are only partially controllable by employers. But because early detection and treatment is considered the least expensive option, "permanent" employees (those hired into preferred professional and managerial positions through civil service systems) are usually provided with extensive preventive education through employee wellness programs, and treatment through employee health plans. Health insurance carriers (and self-insured employers) have responded to the cost of medical care by increasing premium costs, reducing benefits, lengthening the period within which health care benefit claims may be excluded as preexisting conditions, or adopting sub-benefit limitations on coverage for health problems that may be considered preventable because they are "lifestyle choices" (for example, smoking, alcoholism, drug abuse, or AIDS).[15] Benefit managers for self-insured agencies are even responding, on a case-by-case basis, to advance questions from health-care providers about whether reimbursement for specific treatments will be authorized for individual employees.

Second, employers continue to hire managerial, professional, and skilled technical employees through civil service systems into "permanent" positions. The relatively high job status, security, pay, and benefits that go with these positions are considered essential for long-term employee retention and productivity. However, employers have also tried to "cap" benefit costs and liability risks by greater use of the contract or temporary employees to meet fluctuating workloads. These employees typically have less status, lower pay, less job security, and fewer benefits than their civil service counterparts.[16] And because these employees may usually be discharged "at will," employers can externalize costs and liability risks by discharging (on some other pretext) employees who show signs of serious disability or illness.

Whenever possible, given the limits of available technology and the applicability of handicap laws protecting applicant rights,[17] employers have sought to reduce benefit costs by excluding high-risk applicants from "permanent" employment through civil service systems.[18] The ability to predict long-term health risks by evaluating employee health profiles was originally developed as a component of employee wellness programs to prevent serious health problems among current employees. But because "permanent" employees incur high benefit costs,[19] and because these costs correlate with health indicators, medical health indicators are also being used as selection criteria.[20]

In selecting applicants for positions filled through civil service systems, employers are moving from narrowly focused screening methods (such as the use of back X-rays to determine whether laborers are physically able to lift or carry) to more generalized health indicators that may indicate the applicant is a long-term health risk because his or her general indicators are outside normal limits.[21] Examples are: abnormal weight to height, abnormal electrocardiogram, abnormal blood chemistry (such as cholesterol levels), history of heavy drinking (as determined by liver enzyme activity), history of substance abuse (as determined by urinalysis), or likelihood of developing AIDS (as determined by AIDS antibody tests).[22]

OTHER EMERGENT EMPLOYEE BENEFIT ISSUES

To all these items must be added some other employee benefit issues which are either continually in ferment or newly emergent. These include sick leave and vacations, parental leave, child care, tuition reimbursement, and flexible benefit plans.

Sick Leave and Vacations

Employers provide sick leave as a benefit so that employees are not forced to come to work sick, and so that they may accrue enough sick leave to last them through a major illness or injury without loss of pay. In this respect, sick leave is an employer investment in employee health. Unused sick days are usually computed for pension purposes as part of time worked when the employee retires, but are not credited to the employee if he or she leaves the organization prior to retirement eligibility.

Vacation days are provided as a traditional benefit. In contrast to sick leave, they are more the property of the employee (since employees are usually compensated for unused vacation days upon termination of employment). Since the number of days provided usually increases with seniority, they may also provide an incentive against turnover.

Two elements of sick leave and vacation policy are worth examining here because of their implications for employee cost and performance. First, regardless of their differing purposes for the employer, many employees tend to treat sick leave and vacation indistinguishably, taking either type of leave whenever they want to be away from work. Employers can discourage this practice by clarifying the difference between the two types of leave during employee orientation, and by enforcing this distinction (if necessary) through disciplinary action against sick leave abuse. Second, employers should recognize that changing family roles have resulted in numerous single-parent households. Under these conditions, sick leave policies must reflect parental responsibilities to care not only for themselves, but for children and parents as well.

Second, accrued vacation time and sick leave represent an unfunded liability for the agency. It may be accrued at one salary rate and used at another. While this liability is acceptable in the case of sick leave, agencies should prohibit employees from accruing large amounts of annual leave. In addition to the unfunded liability issue, the fact that employees are not choosing to take vacations means that they may become burned out; if supervisors are not allowing them to take vacations because of heavy workload, this indicates more fundamental human resource management problems.

Parental Leave

The major benefit issue most personnel policies fail to address in the United States today is parental leave. *Parental leave* means the legal entitlement of parents to job retention rights if they need to be absent from the workplace to care for a relative. These retention rights apply after a person has exhausted paid sick leave or annual leave; they remain in place for a considerable period of time (six months to a year); and they apply in cases of eldercare, childbirth, or adoption. Either parent would be eligible.

There are several arguments in favor of parental leave. First, the high cost of health care could be reduced if home care provided by a family member were an alternative to hospitalization or care in an extended care facility. Second, because nonworking parents are present in only 11 percent of American households, no home care will be provided unless employees are guaranteed job retention rights. Third, the United States is alone among major industrialized countries in not offering these benefits. Other countries have recognized that, for employees facing childbirth, adoption, or terminal care for a parent, the long-term negative consequences of a forced choice between remaining on the job or giving up their employment rights is not socially justifiable.

In 1990, President Bush vetoed a proposed parental leave bill because of objections by the business community. However, a recent study indicates that parental leave could be implemented easily and inexpensively. The three-year study was conducted in four states that passed parental leave laws during the 1980s. The survey found that 91 percent of respondent personnel directors reported no difficulty with implementation of the laws; 67 percent said they relied on other employees to do the work (rather than hiring replacement employees); and the percentage of working women who took leave and the length of leave were virtually unchanged by the legislation.[23] While opponents of nationally mandated parental leave legislation use this research to demonstrate that most employers are already offering these benefits voluntarily, proponents argue that the same data justify the mandatory extension of these benefits to all employees.

Childcare

The increased number of single parents (and two-parent families where both parents work) has led to increases in employer-operated childcare facilities. At first, this was seen primarily as an employee benefit. But as agencies began to face shortages of qualified employees, childcare has been demonstrated to be necessary to recruit or retain qualified female employees (such as in hospitals or on military bases). In an era of increased workforce diversity, it is simply essential to recognize that employees' ability to find satisfactory childcare arrangements will reduce job stress, turnover, sick leave abuse, and other causes of low productivity.[24]

There are some issues with employer-subsidized child care. These include cost, fee setting, and liability risks. But these are technical concerns rather than major impediments to the adoption of childcare policies and programs. And the fundamental value orientation of childcare remains unassailable. If employees are a human resource and an asset, then children are the seed corn from which future assets are developed for use by the employer and the society.

One innovative proposal allows closer cooperation between employers, parents, and the local school board by allowing parents to place their children in schools close to the job rather than close to home. This reduces the length of time school-age children go without supervision, and makes it easier for parents to leave work for emergencies without so much use of leave or disruption of employer productivity.

Tuition Reimbursement

Employers who value employees as human assets recognize that these assets must be developed. Therefore, they place a high value on employee training and education, often devoting 5 percent of the payroll to this purpose. Unfortunately, training and education is one of the first things cut during a tight budget period because it is considered an expense rather than a capital investment.

Even in the absence of high-profile employee development programs, employers can still encourage individual development and reduce turnover by reimbursing tuition expenses for job-related courses. In particular, state governments can use this as a virtually cost-free employee benefit, especially if enrollment is limited to courses in which vacancies exist. Of still greater benefit—and cost—are programs that provide tuition waivers for entire degree programs for the employee, a spouse, or dependent children. These represent future costs for the employer, yet experience with them in the private sector indicates that they are a valued tool for employee retention.

Flexible Benefit Programs

Flexible benefit programs are sometimes called cafeteria plans because they offer employees a menu of benefits. They are developed by costing the employer's contribution to each of a variety of employer-sponsored benefit programs, and allowing employees to select alternative mixes of benefit packages depending on their needs. This has the major advantage, for the employee, of full utilization of benefits without duplication or gaps. This makes the employer's benefit package of greater value to the employee, and is a tool for recruitment and retention.[25]

There are administrative and financial barriers to flexible benefit programs. First, given the wildly fluctuating cost of alternative benefits, it may be difficult for the employer constantly to calculate (and recalculate) the comparative costs of all options. Second, reconfiguring alternative benefit packages on a constant cost basis may be difficult for employees, who are unable to project benefit usage or the relative utility of alternative benefits accurately. Third, full employee utilization of benefits may increase benefit costs for the employer (who may have been able to reduce costs by relying on such overlaps as duplicate health insurance for two employees in a family). Fourth, increased benefit costs tend to force health and life insurance providers toward uniform defined benefit programs to reduce "shopping" from one program to another. In this environment, the advantages of flexible benefit programs may tend to diminish.

PAY, BENEFITS, AND THE CONFLICT AMONG PERSONNEL SYSTEMS AND VALUES

From the discussion above, it is clear that the conflict between individual rights (pay and benefits for employees) and agency efficiency (reduced pay and benefit costs) is a critical issue. And the outcome of this issue directly affects the conflict among competing personnel systems. For in the short term, at least, the systems that offer the lowest costs are those that provide employees with the lowest pay and least benefits—temporary and contract employment.

It should be noted, however, that despite their relatively short expected tenure in office, political appointees have frequently been able to include themselves in the benefit provisions offered civil service employees. The justification for this is that the relatively low salaries paid to political appointees (compared with their private-sector counterparts) necessitates attracting top candidates with a benefit package as well. Cynics, however, would say that because legislators and judges have the authority to approve statutory benefits for public employees, they have often used their authority to approve pay and benefit increases for themselves as well.

SUMMARY

Pay and benefits are the ways in which the employer rewards employee performance, and the way in which human resources are developed and maintained. Pay setting takes place on the basis of job evaluation and market comparisons, through different processes depending on the personnel system involved. And depending on the personnel system, employee benefits are regarded as an increasingly important motivator of employee retention and performance, or an increasingly uncontrolled employee cost. At least for civil service systems that define employees as a public resource, the emphasis is on providing a range of flexible benefits that will enhance the performance of an increasingly diverse workforce.

KEY TERMS

benefit sharing
broad banding
cost of living allowance (COLA)
defined benefit
defined contribution
disability retirement
discretionary benefits
entitlement benefits
ERISA (Employee Retirement Income Security Act)
Fair Labor Standards Act (FLSA)
flexible benefits
fully funded
Garcia v. San Antonio Metropolitan Transit Authority
labor market
locality pay
merit pay
parental leave
PATC breakdown
pay-as-you-go
pay comparability
portability

seniority pay
time-in-grade
unemployment compensation
vesting
worker's compensation

DISCUSSION QUESTIONS

1. How are job evaluation and market surveys used to set pay in public agencies? How does the choice of pay-setting methods affect comparable worth?
2. What is the relationship of merit pay to performance evaluation, seniority, and cost-of-living allowances?
3. What are the statutory benefits to which employees are entitled by law?
4. What are some of the managerial and public policy issues associated with public pension systems?
5. How have public agencies responded to the dramatic increase in health care costs?
6. How do discretionary benefits (such as sick leave, pensions, parental leave, and child care) relate to employee productivity and workforce diversity?
7. What is the relationship between pay and benefit systems and the conflict among public personnel systems and values?

CASE STUDY

The municipality of Cityville employs 500 people. Last year, excluding vacation time, which averages two weeks per employee per year, the rate of absenteeism was calculated at 3 percent. This 3 percent loss in scheduled work time is attributed to clerical workers (55 percent), blue collar workers (30 percent), and professional staff (15 percent). The average hourly wage for clerical workers is $5.76 with an additional 30 percent in fringe benefits; for blue collar workers $9.62 with an additional 35 percent fringe benefits; and for professional employees $14.42 with 33 percent fringe benefits

Twenty-five supervisors, whose average wage and fringe benefits total $12.50 per hour, handle most of the absentee worker problems and estimate they spent about 30 minutes a day rearranging schedules and trying to organize work to compensate for the unscheduled absences. Cityville's finance director indicates that some $30,000 in incidental costs are associated with absenteeism. These include items like overtime, temporary help,

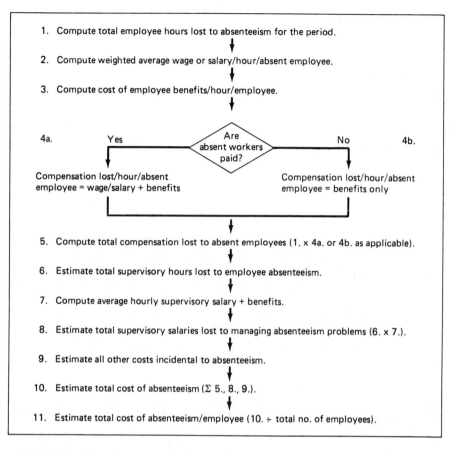

1. Compute total employee hours lost to absenteeism for the period.

2. Compute weighted average wage or salary/hour/absent employee.

3. Compute cost of employee benefits/hour/employee.

4a.   Yes   Are absent workers paid?   No   4b.

Compensation lost/hour/absent employee = wage/salary + benefits

Compensation lost/hour/absent employee = benefits only

5. Compute total compensation lost to absent employees (1. x 4a. or 4b. as applicable).

6. Estimate total supervisory hours lost to employee absenteeism.

7. Compute average hourly supervisory salary + benefits.

8. Estimate total supervisory salaries lost to managing absenteeism problems (6. x 7.).

9. Estimate all other costs incidental to absenteeism.

10. Estimate total cost of absenteeism (Σ 5., 8., 9.).

11. Estimate total cost of absenteeism/employee (10. ÷ total no. of employees).

FIGURE   5-1   Total Estimated Cost of Employee Absenteeism.
Source: Wayne F. Cascio, *Costing Human Resources: The Financial Impact of Behavior in Organizations.* 3rd ed. (Boston: PWS-Kent Publishing Company, 1991), p. 61.

and even an educated guess as to the costs attributed to lower quality of work done by the replacement workers. Problem: Using these amounts and the guide in Figure 5-1, estimate the total cost of absenteeism to the tax-payers of Cityville.

Answers to Case Study Questions

After several years, we and our students have reached reasonable consensus on the answers to these questions:

1. 30,000 hours
2. $8.22/hour
3. $2.68/hour

4. (a) $10.90/hour
    (b) $2.68/hour
5. $327,000
6. 3125 hours
7. $12.50/hour
8. $39.062.50
9. $30,000
10. $396,062.50
11. $792.13

NOTES

[1] A detailed discussion of the impact of the FLSA on state and local governments is beyond the scope of this text. For more information, see *Fair Labor Standards Handbook for States, Local Governments and Schools*, Thompson Publishing Group, 1725 K St. NW, Washington, DC (May 1986), as updated; and James Buford, *Personnel Management and Human Resources in Local Government* (Auburn University: Center for Governmental Services, 1991), pp. 266–271.

[2] For a more detailed discussion of salary surveys and the wage setting process, see David Belcher and Thomas Atchison, *Compensation Administration*, 2nd ed. (Englewood Cliffs, NJ: Prentice-Hall, 1987).

[3] For example, see the U.S. General Accounting Office, *Federal Pay: Private Sector Salary Differences by Locality*, GAO/GGD-91–63FS (Washington, DC: U.S. General Accounting Office, April 1991).

[4] Suzanne Francis and Matthew McCreight, "Restoring Health to Workers Compensation," *IPMA News* (Alexandria, VA: The International Personnel Management Association, October 1990), 5; Catherine Johnson, "Traditional Methods Reduce Workers' Compensation Claim Costs," *Risk Management* (December 1989), 46–48; Daniel Meylan, "Workers' Compensation: The Issue of the 1990's," *Business*, April 20, 1990, p. 42; Susan Werner, "Light-Duty Programs Cut Workers' Compensation Costs, Reduce Work Days Lost," *Business Insurance* (April 9, 1990), 19; and Arthur Parry, "How to Tighten the Reins on Workers' Compensation Costs," *Healthcare Financial Management*, May 1990, pp. 109–10.

[5] Gene Dent, "Effective Disability Management: Employers Often Overlook Ways to Help Worker, Save Money." *Business Insurance 24* (July 9, 1990), 21; and Stacey Lucas, "Putting a Lid on Disability Costs," *Management Solutions*, April 1987, p. 16.

[6] *Equal Employment Opportunity Commission v. Commonwealth of Massachussetts*, Docket Nos. 90–10640-H and 90–10150-Z, November 1, 1990.

[7] Neil Reichenberg, "President Signs ADEA Bill," *IPMA News* (Alexandria, VA: The International Personnel Management Association, December 1990), 10–11.

[8] "County Government Sues Financial Advisors: Out-of-Court Settlement Reached," *PA Times 14*, 4 (April 1991), 1.

[9] U.S. General Accounting Office, *An Actuarial and Economic Analysis of State and Local Pension Plans*, PAD-80–1 (Washington, DC: U.S. Government Printing Office, February 26, 1980).

[10] Fred Luthans and Elaine David, "The Healthcare Cost Crisis: Causes and Containment," *Personnel 67* (February 1990), 24.

[11] Deborah Chollet and Robert Friedland, "Health Care Costs and Public Policy Toward Employee Health Plans," *Review of Public Personnel Administration 7* (Summer 1987), 68.

[12] Ian Allan, "Financing and Managing Public Employee Benefit plans in the 1990's," *Government Finance Review 4* (October 1988), 32.

[13]Because 90 percent of major employers have workplace drug abuse policies (see the discussion of this topic in Chapter 11, and Reichenberg, cited above), it is relatively easy to analyze them. Because only about 10 percent of major employers have workplace AIDS policies (see Dale Masi, "AIDS in the Workplace: What Can Be Done?," *Personnel 64* (July 1987), 57–60), information on their responses to AIDS must be gathered from a wider range of sources, including insurance carriers and state insurance regulatory agencies (see, for example, Donald Klingner with Nancy O'Neill, *Workplace Drug Abuse and AIDS: A Guide to Human Resource Managment Policy and Practice* (Westport, CT: Greenwood/Quorum), 1991, ch. 9 and app. B; H. Turk, "AIDS: The First Decade," *Employee Relations Law Journal 14*, 4 (Spring 1989), 531–47; A. Emery, "AIDS Strategies That Work," *Business and Health*, June 1989, pp. 43–46; M. Heacock and G. Orvis, "AIDS in the Workplace: Public and Corporate Policy," *Harvard Journal of Law and Public Policy 13*, 2 (1990), 689–713; and World Health Organization, *Guidelines on AIDS and First Aid in the Workplace*, WHO AIDS Series 7 (Geneva: World Health Organization, 1990).

[14]A. Blostin, T. Burke, and L. Lovejoy, "Disability and Insurance Plans in the Public and Private Sector," *Monthly Labor Review*, December 1988, pp. 9–17.

[15]R. Faden and N. Kass, "Health Insurance and AIDS: The Issue of State Regulatory Activity," *The American Journal of Public Health 78* (April 1988), 437–38.

[16]A. O'Rand, "The Hidden Payroll: Employee Benefits and the Structure of Workplace Inequality," *Sociological Forum 1*, 4 (Fall 1986), 657–83.

[17]J. Jenks, "Protecting Privacy Rights," *Personnel Journal 66* (September 1987), 123–26.

[18]Donald Klingner, Nancy O'Neill and Mohamed Sabet, "Drug Testing in Public Agencies: Are Personnel Directors Doing Things Right?" *Public Personnel Management 19*, 4 (Winter 1990), 391–97; and Dale Masi, "Company Response to Drug Abuse from the AMA's National Survey," *Personnel 63* (March 1987), 40–46.

[19]R. Holton, "AIDS in the Workplace: Underwriting Update," *Best's Review, Property-Casualty Edition*, September 1988, pp. 96–98; and A. Solovy, "Insurers, HMOs and BC-BS Plans Talk About AIDS," *Hospitals 63* (January 20, 1989), 24.

[20]M. Rowe, M. Russell-Einhorn, and J. Weinstein, "New Issues in Testing the Work Force: Genetic Diseases," *Labor Law Journal 38* (August 1987), 518–23.

[21]L. Uzych, "Genetic Testing and Exclusionary Practices in the Workplace," *Journal of Public Health Policy* (Spring 1986), 37–57.

[22]K. Slater, "Likely Methuselahs Get More Life-Insurance Breaks," *The Wall Street Journal*, June 7, 1990, pp. C1, C8.

[23]Paul Taylor, "Study of Firms Finds Parental Leave Impact Light," *The Washington Post*, May 23, 1991, p. A9.

[24]"Child Care and Recruitment Boost Flexible Plans," *Employee Benefit Plan Review*, March 1987, pp. 32–33.

[25]"Cafeteria Plans, Wellness Programs Gaining in Popularity," *Employee Benefit Plan Review*, July 1990, pp. 90–92.

AFFIRMATIVE ACTION

Today, the man or person or corporate entity "offering the job" is, in fact, probably hiring for reasons other than somebody's personal preference or qualifications or demonstrated performance. Like it or not, the present-day employer is operating under orders from the government, and the government's first priority is to maintain the officially approved mix of genders, races, ethnic backgrounds and so on, not to hire the people best equipped to meet the stated goals of the organization.

—Jim Wright
Dallas Morning News, September 4, 1990

This controversial editorial statement is hardly true, although it reflects the perceptions of a number of Americans, especially those who have not gotten a job they thought they were qualified for. "Orders" from the executive branch of government or the courts are rare, but social equity considerations attract attention and scrutiny and seem to challenge the belief that personnel decisions should be made solely on the basis of knowledge, skills, and abilities.

Affirmative action supports using public jobs to remedy the effects of employment discrimination. Specifically, it favors achieving the value of social equity in recruiting, hiring, and promoting qualified people from different social groups in proportion to their percentage of a relevant and qualified labor market. In other words, if 10 percent of the plumbers in Los Angeles County are African-American, and only 2 percent of the plumbers in the county's workforce are African-American, the imbalance may suggest the need for affirmative action.

This objective conflicts with other selection criteria and values, among them seniority, administrative efficiency, and political responsiveness. For example, it challenges the traditional emphasis of collective bargaining on seniority as the basis for promotion or retention, particularly during periods of limited growth or cutback management. Second, in questioning the job relatedness of traditional selection criteria, it challenges managers' predictable bias toward test scores, educational credentials, and experience as indicators of applicant quality. Last, by increasing the pressure on elected officials to fill appointive jobs with women and minorities, it indirectly attacks the "old boy" network and political loyalty criteria by which top administrative positions have traditionally been filled.

On the other hand, the positive connection between social equity and other values can be seen as well. If pressure for affirmative action opens recruiting procedures to a wider range of people, it is more likely that more applicants with better knowledge, skills, and abilities and those who are not part of "the old boys' network" will join the applicant pool. Also, if an elected official's constituency includes a significant number of minority citizens, it makes political sense to appoint to non-merit positions minority members who are politically loyal to the elected official. Further, minority managers overseeing service delivery to minority communities may enhance service delivery by establishing more rapport with citizen-customers when they hire members of the community they are serving.

According to Henry L. Warren, vice-president for planning and control at Arkansas Power and Light, "Corporate America isn't stupid. . . . Companies are able to see that the customers they'll provide service to are changing." Thus, according to *Business Week*, "To serve these nonwhite customers, companies need a multiracial work force. Furthermore, for a company to ignore the rising numbers of minority workers . . . is to let a valuable talent pool go untapped." In other words, affirmative action "is not just the right thing to do . . . it's a business necessity," according to American Telephone and Telegraph Chairman Robert E. Allen.[1]

Despite its apparent declining political acceptability, affirmative action will have a significant effect on public employment, although probably not the same effect as was initially intended. Its legacy may be found in the judicial influence it has spawned over personnel decisions in all the core personnel functions. The *Uniform Guidelines to Employee Selection Procedures* have asserted that equal employment opportunity provisions extend to all employment decisions involving the distribution of organizational resources. Clearly, some progress in the hiring of women and minorities has been recorded over the past three decades. But the critical test of affirmative action is whether the value of social equity has penetrated the core personnel functions and become a routine consideration in public personnel management, even though the political salience of affirmative action itself may have declined.

In addition to this legacy, the words of corporate executives Warren and Allen suggest a very different way of thinking about affirmative action. Workforce diversity growing out of the demand for productivity and effective service delivery and recognition of the changing demographic composition of the labor pool in America may overshadow affirmative action driven by compliance with laws and regulations. This chapter begins with a discussion of equal employment opportunity, then looks at affirmative action, and concludes with a section on the relationship among productivity, workforce diversity, and equity.

By the end of this chapter you will be able to:

1. Understand why confusion exists between equal employment opportunity and affirmative action, and distinguish between them.
2. Discuss legislation and executive orders that require affirmative action compliance by public employers.
3. Describe the process of voluntary and involuntary affirmative action compliance.
4. Describe the impact the judicial system has in interpreting and enforcing affirmative action laws.
5. Discuss the relationship among workforce diversity, productivity, and fairness.

EQUAL EMPLOYMENT OPPORTUNITY AND AFFIRMATIVE ACTION

Affirmative action began legislatively as an attempt to reinforce equal employment opportunity by challenging conventional recruitment and selection procedures. It has evolved, largely through judicial interpretations of the law, into a tool to remedy the effects of long-standing discrimination in employment.

Given that EEO and AA are often referred to in the same breath and are almost invariably the enforcement responsibility of the same public agencies, it is understandable that distinguishing them is confusing. The distinction can be clarified by remembering that *equal employment opportunity* is designed to protect individual rights and promote employment opportunities and fairness in employment processes and decisions. Affirmative action is oriented more toward the value of social equity. It is more results-oriented and is designed to promote a more diverse and demographically representative workforce. It is often mistakenly associated with quotas.

With a few exceptions, *Title VII of the Civil Rights Act of 1964*[2] prohibits public or private employers, labor organizations, and employment agencies from making employee or applicant personnel decisions based on race, color, religion, gender, or national origin. Although originally applied to private employers, the concept of EEO was extended to state and local governments by the Equal Employment Opportunity Act of 1972.[3] The EEO Act of 1972 also increased the authority of the designated compliance agency, the *U.S. Equal Employment Opportunity Commission.*

In contrast with equal employment opportunity, affirmative action not only prohibits discrimination, but *requires* employers, unions, and employment agencies to take positive steps to reduce underrepresentation through the preparation and implementation of affirmative action plans (AAPs). The two most critical governmental acts enforcing the value of social equity, through the achievement of proportional representation, are Executive Order 11246 and the 1972 Equal Employment Opportunity Act (which really concerns AA rather than EEO). Table 6-1 summarizes several EEO/AA laws.

Executive Order 11246, signed by President Johnson in 1965, prohibited discrimination by most employers providing goods or services to the federal government. Furthermore, it required those with 50 or more employees and government contracts of $10,000 or more annually to prepare a written plan identifying any underutilization of women and minorities and establishing goals and timetables to correct it. This executive order has had great impact, since all subcontractors of covered contractors must also comply—regardless of the size of their contracts or number of employees. By 1990, this executive order covered some 27 million workers and over $194 billion in federal contracts.[4] A subunit of the U.S. Department of Labor (the *Office of Federal Contract Compliance Programs*) prepares regulations and enforces this order. Under the 1972 Equal Employment Opportunity Act, state and local governments were also required to file affirmative action plans, and to take the same types of remedial action required of federal contractors. In addition, this act granted the courts broad power to remedy the effects of employer discrimination.

Given the different objectives of EEO and AA, it is easy to see how enforcement strategies might conflict. Under AA, a plan might establish a goal of hiring more minorities or women until the percentage of employees in an organization equaled an appropriate percentage in a relevant labor market. Under EEO, however, concern for the protection of each appli-

TABLE 6-1   Federal AA/EEO Laws and Compliance Agencies

LAW	PRACTICE COVERED	AGENCIES COVERED	COMPLIANCE AGENCY
Age Discrimination in Employment Act of 1967, as amended in 1974 (29 U.S.C. Sec. 631 and 630B)	Age discrimination against employees over 39 years of age	Virtually all employers	Equal Employment Opportunity Commission (EEOC)
Americans with Disabilities Act of 1990 (P.L. 101–336)	Discrimination against qualified individuals with handicaps	Employers with 15 or more employees	EEOC
Civil Rights Act of 1964 as amended by the Equal Employment Opportunity Act of 1972 (40 U.S.C. Sec. 2000e) as amended by the Civil Rights Act of 1991 (P.L. 102-166)	Discrimination based on race, color, religion, gender, or national origin	Employers with 15 or more employees	EEOC
Equal Pay Act of 1963 (29 U.S.C. Sec. 206d)	Discrimination in pay based on gender	Employees covered by the Fair Labor Standards Act	EEOC
Executive Order 11246	Discrimination based on race, color, religion, gender, or national origin	Employers with federal contracts and their subcontractors	U.S. Department of Labor
14th Amendment to the U.S. Constitution	Prohibits application of law unequally	All public employers	Various federal courts

(continued)

TABLE 6-1   (Continued)

LAW	PRACTICE COVERED	AGENCIES COVERED	COMPLIANCE AGENCY
Vietnam Era Veterans' Readjustment Act of 1974 (38 U.S.C. Sec. 2012, 2014)	Promotion of employment opportunity for disabled and other Vietnam era veterans	Federal government and employers with federal contracts and their subcontractors	U.S. Department of Labor
Vocational Rehabilitation Act of 1973 (29 U.S.C. Sec. 701)	Discrimination against qualified individuals with handicaps	Federal agencies, federal contractors, and other recipients of federal funds	U.S. Department of Labor

cant's or employee's rights would prevent the establishment of a hiring quota ("three of the next ten employees hired must be African-American," for example) unless such a quota were established by a court order or consent decree.

AFFIRMATIVE ACTION COMPLIANCE: VOLUNTARY AND INVOLUNTARY

Voluntary affirmative action compliance occurs when a public employer recognizes a compensatory need to diversify its workforce and complies with affirmative action laws (and pursuant regulations issued by compliance agencies) through the preparation of an affirmative action plan that (1) identifies underutilization of qualified women and minorities compared to their presence in a relevant labor market, (2) establishes full utilization as a goal, (3) develops concrete plans for achieving full utilization, and (4) makes reasonable progress toward full utilization.

Involuntary affirmative action compliance occurs when a private employer or public agency alters its personnel practices as the result of investigation by a compliance agency that ends in a negotiated settlement, when the employer settles out of court with a compliance agency by means of a consent decree, or by court order. Understanding these three types of involuntary compliance mechanisms requires some background knowledge of the process by which compliance agencies investigate employers.

An applicant or employee who believes he or she has been discriminated against usually seeks redress through administrative channels within the organization where the alleged discrimination occurred. This may involve an appeal, informal and then formal, to the personnel office, affirmative action officer, or through union channels if available. If dissatisfied, the employee may file a formal complaint with the appropriate compliance agency (that is, with the government agency responsible for execution of the particular law).

Filing a complaint results in a formal investigation in which the investigating officer contacts the employer, asking for a written response to the applicant's or employee's charge of discrimination. The investigation may result in the complaint being rejected or the compliance agency filing a formal complaint against the employer. Frequently (in nearly half the EEOC's cases), complaints have been resolved "administratively" (with a finding in favor of neither the applicant nor the agency). This might occur when an applicant moves or changes jobs.

For FY89 the Office of Federal Contract Compliance Programs in the Department of Labor conducted over 6,000 compliance reviews of previous settlements or consent decrees and investigated some 1,300 complaints, a 24 percent increase over FY85. Of the complaints, some 190 resulted in violations with remedies.[5] In FY88 the Equal Employment Opportunity Commission processed some 59,000 complaints. Some 9,000 of these were settled with remedies. Combined, the EEOC and state and local fair employment practices agencies received some 118,000 complaints in FY88.[6]

Once a complaint is filed by the compliance agency, the employer may agree to the changes in its employment practices plus whatever specific remedies will "make whole" the injury to the aggrieved employee or applicant. This acknowledgment is called a *conciliation agreement.* It is entered into by the employer primarily to avoid costly litigation and court interference in cases where a court decision would likely go against the employer.

A *consent decree* is a second type of involuntary affirmative action compliance. It results when an employer and a compliance agency negotiate an agreement subject to the approval of a court and judicial oversight. Unlike the conciliation agreement, it is usually entered into by an employer in litigation who "smells" defeat. In such cases, the employer may consider it beneficial not to admit guilt, and to agree to terms which may be more advantageous than those resulting from a guilty verdict. Some consent decrees have resulted in the payment of substantial damages—such as the 1973 settlement between American Telephone and Telegraph and the EEOC, which cost AT&T about $15 million.[7]

For an employer, the most damaging form of involuntary compliance is a *court order.* In situations where a compliance agency or individual has taken an employer to court over alleged affirmative action violations and neither a conciliation agreement nor a consent decree can be agreed upon, a guilty verdict against the employer will result in court-ordered remedies.

Cases involving "egregious" and "pervasive" discrimination may result in mandatory hiring quotas, changes in personnel policies, and back pay for the victims of discrimination. Because of the cost and unfavorable publicity associated with lengthy litigation resulting in a guilty verdict, public officials will generally do their best to avoid this outcome.

FROM EQUAL EMPLOYMENT OPPORTUNITY TO AFFIRMATIVE ACTION

Tracing the history of employment discrimination since passage of the Civil Rights Act of 1964 requires an understanding of how the Supreme Court has interpreted civil rights legislation and the Constitution. The earliest opinions strongly endorsed EEO and traditional merit system values of individual rights and efficiency. But as the Court encountered unexpected cases of systemic and pervasive employment discrimination, it became more sympathetic to the value of social equity, reinforcing affirmative action programs and race-based remedies.

The Court's initial approach in interpreting the Civil Rights Act of 1964 was contained in its unanimous opinion in *Griggs v. Duke Power Company*.[8] Willie Griggs was a laborer at the Duke Power Company in North Carolina where for years the workforce was segregated, with African-Americans doing manual labor. In the early 1960s Duke Power company acknowledged that it had discriminated in the past but argued that in good faith it had recently instituted objective testing of applicants for selection and promotion. Griggs sued on the grounds that the tests unfairly discriminated against African-Americans and were unrelated to job performance. In a unanimous opinion written by the Chief Justice, Warren Burger, the court established several points that prevailed until 1989. First, regarding Congress's intent, the Court said: "The objective of Congress in the enactment of Title VII is plain from the language of the statute. It was to achieve equality of employment opportunity and remove barriers that have operated in the past to favor an identifiable group of white employees over other employees."[9] Thus, the act was interpreted to have a remedial as well as prospective intent. That is, an employer could not simply say, "We discriminated in the past, but no longer do so." Second, the Court said that if an employer's personnel practices resulted in discrimination, lack of intent to discriminate would not constitute a valid defense. In other words, the consequences of employment practices were more important than their intent. Third, the Court said that once an inference of discrimination could be drawn, the burden of proof shifted to the employer to show that the personnel practices that had the discriminatory effect were in fact job related. In other words, the employer must be able to demonstrate objectively that those applicants who performed better in the selection process would, in fact, do better on the job than those who did not fare as well in the selection process. Each of these findings sent a significant message to employers, and the case is viewed as a landmark employment discrimination decision.

From a values perspective, the Court's opinion emphasizes the traditional merit system values of individual rights and efficiency. The Court would protect *individuals* subject to discrimination and would open doors to allow them to compete on the basis of their knowledge, skills, and abilities (efficiency). It would not sacrifice job qualifications in favor of minority origins. In fact, writing for a unanimous court in 1971, Chief Justice Burger observed:

> Congress has not commanded that the less qualified be preferred over the better qualified simply because of minority origins. Far from disparaging job qualifications as such, Congress has made such qualifications the controlling factor, so that race, religion, nationality, and sex become irrelevant. What Congress has commanded is that any tests used must measure the person for the job and not the person in the abstract.[10]

From 1971 to 1987 the Court confronted challenges which Congress had not anticipated with passage of the Civil Rights Act of 1964 and the Equal Employment Act of 1972.

- What should the Court decide if discrimination was systemic rather than isolated to identifiable victims?
- What should the Court decide about cases where employers voluntarily showed racial preference to remediate a discrimination problem that had not been litigated or formally alleged?
- What should the Court decide in the case of seniority systems that in their routine application discriminated against minorities, but that were not originally conceived with that purpose in mind?
- What balance should be drawn between compensation for those discriminated against and the innocent non-minorities who might have to bear some of the cost in delayed promotions or loss of training or advancement opportunities?

Answers to these questions could not be found in the wording of civil rights legislation or the Constitution. Further, the legislative debates leading up to the Civil Rights Act of 1964 and the EEO Act of 1972 were so entangled that *any* answer to these questions could be justified with reference to legislative intent. The court had to use the letter of the law, its intent as interpreted by the Court, and its own precedents in deliberating and reaching answers to these and other questions. *Griggs* was the last unanimous vote the Court recorded on an affirmative action case.

By 1987 the Court had moved away from its color blind interpretation in *Griggs* and embraced the value of social equity, struggling to find a balance between social equity, individual rights, and to a lesser extent efficiency. Sixteen years after *Griggs*, the Court confronted two very different cases. Litigation leading to a Supreme Court review in *United States v. Paradise*[11] began in 1972 when a district court found pervasive, systemic, and obstinate exclusion of African-Americans from employment with the Alabama Department of Public Safety. Continued failure to comply with consent decrees led the district court in 1983 to order the state to promote to the rank of corporal African-American troopers at a 1-1 ratio with Caucasian troopers. This order would be enforced until at least 25 percent of the corporals were African-American or the department could produce a valid promotional examination—that is, one which had no adverse effect on qualified minority candidates. Supporting the State of Alabama, the federal government appealed the ruling to the Supreme Court, claiming it violated the individual rights, protected by the Fourteenth Amendment to the Constitution, of the innocent non-minorities in the Department of Public Safety. The innocent non-minorities were the Anglo troopers who may have benefitted from the discrimination, but could not be shown to be party to it.

Also in 1987 the Court reviewed the reverse discrimination case of *Johnson v. Transportation Agency*.[12] The transportation agency in Santa Clara County, California, noting a substantial imbalance in the number of women working in the agency compared to those available in the county workforce, voluntarily developed an affirmative action plan designed to ameliorate the imbalance by considering gender as one factor in employment decisions. After adopting the plan, the agency promoted Diane Joyce to the position of road dispatcher over Paul Johnson, who had achieved a nominally higher score than Joyce in a promotional interview. Johnson claimed reverse discrimination based on Title VII of the Civil Rights Act and the case eventually reached the Supreme Court. Joyce's promotion was upheld.

To decide whether the use of race and gender preference were lawful in *Paradise* and *Johnson*, the Court employed a two-pronged analytical framework it had developed since *Griggs* in 1971. First, employing the *strict scrutiny* standard for evaluating the use of affirmative action, the Court asked: "Is there a compelling justification for the employer to take race into consideration in its affirmative action program?" In *Paradise*, all the justices answered this question in the affirmative, agreeing that the "Alabama Department of Public Safety had undertaken a course of action that amounted to 'pervasive, systematic, and obstinate discriminatory conduct.'"[13] Therefore, the use of race to remedy the effect of this conduct was justified.

In *Johnson*, a majority of the Court answered in the affirmative as well. The majority inferred discrimination based on gender from a comparison of the number of women working in several of the transportation agency's job classifications compared to their numbers in the county's total labor pool. Thus, they found justification for the use of gender in the county's affirmative action plan.

In both cases, the Court then turned to the second and usually more important question involved in the strict scrutiny standard: Is the affirmative action plan narrowly tailored to solve the discrimination problem, or does it create additional, unacceptable problems? In asking this question, the Court is concerned with the effect the remedy will have on the lives of the innocent non-minority employees who may have to bear part of the cost of the affirmative action. With this question the Court tries to avoid remedying past discrimination with a solution that in itself discriminates.

In *Paradise*, a majority noted that the order to promote African-American troopers to the rank of corporal at a 1–1 ratio with Caucasian troopers was "narrowly tailored" and minimally intrusive on the innocent non-minority troopers for the following reasons: The promotion quota was in effect only until a valid promotion procedure could be developed or until 25 percent of the corporals were African-American; the requirement could be waived if no qualified African-American troopers were available; it would apply only when the department needed to make promotions; because it was limited in scope and duration, the remedy imposed a *diffuse* burden on the Caucasian troopers, and no individual non-minority employee must bear the entire cost of the remedy.

In *Johnson*, a majority of the Court found the county's plan was narrowly tailored, and it did not "trammel" the rights of male employees. The Court noted that the plan did not set aside any positions for women; it did authorize consideration of gender as one factor in promotion decisions. It found that Johnson had no absolute right to the position; he and Joyce were among several "acceptable" candidates whose names were sent to the person who finally decided who would be promoted. The Court noted that Johnson retained his employment and seniority and would be eligible for a future promotion. Last, the Court found that the county's plan was intended to "attain" a gender balance, not "maintain" one, which would have been illegal.

In both *Paradise* and *Johnson*, the Court showed its willingness to attack the barriers of discrimination with remedies benefitting those who had not been the specific or identifiable victims of discrimination. None of the troopers who might benefit from the court's order in *Paradise* claimed to have been specifically discriminated against; and Diane Joyce did not claim gender discrimination. Nevertheless, they were members of a class who had been discriminated against. This shows the Court's willingness, in contrast to *Griggs*, to endorse the value of social equity. But in both 1987 cases the Court was unwilling to dismiss the value of individual rights, as it considered the effects the affirmative action in both cases would have on the lives of the innocent non-minorities. Further, the Court acknowledged the value of efficiency by requiring that the minority troopers in Alabama be qualified and by noting that Diane Joyce was qualified.

By 1989, with the inclusion of President Reagan's appointees, the minority in *Paradise* and *Johnson* became a majority on the Supreme Court. As could be expected, the value of individual rights grew and the value of social equity declined. In *Richmond v. Croson*[14] the Court signaled the change in emphasis advocates of affirmative action feared. The Court ruled 6 to 3 against the City of Richmond's voluntary plan that required at least 30 percent of each city contract to be sublet to minority contractors. While recognizing that the city's population was 50 percent African-American and less than 1 percent of the city's prime contracts had gone to minority business enterprises, and despite substantial anecdotal evidence of widespread discrimination against minority contractors, the Court ruled that the city had shown no direct evidence establishing discrimination *by the city* against minority contractors. Thus, the City of Richmond's plan failed to meet the Court's first test in its two-part analytical framework: It failed to establish a compelling reason for the affirmative action by the city in minority contracting. In addition, it failed to meet the narrowly tailored test because it could not tie the derivation of the 30 percent figure to the actual degree of discrimination that could be attributed to the city's actions.

Also in 1989 the Court made it easier for an employer to demonstrate that a racial imbalance in the employer's workforce was justifiable. In *Wards Cove Packing v. Atonio*,[15] the Court ruled 5 to 4 that to draw an inference of discrimination, the plaintiff must identify the specific employment practice that resulted in discrimination. Prior to this case, inferences of discrimination could be drawn simply from comparisons between the percent minority in the workforce compared to the percent of qualified minorities available in the appropriate labor market. The plaintiff did not have to identify which employment practice caused the imbalance. Also with *Wards Cove Packing* the Court appears to have challenged what it said in *Griggs* some twenty years earlier. In *Griggs*, once discrimination could be inferred, the burden of proof shifted to the employer to show convincingly that the employer's personnel practices were based on business necessity or job-related factors. If the employer failed in this requirement, the employer would be found guilty by default of discrimination. In *Wards Cove Packing*, the Court said: "'The ultimate burden of proving that discrimination against a protected group has been caused by a specific employment practice remains with the plaintiff *at all times*.'"[16]

Let us look back over the three time periods we have briefly reviewed. In 1971, the Court interpreted the Civil Rights Act as protecting individual rights and efficiency and saw no conflict between the two. By 1987, the Court had adopted the value of social equity but recognized its conflict with the individual rights of non-minority employees and to a lesser extent with efficiency, and it sought a balance among the three values. In 1989, the Court signaled a shift away from the value of social equity. One infers from the Court's decisions in *Richmond* and *Wards Cove Packing* an inclination to return to the days when affirmative action focused on specific acts of discrimination and on protecting only identifiable victims.

Reacting to *Wards Cove Packing* and other decisions by a Supreme Court President Reagan's appointees dominated, a Democratic Congress counterpunched legislatively with the Civil Rights Act of 1991, signed by President Bush after considerable partisan wrangling. The authors of the act sought to overturn *Wards Cove Packing* and related Court decisions that had increased the difficulty of successfully proving unintentional employment discrimination. To some extent the act does this, and it contains a new provision permitting payment of compensatory and punitive damages for intentional discrimination, including discrimination against the disabled. But, according to the *New York Times*, the compromises required to pass the legislation are "riddled with confusing and ambiguous provisions that will take the courts years to straighten out."[17] That is, because the legislative history is so conflicting, the courts will have little recourse but to rely on their own values and judgment in interpreting the law.

IMPACT OF AFFIRMATIVE ACTION

Has civil rights legislation and employment discrimination litigation reduced discrimination and opened doors for minorities and women? The answer appears to be "yes," but it is difficult to marshall convincing statistics to answer the question.[18] It does seem clear that the kinds of discrimination reported in cases that came before the Court in the 1970s have decreased. It is difficult to conceive today of a case of intentional racial discrimination in employment like that reported in *Griggs* (1971) or *Paradise* (1987). Further, it is clear that the value of social equity has challenged merit systems to demonstrate that personnel practices once assumed to be job-related are, in fact. In this way, the force of affirmative action has benefitted all employees, regardless of race or gender. It has become standard operating procedure to advertise jobs publicly and widely; to tailor interview questions and tests to specific jobs. Performance appraisal instruments have become more job related, and pay systems have become more equitable and sensitive to gender differences even if they have not erased them.

In addition to its specific impact on the public personnel manager, affirmative action has a more general impact on all public managers and supervisors because it affects the rules by which the acquisition function is carried out. Conflicts between social equity and merit, or even among alternative definitions of social equity, result in the application of confusing and contradictory decision rules regulating the acquisition function.

During periods of agency growth, such as the 1960s and 1970s, managers could overcome these conflicts by hiring more people from all groups—as long as the pie was getting larger, everyone could get a bigger piece. Consequently, it was relatively easy for agencies to overcome barriers to compliance. For example:

- Agencies unable to recruit sufficient minorities or women were advised to target recruitment efforts toward community organizations, schools, or media oriented toward these groups.
- Agencies unable to find sufficient minorities or women, even after targeted recruitment efforts, were encouraged to consider lowering the job qualifications to increase the size of the applicant pool.
- Agencies unable to promote sufficient minorities to more responsible positions were advised to consider remedial training, revision of qualifications for the promotional position, or promotional quotas enforced by being incorporated into the organization's reward system for managers.

FROM AFFIRMATIVE ACTION TO WORKFORCE DIVERSITY

During the 1980s, when allocation issues were paramount, and where the political tide seemed to turn against social equity, affirmative action suffered. What can we expect in the future? Consultant Terry Simmons, speaking on workforce diversity, contrasts it with EEO and affirmative action. He says:

> When people first thought about equal opportunity, it was a great concept. The same with affirmative action. You know, taking positive steps. But most organizations implemented them in a negative way, a defensive way: 'Watch out for the law.' Diversity is a movement away from strictly legalistic approaches and toward more of a productivity and a maximization of resources approach.[19]

In other words, the impetus to implement affirmative action was compliance with the law. In the future, economic and demographic pressures may enhance workforce diversity because it makes good business sense.

This transition from affirmative action to workforce diversity sees the social differences in our society as assets, as sources of creativity, rather than sources of conflict. It transforms them from political issues of equity into business and administrative issues having to do with productivity and efficiency. Simmons continues:

> A different style and a different way of thinking are actually healthy because they will allow us to challenge our processes. If you can manage that in a positive way, then this challenge is good because it helps you get new ways of problem solving. It adds to your creativity. It helps you understand the views of your marketplace, which are different from what your traditions happen to be. So, if managed well, this diversity can create a rebirth of thinking in an organization and revitalize it from the inside out.[20]

This view is wholly consistent with the human resources rather than economic view that employees are assets rather than costs of production.

Further, from this perspective we might observe that affirmative action was a transition policy between EEO and workforce diversity; the interim permitted time for traditional merit systems to begin adapting to the demographic realities of the 1990s and beyond. Because workforce diversity is associated with traditional merit values and productivity, it carries little of the political baggage associated with affirmative action. The depoliticization of affirmative action is accompanied by the adoption of less emotionally charged language. "Affirmative action" gives way to "workforce diversity"; "equity" is replaced with "representation"; and "racial" differences are discussed as "ethnic" differences. In the United States, we find it more comfortable to discuss workforce diversity in terms of ethnic differences rather than racial differences.

To the extent that economic markets can influence personnel policies and practices, the forecast connecting workforce diversity and productivity seems on target. But the strength of the marketplace contains its weakness as well; it is driven by the value of efficiency, not by concerns of equity, fairness, or justice. While the connection between productivity and diversity may increase representation of racial and ethnic minorities in the workplace, history suggests that if it does so fairly, it will be coincidental. It appears safe to observe that in the 1990s, the value of social equity is being carried into the political arena more by demographic reality than by legislation, litigation, and conscience. At least in large urban areas, the composition of the labor force and the increasing political pressure of racial and ethnic groups should open access to public jobs even wider. From a values perspective, we may see increasing alliances of responsiveness/representation, efficiency, and social equity. While the courts will continue to orient themselves to the protection of individual rights, demographic realities will force legislatures and administrative agencies to respond to representation and the broader political concern of workforce diversity. Further, increasing emphasis on customer satisfaction in multigroup communities may very well connect workforce diversity to productivity.[21] In sum, while workforce diversity in an era of affirmative action in large measure has been forced upon employers, in a multicultural community, it may be seen as a requisite for productivity.

SUMMARY

Affirmative action is a mediating function that has had a profound effect on all personnel functions. It is based on the value of social equity, which is embodied in many federal laws and enforced by many affirmative action compliance agencies.

For the public personnel manager, affirmative action means preparing an affirmative action plan that determines underutilization and provides for various programs to correct it. For the public manager in general, affirmative action exacerbates existing conflicts over two questions: What criteria control employment decisions? How are conflicts among these criteria resolved?

Despite the current eclipse of social equity due to the renewed emphasis on other values (primarily administrative efficiency, political responsiveness, and individual rights), affirmative action will continue to have a profound impact on public administration because of its control over the acquisition process and the increasing role of the judicial system in regulating employment decisions and ensuring procedural due process. Furthermore, one might speculate that affirmative action is simply a political stage America needed to transit on its way to accepting increasing cultural and therefore workforce diversity. The cultural fabric of American society is changing even if its fundamental values remain relatively stable; and in the future, the value of social equity may be advanced by demonstrating a connection between the concept of a culturally representative workforce and organizational productivity.

KEY TERMS

affirmative action
Civil Rights Act of 1991
conciliation agreement
consent decree
court order
equal employment opportunity
EO 11246

Griggs v. Duke Power Company
Johnson v. Transportation Agency
Office of Federal Contract Compliance Programs (OFCCP)
Richmond v. Croson
strict scrutiny
Title VII
Uniform Guidelines to Employee Selection Procedures
U.S. Equal Employment Opportunity Commission (EEOC)
United States v. Paradise
Wards Cove Packing v. Atonio

DISCUSSION QUESTIONS

1. What are the definitions of equal employment opportunity and affirmative action, and what is the distinction between them?
2. What federal agencies are responsible for affirmative action compliance? Do you think compliance agencies should spend more time assisting employers in meeting their affirmative action obligations or in regulating employer behavior?
3. Describe the different mechanisms involved in voluntary and involuntary compliance with affirmative action law.
4. Describe the different orientations and values the Supreme Court has endorsed from 1971 to 1989 in interpreting EEO/AA law. Do you think the Civil Rights Act of 1991 will reverse the trend set in 1989 by the Supreme Court?
5. What role do you think the public manager should take in advancing affirmative action and workforce diversity in an environment of conflicting values?
6. What do you believe is the relationship among affirmative action, workforce diversity, and productivity in a culturally diverse community?

CASE STUDY

Read the following passages from Supreme Court opinions, and then answer the questions which follow.

It is plainly true that in our society blacks have suffered discrimination immeasurably greater than any directed at other racial groups. But those who believe that racial preferences can help to "even the score" display, and reinforce, a manner of thinking by race that was the source of the injustice and that will, if it endures within our society, be the source of more injustice still. The relevant proposition is not that it was blacks, or Jews, or Irish who were discriminated against, but that it was individual men and women, "created equal," who were discriminated against. And the relevant resolve is that should never happen again. Racial preferences appear to "even the score" (in some small degree) only if one embraces the proposition that our society is appropriately viewed as divided into races, making it right that an injustice rendered in the past to a black man should be compensated for by discriminating against a white. Nothing is worth that embrace.

—Justice Scalia, *Richmond v. Croson*, 102 L Ed 2d, 854, 905 (1989).

A profound difference separates governmental actions that them-selves are racist, and governmental actions that seek to remedy the effects of prior racism or to prevent neutral governmental activity from perpetuating the effects of such racism. . . . Racial classifications "drawn on the presumption that one race is inferior to another or because they put the weight of government behind racial hatred and separatism" warrant the strictest judicial scrutiny because of the very irrelevance of these rationales. . . . By contrast. . . . [b]ecause the con-sideration of race is relevant to remedying the continuing effects of past racial discrimination, and because governmental programs em-ploying racial classifications for remedial purposes can be crafted to avoid stigmatization, ... such programs should not be subjected to conventional "scrutiny"—scrutiny that is strict in theory, but fatal in fact.

—Justice Marshall, *Richmond v. Croson*, 102 L Ed 2d, 854, 920 (1989).

Congress has not commanded that the less qualified be preferred over the better qualified simply because of minority origins. Far from disparaging job qualifications as such, Congress has made such quali-fications the controlling factor, so that race, religion, nationality, and sex become irrelevant.

—Chief Justice Burger, *Griggs v. Duke Power Company*,
401 L Ed 2d, 158, 167 (1971).

Questions:

1. Identify the values in each of the passages.
2. Which passages do you agree with most/disagree with most?
3. Read the following scenario and complete the assignment in the last paragraph.

In 1982 a group of Hispanic-Americans sued the city government for discrimination in employment practices in the police and fire departments. The court encouraged the parties to enter a consent decree, which they did. The consent decree called for the city to cease its discrimination, to identify the victims of discrimination, to make the hiring of the qualified victims a priority, and to establish hiring and promotion goals that would bring the percentage of Hispanic-Americans in the public safety departments on par with the number of qualified potential Hispanic-American applicants in the surrounding labor market.

By 1984, although the city had hired a few of the plaintiffs who had not already found other jobs, the city had shown little effort to comply with the consent decree, and the racial imbalances were hardly affected. The Hispanics complained that those who were hired had been kept in lower-paying job classifications longer than their Anglo peers and were subjected to racial jokes; they were paired with each other in the police department and assigned to Hispanic-American high-crime areas. In the fire department they were isolated in the day-to-day informal activities of the department. It was rumored about city hall that the mayor had encouraged the personnel director to "do as little as possible" in complying with the consent decree.

In 1985 the Hispanic advocates went back to the court, requesting judicial intervention. The court summoned the parties, and a revised consent decree was entered. It provided for a court-ordered trustee to monitor the consent decree. In 1986 the city halted all hiring, citing budgetary problems. By 1988, the city began to hire on a case-by-case basis in other departments, but not in public safety, citing the lack of need for additional officers and firefighters.

The Hispanic plaintiffs returned again to the court, seeking relief. After consulting with the trustee, the judge, citing the court's exasperation and failure to note good faith on the part of the city, was determined to craft a solution that would make a difference. At this point, the mayor announced the hiring of a chief administrative officer and assigned the CAO the responsibility of coming up with a plan to "deal with this mess." The city successfully persuaded the judge to give it six more months to rectify the problems. The judge reluctantly agreed.

You are the CAO. Develop a plan, recognizing that it will have to be approved by a judge who will tolerate no more delays. At the same time, you must understand that the judge is bound to analyze the plan according to the strict scrutiny standard. Thus, you must remedy the effects of the discrimination, but your plan must not place too much of a burden for the remedy on innocent non-minority workers.

NOTES

[1]"Race in the Workplace: Is Affirmative Action Working?" *Business Week*, July 8, 1991, p. 53.

[2]*The Civil Rights Act of 1964*, P.L. 88–352, 78 Stat. 241, 28 USC ss. 1147 [1976].

[3]*The Equal Employment Opportunity Act of 1972*, P.L. 93–380, 88 Stat. 514, 2–0 USC 1228 [1976].

[4]Employment Standards Administration, U.S. Department of Labor, *Office of Federal Contract Compliance Programs: Director's Report Fiscal Year 1989* (Washington, DC, undated).

[5]Ibid.

[6]United States Equal Employment Opportunity Commission, *Combined Annual Report Fiscal Years 1986, 1987, 1988* (Washington, DC, undated).

[7]Equal Employment Opportunity Commission, *Eliminating Discrimination in Employment: A Compelling National Priority* (July 1979), pp. III-(5–11).

[8]*Griggs v. Duke Power Company*, 28 L Ed 2d 158 (1971).

[9]*Griggs v. Duke Power Company*, 28 L Ed 2d 163 (1971).

[10]*Griggs v. Duke Power Company*, 28 L Ed 2d 167 (1971).

[11]*United States v. Paradise*, 94 L Ed 2d 203 (1987).

[12]*Johnson v. Transportation Agency*, 94 L Ed 2d 615 (1987).

[13]*United States v. Paradise*, 94 L Ed 2d 239 (1987).

[14]*Richmond v. Croson*, 102 L Ed 2d 854 (1989).

[15]*Wards Cove Packing v. Atonio*, 104 L Ed 2d 733 (1989).

[16]*Wards Cove Packing v. Atonio*, 104 L Ed 2d 733 at 755 (1989) citing *Watson v. Fort Worth Bank and Trust*, 101 L Ed 2d 827 (1988).

[17]Steven A. Holmes, "Lawyers Expect Ambiguities in New Rights Law to Bring Years of Lawsuits," *New York Times*, December 12, 1991, p. A-12.

[18]J. Edward Kellough, *Federal Equal Employment Opportunity Policy and Numerical Goals and Timetables* (New York: Praeger, 1989); Finis Welch, "Affirmative Action and Discrimination," in Steven Shulman and William Darity, Jr., *The Question of Discrimination* (Middleton, CT: Wesleyan University Press, 1989), pp. 153–198.

[19]Terry Simmons, "Diversity at Work," *USA Today*, August 26, 1991, p. 9A.

[20]Ibid.

[21]Taylor H. Cox and Stacy Blake, "Managing Cultural Diversity: Implications for Organizational Competitiveness," *Academy of Management Executive 5*, 3 (1991), 45–56; Troy Coleman, "Managing Diversity at Work: The New American Dilemma," *Public Management 72* (October 1990), 2–6.

RECRUITMENT, SELECTION, AND PROMOTION

In government jurisdictions with strong merit systems, recruitment, selection, and promotion activities are frequently viewed as routine administrative functions. This perspective masks the dynamic political conflicts that frequently characterize policy debate over the appropriate criteria to use in the recruitment and selection of job applicants and the promotion of employees. This chapter reviews the value conflicts and the compromises that take place over the criteria used in these acquisition and planning functions in addition to describing some of the technical aspects of recruitment and selection.

By the end of this chapter you will be able to:

1. Describe the influence different values have on the objectives of the recruitment and selection process.

2. Describe briefly the differences in perspective between political appointees and career civil servants.

3. Describe several external factors that influence the recruitment and selection of public employees.

4. Contrast centralized and decentralized recruitment and selection techniques.

5. Describe the concept of test validation and three validation strategies.
6. Describe the relationship between job analysis, test validation, and performance evaluation/productivity.
7. Describe eight steps in the recruitment and selection process.
8. Identify four types of written tests used in the selection process.

As he faced a reelection campaign in late summer 1988, Mayor Tom Bradley of Los Angeles was being pressured to appoint more Latinos to top City Hall vacancies.[1] The growing Latino population had topped 30 percent in Los Angeles, while the number in top city jobs reached only 7 percent. Bradley faced a unique opportunity—to fill five top vacancies at once. Three of the vacancies came because of mismanagement, nepotism, and falsification of a résumé. The mayor thus could not ignore the knowledge, skills, and abilities of candidates for these positions. Moreover, as he prepared for a stiff challenge in the upcoming election, he could use the appointments to shore up his traditional base of support among African-Americans. Complicating the situation was a mayoral challenger who claimed his strength in the largely Anglo-populated Westside of Los Angeles.

Bradley's recruitment and selection of candidates to fill these positions reflects a combination of values and the interaction of recruitment, selection, and promotion practices. Bradley was required by law to select from lists of finalists developed by the personnel department in accordance with civil service rules, giving the impression that knowledge, skills, and abilities would dominate the selection criteria. But the Latino employee association worked hard to ensure adequate representation of Latinos on a list that, according to the *Los Angeles Times*, was pared down through an examination and interviews by a panel of citizens.

Bradley chose two African-Americans, one Latino, and two Anglos for the positions, with each evidently bringing substantial knowledge, skills, and abilities to their new positions. Two weeks prior to making the appointments, the mayor announced the promotion of a Latino firefighter to the position of deputy chief, making him the highest-ranking Latino on the force.

From these appointments, one might infer the complicated set of factors the mayor and his closest aides weighed before making their choices. Clearly the racial-ethnic mix of the appointments entered the picture; the inclusion of the promotion in the fire department may have given Bradley some flexibility in his other appointments. The scandalous departures of previous appointees also played a role. Driving the entire process were the mayor's concerns about the upcoming election.

It would be a mistake to conclude that most recruitment, selection, and promotion decisions are made within such a highly politicized environment. But it would be naive to argue that all are conducted according to routine procedures designed only to reward knowledge, skills, and abilities. In addition to political pressures, for example, advocates of seniority systems heavily influence promotion decisions in many jurisdictions and especially at the local level in police and fire departments. Similarly, affirmative action concerns are incorporated in many recruitment, selection, and promotion procedures today and may result in some preference being shown for members of protected classes.

It is safe to observe that policy-oriented and politically sensitive positions in government jurisdictions are subject to the criterion of political loyalty, with factors like efficiency, affirmative action and seniority as secondary considerations, although in many cases they are very important. In contrast, technical and professional positions are more likely to be filled according to knowledge, skills, and abilities, with seniority and affirmative action having secondary influence and political loyalty having little influence at all, except where patronage systems prevail. Entry- and basic-skill-level jobs are most often filled with primary attention to knowledge, skills, and abilities and affirmative action, although they can be subject to patronage hiring as well.

THE ACQUISITION FUNCTION

The second of the four functions every comprehensive personnel system must fulfill involves the acquisition of knowledge, skills, and ability (KSA). Along with motivation, the knowledge, skills, and abilities employees bring to their work is essential to mission accomplishment. When an organization recruits and hires employees, it is acquiring needed knowledge, skills, and abilities. It may seem cold and impersonal to talk about the recruitment and hiring of people in terms of acquisition. But traditionally, the impersonality of merit systems—the most comprehensive and pervasive personnel systems in government—has been a virtue. In merit systems personnel decisions are suppose to be made not on the basis of who an applicant or employee knows, but on the basis of that applicant's knowledge, skills, and abilities and the performance that results from the employee's application of his/her KSA to the agency's work. When we talk about the acquisition of labor, we are talking about an employer's acquisition of knowledge, skills, and abilities through recruitment and selection processes. The emphasis on KSA in merit systems often masks the tacit understanding that an employee's motivation and ability to get along with others and to fit into a work setting make a difference to a hiring agency. The focus on KSA, as set out formally in job descriptions, is less often a guide to how applicants are hired than they would like to believe or are led to believe.

Objectives of Recruitment

Public agency recruitment has several major objectives connected to the values of responsiveness, efficiency, social equity, and individual rights. Advocates of political responsiveness view recruitment of political executives as the means by which elected officials can fulfill policy promises, reward political loyalty, and maintain control over career bureaucrats in government agencies. Advocates of administrative efficiency see recruitment as the process by which qualified employees are attracted to government jobs. Advocates of social equity regard recruitment as the initial step in placing more employees from protected groups in government jobs. Last, advocates of individual rights and collective bargaining systems see the recruitment process as the entry opportunity for potential new union members. But aside from apprenticeship programs, the major staffing interest of unions is in the promotion process, where they advocate seniority as a critical factor in deciding who gets promoted.

Public personnel managers are primarily involved with the recruitment of employees who occupy civil service positions in local, state, and federal agencies. These are the bureaucrats—police officers, office workers, engineers, lawyers, scientists, teachers, and administrators—who comprise most of the government's employees. Personnel managers work closely with line managers to attract qualified applicants to available positions. After all, the credibility and status of personnel officers derives in large measure from the degree to which they are regarded as a help to line managers. But personnel managers must adhere to other standards as well. For example, they attempt to fulfill the acquisition function while keeping recruitment and selection costs low. Further, personnel managers trained in merit systems attempt to develop recruitment and selection processes which instill confidence that applicants are being treated fairly and will be selected according to their knowledge, skills, and abilities. Obviously, these criteria do not always coalesce harmoniously, and part of the ongoing tension in the professional personnel manager's role definition is the struggle between facilitating the work of line managers and regulating their decisions to keep them in line with accepted personnel practices.

Recruitment of Political Appointees

Recruitment is seen as a method of enhancing managerial efficiency through the acquisition of employees with desired knowledge, skills, and abilities and as a tool to advance the aims of social equity advocates. But recruitment takes a different shape when it is aimed at advancing political responsiveness. The public often views government employees who they see issuing statements on television, holding press conferences, and making visible and critical decisions as government bureaucrats. Yet few of these individuals actually are career government employees. Almost all agency heads at the state and federal levels of government, and many at the local level, are political appointees. That is, they are not appointed as a result of a competitive examination, and they serve at the pleasure of the elected officials who appointed them.

At the federal level, political appointments include people like cabinet secretaries, assistant secretaries, and other ranking agency officials; employees who work in the Office of the President; many legislative employees; and ranking officials of independent agencies. Similar positions are available in state government. Depending on the form of local government, the chief administrative officer and department heads may serve at the pleasure of the governing body or perhaps the mayor. If one is unfamiliar with a particular organization or government, the difference between politically appointed versus career officials can usually be determined by asking which positions are part of the civil service system. Career civil servants usually occupy "classified" positions covered by policies, rules, regulations, and procedures that constitute a merit system—a comprehensive personnel system where decisions are made primarily on the basis of knowledge, skills, and abilities.

Political appointees view public employment from different perspectives than do career civil servants.[2] Political appointees owe primary allegiance *upward*—to the elected official who appointed them. Incumbents of political positions value loyalty to a political philosophy or elected official or party, and they are frequently unfamiliar with the structure and operations of the agency they are being called upon to run, even though they may bring impressive political qualifications and a solid background of experience in the private sector to their posts.

Political appointees usually bring a short-term perspective to their work, and they frequently regard career civil servants as politically unresponsive, believing their loyalties are to programs or policies that have been part of previous administrations. Hence, appointed officials may view civil service protections as "red tape" that keeps "unproductive and unresponsive" civil servants in jobs, frustrating the political aims of the elected leadership. Over time, career civil servants begin to value continuity and stability in public policy and consistency in the application of public policy, and they are less likely to embrace short-term initiatives they see as having little chance of long-term success or to grant exceptions to rules.

These differences in the perceptions and objectives of career bureaucrats and political appointees highlight one of the continuing tensions within public employment—the conflict between the values of managerial efficiency and political responsiveness. Often this conflict is focused in the recruitment and selection process, since advocates of these two values advance such different criteria when sorting through an applicant pool and a job applicant's credentials.

External Influences on Recruitment

The demand for and supply of labor for government employers are influenced by demographic factors, and the economic, political, and legal environment of public employment.[3] The demand for labor is determined by the specific knowledge, skills, and abilities needed to fulfill public agency missions and objectives. Fundamentally, financial resources, authorized positions, and the formulation and content of agency missions influence the demand for labor.

Regarding the supply of labor, several questions are relevant: Who is available in the relevant labor market, and what knowledge, skills, and abilities do they possess? Where can potential employees be found, and how can they be reached and recruited for public employment?

Analyzing age demographics, Lane and Wolf[4] suggest that the overall problem affecting recruitment and retention in the near future is too many baby boomers (those born between 1945 and 1965), too few younger workers, and too many older workers leaving the workforce prematurely. The problem associated with the baby boomer generation is too many competent workers competing for limited opportunities for upward mobility. Simultaneously, a shortage of younger workers is anticipated. Finally, as increasing numbers of public employees become eligible for retirement, critical shortages can be anticipated.

Women will represent some two-thirds of those who enter the workforce between 1990 and the year 2000. African-Americans, who constituted 11 percent of the national workforce in 1987, are expected to increase to 17 percent of those entering in the decade of the nineties. Hispanics, who constituted some 7 percent, are expected to comprise 29 percent of those entering the workforce in this decade. Lane and Wolf observe that the knowledge, skills, and abilities required of the future labor force are not yet commonly held by these new African-American and Hispanic entrants. Assessing the needs of the federal government, they conclude that the greatest demand for labor in this decade is likely to occur in the engineering and scientific occupational categories.

In addition to demographic influences on recruitment and retention, political factors play a role as well. Changes in program priorities affect the demand for and supply of labor. For example, increased emphasis on the space program in the 1970s created thousands of jobs for aerospace workers; then financial concerns resulting in cutbacks decreased demand for these same workers. Similarly, as Hispanic and other immigrant populations grow, political pressure on educational systems for bilingual education will increase the political demand for bilingual teachers.

The sheer size of government means that agency needs will have a significant impact on the labor market. As the federal government has shed itself of direct service delivery, state and local governments have begun

---

ECONOMIC GROWTH:

1. Scarcity of qualified applicants
2. High demand for internal promotions and external recruitment
3. Open and continuous recruitment

ECONOMIC DECLINE:

1. Surplus of qualified candidates
2. Low demand for internal promotions and external recruitment
3. Recruitment managed or targeted toward shortage-category occupations

---

FIGURE   7-1   Economic Conditions and Recruitment

to fill the void, requiring increases in the numbers of state and local employees.

As shown in Figure 7-1, economic conditions influence recruitment and retention of public employees as well. Public jobs are commonly seen as being less susceptible to recession, and economic setbacks commonly see increasing numbers of available applicants for public jobs. At the same time, economic recession decreases the number of people resigning from jobs in public agencies. Lower revenue projections will diminish recruitment efforts, since the demand for new employees will be reduced.

The legal environment influences recruitment and retention practices as well. Laws affecting retirement age directly influence retention rates and the supply of existing labor. Affirmative action laws require more outreach in recruitment practices and have significantly affected not only the criteria used to make selection decisions but testing and interview practices. Residency requirements may affect the availability of individuals with critical knowledge, skills, and abilities.

RECRUITMENT TECHNIQUES

Centralized Techniques

Public agency recruitment techniques may be centralized or decentralized. If the agency has several thousand employees, and if different departments recruit large numbers of clerical or technical employees for the same types of positions, centralized recruitment will frequently be used because it is more efficient. If recruitment is centralized, the central personnel agency will be responsible for requesting from agency personnel managers periodic estimates of the number and type of new employees needed in the future (the next quarter or fiscal year). The staffing needs of all agencies are entered into a computer, after being classified by occupational code and salary level, and a summary listing of all projected new hiring needs is produced.

In reality, producing an accurate projection of new hiring needs is rarely this simple. To begin with, it is not always possible for agencies to predict their needs a year ahead of time. A political crisis or budget cut can drastically affect recruitment needs, and hence the quality of the estimate. Central personnel agency recruiters also realize that agency personnel managers will tend to overestimate the number of employees they require, just because from their point of view it is better to have too many applicants than too few. Naturally this conflicts with the need of the central personnel agency to reduce selection costs by reducing the number of applicants to the minimum number needed to ensure that all available positions are filled with qualified applicants. In addition, specialized positions require a greater ratio of applicants to projected vacancies, because a higher percentage of applicants is likely to be rejected by the selecting agency as not meeting the specialized requirements of the position.

Based on all these considerations, the central personnel agency will issue a job announcement that formally notifies applicants a vacancy exists. To meet affirmative action laws and regulations, each job announcement might include the following information:

1. Job title, classification, and salary range
2. Duty location (geographic and organizational unit)
3. Description of job duties and responsibilities
4. Minimum qualifications
5. Starting date
6. Application procedures
7. Closing date for receipt of applications

The extent of recruitment efforts once a vacancy is announced will depend upon several considerations: the geographic area, the length of time during which applications are accepted, and the necessity for targeted recruitment efforts. Typically, professional and managerial positions have a larger geographic job market than do clerical or technical positions. While recruitment for the latter may be local (conducted through newspaper advertisements or phone calls to the local office of the state employment service), recruitment for the former may be regional or national (involving recruiting agencies or advertisements in national professional newsletters). Generally, job vacancies are open longer if the position is managerial than if it is clerical. This is because the creation of a larger geographic job market means that applicants take longer to learn about the vacancy and to submit their applications and because agencies are generally able to predict managerial vacancies further in advance than clerical or technical ones.

If the agency underutilizes women or minorities, it will be interested in targeting recruitment efforts toward individuals from these groups. Community organizations, churches, shopping centers, minority newspapers, state employment services, and minority recruitment centers are all possible avenues for targeted recruitment. Given the hesitancy of many minorities and women to apply for jobs in public agencies in which they have historically had little opportunity for employment, it is to be expected that recruitment will also occur over a longer period of time if it is targeted toward these individuals.

Decentralized Techniques

Decentralized recruitment is most likely to occur in agencies that are relatively smaller, for which recruitment needs are limited, and where each agency employs different types of workers. It is almost always used for professional, scientific, or administrative positions peculiar to a particular agency. For example, smaller municipalities may not have enough vacancies to utilize the services of a central personnel department. Or the department heads may have successfully argued that their particular employees are unique to their own department and that it is more appropriate to handle recruitment and selection on a departmental level. Police and fire departments are likely to make this argument at the municipal level. Particularly during a recession, many agencies will find it more effective to utilize decentralized recruitment, because no cost savings can be gained through centralized recruitment when demand for public jobs is great but the number of available openings is small.

If recruitment is decentralized, individual public agencies will go through essentially the same steps required for centralized recruitment, except that dealings with the central personnel agency are limited. Agency personnel managers will work directly with the supervisors in their agencies to make periodic estimates of hiring needs. Then agency recruiters will meet with agency affirmative action specialists to determine whether recruitment efforts should be targeted toward specific minority groups. After evaluating both the need for new employees and the affirmative action goals of the agency, the agency personnel director will determine what recruitment efforts are required. The job announcement process is exactly the same as that of a central personnel agency, except that applicants are requested to send their applications to the specific agency.

While individual agencies are likely to favor decentralized recruitment because it gives them more control over the process, it has the disadvantage of reducing the control the chief executive has over expenditures or affirmative action compliance. In a centralized personnel system, for example, the chief executive will be able to stop new hiring simply by forbidding the central personnel agency from recruiting any new applicants and from sending the names of any applicants already on the register (list of eligibles) to individual agencies. In a decentralized system where the chief executive has no direct control over the recruitment process, it is more likely that individual agency directors will insist on their right to recruit people to meet program needs, and to manage their own budgets more autonomously.

In addition, decentralized recruitment is more likely to result in reliance upon word-of-mouth recruitment techniques, particularly in smaller agencies. If underutilization of women or minorities is a problem, word-of-mouth recruitment will probably make it worse; existing employees will be those most likely to discuss the job vacancy with their friends. Group pressure will make it unlikely that they will seek out qualified applicants who might be regarded by their co-workers as "different." In this situation, it is particularly important that formal job announcement and application procedures be scrupulously observed, and that recruitment efforts targeted toward the appropriate groups be carried out.

Some agencies utilize a combination of centralized and decentralized recruitment. For example, a central personnel agency may authorize individual agencies to recruit and test applicants independently, subject to audit by the central personnel agency once they have been hired. This compromise will provide for greater degree of centralized control than is possible with a decentralized system, while simultaneously providing agencies with timelier and more flexible recruitment than may be available from a central personnel agency.

SELECTION

Recruitment of employees is the initial phase of the selection process. The same discussion of value influences on recruitment apply to selection and, to a large degree, to the promotion process as well. In merit systems, the central tension is between the values of responsiveness and efficiency. Obviously, these values can coincide in the selection process as they did in the example involving Mayor Bradley at the beginning of the chapter. But the potential for conflict is great.

In order to realize the values of responsiveness and efficiency and also routinize recruitment and selection processes, most public jurisdictions set aside certain positions for political appointments, with the vast remainder covered by merit system procedures and protections. Tension occurs when the elected leadership believes it could accomplish more to advance its political platform—legitimized through an election—if it had more influence over top-level classified positions. In these cases, partisan pressures crop up either formally or informally to influence career appointments. Over time, if these attempts are successful, the response is that the knowledge, skills, and abilities necessary for informed public policy formulation and implementation are eroded. If the inroads result in notoriety or scandal involving political appointees, counterpressure is felt to strengthen the merit system.

While this pendulum swings, the values of social equity and individual rights often throw it on another course. Not only does the merit system have to respond to political pressures to accommodate the value of responsiveness, it must also adapt to public-policy initiatives and political pressure stemming from the values of social equity and individual rights.[5]

The most effective way of realizing social equity claims is through the establishment of quotas—for veterans, women, or racial and ethnic minorities. But the historic strength of merit systems and the ongoing appreciation of the need to bring expert knowledge to bear on public-policy formulation and implementation decreases the availability of this solution. In fact, even though quotas are commonly associated with affirmative action, they are rarely part of affirmative action programs. It is useful to remind ourselves that where hiring or promotion ratios do exist, they have resulted from a court order that usually follows convincing evidence of egregious and systematic discrimination. Even when hiring ratios are present, they are usually tempered by the phrase "qualified minorities," and they are not enforced if legitimate budgetary constraints place limits on hiring.

Nevertheless, affirmative action that calls for some kind of preference to protected classes rather than a program aimed simply at broadening the recruitment net and making sure that selection processes are impartial will challenge the traditional concept of the merit system. For example, if two applicants have similar scores on an examination, preference might go to the woman or minority applicant. These kinds of accommodations and adaptations make it impossible to describe a merit system definitively. What is clear is that whether in form or in substance, where personnel decisions are made primarily on the basis of knowledge, skills, and abilities, the force of merit is present.

The value of individual rights enters selection procedures as protection from partisan political influence. Thus, acquisition routines that include open access and selection criteria based on knowledge, skills, and abilities derived from the job to be performed have the effect of protecting the rights of individual job applicants to fair treatment. But the value of individual rights is also expressed significantly in the promotion process, where upward mobility is allocated, or in layoffs, where jobs themselves are allocated through the planning and sanction functions. Collective bargaining systems, seeking to protect the rights and treatment of their members, are particularly oriented toward these kinds of allocational decisions rather than acquisition—recruitment and selection—decisions.

Even though a union may not seek to influence recruitment and selection decisions in nonapprenticeship positions, it will make every effort to convince newly appointed employees to join the union if the job falls within the union's bargaining unit. In Kansas City, Missouri, every newly appointed firefighter joins the union, even though Missouri is a right-to-work state. During the initial training period, peer pressure is applied to accomplish this goal.

One of the ways unions protect their members from management favoritism is by insisting that seniority play a major role in allocational decisions like promotion and layoffs. Similarly, they argue against contracting out of city services if those services are currently performed by unionized city employees. Again, where merit systems exist along side collective bargaining systems, compromises are commonly reached. For example, it would not be unusual to see promotion scores calculated according to a formula that includes credit for an examination score and credit for years of service.

A major thesis of this book is that these value conflicts cannot be avoided because the values themselves are fundamental to the political culture. As long as public jobs are considered scarce resources, these values will be brought to bear on acquisition and planning or allocation personnel decisions. This results in merit systems under continual pressure from advocates of values other than efficiency (KSA), and public-policy compromises that eventually are reflected in personnel routines and techniques and regulations.

SELECTION, PROMOTION, AND AFFIRMATIVE ACTION: TESTING

Social equity advocates are often associated with promoting preferential treatment of minorities and women. But their greatest and most lasting impact may be in the area of testing for knowledge, skills, and abilities. Testing often provides clear indication that a public employer conducts business according to merit principles. In the 1970s, when the Civil Rights Act of 1964 was first being litigated, tests that discriminated against minorIties were scrutinized to see if those who scored highest really did turn out to be high performers. In other words, were the tests which purported to assess appropriate knowledge, skills, and abilities truly measuring qualities necessary for on-the-job performance? This focus challenged personnel practices at the merit system's core and over time resulted in more impartial and job-related selection tests and other selection devices. Examples include interviews conducted by boards rather than individuals in order to decrease the likelihood that individual bias will enter the selection process. In public safety positions, in particular, testing has been subject to continual review, and ad hoc height and strength requirements have given way to those empirically derived from an understanding of what kinds of knowledge, skills, and abilities are truly needed to perform police work and firefighting.

The purpose of testing is to distinguish those who will do better on the job from those who will not. If a test does this, regardless of its effect on women and minorities, it is a fair test. This kind of discrimination is legally acceptable. But before deciding whether a test or other employment requirement *unfairly* discriminates against minorities and women, we must first know whether it discriminates against them at all. Two methods for determining whether selection devices discriminate against minorities have developed over the years. One method of detecting discrimination or the adverse impact of selection procedures against minorities or women is by comparing the percentage of minority individuals employed by the organization in specific jobs with those qualified minorities present in the relevant labor market. Statistical analysis can determine the likelihood of these ratios occurring by chance.

Another method more clearly aimed at testing itself involves the 80 percent rule. This rule, presented in the 1978 *Uniform Guidelines to Employee Selection Procedures*, states that discrimination has occurred against a particular group if the selection rate for that particular group is less than 80 percent of the selection rate for the group with the highest selection rate. Table 7-1 illustrates the 80 percent rule showing that discrimination has occurred against Anglo and Hispanic males and Hispanic females. The passing standard is established by the Anglo females, and African-American males and females pass at a rate between 80 and 100 percent of the Anglo females. The 80 percent rule applies to all parts of a selection process, not just the overall selection rate.

TABLE 7-1 The 80 Percent Rule

ETHNIC GROUP	NO. OF APPLICATIONS	NO. OF SELECTIONS	PERCENT SELECTIONS	PERCENT SELECTIONS COMPARED TO HIGHEST	DISCRIMINATION?
W Male	20	5	25%	62.5%	yes
W Female	20	8	40	(highest)	—
B Male	15	5	33	82.5	no
B Female	20	7	35	87.5	no
H Male	15	3	20	50.0	yes
H Female	20	0	0	0	yes

Test Validation

A The impact on selection processes stemming from affirmative action, then, concentrates on what constitutes acceptable qualifications and how job qualifications are determined. This emphasis is seen in the area called *test validation*—the determination of the extent to which a selection device is related to a job. Even though validity is stimulated by a concern for social equity, it is theoretically consistent with the value of administrative efficiency as well.

A The Uniform Guidelines established three validation strategies as acceptable: empirical, construct, and content validation. *Empirical validation*, also known as *criterion validation*, requires that a test score be significantly correlated, in a statistical sense, with important elements of job performance. For example, let's assume that we have developed a written test to examine applicants for the position of personnel director. Over the past several years we have given this test to several hundred applicants, hired them regardless of the results, and later evaluated them on the basis of a performance evaluation test (which actually measures desired work performance). When we compare the written test results with the performance evaluation scores, we get the results shown in Table 7-2.

This test is unquestionably a good predictor of subsequent performance as a personnel manager. If you had to state the relationship between preemployment test scores and subsequent job performance, you would conclude that the test score, divided by 10, was a very close approximation of the subsequent performance evaluation. Of course, this assumes that a satisfactory performance can be established and measured by the organization's performance evaluation system.

The relationship between these test scores and subsequent job performance scores is plotted in Figure 7-2. The matrix is divided into four quadrants separated by a passing grade of 70 on the test and a minimum performance rating of 7. The goal of any selection device is to place most "hires" into the upper-right quadrant. These are the people who score well

TABLE 7-2 Empirical Test Validation

APPLICANT NAME	TEST SCORE	PERFORMANCE EVALUATION SCORE
Allen	70 (out of 100)	7 (out of 10)
Smith	45	4
Jones	93	9
Hammell	94	10
Wolfe	88	9
Kendall	62	6
Taylor	55	6
Mendoza	82	8

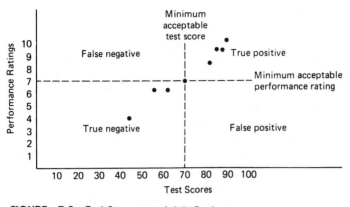

FIGURE 7-2 Test Scores and Job Performance

on the selection device and then also turn out to do well on the job. Another goal of a good test is to place applicants in the lower-left quadrant, such that those who do poorly on the test would also be those who do poorly on the job.

The more scores that fall in these two quadrants, the more valid a test is; in other words, the better job it will do of predicting subsequent performance. Most tests do not have anything near the predictive quality of our example. This means that people who do poorly on the test might end up doing well on the job (the upper-left quadrant), or that other applicants might score high on the test but not perform well on the job (the lower-right quadrant). Table 7-3 summarizes these relationships. The more valid the test, the easier it is to produce *true positives* and *true negatives*; the less valid the test, the greater the occurrence of *false positives* and *false negatives*.

Construct validation involves identifying psychological traits or aptitudes that relate to successful job performance and devising a test that measures these traits. For example, most insurance companies give psychological tests to applicants for sales positions. These test purport to measure

TABLE 7-3 Test Scores and Job Performance

	TEST SCORE	JOB PERFORMANCE
1. True positives (hire, do well)	high	high
2. True negatives (not hire, do poorly)	low	low
3. False positives (hire, do poorly)	high	low
4. False negatives (not hire, do well)	low	high

the applicant's congeniality, outgoing nature, liking for people, and other traits supposedly related to ability to sell. Police departments require a psychological profile on new recruits. In the sales example, tests have been developed by identifying the best salespeople in the organization, giving them a psychological test measuring a variety of traits, and establishing a personality profile of the "ideal salesperson." Police professionals are trying to eliminate individuals with unacceptable traits—overly aggressive, prejudiced—from the applicant pool. Profiles are then used as a yardstick against which the characteristics of applicants are measured. Those who approximate this yardstick move on in the selection process; those who do not are eliminated from the applicant pool.

Content validation requires that the job be analyzed to determine its duties; the particular conditions that make work easy or difficult; realistic performance standards; the skills, knowledge, and abilities required to perform these tasks up to these standards under these conditions; and the minimum qualifications required to ensure that an applicant would have these KSAs (knowledge, skills, and abilities). For example, it is logical to assume that a prison guard, responsible for transporting prisoners by car from one location to another, would need to know how to drive. An example of the application of the relationship between content validation and job analysis is given in the section on results-oriented job descriptions (RODs) in Chapter 4.

Content validation, therefore, links the functions of affirmative action and job analysis. In addition, it connects them with a third function, productivity. This is because the establishment of a logical relationship between duties and qualifications is not only a defense of validity, it is also a justification for discriminating between qualified and unqualified applicants on the basis of their anticipated performance. It would follow from this that a content-valid job description (such as a ROD) could be used to assess the validity of a selection or promotion criterion by measuring the performance of an employee hired on the basis of that criterion. As we will see in Chapter 10 on performance evaluation, one appraisal method—the behaviorally anchored rating scale (BARS)—has been developed with this objective.

Although each of these validation methods is equally acceptable to the EEOC (and other federal affirmative action compliance agencies), each is considered appropriate for different circumstances. Empirical validation requires that the organization hire many employees in the same type of work during a short time period, and some authors suggest that a group of several hundred employees is necessary.[6] Under the best of conditions, it would also require that the agency hire people who fail the test. After all, going back to Table 7-3, a valid test will minimize false negatives. In sum, empirical validation takes time and money, and it can be impractical for organizations that hire few people in a job class.

Construct and content validation both require a relatively thorough

TABLE 7-4 Comparative Advantages of Alternative Validation Procedures

	VALIDATION PROCEDURE		
APPROPRIATE CONTEXT	Criterion	Construct	Content
1. Meets federal guidelines	yes	yes	yes
2. Requires job analysis	some	thorough	thorough
3. Requires large sample	yes	no	no

job analysis to determine, respectively, the psychological traits or skills required for the position. Construct validity can be determined for a variety of jobs in different organizations. But because it requires the services of research psychologists, construct validation is beyond the abilities of most smaller public agencies. Its validity also depends upon the relationship between traits and performance, a link that is sometimes difficult to establish. This leaves content validation as the method of choice for the overwhelming majority of public employers. Its advantages are strengthened when we realize that the development of RODs can result not only in content validation, but also in the enhancement of productivity and clarity of performance expectations between employees and their agencies.

Table 7-4 shows the comparative advantages of alternative validation methods.

Test Validation Strategies

Our discussion of test validation procedures reveals a time-consuming and costly process. Given the limited resources of many personnel departments—and the unwillingness of personnel directors to devote resources to validation studies unless a selection or promotion system is questioned—how should public personnel managers treat the entire issue of validation? Our previous discussion has indicated that validation is theoretically useful to advance the values of social equity and administrative efficiency. That is, a test that is valid will not only be legally defensible under affirmative action laws, but will also result in the hiring of true positives and the rejection of false negatives.

Yet while it is theoretically sound to validate all criteria for employment, personnel professionals may wish, or be forced by circumstances, to adopt the next best approach, summarized as follows:

1. **Identify the classes of positions with the largest number of employees.** Since most public organizations are pyramidal in nature, these are likely to be entry-level positions or first-level supervisory positions. It is easier to conduct empirical validation studies with large groups of

employees, and these positions are likely to be those subject to the greatest pressure for access by different groups.

2. **Identify the positions most likely to be the subject of an affirmative action investigation or lawsuit.** Indications of this might be the rate of internal complaints, the experience of other similar organizations, or the presence of a high percentage of minority group members or women in lower-level positions from which the position in question is considered a promotion or a desirable lateral reassignment.

Given these two factors, personnel managers should prepare a schedule according to which selection procedures for all organizational positions will be periodically reevaluated. In presenting a budget request to upper management, personnel managers should emphasize the comparative costs and consequences of validation procedures versus affirmative action investigations or lawsuits. Remember—it can cost several thousand dollars to validate a test, but a successful lawsuit will cost several times this amount in court costs and attorneys' fees and compensatory damages.

The existence of a schedule for test validation will not in and of itself validate tests, but it may convince an EEOC investigator that your organization is making a "good faith effort" to improve the job-relatedness of selection and/or promotion procedures. In such cases, the personnel manager should consider using the level of impending administrative or legal sanctions to improve their bargaining power vis-á-vis management for additional funding for validation studies. In addition, the relationship between test validation and productivity would be an additional argument in its favor.

As *Griggs v. Duke Power Company* concluded, the use of a professionally developed test (aptitude or ability) does not in and of itself qualify the test as legal under Title VII. Although the Tower Amendment to the 1964 Civil Rights Act of 1964 (Section 703[h] specifically approves the use of "professionally developed ability tests," provided that such tests are not "designed, intended or used to discriminated because of race, color, religion, sex or national origin,"[7] other court decisions have held that the mere fact that a test is professionally developed does not guarantee that its use is proper in all circumstances.[8]

In addition, what would normally be classified as non-merit factors (for example, race, sex, or religion) may be used to exclude members of a particular group from employment consideration if membership in a certain race, religion, or sex is a legitimate job requirement. For example, chaplains may be required to be of a certain religion. However, the exclusion must be based on *business necessity* rather than mere convenience. For instance, the lack of separate bathroom facilities is not sufficient grounds for excluding women from a work site. It may be costly to build additional facilities, but this is not an insurmountable hardship; it is a reasonable accommodation.

SELECTION AND PROMOTION METHODS

Before proceeding with a discussion of selection methods, it will be useful to identify various steps and responsibilities in the staffing process:

1. Identify human resource needs
2. Seek budgetary approval to create and/or fill the position
3. Develop valid selection criteria
4. Recruit
5. Test or otherwise screen applicants
6. Prepare a list of qualified applicants
7. Interview the most highly qualified applicants
8. Select the most qualified applicant

Different jurisdictions or agencies will carry out these steps in different ways. The important point to be made here is that the line manager—the person the potential hire will actually be working for—is most heavily involved in steps 1, 2, 3, 7, and 8. The job of the personnel department is to assist the line manager in finding and hiring the best applicant (a staffing role), and to ensure that the staffing process takes place without the undue influence of politics or favoritism (a regulatory role).

The next step is establishing the minimum qualifications for a position through job analysis. This concerns the particular methods used to measure the extent to which applicants or employees possess these qualifications. Nine methods are commonly used: review of biographical data, aptitude tests, ability tests, performance exams, references, performance evaluation (for promotional assessment of current employees only), interviews, assessment centers, and a probationary period.

A review of an applicant's education and experience, through a standardized application form, is fundamental to the selection process. Levine and Flory estimated in 1976 that over *one billion* résumés and job applications are completed and reviewed annually. One can imagine what that number is today! Even if education and experience are not important selection criteria, they do serve other important purposes: They are a tally of the number and the qualifications of applicants for research and recordkeeping purposes; they provide a basis for interviewing; and they serve as a component of the personnel record of selected applicants. Research suggests that the data provided through job applications are more valid and reliable than information provided during interviews.[9]

Four types of written tests are commonly used for selection purposes: aptitude, characteristics or traits, ability, and performance. Aptitude tests measure general intelligence or cognitive ability (for example, the federal government's now-discontinued Professional, Administrative Career Entrance (PACE) examination, or the Otis-Lennon). Aptitude tests are both relatively inexpensive to administer and score, and highly reliable. Some commentators are wary of the ease with which responses to psychological tests can be "faked" to match the presumed desired responses to the set of the test scores. However, interim reliability checks can reduce the likelihood of this happening. The validity of such tests, however, can range from minimal to moderate, depending on the quality of the job analysis and the resulting construct validation of the aptitude as a predictor.

Several factors contribute to low validity. For one thing, as standardized tests, they are not adaptable to the particular objectives, conditions, or circumstances of different positions having the same title and general range of duties. As a consequence, some experts consider aptitude tests generally reliable for training purposes but less so for selection.[10] Others consider them particularly useful for screening large groups of employees,[11] particularly if they are carefully validated so that they are not inherently biased against minority group members.[12]

A second type of paper-and-pencil test measures personality traits or characteristics. The resulting personality profiles are then compared against profiles of current employees considered successful in the position, or against traits judged as job-related through construct validation. Examples are the Edwards Personality Preference Scale (EPPS) and the Minnesota Multiphasic Personality Inventory (MMPI).

Ability tests measure the extent to which applicants possess generalized abilities or skills related to job performance through empirical or construct validation. Examples would be verbal or mathematical ability, such as the Scholastic Aptitude Test (SAT) or the Graduate Record Examination (GRE). The more closely an ability test simulates actual job tasks and context, the more it becomes a performance test. A realistic typing or word processing test would be a good example. A performance test would be position-specific in that it would measure an applicant's ability to type a given kind of material on the specific machine used on the job. Research studies generally confirm that ability tests which result from job analysis are logically related to subsequent job performance.[13]

References are another selection tool. They are usually used to verify educational and employment records or to obtain information about the applicant's skills or personality. Their validity depends upon the opportunity that the writer has had to observe the applicant, and upon the relatedness of this relationship to the prospective job. Understandably, references are usually positive, limiting their effectiveness as selection tools. Because recommendation letters are overwhelmingly positive, readers frequently fall into the trap of looking for the smallest of differences as they attempt to distinguish one applicant from another. A better use of reference letters is to stimulate questions that can be asked in an interview.

Previous performance evaluations are often used to assess potential for reassignment or promotion. They are valid to the extent that the ratings are based on job performance and this performance involves the same skills or abilities required in the prospective job. Their reliability is based on the extent of inter-rater agreement among previous supervisory evaluations.

Interviews are a popular selection or promotion method. Most organizations will not hire an employee without one because they believe the interview gives them the opportunity to observe an applicant's appearance and interpersonal skills and to ask questions about subjects not adequately covered on the application form. However, interviews are not recommended as a primary selection method. Not only do they take a good deal of the supervisor's time, but they also require the supervisor to be a trained interviewer.[14] Since interviews are a prime method of rejecting candidates who look good on paper but might not fit into an organization, they are subject to close scrutiny as potentially invalid selection criteria.[15]

What, then, are some good guidelines to follow concerning interviews? If they are used to screen applicants, they must be validated by the same methods as are other selection devices, that is, justified by job analysis and supported by a content validation strategy.[16] Structured interviews, those using a prepared series of questions relating to the position, previous experience, career objectives, and so on, are preferable to unstructured ones. Panel interviews (those involving more than one interviewer) are more reliable than individual interviews, though they also increase the cost of this already expensive selection method.[17]

Assessment centers attempt to present several applicants with simulated job situations in order to stress performance on job-related tasks. They are used in both the public and the private sectors; in the public sector, their use is most prevalent among law enforcement organizations. If performance criteria are validated, they can be useful in selection, promotion, and career development.

The last selection or promotion method is the probationary appointment. This technique possesses the highest possible validity and reliability factors because it measures actual performance on the job. However, it also carries the highest cost and greatest risk to the organization, since a potentially unqualified employee may occupy a critical position until he or she makes enough serious mistakes to be considered unfit. The use of the probationary period places upon supervisors the responsibility of weeding out unsatisfactory or marginal employees before they attain career status (and hence the right to grievance hearings to protest a discharge after they have attained a "property interest" in their jobs) and upon personnel managers the responsibility of developing valid probationary period evaluation systems.

As might be expected, choosing among these alternative selection and promotion methods is difficult. The methods have differing degrees of validity or job-relatedness. They have varying degrees of reliability, or the

TABLE 7-5 Comparison of Selection Methods

METHOD	VALIDITY	RELIABILITY	COST
1. Biodata	moderate	high	low
2. References (letters of recommendation)	low	low	low
3. Aptitude tests	moderate	moderate	low
4. Characteristics of trait tests	moderate	moderate	low
5. Ability tests	moderate	moderate	moderate
6. Performance tests	high	moderate	moderate
7. Interviews	low	low	high
8. Assessment centers	moderate	high	high
9. Probationary appointment	very high	very high	very high

consistency of scores for one applicant over time. They range from the inexpensive to the costly. Even beyond the three criteria of validity, reliability, and cost are the values alternative methods can enhance or retard. Those who favor agency efficiency tend to support selection methods that measure quantifiable qualifications cheaply and easily: biodata, tests, and credentials. Those who favor political responsiveness support selection methods that provide information about an applicant's values or personality, or those that maximize flexibility for the hiring officials: references, interviews, and the probationary period. Advocates of social equity favor reliance on the probationary period. They fear that tests and minimum education and experience requirements, while easy to measure and effective at reducing the size of the applicant pool, will reject minority applicants who could perform well if hired ("false negatives").

Because each of these methods differs in value orientation, cost validity, and reliability, organizations must compare them.[18] Table 7-5 summarizes their comparative advantages. Usually standardized test scores are used to screen out persons unable to meet the basic requirements for a position, while interviews, assessment centers, or a probationary period are used to select the most qualified applicant from among all those who are basically qualified.[19]

FOUR RECRUITMENT AND SELECTION MODELS

Table 7-6 depicts four recruitment and selection routines that take place in Lawrence, Kansas, a council-manager city with a permanent population of some 65,000. By reviewing the information, we can find a number of the steps and methods already discussed as well as the influence of the values of efficiency, social equity, responsiveness, and individual rights. Knowledge, skills, and abilities are weighted very heavily in each of the selection proc-

TABLE 7-6   Recruitment and Selection Process in Lawrence, Kansas

ENTRY-LEVEL POSITIONS (NON-PUBLIC-SAFETY)	PUBLIC-SAFETY POSITIONS	DEPARTMENT DIRECTOR	CITY MANAGER (CHIEF ADMINISTRATIVE OFFICER)*
Recruitment:			
• Local newspaper • Announcements to 50 local agencies, including Job Service Center, NAACP, Haskell Indian Junior College, Kansas University	• Local and regional newspapers • Announcements to 50 local agencies and law enforcement and fire agencies • Special efforts to recruit women and minorities	• Local and regional newspapers • Professional associations (national) • Announcements to 50 local agencies	• Local and regional newspapers • Professional associations • Announcement to 50 local agencies
Selection:			
• Applications screened by personnel office • Reduced applicant pool reviewed by hiring authority • Test where appropriate • Interview with board • Reference checks • Preemployment physical, including drug screening • Appointment by hiring authority	• Written test • Physical fitness evaluation • Psychological test for police officer • Interview with board • Interview by department director • Reference checks • Preemployment physical, including drug screening • Appointment by department director	• Applicants screened by: personnel office/ selection committee/ city manager • Reduced pool reviewed by city manager • Assessment lab • Committee interview • Interview with city manager • Reference checks • Preemployment physical, including drug screening • Appointment by city manager	• Applications screened by: consultant/ personnel department/ committee of the governing body/ entire governing body • Reference checks • Interview with governing body (may also include visits with department heads) • Preemployment physical, including drug screening • Appointment by governing body
Length of Total Process:			
4–8 weeks	3–4 months	2–3 months	3–5 months
Training:			
On the job	Law enforcement academy	On the job	On the job

*Recruitment and selection may be conducted in-house or by an executive search consultant.

esses. For both the non-public-safety and public-safety-entry level positions, usually the city administers a test of knowledge or skill supplemented by interviews and reference checks. For all positions in the city, a pre-employment physical includes a drug screening test. Oral interview boards have replaced interviews with individual supervisors in order to get a broader range of opinion on the suitability of applicants. Interview boards also protect the individual rights of applicants to fair and equal treatment.

No paper-and-pencil testing takes place for department heads or for the city manager, but the national recruitment procedure indicates a desire to secure professionally trained talent. In addition, the interview board usually includes a professional in a related field who is not a member of the city staff. For example, selection of a new finance director might include a banker or the city's auditor as a member of the interview board.

Social equity is particularly noticeable in the public-safety positions, where special efforts are made in the recruitment process. Recent *recruitment* efforts for police and firefighters featured a poster advertising the positions and showing minority and female officers and firefighters; special booths at a shopping mall in the metropolitan Kansas City area with concentrations of minority populations; special visits to a junior college with a large minority population; and special outreach in the Topeka, Kansas area working with the YWCA to identify female candidates. No special efforts were made to show preference to women and minorities in any of the four *selection* processes.

The value of responsiveness is apparent only in the selection for city manager. The manager serves at the pleasure of the governing body, and elected officials are heavily involved in all phases of the selection process, whether they hire an executive search consultant or handle the process through their own personnel department. They employ criteria designed to determine whether the manager will work well with the governing body and will fit in with the political and social culture of the city.

SUMMARY

Because public jobs are regarded as scarce resources, competition for them reflects the competing values of responsiveness, efficiency, individual rights, and social equity. The goal of most public employers is to hire and promote those with the best knowledge, skills, and abilities to perform the job. But other interests, represented by political, collective bargaining, and affirmative action systems, frequently challenge this goal. Ultimately, the differences in value and policy orientations must be transformed into workable recruitment, selection, and promotion procedures that permit routine, cost-effective application and promise fair treatment for applicants.

KEY TERMS

acquisition function
career civil servant
centralized recruitment and selection
construct validity
content validity
criterion validity
decentralized recruitment and selection
political appointees
test validation
true and false positives and negatives
Uniform Guidelines to Employee Selection Procedures

DISCUSSION QUESTIONS

1. How does one's value perspective influence the objectives of the recruitment and selection process?
2. Describe the different basic values and perspectives of political appointees and career civil servants. How do these differences affect their working relationship?
3. Describe several external environmental factors that influence the acquisition of public employees.
4. Compare and contrast centralized and decentralized recruitment techniques.
5. Describe the concept and importance of test validation and three validation strategies. How have affirmative action and advocates of social equity and individual rights advanced the importance of test validation, and therefore the value of efficiency?
6. What is the theoretical relationship between job analysis, test validation, and performance evaluation/productivity?
7. Review the recruitment and selection processes in Table 7-6 and identify the values emphasized in each model. How would you improve these processes?

CASE STUDY

The following conversation takes place among three members of a state government: Brenda Simon, secretary of the Department of Corrections; her administrative assistant, Mary Rodriguez, and Larry Gordon, from the governor's office. They are talking about applicants for the recently vacated unclassified position of deputy secretary in the Department of Corrections.

1. Citing specific language in the conversation, identify evidence of different values.
2. Which candidate would you choose for this job and why?
3. What would happen if this kind of conversation took place every time a job opening occurred in a public organization? How do public organizations avoid these kinds of conversations every time a job opening occurs?

BRENDA: Well, I don't know about you two, but in my book this John Simpson seems to have enough experience to handle the job. I need someone who can take over the internal operations of the agency while we get this new program off the ground. But what really impressed me was his commitment to the policy direction we're headed in.

MARY: You know I admire your judgment, Brenda, but does he really have the skill to pull off the job? We know Don Johnson is doing a fine job now as a division director. He already knows the ropes around here, and I think he's ready for a bigger job. Besides, it's about time we got another minority into this sacred secretarial hut!

BRENDA: Hold on, Mary. You know I support our affirmative action program. I gave you a boost some time ago, I remember.

MARY: Now wait a minute! Let's not dredge up the history on that one. You know very well I was qualified for this job. This is now, and Don's qualified.

BRENDA: Mary, Don may be able to do the job; I'm not as convinced as you, but this Simpson is on target when it comes to supporting the philosophy behind the new program. And the more I think about it, the more I need that commitment to make this thing go. There's a lot at stake in making the program a success. Don's pretty hardheaded when it comes to seeing us turn this agency into what he feels is a softhearted bunch of social workers.

LARRY: Look folks, I hate to complicate things for you, but the governor's been getting pressure to find a spot for Jim Masington.

MARY: Jim who? I've never heard of him.

BRENDA: Well, I have. He worked pretty hard in the governor's last campaign, didn't he?

MARY: Oh no! I can see it coming.

LARRY: Don't get excited. Just give the guy some consideration. Brenda, you know the governor went out on a limb with the legislature to give you the chance to experiment with this new program, and he may need a favor here.

MARY: I just don't like the politics in all this.

BRENDA: Look, Larry, I want to help, but I need someone who is committed to this program.

MARY: And I think we'd better get someone who can manage the internal operations of this agency.

LARRY: Well, I think that you ought to look at Masington's application. You know that's all the governor is asking.

BRENDA: Thanks, Larry. I want to think about this. Mary, let's get together on this tomorrow afternoon.

MARY: Politics!

NOTES

[1]Rich Connell, "Bradley Comes Under Pressure to Name Latinos to Top City Jobs," *Los Angeles Times*, August 12, 1988, pp. II-1, 8.

[2]Joel D. Aberbach, Robert D. Putnam, and Bert A. Rockman, *Bureaucrats and Politicians in Western Democracies* (Cambridge, MA: Harvard University Press, 1981); Hugh Heclo, *A Government of Strangers: Executive Politics in Washington* (Washington, DC: The Brookings Institution, 1977).

[3]Larry M. Lane and James F. Wolf, *The Human Resource Crisis in the Public Sector* (New York: Quorum Books, 1990).

[4]Ibid., Chap. 2.

[5]Frederick C. Mosher, *Democracy and the Public Service*, 2nd ed. (New York: Oxford University Press, 1982).

[6]Frank L. Schmidt et al., "Statistical Power in Criterion-Related Validation Studies," *Journal of Applied Psychology 61*, 4 (1974), 473–85.

[7]The Civil Rights Act of 1964, P.L. 88–352, 78 Stat. 241, 28 U.S.C. s. 1447 [1976].

[8]*Albemarle Paper Company v. Moody*, 422 U.S. 405, 1975.

[9]Edward L. Levine and Abram Flory III, "Evaluation of Job Applications—A Conceptual Framework," *Public Personnel Management*, November–December, 1976, pp. 378–85.

[10]Edwin E. Ghiselli, "The Validity of Aptitude Tests in Personnel Selection," *Personnel Psychology 26* (1973), 461–77.

[11]Craig C. Pinder, "Statistical Accuracy and Practical Utility in the Use of Moderator Variables," *Journal of Applied Psychology 97*, 2 (1973), 214–21.

[12]William Jasper, "Results of Study of Fairness of Written Tests," *The Personnel Research Reporter V 2*, 3 (July 1972), 1–6.

[13]I. von Raubenheimer and Joseph Tiffin, "Personnel Selection and the Prediction of Error," *Journal of Applied Psychology 55*, 3 (1971), 229–33; and Herbert S. Field, Gerald A. Bayley, and Susan M. Bayley, "Employment Test Validation for Minority and Nonminority Production Workers," *Personnel Psychology 30*, 1 (1977), 37–46.

[14]S. W. Constantin, "An Investigation of Information Favorability in the Employment Interview," *Journal of Applied Psychology 61*, 6 (1976), 743–49; and Neal Schmitt and Bryan W. Coyle, "Applicant Decisions in the Employment Interview," *Journal of Applied Psychology 61*, 2 (1976), 184–92.

[15]Robert L. Dipboye, Howard L. Fromkin, and Kent Wiback, "Relative Importance of Applicant Sex, Attractiveness and Scholastic Standing in Evaluation of Job Applicant Resumes," *Journal of Applied Psychology 60*, 1 (1975), 39–43; Manuel London and John Poplawski, "Effects of Information on Stereotype Development in Performance Appraisal and Interview Contexts," *Journal of Applied Psychology 61*, 2 (1976), 199–205.

[16]Enzo Valenzi and I. R. Andrews, "Individual Differences in the Decision Process of Employment Interviews," *Journal of Applied Psychology 58*, 1 (1973), 49–53; Glen D. Basket, "Interview Decisions as Determined by Competency and Attitude Similarity," *Journal of Applied Psychology 57*, 3 (1973), 343–45.

[17]Milton D. Hakel, "Similarity of Post-Interview Trait Rating Intercorrelations as a Contributor to Interrater Agreement in a Structured Employment Interview," *Journal of Applied Psychology 55*, 5 (1971), 443–48.

[18]Alan L. Gross and Wen-huey Su, "Defining a 'Fair' or 'Unbiased' Selection Model," *Journal of Applied Psychology 60*, 3 (1975), 345–51.

[19]Yoash Wiener and Mark L. Schneiderman, "Use of Job Information as a Criterion in Employment Decisions of Interviewers," *Journal of Applied Psychology 59*, 6 (1974), 699–704.

CHAPTER

8

Improving Employee Performance through Leadership

If the 1980s taught public personnel managers anything, it was that personnel systems must be increasingly responsive to external pressures for productivity, work measurement, and political accountability. With the exception of the staunchest proponents of civil service systems, stakeholders are not particularly interested in merit system principles or the problems caused by the spoils system, except insofar as these systems result in public agencies that are ineffective or unaccountable. This means that the focus of public personnel management must change from management of positions, as was the case under traditional civil service systems, to accomplishment of agency mission.

For public personnel managers working primarily within civil service systems, this means the need for increased flexibility and experimentation in many areas: rank-in-job versus rank-in-person personnel systems, work classification and evaluation versus job classification and evaluation, impact of person on job, individual versus group performance evaluation and reward systems. It also means that public personnel managers must lay aside any biases they may have in favor of civil service systems and objectively evaluate the comparative advantages of alternative systems in accomplishing agency missions under a variety of conditions. To put it bluntly, the evolving role of the public personnel professional requires experimentation and testing of alternatives in an uncertain environment, with agency performance as the objective and point of reference.

To be fair, elected officials and agency managers must also recognize the ways in which their views have been bounded by traditional views of personnel management. Elected officials must recognize that they are largely responsible for the creation of position management through their focus on external control of agency resources (through line item budgets, control over appropriations, and control over number of positions and average grade level). Instead, elected officials must take a "leap of faith" and begin to trust agency managers to manage for results once they are given flexibility over budgets and human resources. True, some managers are so used to living with external controls that they will not be able to function in an environment where they are given greater flexibility over resources and greater accountability for results. But this question will be moot unless elected officials are willing to take the risk and see what happens.

For their part, managers must insist on flexibility of resources, on the freedom to experiment with a variety of personnel systems and techniques, in order to find those that are most effective at achieving the agency's mission. They must train themselves to thrive in a contingent environment where objectives are diverse and means-end relationships are uncertain. And they must reward subordinates for taking similar risks, and for learning from them. It is only through leadership from the top, leadership that speaks directly to employees' highest aspirations rather than to their deepest fears, that the organizational culture will change from hierarchy, mistrust, and inertia to self-motivated networks of employees.

This means that personnel directors must work with supervisors and agency managers to underscore the connection between agency effectiveness and the vast body of social science research that focuses on individual and group performance in organizations. Personnel directors must glean from this body of research the insights they need to be "interocular trauma specialists" within their own agencies. That is, they must use research findings to propose and defend new ways of organizing work and managing people, ways based on the imperatives of environmental demands on agencies, and on what people really want from their jobs. They must hit people between the eyes with information, and use it to help transform the organization in ways that are at once more pleasant and more productive.

By the end of this chapter, you will be able to:

1. Discuss ways that political leaders (elected executives and legislators), personnel directors, and agency managers can create conditions that enable public employees to be more productive.

2. Discuss the importance of supervisors in ensuring that employees have adequate skills, orientation, feedback, and consequences (the four "building blocks" of productivity).

3. Discuss and evaluate the findings of social science research (especially equity theory and expectancy theory) on employee motivation and performance.

4. Tell how the personnel director can work with supervisors to design alternative work systems that enhance performance by changing job design and organizational culture, and discuss why this is particularly important with a diverse workforce.

PRODUCTIVITY IMPROVEMENT THROUGH POLITICAL LEADERSHIP

With the decline in resources available to public agencies for productivity improvement through technological innovation, it is even more important that public employees work under conditions that allow and encourage them to be more productive. Organizational productivity was discussed generally in Chapter 3. This chapter will focus on the shared role of political leaders (executives and legislators), appointed agency managers, and the personnel director in creating the conditions under which public employees can be productive. Today more than ever, political leadership means productivity improvement from the top down.

What can these key public officials and managers do to enable public employees to be more productive? In a word, everything! Employee productivity depends on individual ability and effort. But these conditions alone are not sufficient. Employees also need the opportunity to perform well, and clear objectives for which to strive.

Ability

Legislatures and administrative executives have the most significant effect on the ability of the worker through the wage-setting process. The more money allocated to salaries, the more competitive a governmental employer will become in the labor market and the more talent it will attract. Similarly, salary level and working conditions affect an employee's intention to stay with an employer. Unfortunately, public agencies often serve as training centers for the private sector by paying relatively low salaries for experienced employees. For example, social workers hired by a state human service agency are usually paid competitive entry-level salaries, but are not given pay increases as they gain experience. As a result, many of the best new employees (up to 30 percent after one year) choose to leave state employment for private sector jobs. This "brain drain" reduces productivity by making case tracking more difficult, hampering management development, and diminishing organizational memory.

Within the agency, department managers and personnel directors affect productivity most significantly through employee selection. Assuming that a market wage will attract talent to the public employer, it is now necessary to select potential employees with the most ability to perform current responsibilities and learn new skills as as well. Other important departmental influences on the employee's ability to perform include the quality of on-the-job training (coaching), and the quality and timeliness of feedback regarding performance.

The personnel department has a significant effect on the ability factor as well by conducting training needs assessments and locating training opportunities, by emphasizing and researching the validity of selection methods, by working with supervisors and employees to develop performance-based appraisal methods, and by increasing supervisory skill in communicating constructive feedback to employers. In some cases, the personnel department may keep track of labor market conditions and gather data on prevailing wage rates for input into legislative decisions regarding allocation or collective bargaining positions.

Effort

Assuming that agencies can hire and retain employees with the ability to perform public services, employee effort (motivation) is similarly affected by an array of organizational and environmental factors. Political leaders, agency managers, and personnel directors are responsible for creating and funding personnel programs that provide incentives for superior performance. These include merit pay, bonuses for employee suggestions, and recognition for detection of client fraud and abuse. At the departmental level, linking incentives to desired performance will critically affect the employee's belief that high performance will be rewarded and poor performance dealt with. The creation of challenging jobs will tap the intrinsic desire people have to master their work and avoid boring, fatiguing activities that hold few positive outcomes. Moreover, establishing career paths allows employees to look ahead to a future with their employer. In addition, endorsement of fair but streamlined disciplinary procedures will carry the message to managers as well as employees that unsatisfactory performance will not be overlooked.

Perhaps the greatest influence on employee performance involves the fairness with which employees feel they are being treated. While this is primarily a supervisory responsibility, the personnel office can affect an employee's motivation indirectly by training supervisors in how to motivate employees and how to enhance perceptions of equity in the workplace. They can monitor pay and evaluation processes to ensure no obvious abuses are occurring. They can assist departments in the design of challenging jobs and can work toward developing classification and compensation plans that foster innovative work design, assignments, and availability of monetary incentives.

One last factor affecting public employees' effort is the example set by their political and administrative leaders. Given that Americans currently express a high degree of cynicism about political leaders and institutions, it is important that employees view their leaders as appropriate ethical and professional role models. Otherwise, the message they send to employees will be hypocritical and negative.

Opportunity

Frequently overlooked among the factors connected to productivity is the employee's opportunity to perform well. Yet political leaders, agency managers, and personnel directors have the primary responsibility for ensuring that the opportunity to perform well exists. First and foremost, political leaders can create agencies with clear missions, adequate resources, and internal administrative stability. Or they can tie public employees' hands by allowing the continuation of organizational factors that hinder performance: unclear objectives, inadequate budgets, frequent internal reorganizations, lack of realistic work planning or scheduling, and constant harassment of agency managers for partisan political objectives (also known as "bureaucrat bashing").

Employees must also be given reasonable expectations. Included here is not so much the clarity of goal statements, but the feasibility of the goal at all. For example, measuring police officers' performance by variations in the crime rate discounts the variety of factors not under a police department's control which influence crime in a community. Similarly, the National Education Association and the American Federation of Teachers have hotly criticized what they feel is the simplistic notion that incentive pay for teachers will improve student performance. These professional associations cite a host of factors outside the classroom that can have more effect on student performance than teacher behavior.

From a more positive perspective, rather than just demanding that employees work harder, political leaders and agency managers can provide the technology that enables employees to "work smarter." For example, an on-line computer database is likely to allow an employee to do better work than a manual file of index cards. The availability of the tools of one's trade, be they reliable snowplows or microcomputers and spread sheets, is essential to employee performance.

Another factor related to productivity involves attention to safe equipment and working conditions. Sick leave and worker's compensation cost public employers a great deal, and unsafe working conditions reduce the employee's opportunity to work productively.

A final factor at this level has to do with the personnel system itself. If a system is too rigid there may be few opportunities for flexibility in work assignments, career mobility, and implementation of incentive plans. On the other hand, a system too flexible might encourage favoritism, capricious personnel actions, and an undermining of morale and confidence in the overall merit concept.

At the departmental level, opportunity is made available to employees with the appropriate allocation of resources to mission and with the specification of feasible performance objectives. Safety in the workplace often depends on its emphasis at this level. The personnel department, through its interpretation of personnel rules, enhances the employee's opportunity to perform. This, of course, is a tricky area, because too much flexibility leads to favoritism and organizational instability; too rigid interpretation stifles innovation in the awarding of incentives, work assignments, and career mobility. The personnel department also bears the responsibility for monitoring safety goals and establishing employee assistance programs.

Goal Clarity

Another factor that advocates of productivity in government easily overlook is goal clarity. Measurement of productivity in the provision of social services is often impeded by ambiguous notions of what constitutes acceptable output, or simplistic counting of service activities rather than a focus on agency mission. Yet an employee must know what the organization considers a satisfactory level of performance in order to do well. At the legislative level, this means specification of legislative priorities and program objectives. At the departmental level, managers and supervisors must translate these priorities into specific work unit and individual objectives and must provide feedback to employees about performance. The personnel office can contribute to goal clarity by conducting timely job analyses, and by training supervisors in the writing of performance standards and in the assessment process.

In sum, at the legislative and agency corporate level, productivity of employees will be enhanced by the allocation of wages and working conditions competitive with other employers, by provision of incentives, and by adoption of equitable human resource management policies. Elected officials and agency managers will be most effective if they establish program priorities and provide adequate resources to accomplish feasible objectives.

The personnel department, as we have stressed throughout, takes on a supporting role in the effort to improve productivity. Activities connected with this role include conducting training needs assessments, locating training and career development opportunities, providing supervisors with knowledge of the factors affecting employee motivation and perception of fair treatment, assisting in the development and maintenance of an equitable pay and benefit plan, assisting supervisors in testing the limits of classification and pay systems to create jobs that reflect emphasis on agency mission and that are challenging to employees, monitoring safety goals, setting up an employee assistance program, and training supervisors in writing performance objectives and communicating constructive feedback to employees.

SUPERVISORS AND THE BUILDING BLOCKS OF PRODUCTIVITY

In order to do their jobs well, employees need the organization to provide them with four things—the building blocks of productivity. These building blocks are the combined responsibility of the supervisor, other managers, and the personnel department.

1. **Clear instructions**. Employees cannot perform well unless they know what is expected of them.
2. **Adequate skills**. Employees cannot perform well unless they are able to do the job they are given.
3. **Feedback**. Employees do not know how they are doing unless someone tells them.
4. **Appropriate consequences**. Good performance must be rewarded, and bad performance punished, if employees are to perform well.

As a supervisor or manager, you may feel that you can quickly and instinctively tell the difference between "good" and "bad" employees. But good supervisors know that first impressions are not always accurate. Before you decide that you need to discipline an employee, ask yourself if you have done your job as a supervisor by making sure the employee has the building blocks necessary to be productive.

CLEAR EXPECTATIONS

- Have you asked the employee to develop an informal job description for his or her position which emphasizes the major tasks, and some reasonable performance standards (stated objectively in terms of quantity, quality, or timeliness of service)?
- If the position is hopelessly misclassified, did you request a desk audit of any positions for which these informal job descriptions appear unrelated to the formal position description?
- Have you used the supplemental job description to give the employee a clearer idea of what is expected?
- Have you reached clear understanding with the personnel department over shared responsibilities for new employee orientation? Do you use your best employees for unit orientation?

ADEQUATE SKILLS

- Having identified the major elements of the job before filling a vacancy, are you sure the employee has the skills, ability, and knowledge to perform satisfactorily within 3 to 6 months after hiring?
- If all applicants are unqualified, have you asked for an audit or reclassification?
- Have you provided orientation and training where needed?

FEEDBACK

- Do you document performance?
- Do unproductive employees know, directly from you, that they are not productive? Do you use immediate feedback, rather than waiting for performance evaluation periods?
- Do you praise in public and critique in private?

CONSEQUENCES

- Do you support the development of a merit pay system which allocates a large sum of money—up to 25 percent of base salary in exceptional cases? Do you push for the right of supervisors to allocate merit pay at their own discretion, based on objective performance relative to previously established performance standards?
- Do you support the need to separate merit pay for any systems that adjust pay based on cost of living or seniority (these are not related to merit)?
- Do you use noneconomic rewards lavishly?
- Do you continue to lobby the personnel department on the need to clarify personnel regulations regarding employee conduct? These are necessary not only to improve employee productivity, but to safeguard the union contract and protect against legal liability in case of a civil suit.
- Are you aware that the doctrine of "vicarious liability" means that you are responsible for employee behavior that violates the rights of clients and other employees?

MOTIVATION, EFFORT, AND EMPLOYEE PERFORMANCE

Human resources constitute between 50 and 75 percent of a public agency's budget. Given the size of these outlays, it is evident that the more efficient use of human resources requires a more concentrated analysis of employee performance related to two issues: the willingness or motivation of the employee to perform (which produces employee effort), and the employee's ability to perform.

An individual employee's satisfaction or dissatisfaction with work is a subjectively derived conclusion based on a comparison of what the employee receives from working compared to what the person expects, wants, or thinks he or she deserves. Satisfaction is an overall concept that includes the employee's subjective weighting of satisfaction with pay, job security, interpersonal relations at work, future opportunities, and the work itself. Two theoretical tools help explain the relationship between job satisfaction and motivation—equity theory and expectancy theory.

Equity Theory

Equity theory helps us understand how a worker reaches the conclusion that he or she is being treated fairly or unfairly. The feeling of being treated equitably is an internal state of mind resulting from a subjective calculation of what one puts into a job and what one gets out of it in comparison to some other relevant person. Inputs can include anything of value the employee brings that he or she thinks deserves special recognition in comparison with others—seniority, expertise, type of work, difficulty of work. Inputs can also include the less formally recognized but still frequently claimed credit for age, sex, race, political influence, and other "non-merit" factors. Outcome credits have equal range: pay, future opportunity, promotion, recognition, organizational climate, work schedule, autonomy, a reserved parking space, a certain size and location of office.

Equity calculations involve two types of subjective comparisons: input to output, and comparison with other employees. Equity does not require that all employees receive equal outputs, only that outputs be proportional to inputs, and that employees with comparable inputs receive comparable outputs. Equity issues are confronted in an organization at two levels, in terms of policies regarding human resource management and in the supervisor-subordinate relationship. At the policy level (at least within civil service and collective bargaining systems), considerable attempts are made in public organizations to prevent equity issues from surfacing. Job classification, performance evaluation, and grievance systems are built around the idea of equal pay for work of equal worth. Yet political systems and affirmative action are built around the opposite premise. Affirmative action proponents believe that institutional sexism or racism prevent equity for minorities and women; political systems believe that perceived pay inequities in fact reflect the personal value of subordinates to the organization, and that these are in fact equitable ("go for as much salary as you can pull down").

Inevitably, questions of equity will occur at the working level in any organization. There are several ways to deal with an employee's feeling of being treated unfairly. First, the supervisor must recognize that reaching a conclusion that one has been treated unfairly is the product of someone's unique internal logical processes, driven in many cases by a gnawing sense of injustice. Also impeding simple resolution of equity issues is the facility human beings have to distort input-output ratios to justify feeling ill-treated. The supervisor should try to find out what the employee perceives his or her rewards and contributions to be and who an appropriate person for purposes of comparison might be, in order to clarify the source of perceived injustice. Finally, the supervisor can attempt to forestall equity claims by making clear to others what he or she feels deserves organizational rewards, and then consistently applying organizational rewards and punishments and specifying the reasons behind the actions.

Expectancy Theory

Expectancy theory augments equity theory by showing how employees' feelings of job satisfaction are translated into performance. Expectancy theory attempts to reconstruct the mental processes that lead an employee to expend a certain amount of effort towards meeting a work objective. It assumes that effort results from three factors:

1. The employee's subjective probability that he or she can do the job
2. The employee's subjective assessment that identifiable rewards or consequences will occur as a result of doing (or not doing) the job
3. The value the employee places on these rewards or punishments

In reality, employees do not make these calculations explicitly or formally. Rather, they adjust their level of effort (or change its focus from one task to another) based on implicit and intuitive responses to these issues. For example, an employee who is promised a promotion for performing a task well will probably do so, provided that the employee thinks he or she can do the task, and that he or she wants a promotion. Given the same circumstances, an employee who wants to spend more time with his family may turn down the promotion because it means more work (an undesirable consequence), even though he believes he could do the job.

The expectancy model provides an excellent diagnostic tool for analyzing an employee's work behavior because it focuses attention on the ways the organization affects employee effort and performance. First, the probability that effort will result in task performance is low if the task is difficult, and high if the task is easy. But since easy jobs are usually boring, supervisors must delegate responsibility appropriately by striking a balance between setting a performance level so high as to be perceived as unattainable, or so low as to be seen as attainable but boring. Second, the perceived equity and adequacy of performance evaluation and reward systems have a major influence on the employee's perception that performance will lead to rewards (or punishment). Performance appraisal systems that do not distinguish high and low performers, or that do not result in differential rewards (or punishments) for them, will lead under equity theory to downward adjustment of inputs to meet outputs. Finally, consequences must be desirable to result in effort. A probation officer who is rewarded for resolving cases quickly and well by being assigned more cases and more difficult ones, will soon learn to work more slowly.

Some Conclusions

One of the biggest problems public agencies face is developing merit pay systems that reflect the realities of equity theory and expectancy theory, at least as employees view them. Most merit pay systems in fact are underfunded, and end up being used as devices to provide small cost-of-living increments to a large proportion of employees. If rewards were large enough (20 to 30 percent of base pay) to generate effort and performance, they would be the target of politicians ("Why should we pay people bonuses for doing what they should be doing in the first place?") and budget cutters ("What's this large, variable expense item doing in our budget?").

Equity theory and expectancy theory lead thoughtful supervisors away from more prescriptive, universal theories of human motivation and performance (such as Maslow's hierarchy of needs or Herzberg's motivator-hygiene theory). In reality, employees are individuals, with subjective perceptions of their own needs and abilities. Good personnel managers are those who can develop personnel functions so as to recognize the impact of organizational climate on employee performance, and good supervisors are those who can use these systems to develop relationships based on open communication and trust.

ALTERNATIVE WORK SYSTEMS THAT ENHANCE PERFORMANCE

Performance management is the management of resources toward agency mission. This includes not only financial resources, but human resources as well. It is here that human resource managers have an advantage over their financial counterparts. Financial resources are finite and fixed. In an era where policy and program initiatives are predicated on "budget neutrality," managers and supervisors have come to conclude that financial managers respond to problems by telling the organization to do the same with less, or more with the same amount of money. Human resource managers recognize that employees are a resource, and a variable one. That is, even in the absence of significant financial rewards, employee performance will continue to improve if the characteristics of work and the climate of the organization are appropriate.

Figure 8-1 summarizes this approach to designing work and organiza-

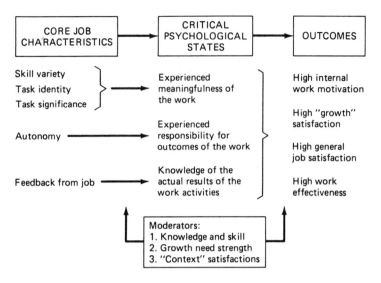

FIGURE   8-1   Job Characteristics Model.

Source: Richard Hackman/Greg Oldham, *Work Design,* © 1980 by Addison-Wesley Publishing Company. Reprinted with permission of the publisher.

tions. The model depicts the following line of argument: High internal work motivation, "growth" satisfaction, general job satisfaction, and work effectiveness result when people experience their work as meaningful, when they feel responsible for the quality and quantity of work produced, and when they have first-hand knowledge of the actual results of their labor. These psychological states are likely to result from work designed to incorporate the following characteristics: variety, work with a beginning and identifiable end, work of significance, and work characterized by autonomy and feedback.

Jobs that are high in these qualities are said to be "enriched" and to have a high motivating potential. Whether high internal motivation, satisfaction, and productivity actually do result in holders of these kinds of jobs depends on differences in the workers' knowledge and skill, their growth need strength (such as the need for self-esteem or the esteem of others), and by context satisfaction (including such aspects of work as pay, supervision, and working conditions).

Results of research into this model have been generally supportive. At an operating level, they have resulted in the adoption of personnel policy innovations first as experiments, and then as options in the "tool kit" the supervisor and personnel director use to match employees with work, and to generate good individual and team performance. These include delegation, flexiwork, management by objectives (MBO), and total quality management (TQM).

Delegation

Delegation is the developmental reassignment of work from supervisors to subordinates. If it is done well, it is not only developmental for the employee, but it also frees the supervisor's time for supervision and planning rather than production work. Also, delegation increases employees' sense of participation and internal motivation, thereby increasing productivity.

There are many reasons why supervisors may fail to delegate: lack of faith in subordinates, fear of superiors should the delegation be unsuccessful, desire for personal credit, and misjudgment of time. Here are some tips for successful delegation:

1. Select the task carefully—delegate a task that you do not need to do, and that an employee will consider developmental.
2. Select the person carefully—match the delegation with the employee's skills, and do not use favoritism.
3. Prepare the setting carefully—change is threatening, even if the employee considers it desirable. Turn over the assignment skillfully:
   (a) Meet in private where you will not be interrupted.
   (b) Allocate sufficient time to delegate carefully and thoroughly.
   (c) Go over the new job carefully, step by step.
   (d) Ask the employee for verbal feedback on all steps to avoid misunderstanding.
   (e) Give the employee a chance to ask questions.
4. Provide feedback—follow up soon to determine how things are going. Remember, either positive or negative feedback is better than no feedback at all.
5. Offer rewards or other consequences—praise good work to build confidence and transmit enthusiasm. Praise in public; criticize in private.

Flexible Work Locations and Schedules

In the past, all employees were expected to have identical working hours and a fixed job location, but this is no longer true. First, changes in technology (primarily communications and computers) have meant that employees can work productively at decentralized work stations, or even at home (*flexiplace*). Second, the need for more flexible service delivery, and the complex child care and eldercare arrangements necessitated by two-career families, have resulted in the development of part-time and flexible work schedules. Last, the focus on employees as resources has led to the development of variable models of resource use that have proved effective at achieving performance.

Under *flextime*, all employees are expected to work during core hours (such as 9:00–3:00). Depending on agency needs and personal preferences, each employee is free to negotiate a fixed work schedule with different start or end times. Research on flextime experiments in both the public and private sectors generally reveals positive results in employee attitudes and in the reduction of absenteeism, tardiness, and in some cases even increases in productivity.

Job sharing is the splitting of one job between two part-time employees on a regular basis. There are obvious advantages for employees (flexible part-time work rather than a choice between full-time work or no work at all) and the agency (mentoring, light duty work). But the employees must coordinate their activities with each other, with their supervisor, and with clients/customers inside and outside the agency. And the agency must develop policies for contributions and division of pensions, health care, and other benefits.

Under *flexiwork*, employees may work away from the office, provided a suitable outside workstation is available. This works best for professionals who can work independently, and yet remain in contact with the agency through phone systems, a computer, and a modem. The advantage to the agency is that it may be able to get work done just as well, and to attract individuals who value independence and flexibility. The downside, of course, is predictable things like communication and control, and unpredictable ones like workplace health and safety, and worker's compensation claims.

Management by Objectives (MBO)

Management by objectives (MBO) is a technique for giving employees clear performance objectives which are related to organizational goals. It requires goal clarity, and relating these goals to individual performance goals in a goal-setting interview between supervisor and employee. Next, both supervisor and employee evaluate the employee's performance using these predetermined goals, with objective performance standards (critical incidents). Naturally, unforeseen changes in conditions lead to revision of the performance contract.

But MBO is not just a technique for delegating responsibility and following up to ensure that the work has been done; MBO is also a philosophy of human relationships which requires that employees "buy into" organizational goals by having shared responsibility for their achievement. It thus requires, and emphasizes, mutual respect, trust, and teamwork.

Total Quality Management (TQM)

Total quality management (TQM) is a participative management technique that focuses on increased employee involvement in and commitment to agency mission. Essentially, TQM consists of small groups of employees who volunteer to meet regularly and identify, analyze, and solve problems in their common work area. These problems most often focus on customer/client service, quality control, production, cost savings, and accident prevention. Frequently, quality circle participants are trained in problem-solving techniques, including the development of communication and problem-identification skills, and data gathering and analysis. Their focus is on problems that can be identified and resolved at the participant's level within the agency.

Performance Management and Workforce Diversity

All these examples of managing for performance have a common thread—working with employees as unique human resources rather than as uniform inputs to a production process. For example, delegation and MBO are fundamentally not management techniques, but assumptions and values related to the human resource development and employee involvement in accomplishing the mission of the agency.[1] Flexible work scheduling and locations are not just troublesome exceptions to normal working hours and duty stations, they are innovative ways of using people's talents which are possible because of new work technologies.[2]

Not only that, they are necessary because of changing role expectations and cultural norms. Those who promote workforce diversity as a new approach to productivity (rather than just a new name for affirmative action) believe that different races, ethnicities, and sexes bring diversity to the workplace, and that this diversity introduces variations on white male management styles which can make organizations dramatically more effective. For example, some researchers conclude that women have a more interactive and nurturing management style which makes organizations more flexible and effective utilizers of human resources.[3]

SUMMARY

Human resource managers and supervisors have a unique and irreplaceable role in the agency. Within the parameters set by legislators and chief executives, they must develop and implement corporate human resource systems for maintaining and improving the performance of individual employees and work groups. This requires an understanding of what employees need to perform well (adequate skills, clear instructions, feedback, and rewards); and insight into the impact of equity theory and expectancy theory on employee effort and performance. Most important, it requires understanding of the critical role played by human resource specialists in managing a variable, strategic resource (employees) so as to achieve agency objectives.

KEY TERMS

delegation
equity theory
expectancy theory
flexiplace
flexiwork
flextime
job satisfaction
job sharing
management by objectives (MBO)
motivation
organizational climate/organizational culture
performance management
total quality management (TQM)
workforce diversity

DISCUSSION QUESTIONS

1. What is meant by the shared role of the personnel director, line managers, and executives and legislators in productivity improvement?

2. What are the four building blocks employees need for effective job performance? What is the role of the supervisor in providing these?

3. What is equity theory? expectancy theory? How do they contribute to our understanding of motivation, effort, and performance?

4. What are some examples of alternative work systems that supervisors and personnel directors can use to enhance individual and group productivity?

CASE STUDY: REQUIEM FOR A GOOD SOLDIER

"How about Rachel Fowlkes?" Gordon asked. "She's certainly in line for the job. Rachel has had all the requisite training and experience to become an assistant director."

Harold Nash, manager of the Department of Health and Welfare, rolled a ballpoint pen between his fingers and rocked slowly in his executive desk chair. "I don't know," he said softly, "I really don't know. Give me another rundown on her experience."

Clifton Gordon opened the manila personnel folder and laid it on Nash's desk. "Six years with this bureau, but she'd been with the old Vocational Rehabilitation Department for almost nine years before the reorganization. She started as a clerk, was in line for assistant director at the time we reorganized."

"We had too many chiefs as a result of that merger," Nash said. "As I recall, a few people were bumped."

Gordon smiled. "I remember that, all right. She was one that was bumped and I was the one who took over as assistant director."

"How did she take it?" Nash asked.

"No problem," Gordon said. "She was a good soldier."

"A good soldier," Nash echoed.

"She was very capable and versatile," Gordon said. "In fact I relied on her heavily for new personnel training. Many of those green young men she trained are now directors and assistant directors." Gordon pointed to the personnel folder. "Rachel was made acting assistant director of the information and public assistance section four years ago and apparently was seriously considered for the position of assistant director when Tom Walters retired."

Nash shook his head. "Regrettably, I had a difficult choice then as well. I had to choose between a capable career woman and an equally talented young man. Both were on the cert as best qualified. In the end I felt Manpower Research was not the right place in which to place our first female assistant director."

"Now would be a perfect time," Gordon said, "especially in view of the governor's recent order on the EEO Act and the stress on the utilization of minorities and women. I think that's what all this talk of affirmative action is all about. Wouldn't promoting Rachel be an affirmative action?"

Nash winced. "Don't remind me. That report to the governor is due shortly! But back to Rachel; promotions must ultimately be based on merit and not on sex or color of skin."

"I agree completely," Gordon replied quickly, "but with all other things being equal, why not select a woman?"

"If that were true, I just might. But all other things are not equal. Not only do I again have several capable candidates along with Rachel on the cert, but there have been problems with Rachel lately."

"I wasn't aware of that. What's happened to Rachel, the good soldier? I can't imagine her causing problems for anybody."

"That's what I'd like to know," Nash said. "For the past six months I've given her several responsibilities and she just hasn't responded the way she used to. Her work output is definitely deteriorating and her attitude is, too."

"What's her complaint?"

"No one seems to be able to put his finger on the problem: I even had her in the office once for a casual chat, but she claimed there was nothing causing her any concern. I mentioned her slipping work performance and she promised to improve."

"And?"

"Oh, she's improved. I guess her work is O.K., but that old spark is gone."

"That's a shame," Gordon said. "Rachel has done so well . . . for a woman."

Nash nodded, "Yes, it is a shame. I'm afraid we'll have to look elsewhere to fill that assistant director position."

Source: U.S. Civil Service Commission Bureau of Training, *The Equal Employment Opportunity Act: Implications for Public Employers.* U.S. Government Printing Office, Washington, D.C., 1973.

Questions:

1. Using equity theory, analyze how and why Rachel's behavior has changed during the time period of the case.

2. What are the important inputs and outcomes from Rachel's point of view? Who is the focus of her social comparison?

3. What factor(s) has Harold Nash given input credit for that Rachel may have overlooked?

4. Utilizing expectancy theory, analyze how Rachel's behavior has changed during the time period in the case.

5. How has Rachel's estimation of her ability to perform as assistant director changed? Has the value she places on different outcomes associated with being assistant director changed? Has her expectation changed that good performance in her current job will lead to a promotion?

6. How would you define "old spark" in terms of a performance goal or job standard? How would you feel as an employee if someone failed to promote you justifying it, in part, by your loss of the "old spark"?

7. How do you think Rachel feels at this point in her job? How do you think you might feel? How common do you think the case of Rachel is in modern organizations?

8. Who is responsible for the changes in Rachel's behavior in this case? Who is accountable for them? What is the difference?

9. If you were Harold Nash, would you promote Rachel, given the deterioration of her morale and her apparent competent but lackluster performance?

NOTES

[1] Marshall Sashkin, "Participative Management Is an Ethical Imperative," *Organizational Dynamics 12*, 4 (Spring 1984), 5–21.

[2] C. Mellado, R. Mellado, and F. Armendariz, "Apple's New Approaches to Affirmative Action," *Hispanic Engineer*, Spring 1989, pp. 32–36.

[3] Judy B. Rosener, "Ways Women Lead," *Harvard Business Review 68*, 4 (November-December 1990), 119–25.

CHAPTER 9

TRAINING, EDUCATION, AND STAFF DEVELOPMENT

The need for enhanced investment in the training and development of public employees in the 1990s and beyond is widely recognized. Several factors are responsible for projected shortages in valued knowledge, skills, and abilities and the resultant need for training. Demographic projections of the future workforce coupled with heightened demand for professional and technical skills suggest critical gaps. Rapid technological change suggests that the knowledge, skills, and abilities of workers today will be obsolete tomorrow. The capability of public organizations to seek continual improvement requires workers who themselves are committed to continuing education. Finally, the *acquisition* of new knowledge, skills, and abilities by hiring new employees will be limited by the public's willingness to invest more taxes in more government. If new knowledge, skills, and abilities cannot be hired, they must be developed internally.

In contrast to these needs is the dismal picture painted generally about our ability to educate ourselves with basic knowledge and skills.[1]

- At New York Telephone, 60,000 applicants had to be tested for 3,000 openings.
- An advertising company in Minnesota reported that 20 applicants

were required to fill each secretarial position and 10 for a supply or mail clerk.

- 60 percent of the young people applying for jobs in Colorado had insufficient skills to be competitive, according to a research study.
- An Oregon electronics manufacturing firm found that 20 percent of its workers did not have the basic skills needed to make the transition from a traditional assembly line to newer manufacturing methods.
- Kansas employers report deficiencies among current and new employees in basic job performance skills like goal setting, personal motivation, work habits, listening and communication, and problem solving.[2]

By the end of this chapter you will be able to

1. Distinguish between training, education, and staff development as part of the development function.
2. Discuss why the present orientation toward training may be short-sighted.
3. Identify and discuss contemporary development trends.
4. Describe three roles for the human resources developer.
5. Identify when training is appropriate.
6. Briefly describe training needs assessment, design, and evaluation.
7. Discuss the implications of contemporary trends in human resource development for four personnel systems.

WHAT IS THE DEVELOPMENT FUNCTION?

Organizations rely on the knowledge, skills, and abilities of their employees to produce goods and services efficiently, effectively, and responsively. Because missions change, employees change jobs, and knowledge, skills, and abilities become outdated, organizations must continually renew their human resources—their employees.

The most common way of doing this simply is to hire new employees, thus acquiring new knowledge, skills, and abilities. Alternatively, an organization can negotiate with other organizations to purchase or lease needed knowledge, skills, and abilities. Some cities, for example, contract with the surrounding counties for police protection. In this chapter, we explore a third way of renewing human resources, working with existing employees to develop new knowledge, skills, and abilities.

Every organization must invest time and money developing employees. At the simplest level, we saw in Chapter 8 that the building blocks of effective supervision center on communicating expectations, building employee skills, providing feedback on performance, and creating an environment of fair play in an organization. This is easier to accomplish in organizations where employees are seen as assets rather than simply a cost of production, and training is seen as integral to mission accomplishment.

Nadler and Nadler have identified three categories of development activities—training, education and staff development.[3] Commonly, the development function is associated with *training* of employees to perform existing jobs more efficiently, effectively, and responsively. But in many organizations the development function includes more than training for short-term improvement. It is not uncommon for organizations to *educate* employees for the longer term, to build the knowledge, skills, and abilities they will need for promotions to specific jobs in the career ladder. For example, some agencies offer supervisory training for nonsupervisory employees who might be in line for a promotion to a supervisory position. *Staff development* is designed to open the organization to broader vistas and new ways of thinking. Staff development aims to build the knowledge, skills, and abilities of employees to enhance the general knowledge base of the organization and to prepare a cadre of people to think strategically even if strategic thinking is not required in their present jobs.

Training: Too Often Shortsighted and Underfunded

While it is common to speak of training, education, and staff development, the bulk of investment in the development function goes into short-term training activities designed to improve performance in an employee's current job. Training is not a new personnel activity, but in many organizations it is one largely taken for granted. Training funds are viewed as discretionary, and somber revenue forecasts usually have a negative impact on training budgets. In addition, often training staff have little formal educational background in learning theory and minimal experience qualifying them to staff a training office.

The low priority established for the development function as well as shortcomings in development staffing have contributed over the years to several serious problems.[4]

- The human resources development function is usually evaluated in terms of activities and costs and not business results whether the focus is on training, education, or staff development.
- Human resources development staff are usually held accountable for the design and number of programs they deliver, rather than the impact of the programs.
- The dynamics of transferring knowledge, skills, and abilities from the development setting to the job is not well understood in most organizations.

- The connection between the development function and the strategic goals of the organization or agency frequently are never made.
- The shared development responsibility between the human resources development staff and line management goes largely unexplored. Frequently, for one reason or another, poor performers are sent to training rather than being disciplined or otherwise counseled.

Some public organizations, especially larger federal agencies with accomplished development staff, have recognized these problem areas and have worked for years to overcome them. But for most of the some 83,000 units of government in the United States, the development function still focuses on the individual employee, the short term, and activities rather than results measured in the successful application of knowledge, skills, and abilities.

Trends in the Development Function

In a study, *Workforce 2000*, funded by the Department of Labor, Johnston and Packer observe: "The income generating assets of a nation are the knowledge and skills of its workers."[5] As business and government come to recognize the growing importance of building the knowledge and skills of America's workforce, they realize the necessity of addressing the shortcomings that characterize much of today's training. Human resources development managers and academicians are exploring new development concepts and reexamining some that have been around for a while.

Training Connected to Business Strategy. Bernhard and Ingols, a human resources development executive and an academician, have commented that in many organizations the development function produces "pleasant but basically irrelevant" activities resulting from corrective but not strategic goals.[6] According to Rosow and Zager, "Today a new notion has begun to take hold—that the sole objective test of relevance for a training program is whether the corporation's business strategy requires it."[7] Aligning a development strategy with agency goals has several advantages.[8] First, it helps to clarify budget options in the human resources development area. It provides guidance for determining how much money an agency is going to invest in development. Also, alternative investments can be evaluated in terms of how well they advance agency goals. Second, the alignment provides a framework to evaluate whether or not the development activity has actually produced a cost-effective result. Last, it provides additional resources and mechanisms to advance agency goals. It facilitates communication about agency goals, and can advance commitment to agency goals through participative and team-based discussion, design, and implementation of development activities.

Commitment to Continuous Learning. Underpinning many innovations in the development area is the overriding precept that organizations increasingly must prepare themselves to adapt to change. They can do this by seeing themselves as learning systems, with employees serving as both learners and teachers. Continuous learning requires that the organization teach its employees new skills. It assumes that the more employees know about their equipment and work processes, the better prepared they will be to discover problems and ideas for solutions. The commitment to continuous learning also requires that employees use their knowledge and skills to discover administrative and production problems they can then help to solve.

At first, the concept of continuous learning seems simple. No one consciously would oppose continuous learning, yet there are many resisting forces. Argyris identifies organizational norms like avoiding conflict and "straight talk" that work against questioning an agency's basic assumptions and operating procedures.[9] In addition, managers are more likely to reward workers who solve problems rather than discover them. Further, in a hierarchical system, workers are always reminded that management has the upper hand, and improvements in work methods may threaten job security. Finally, history would suggest that organizations are more likely to make technical work simple and mask its complexity in order to accommodate basic employee skills rather than investing in an upgrade of basic skills so that employees could learn more about their equipment. Rosow and Zager observe: "The amount of training required to profit from a new technology varies directly with the amount of diversity of new knowledge embodied in it."[10] In sum, a commitment to continuous learning takes more than a slogan on the wall or a phrase in a mission statement; it requires a philosophical orientation that challenges many of the ways Americans are used to conducting business and government.

Organizational Development and Team Building. Managers and supervisors are responsible not only for training individual employees to improve their work skills, but also for helping to improve the quality of those employees' work relationships. This process is called *organizational development* (OD). It developed in the 1960s as a combination of *sensitivity training*, a focus on the emotional side of interpersonal work relationships, and *action research*. Action research is based on gathering data about practical problems and feeding the data back to employee participants for interpretation and assessment. These phases are followed by an employee-centered problem-solving process. OD is similar to training in that both are change-oriented. However, OD is usually participant-focused rather than trainer-oriented; it seeks to increase productivity by increasing employee identification with the objectives of the organization rather than by increasing employee job skills; it focuses on the process variables that comprise human interaction rather than the work product itself; and it tends to be systems- and group-oriented rather than aimed at building the knowledge and skills of individual employees.

One widely used method of organizational development is *team building*. Team building activities are designed to assist members of a work group to increase their productivity as a group. Typically, team building begins when a consultant is called into an organization to diagnose and correct a problem in the relationships within a department or between one department and another. Rather than define the problem alone, the consultant will invite members of the work group(s) to engage in diagnostic exercises aimed at assessing how well the group is working together and where the problem areas might be. Data are collected through questionnaire or through discussion and then summarized and fed back to the participants. Work group members are asked to help the consultant interpret the results. "What do these data tell you about how well you are working as a group?" the consultant might ask. Problems are identified, discussed, given a priority and then a process for dealing with them is devised by the group with the help of the consultant.

The steps involved in team building illustrate a general organizational development effort. An OD project moves through six phases:[11]

- *Problem perception*—sensing that a problem exists because previous work methods or relationships are no longer effective
- *Diagnosis*—defining the nature of the problem
- *"Unfreezing"*—reducing reliance on unsuccessful methods and exploring reasons why standard operating procedures are not working
- *"Movement" or increased experimentation*—committing time and money to testing alternatives and working to reduce the forces resisting change
- *"Refreezing"*—integrating changes into the organization's natural work processes and anchoring them to reward and other administrative systems
- *Limiting change efforts* to the appropriate organizational activities or relationships

Total Quality Management (TQM). W. Edwards Deming, a statistician, developed the idea of total quality control in the United States, but the movement has gained popularity in America only recently after its considerable successes in post-World War II Japan.[12] Total quality management advocates point out that TQM is a philosophy, not a technique. The philosophy views the organization as a learning system; highlights the intelligence of employees and their willingness to commit to their work; places faith in statistical methods to uncover system problems; and pinpoints trust in customer satisfaction as the ultimate measure of quality.

Quality is defined as the ability to meet, and even exceed, customer needs and expectations. TQM emphasizes quality through continuous improvement. In other words, quality is never realized, it is always sought. The ultimate test of quality is customer satisfaction. The attraction of TQM results from two diverse orientations to the development function—human relations and scientific management. First, TQM depends upon employee participation to produce continuous improvement. Continuous improvement requires an employer's commitment to investments in employee training and education. The more employees know about production processes, the better equipped they are to participate in problem identification and solving. TQM attempts to build an organizational culture where the cornerstone is pride in quality.

Second, continuous improvement focuses on detailed statistical analysis of production processes. According to TQM precepts, quality problems stem from system problems, not people problems. System problems require employee knowledge and disciplined data gathering and analysis to identify and solve. Thus, the TQM scientific management heritage appeals to advocates of an administrative science approach to quality control as well as human relations proponents.

Madison, Wisconsin, is home to model TQM programs in both state and local governments and offers some examples of how TQM principles have been applied in the public sector. The Madison police department began implementing quality improvement methods in 1981, beginning with an elected employee council. Under the leadership of its chief, David C. Couper, the department began applying the principles of the total quality approach through several project teams. One team came up with new and creative ways to improve employee (internal customers) and citizen (external customers) satisfaction. Data were collected and analyzed using control charts and other fairly simple statistical tools. Another team focused on improving the promotional system within the department; the plan was implemented two years later. Eventually the entire department was reorganized into teams.

Another effort was conducted in the motor equipment division of the city's department of public works. With the help of an internal organizational development consultant and a faculty member at the nearby university, the department used tools like customer surveys, brainstorming, Pareto charts, and flow diagrams as well as team meetings and participative decision making to better understand their customers' needs and to identify basic underlying causes for excessive vehicle downtime. The time invested in these efforts led to improved customer satisfaction and procedures throughout all departments to reduce repair downtime. At a time when staff was reduced by 17 percent, vehicles serviced increased by 25 percent.

In the Wisconsin Department of Revenue, a team consisting of managers, workers, and internal customers worked on reducing the turn-around time for items going to the word processing pool. Through data collection and team discussions they were able to discover the true nature of the work flow processes and then implement solutions that eliminated the causes of problems. After improvements in quality were implemented at each step in the process, turnaround time decreased from two to three weeks to two days and then to eight hours.

Training for Diversity. One of the biggest development challenges for public employers in the 1990s and beyond will be accommodating administrative processes and human relations to differences in culture and ethnicity. America's minorities will be entering the workforce at a faster rate than ever before; immigrants will constitute a larger proportion of the workforce than at any time since World War I; and women will make up 60 percent of the new entrants into the workforce.[13] A generalized tolerance for differences and adherence to procedural rules simply cannot be expected to absorb the organizational shocks these demographic changes are bringing.

The nature of bureaucracy itself may mitigate some of the differences. That is, job descriptions, work goals, performance standards, and the general impersonality of bureaucracy can be expected to have a homogenizing effect on diversity. Nevertheless, the remarks of Bellah and associates provide words of caution. They observe: "Americans, it would seem, feel most comfortable in thinking about politics in terms of a consensual community of autonomous, but essentially similar, individuals. . . . For all the lip service given to respect for cultural differences, Americans seem to lack the resources to think about the relationships between groups that are culturally, socially, or economically quite different."[14]

It seems reasonable to think that investments will be needed in training and educating employees to understand and deal with diversity. But training and education will not be enough. In some cases, organizations will have to come to grips with prejudice not only among Anglos, but among the minorities as well. In such cases, organizational expectations will need to be clarified and rewards and discipline may be required to make the point that at a minimum, differences are to be tolerated if not valued.

Training in workforce diversity may include several components:[15]

- Skilled instructors sensitive to multicultural awareness
- Experiential learning, including role playing, exercises, discussions and group experiences
- Flexibility and latitude for tailoring to specific work group circumstances

- Clearly identified goals that connect to a larger organizational philosophy and effort
- Evaluative instruments to assess effectiveness
- Follow-up programs because increasing awareness may occur in a half-day training session, but changing attitudes and behavior takes much longer

Training for Basic Skill Development.   Public employers are no different from private employers in their need for job applicants with increasingly sophisticated basic skills. Estimates are frightening of the number of Americans whose reading, writing, and computing skills limit their employment opportunities. These estimates bear heavily on job opportunities for disadvantaged minorities.

According to the Hudson Institute, while disadvantaged minorities will be entering the workforce in larger numbers, it is not clear whether their economic outlook will improve: "The jobs that will be created between 1987–2000 will be substantially different from those in existence today. A number of jobs in the least-skilled job classes will disappear, while high-skilled professions will grow rapidly. These occupational changes will present a difficult challenge for the disadvantaged, particularly for black men and Hispanics, who are underrepresented in the fastest growing professions and overrepresented in the shrinking job categories."[16] They continue: "Many workers will need advanced skills simply to give them access to useful job training. For example, assembly-line workers in many manufacturing plants are learning statistical process control, a system that is beyond the reach of those without a solid grounding in mathematics."[17]

The Hudson Institute's report *Workforce 2000* paints a bleak picture, and one that makes basic skills training not only an organizational problem, but probably more important, a public policy problem of significant proportions. Just as many have assumed that government employers should take the lead in affirmative action, it may be that public agencies will be seen as primary agents of public-policy initiatives emphasizing basic skills training in the workplace.

THREE ROLES FOR THE HUMAN RESOURCES DEVELOPER

Trends in the development function seem to be having an effect on the way the role of the human resources developer is envisioned, independent of fluctuations in funding for training, education, and staff development. The trend away from canned training packages to training designs tailored to strategic agency thinking places the HR developer in a more essential organizational position.

Nadler and Nadler have conceptualized the HR developer's role in three ways.[18]

LEARNING SPECIALIST

- Facilitator of learning
- Designer of learning programs
- Developer of instructional strategies

MANAGER OF HRD

- Supervisor of HRD programs
- Developer of HRD personnel
- Arranger of facilities and finance
- Maintainer of relations

CONSULTANT

- Expert
- Advocate
- Stimulator
- Change agent

Although all roles must be filled if the development function is to operate comprehensively and effectively, they can be merged, and one is not necessarily exclusive of the others. The list roughly approximates the historical evolution of the human resources developer role.

In general, human resources development staff must demonstrate several competencies to fulfill these roles: knowledge of the organization, its purposes and structure; knowledge of adult learning; knowledge of the relationship between an organization's culture and its learning environment; and knowledge of organizational and individual change.

These competencies and the trends in the development function create a career track for the human resources developer that requires formal management education and a consultant orientation. It is no longer adequate for the HR developer oriented to organizational productivity simply to receive vendors and decide which training packages to buy.

TRAINING ISSUES

There are a number of practical issues connected to training that human resources developers face. For example, when is training appropriate? How does one design and evaluate training development programs? What should be included in a new employee orientation? Even though we will concentrate in this section specifically on training programs as opposed to education and development, much of the information will be applicable to all three categories of development interventions.

When Is Training Appropriate?

Training is frequently used as a solution to a performance problem without considering alternatives. Table 9-1 summarizes the causes of performance problems, the preferred organizational responses to them, and the personnel activity involved.

Many organizations ignore the performance problem if it is insignificant or if there is no readily apparent solution. The second response to a performance problem involves examining selection criteria to determine if they really reflect the KSAs needed to perform the job; and if not, raising the standards or reexamining the criteria themselves. This involves a trade off between the higher salaries that must be paid to attract more qualified people and the higher cost of on-the-job training after they are hired, plus the greater risk of losing them to a competitor once they are trained. The third response is deceptively simple, for it involves merely clarifying standards by providing orientation or feedback to employees. This assumes, of course, that performance standards have already been established for the job—a big assumption in many cases. The fourth possible solution is to train employees by giving them the job-related skills needed to meet current performance standards. Finally, supervisors may offer greater rewards

TABLE 9-1   Organizational Responses to Performance Problems

SITUATION	ORGANIZATIONAL RESPONSE	PERSONNEL ACTIVITY
1. Problem is insignificant	Ignore it	None
2. Selection criteria are inadequate	Increase attention to selection criteria	Job analysis
3. Employees are unaware of performance standards	Set goals and standards and provide feedback	Orientation, performance evaluation
4. Employees have inadequate skills	Provide training	Training
5. Good performance is not rewarded; poor performance is not punished	Provide rewards or punishments and connect them to performance	Performance evaluation, disciplinary acton

to employees who meet performance standards, or initiate disciplinary action against those who do not.

Some of these options are more difficult to implement than others. Changing selection criteria or rewards and punishments may be difficult, since these involve changes in job evaluation and flexible compensation plans. Because training is one of the easiest options to implement, the chance is relatively great that it will be used regardless of its appropriateness to the situation.

Employers can train their employees and increase their ability to perform the work, but generally they are in for a disappointment if they think one can *train* people to expend more energy on the job. If the person could perform up to standard if his or her life depended upon it, low performance is not a training problem![19]

Before designing a training program or a series of training programs, the human resource developer will conduct some kind of assessment. What problems exist? Are they suitable for a training solution? Then the content of the program is designed. Once the program is completed, an evaluation is conducted to measure the reactions of the trainees and, where appropriate, the objective impact of the training on the original problem area.

Assessing Training Needs

Management may require training for all employees in a job classification without regard for data concerning a particular employee's performance. For example, all newly appointed supervisors may be required to take training in supervisory methods and delegation; or employees whose jobs require extensive public contact may be required to take communications training. This type of training-needs assessment may be called a *general treatment need*.

A second type of training-needs assessment is based on *observable performance discrepancies*. These are indicated by problems such as standards of work performance not being met, accidents, frequent need for equipment repair, several low ratings on employee evaluation reports, high rate of turnover, the use of many methods to do the same job, and deadlines not being met. In this case, management's job is to observe the jobs and workers in question and uncover the difficulties. This may be done through observation, interviews, questionnaires, and performance appraisal, and by requiring employees to keep track of their own work output.

A third type of development assessment is related not to present performance discrepancies, but to future human resource needs. Nadler and Nadler would call these educational and staff development needs. For example, an organization contemplating the purchase of microcomputers will need to hire people skilled in their use, or train existing employees to use them. This type of needs assessment is based on the anticipation of a future discrepancy caused by technological advances and changes in mission and strategic goals.

Designing a Training Program

Once a problem area is identified, an intervention can be planned. Often sending someone to training is a naively simple solution. To reiterate, training can only benefit an employee who does not know how to work effectively; it should not be used in cases where employees know how to perform effectively, but for one reason or another do not perform up to standard.

If training is an appropriate intervention, the appropriateness of a particular training method depends upon the target of the change. The simplest distinction in training objectives is whether or not the change will involve an interpersonal dimension. Traditional training methods, which are more directive, teacher-oriented, and have as their objective transferring knowledge, work best where the trainees are motivated to change, see the value in the change, and where the change can be readily incorporated into the way the employee currently performs the job.

The more significant the change anticipated, the more likely it will involve rejection of something the employee already knows and relies upon. Training techniques appropriate to these situations must be trainee-oriented, with the trainer taking a more facilitative role. If the anticipated change is tangible and involves technical training, the trainer must maintain a delicate balance between getting the material across and recognizing that not all the trainees may be eager to reject what they already know and what may still serve them well.

Supervisory training is probably as difficult as any other because it involves a degree of new knowledge, but knowledge that has to be filtered through an interpersonal and cognitive screen unique to each individual. Further, there is no one best way to be an effective supervisor. Mass production supervisory training falls victim to the charge that it is activity-oriented rather than results-oriented. Results-oriented supervisory training must at some point be tailored to individual supervisors. Regardless of the goal of the intervention, group discussion, case studies, and role play are techniques commonly used to get trainees involved and invested in the learning process. By encouraging the trainee to integrate material presented with his or her own knowledge, and by reinforcing the integration through performance at the training session, the likelihood increases that training will result in the learning of new behaviors.

Evaluating Program Effectiveness

To be effective, training must be an appropriate solution to an organizational problem; that is, it must be intended to correct a skill deficiency.

For optimum learning, the employee must recognize the need and want to acquire new information or skills. Whatever performance standards are set, the employee should not be frustrated by a trainer who requires too much or too little.

Many learning theories revolve around the idea of reinforcement. It is natural for people to repeat behavior that is followed by rewards and to avoid actions they associate with negative outcomes. If employees in a training situation are given no feedback, there is no opportunity to guide the desired learning.

It is extremely important that supervisors understand the value of positive reinforcement. Supervisors are in the best position to observe performance problems, show employees the correct work method, provide feedback, and connect subsequent rewards or punishments to performance. Most organizational training is informal and occurs on the job, through precisely this process.

To justify itself, training must demonstrate an impact on the performance of the employee. By determining how well employees have learned, management can make decisions about the training and its effectiveness. The mere existence of a training staff, an array of courses, and trainees does not ensure that learning is taking place. Because development activities consume both time and money, evaluation should be built into any program.

Training can be evaluated at five levels: reaction, learning, behavior, results, and cost effectiveness.

Reaction	How well did the trainees like the training? Do they feel they benefitted from the training?
Learning	To what extent did the trainees learn the facts, principles, and approaches that were included in the training?
Behavior	To what extent did the trainee's job behavior change because of the program?
Results	What increases in productivity or decreases in cost were achieved? To what extent were unit or organizational goals advanced?
Cost effectiveness	Assuming the training is effective, is it the least expensive method of solving the problem?

The first two measures of effectiveness can be demonstrated by interviews or questionnaires administered to trainees at the training site. Changes in job-related behavior or results are best measured by comparing employees' responses with data gathered from supervisors concerning employee behavior or productivity. There is little doubt that this criterion of effectiveness is important. George Odiorne has observed:

> The systems approach to evaluation of training starts with a definition of behavior change objectives sought through a conscious development effort. This definition then remains a yardstick for measurement throughout the course and achievement against the stated goals is the measure of success. All other forms of evaluation measure the internal character of the activity itself, not the effectiveness of training.[20]

While training may be an appropriate solution to an organizational performance problem, and while it may be effective in changing employee behavior, it is not cost effective unless the cost of the training program is less than the cost of the problem, and less than the cost of alternative solutions. The cost effectiveness of a training program is determined by subtracting the cost of the program from the cost of the problem. *Problem costs* are the tangible economic losses an agency suffers as a result of using untrained personnel. These include:

Equipment breakdown	Cost of downtime and repair
Salaries and benefits	Wasted compensation for unproductive employees
Monitoring and quality control	Cost of supervision
Personnel costs:	Increased recruitment, selection or sick leave abuse costs

Training program costs are the expenses incurred in developing, implementing, and evaluating the training program:

Program development	Salary and fringe benefits for the training specialist's time spent in assessing needs, setting training objectives, and selecting training methods
Program presentation	Costs of room rental, supplies, equipment, marketing, handouts, refreshments, and trainers' salaries
Trainee expenses	Trainees' salaries and fringe benefits during training, travel, lodging, and per diem (if applicable)

Training program proposals should also consider intangible problem costs such as reduced employee morale, client complaints, or loss of legislative support. Although dollar figures cannot realistically be assigned to these costs, they are often influential in the decision about whether to hold a training program. If the training program will cost less than the projected cost of the problem, it is cost efficient.

Several factors inhibit the evaluation of training program effectiveness. The effectiveness of training depends upon how relevant the chosen criteria of effectiveness are to the development purposes of the program. While we have used the term training to stand for all development activities, assessing the success of activities with educational and development purposes requires a less stringent attitude toward assessment.

Nadler and Nadler point out that with training activities, it is possible to evaluate what the trainees learned at the training session and how the training affected work performance.[21] After all, training is designed to correct a work-related problem. With educational activities, the challenge is greater because the learning is designed to facilitate the employee's performance in a future job. Development activities suffer most under strict evaluation criterion because they are not specifically job-related.

Perhaps the greatest challenge facing those who evaluate training is to recognize that while most development activities are delivered to individual employees, the goal is to get the organization as a whole learning, growing, and pulling together. Modest individual changes directed uniformly toward organizational goals may be highly desired yet difficult to achieve and measure.

IMPLICATIONS FOR DIFFERENT PERSONNEL SYSTEMS

The development function is viewed differently from the perspective of alternative personnel systems. Political executives are selected for their partisan loyalty and partisan policy orientations. Usually, they receive little training prior to or following their appointment, despite the fact that many have little public policy-making experience and few of the skills required to manage complex public organizations. Because training, education, and staff development represent time-consuming investments in the future, political executives who frequently spend a short time in government have little interest in the development function, either for themselves or for those who work for them. The function takes on a special significance, however, if political executives are able to influence the selection of training consultants.

As the permanent bureaucracy, members of the civil service value the development function more than political executives. In fact, many professionals working for public employers, like those in health-related professions, are required to enroll in a minimum number of continuing education hours annually in order to maintain various certifications or licenses.

By its very nature, the civil service houses an abundance of public-policy-related knowledge as well as the knowledge, skills, and abilities needed to translate public policy goals into service delivery and regulatory actions. The quality of public policy making depends on the knowledge of a government's civil servants. Without the ability to acquire and enhance the valued knowledge, expertise, and experience of government employees, civil service systems lose their credibility and focus as the reservoir of society's knowledge about its own problems. One could argue that as result of major cost-cutting measures, the knowledge base of civil service systems has been seriously eroding since the late 1970s.

As we have seen during the discussion of training for basic needs, the development function is of vital importance in advancing the goals of affirmative action. The danger in the next decade is that equity gains for minorities will be lost if disadvantaged minorities enter the workforce without advanced competencies in reading, writing, and computing or if they cannot obtain these skills once hired.

The development function meets with mixed reaction in the collective bargaining personnel subsystem. On the one hand, union members value the continuous development of knowledge, skills, and abilities needed to maintain timely competencies and to involve union members in organizational decisions about work processes. For example, the National Treasury Employees Union has given a positive reception to total quality management initiatives that promise to involve union members in decision-making processes previously off limits to them. Further, the development function is connected to a longstanding apprenticeship tradition involving structured experiences designed to transform the apprentice into a skilled craftsperson. As a counter example, because of perceived threats to job security, Postal Service union members have resisted organizational development efforts designed to improve the quality and efficiency of work processes.

SUMMARY

Even though training budgets seem to be the first to be cut in times of fiscal stress, there is good evidence to suggest that the development function will increase in importance in the 1990s. Demographic trends and changes in technology suggest there will be serious gaps in the number of workers prepared to work in tomorrow's workplace. Revenue shortfalls suggest that public employers will have to find ways of enhancing the knowledge, skills, and abilities of their existing workforce rather than simply procuring needed KSAs in the labor market.

These shortages and the general demand for more customer-oriented and competitive business and efficient government have created an environment of innovation in the development function. Many of these changes can be summarized with the term "continuous learning and improvement." Organizations use the term to indicate their investment in a workforce and a philosophy captured by the belief that quality is never reached, it is continually sought.

Seeking quality requires an employer investment in the KSAs of a workforce that must become intimately acquainted with service delivery systems and committed to a customer orientation. The value of efficiency that is captured in the basic concept of civil service systems provides the foundation for government to face these challenges. However, investments in the development function go beyond traditional training and extend into the areas of education and staff development, where employers indicate their willingness to make long-term investments in their employees. In part, this depends upon whether public employers are able to view their employees as assets rather than liabilities and whether citizens are willing to do the same.

KEY TERMS

basic skill development
consultant role
continuous learning
development function
education
learning specialist role
manager of HRD role
organizational development (OD)
staff development
team building
total quality control (management)
training
training design
training evaluation
training needs

DISCUSSION QUESTIONS

1. Briefly define the development function and the value(s) it reflects. Then, distinguish it from the acquisition function, and then describe the differences between training, education, and staff development.
2. List five problem areas in contemporary training. Which one do you think is the most difficult to overcome? Why? The easiest to overcome?

3. What kinds of challenges do the six trends in the development function pose for the human resources department in public agencies?
4. Distinguish between the three roles of the human resources developer. Which of the roles do you think is most compatible with the traditional human resources developer? What do you think would be the strengths and weaknesses of each role in dealing with contemporary trends in the development function?
5. Describe the role of the development function in each of the four personnel systems.

CASE STUDY 1

You are the director of the human resources development department of a city with a population of 105,000. Your city provides its citizens with a full array of services, including police, fire, water, sanitation, roads, parks, and recreation. Your city employs some 750 employees, including 150 police officers.

Over the years there has been an influx of Asians and Spanish-speaking people into this city, which used to be predominantly Anglo, with about a 5 percent African-American population. Some of the immigrants are joining the city's workforce and racial/ethnic cliques are developing. Over the years, the African-Americans have complained that the police treat them differently than other citizens, and they are being joined by spokespersons for the other minorities.

The values of tolerance, dignity, and fairness were underlying issues in the most recent election for city council. The new council has requested that the chief administrative officer develop a program of diversity training to heighten awareness of the value of differences in the workforce and the community. The CAO calls you into the office and asks you to work on a proposal.

Develop a proposal that includes a plan for assessing the need, designing the program, and evaluating it. What problems do you anticipate with the training program?

CASE STUDY 2: VEHICLE MAINTENANCE IN A CITY'S PARKS DEPARTMENT

Prosperity is a pleasant American city with a population of about 750,000. Its citizens are deservedly proud of their parks. Many years ago, far-sighted civic leaders annexed thousands of acres of woodland into the city limits so that today Prosperity has the highest percentage of incorporated land as parks of any American town.

Yet Prosperity's Parks and Recreation Department has problems maintaining these parks and running recreation programs within a limited budget. The director has chosen to deal with resource constraints by concentrating maintenance activities on the busier parks, and deferring purchases and maintenance of equipment.

However, this strategy is no longer working. As the existing equipment gets older, it spends more time in the department's repair facility. The head of the maintenance department is careful to schedule routine preventive maintenance for all equipment, but this schedule is seldom followed. There is such a demand for the equipment during the spring, summer, and fall that the department director is often forced to choose between performing equipment repair or providing needed park maintenance. Park maintenance crews usually wait until heavy summer thunderstorms to bring equipment in for maintenance work. When this happens, the work crews sit idle because there are no extra vehicles, and the vehicle maintenance staff is flooded with more work than it can handle. Employees are often poorly trained in equipment operation, basically because supervisors are generally overburdened with other tasks. As a result, damage to vehicles, trees, and city property is often heavy.

You are the administrative assistant to the department director. He has just received a phone call from the Mayor's office complaining of poor maintenance, idle work crews, and heavy expenses for equipment maintenance. He orders you, "Do something about the problem!"

Divide the class into groups consisting of four or five students in each group. Within each group, read the case study and develop answers to the questions below, using the information provided. If no information is provided, make your own assumptions about the problem. After you are done, compare your answers with those developed by other groups.

1. To what extent is this problem due to inadequate selection criteria, inadequate feedback, a skill deficiency, or inadequate rewards and punishments? In the space supplied, indicate the percentage of the problem that is due to each problem, and what (in general) you would do about it.

CAUSE	PERCENTAGE	SOLUTION
Inadequate selection criteria	_____	_____
Inadequate feedback	_____	_____
Skill deficiency	_____	_____
Inadequate reward	_____	_____

2. What are the observable performance discrepancies that are due to a skill deficiency?

WHOSE DISCREPANCY?	WHAT DISCREPANCY?
_____	_____
_____	_____
_____	_____
_____	_____

3. For each group with an observable performance discrepancy, define the training objective.

GROUP	TRAINING OBJECTIVE
_____	_____
_____	_____
_____	_____
_____	_____

4. For each group, what training methods are appropriate? Specify type of training, location, format, and trainer.

GROUP	METHOD
_____	_____
_____	_____
_____	_____
_____	_____

5. What would the training cost? For each training program, include the cost for trainer's salary, trainees' salaries, training materials, and any other necessary expenses. Use the following information to compute these costs.
   (a) Training can be performed by manufacturer's representatives free of charge, by city trainers at $45 per hour on a reimbursable basis, or by department employees and supervisors at the cost of their salary and benefits.
   (b) The department employs 40 park maintenance employees at an average hourly salary of $6.50, plus 25 percent for benefits.
   (c) The department employs 12 equipment and vehicle maintenance employees at an average cost of $10.50 per hour, plus 25 percent for benefits.

TRAINING PROGRAM	COST
_____	_____
_____	_____
_____	_____
_____	_____

6. Would training be cost effective? Compare the cost of each of the above training programs with the costs of the problem they are designed to correct. Use the information provided below, and compute costs and benefits over a three-month period.

   On an average work day, 25 percent of the park maintenance equipment is in the shop for repairs. Ten percent is scheduled maintenance; 15 percent is emergency repairs. The maintenance director estimates that the total value of equipment and production lost through downtime is $1000 per day.

   When equipment is in the shop, its crew sits idle. There is enough reserve equipment to employ full crews when maintenance is scheduled, but not to utilize them when repairs must be made on an emergency basis.

   During the winter, as many as half of the vehicle maintenance employees are idle because the equipment is not being used.

TRAINING PROGRAM	SAVINGS?	COST EFFECTIVE?
_____	_____	_____
_____	_____	_____
_____	_____	_____
_____	_____	_____

7. Given this information, what combination of personnel practices would you recommend to the department director to solve this problem? Consider changes in human resource planning, job analysis, selection, compensation, and training.

_____

_____

_____

_____

NOTES

[1]Patricia Gold, "A Powerful Solution Meets an Overwhelming Problem," *Instructional Delivery Systems*, September-October 1989, 6–7. Reprinted in Richard B. Frantzreb (ed.), *Training and Development Yearbook. 1990 edition* (Englewood Cliffs, NJ: Prentice Hall, 1990) p. 7.7.

[2]Charles E. Krider, Ronald Ash, and Henry Schwaller, IV, "Adult Basic Kills and the Kansas Workforce," *Kansas Business Review 15* (Fall 1991), 1–2.

[3]Leonard Nadler and Zeace Nadler, *Developing Human Resources*, 3rd ed. (San Francisco, Jossey-Bass, 1989).

[4]Dana Gaines Robinson and James C. Robinson, *Training for Impact: How to Link Training to Business Needs and Measure the Results*. (San Francisco: Jossey-Bass, 1989).

[5]William B. Johnston and Arnold E. Packer, *Workforce 2000* (Indianapolis: The Hudson Institute, 1987), p. 116.

[6]Harry B. Bernhard and Cynthia A. Ingols, "Six Lessons for the Corporate Classroom," *Harvard Business Review 88*, 5 (September-October 1988), 40–48.

[7]Jerome M. Rosow, and Robert Zager, *Training—The Competitive Edge: Introducing New Technology into the Workplace* (San Francisco, Jossey-Bass, 1988), p. 9.

[8]Jill Casner-Lotto and Associates, *Successful Training Strategies: Twenty-six Innovative Corporate Models* (San Francisco: Jossey-Bass, 1988), pp. 5–6.

[9]Chris Argyris, "Making the Undiscussable and Its Undiscussability Discussable," *Public Administration Review 40*, 3 (May-June 1980), 205–13.

[10]Rosow and Zager, *Training—The Competitive Edge*, p. 4.

[11]Wendell L. French and Cecil H. Bell, Jr., *Organizational Development*. 4th ed. (Englewood Cliffs, NJ: Prentice Hall, 1990).

[12]W. Edwards Deming, *Out of the Crisis* (Cambridge, MA: MIT Center for Advanced Engineering Study, 1988).

[13]Johnston and Packer, *Workforce 2000*, Chap. 3.

[14]Robert N. Bellah, Richard Madsen, William M. Sullivan, Ann Swidler, and Steven M. Tipton, *Habits of the Heart: Individualism and Commitment in American Life* (Berkeley: University of California Press, 1985), p. 206.

[15]Charlene Marmer Solomon, "The Corporate Response to Work Force Diversity," *Personnel Journal*, August 1989, pp. 43–53. Reprinted in Richard B. Frantzreb (ed.), *Training and Development Yearbook: 1990 Edition* (Englewood Cliffs, NJ: Prentice-Hall, 1989), pp. 7.59–7.66.

[16]Johnston and Packer, *Workforce 2000*, p. 96.

[17]Ibid., p. 103.

[18]Nadler and Nadler. *Developing Human Resources*.

[19]Paul Mager and Peter Pipe, *Analyzing Performance Problems* (Belmont, CA: Wadsworth, 1980).

[20]George S. Odiorne, *Training by Objectives* (New York: Macmillan, 1970), p. 181.

[21]Nadler and Nadler, *Developing Human Resources*, p. 114.

PERFORMANCE APPRAISAL

Performance appraisal is supposed to play a key role in the development of employees and their productivity. Theoretically, the appraisal of performance provides employees with feedback on their work, leading to greater clarity regarding organizational expectations and to a more effective channeling of employee ability.

When a formal performance appraisal leads to organizational decisions regarding promotion and pay—allocational decisions—the process becomes more complicated; it is accompanied by heightened legal scrutiny for civil rights violations and employee demands for reasons behind the allocational decisions. Further, where the results of an unsatisfactory appraisal lead to disciplinary action or denial of an organizational reward, due process guarantees are invoked through union contracts, merit system rules, or possibly even the United States Constitution. Often these legal, accountability, and due process considerations overshadow the feedback purpose of appraisal systems, forcing a formalism better suited to litigation than management.

Even though the appraisal function is related to employee productivity and employees' desire to know how well they are doing, rarely are supervisors or employees satisfied with the appraisal process. On the one hand, in some organizations it is not taken very seriously and is viewed as a waste of time. In other cases, it plays a major role in the distribution of organizational rewards and frequently becomes the source of considerable tension in the employee-employer relationship. For example, in 1983 President Reagan placed the quality of public education on the nation's political agenda by calling on school districts to provide incentive pay for the best teachers. In contrast, both the National Education Association (NEA) and American Federation of Teachers (AFT) had endorsed compensation schedules based on seniority and educational credits. As a political necessity these unions softened their opposition to incentive pay in 1983, but it is doubtful that many individual teachers followed suit. The fear that pay for performance would lead to favoritism or subjective appraisal was underscored in a statement the NEA convention drew up following the president's initiative. According to a *New York Times* report, the NEA established the following criteria for a merit pay plan:

1. Administrators who do the evaluating must be trained in assessing effective teaching.
2. All plans must be developed with teacher participation.
3. There must be nothing intrinsically divisive about the plan, pitting teacher against teacher or teacher against administrator.
4. No capricious political whim may be involved in the selection process, and academic freedom must be maintained.
5. Eligibility must not be limited to a predetermined percentage of a teaching force.[1]

One can sense the emotional intensity in these statements and can understand that while reward systems based on seniority may not be performance-based, they do protect against the lightly masked fears underscored in this NEA statement.

By the end of this chapter you will be able to:

1. Describe two goals of performance appraisal, including several operational functions.
2. Describe and distinguish among seven performance appraisal methods.
3. Discuss the comparative validity, reliability, and costs of various appraisal methods.
4. Describe the characteristics of an effective rating system.
5. Discuss the conditions necessary for pay to motivate performance.
6. Describe the supervisor's motivation to assess the performance of subordinates.

PURPOSES OF PERFORMANCE APPRAISAL

Performance appraisal is directed toward technical and management goals but rarely toward employee aspirations. The technical part focuses on developing an instrument that accurately measures individual performance on something we call a job. Because personnel decisions like promotions and merit pay increases are connected to individual performance, the instrument used to evaluate performance must withstand serious scrutiny by employees and managers. The management part attempts to advance several operational functions:

1. Communicate management goals and objectives to employees. It is clear that performance appraisal reinforces managerial expectations. After instructing employees what to do, it is management's responsibility to follow through by providing feedback on how performance matches the stated criteria.
2. Motivate employees to improve their performance. The purpose of providing feedback, or constructive criticism, is to improve performance. Appraisal, then, should encourage employees to maintain or improve job performance.
3. Distribute organizational rewards such as salary increases and promotions equitably. One of the primary criteria of organizational justice and quality of employee work life is whether rewards are distributed fairly.
4. Conduct personnel management research. Logic suggests that if jobs have been analyzed accurately, and if people have been selected for those jobs based on job-related skills, knowledge, and abilities, their subsequent on-the-job performance should be satisfactory or better. If not, one might suspect defects in the job analysis, selection, or promotion criteria—or in the performance appraisal system itself.

Title VII of the 1964 Civil Rights Act, as amended (1972), requires employers to validate any personnel technique that affects an employee's chances for promotion. This includes performance appraisal. For this reason it is strongly suggested that personnel managers adopt one of the performance-oriented techniques discussed later in this chapter. Latham and Wexley[2] cite the Civil Service Reform Act of 1978 as providing the model for a sound, straightforward approach to performance appraisal. The act requires most federal agencies to:

1. Develop an appraisal system that encourages employee participation in establishing performance standards
2. Develop standards based on critical job elements

3. Assess employees against performance standards rather than each other or some statistical guide like a bell curve

It is interesting to note the parallel between these requirements and those applying to techniques for the selection of employees. The common ground is found in the overall mandate that personnel decisions be based on job-related criteria.

APPRAISAL CRITERIA

As we saw in the discussion of selection and promotion processes in Chapter 7, the fundamental question is: What factors should be evaluated? There are only two basic criteria, *person-based* and *performance-based*, though some appraisal methods employ a mixture of the two types. Person-based systems assess an employee's personality traits, characteristics, and aptitudes and often lead to very subjective assessments. These systems are being replaced with performance-based systems or a method that merges the two approaches. In the person-based system, the rater compares employees against other employees or against some absolute standard. Performance-based systems measure each employee's behaviors against previously established behaviors.

Each criterion has advantages. Person-based systems are, beyond a doubt, the easiest and cheapest to design, administer, and interpret. Many organizations evaluate employees on the extent to which they possess desirable personality traits—initiative, dependability, intelligence, or adaptability. Ratings are easily quantified and compared with past appraisals or ratings of other people or units through computerization so that the appraisal process can be completed by frequently overburdened supervisors in a minimum of time. However, person-oriented appraisal systems share the same drawbacks as trait-oriented job-appraisal and classification systems—they have low validity, low reliability, and are of dubious value in improving performance.

First, such systems are invalid to the extent that personality characteristics are unrelated to job performance. For example, organizational and environmental characteristics heavily influence the nature of a given position and, by implication, the kinds of skills or characteristics needed for successful performance. It is impossible to specify, for all positions in an organization, a uniform set of desirable personality characteristics that can be demonstrably related to successful job performance. Second, the reliability of trait rating is frequently marginal at best; two supervisors may have very different definitions of loyalty, depending on their views of the job or their level of expectation for their employees. Third, comparative trait appraisals are not useful for counseling employees because they neither identify areas of satisfactory or unsatisfactory performance nor suggest areas where improvement is needed. Since an employee's personality characteristics are central to his or her self-concept, it is difficult for supervisors and employees to discuss them without lapsing into amateur psychology and defensiveness. As a result of their low validity and reliability, person-oriented systems are not very useful for personnel management research aimed at validating selection or promotion criteria.

For these reasons, most performance specialists advocate the use of performance-based systems—namely, those which evaluate job-related behaviors. In fact, person-based systems can rarely stand the test of legal scrutiny that examines their reliability and validity in relation to actual job performance. In contrast to person-based systems, performance criteria communicate managerial objectives clearly, are both highly relevant to job performance and highly reliable, and fulfill the purposes of reward allocation, performance improvement, and personnel management research. If objective performance standards are established between employees and supervisors through some process of participative goal setting, the employee becomes clearly aware of the specific behavioral expectations attached to his or her position.

Second, the fact that desired behaviors are specified makes the evaluative criteria highly valid—that is, the job behaviors themselves are evaluated, rather than personality characteristics *believed* to be related to performance. Third, appraisal is highly reliable because the use of objective performance standards enables raters, employees, and observers to determine whether or not predetermined performance standards have been met. As a result, changes in salary levels, promotions, or firings can be amply justified by reference to employee productivity. Reward allocation decisions can be explained to employees by discussing their performance objectively, rather than by arguing about the desirability of changing certain negative personality traits. Areas where performance improvement is needed can be identified for counseling, training, or job assignment purposes. The performance-based system increases job-related communication between employees and supervisors, primarily because performance standards must be altered periodically to meet changes in organizational objectives, resource allocation, or environmental constraints.

However, performance-based systems are considerably harder to develop than person-based systems. Because performance standards will vary (depending on the characteristics of the employee, the objectives of the organization, available resources, and external conditions), separate performance standards must be developed for each employee, or for each class of similar positions. Second, the organization may wish to specify desired methods of task performance as well as objectives. Third, the changing nature of organizations and environments means that employee performance standards may also change, and seldom at regularly scheduled or administratively convenient intervals. As a result, supervisors will need to spend more time working with employees to develop performance standards and subsequent appraisal interviews. Since supervisors are rewarded primarily for improving their work unit's short-term productivity, they may view developmental counseling as an inefficient use of their time.

Fourth, it is difficult to develop objective performance standards for many staff people or for positions that are complex or interrelated in a job series. Job-related, objective measures are more suited to simple jobs with tangible output that can be attributed to employee performance. Attempts to measure performance in complex jobs objectively can focus attention on concrete but trivial factors. Further, an employee's performance is also subject to other influences: the quality of the performance standards-setting process, the relationship with others in the work unit, and environmental factors. An example would be when teachers point out that in addition to teacher performance, student accomplishments are influenced by home environment, peers, level of ability, class size, and other factors that complicate the assessment of teachers based on student performance. Since evaluative standards are individualized, computerized scoring or interpretation of results is difficult.

Last, it is difficult to compare the performance of employees with different standards. If each of three employees has met previously established performance standards, how does a supervisor decide which of them should be recommended for a promotion?

APPRAISAL METHODS

The criterion question concerns whether personality characteristics or behavior will be the object of appraisal and the difficulty of separating the two; the methods question concerns the format or technique by which the criterion will be evaluated. Seven methods are commonly used:

- Graphic rating (or adjectival scaling)
- Ranking
- Forced choice
- Essay
- Objective
- Critical incident (or work sampling)
- Behaviorally anchored rating scales (BARS)

Some of these techniques, primarily the first three, are more adaptable to person-oriented systems. Others are utilized primarily in performance-based systems.

FIGURE 10-1 Graphic Rating Scale

Appraisal of Personnel

Person Evaluated_____ Position_____

Location_____

PERFORMANCE FACTORS	Out-standing	Very Good	Good	Satis-factory	Unsatis-factory	Un-known
1. Effectiveness						
2. Use of time and materials						
3. Prompt comple-tion of work						
4. Thoroughness						
5. Initiative						
6. Perseverance						

ABILITIES, SKILLS, AND FACULTIES

	Out-standing	Very Good	Good	Satis-factory	Unsatis-factory	Un-known
7. Technical skills						
8. Communication skills						
9. Judgment						
10. Analytical ability						
11. Ability to organize						
12. Ability to inspire and influence staff						
13. Ability to inspire and influence others than staff						
14. Flexibility and adaptability						
15. Imaginativeness and creativity						
16. Ability to develop subordinates						
17. Breadth of concepts						

ETHICAL CONSIDERATIONS

	Out-standing	Very Good	Good	Satis-factory	Unsatis-factory	Un-known
18. Loyalty to department						
19. Loyalty to peers						
20. Loyalty to sub-ordinates						

(continued)

FIGURE 10-1 (Continued)

	Out-standing	Very Good	Good	Satis-factory	Unsatis-factory	Un-known
21. Sense of ethics						
22. Cooperativeness						
23. Responsibility						
24. Commitment of service						
25. Open-mindedness						

Date Evaluated _____ Evaluator_____

The above appraisal was reviewed with me on _____

_____

(Signature of Person Evaluated)

Comments_____

1. *Graphic-rating scales* are the most easily developed, administered, and scored format. They consist of a listing of desirable or undesirable personality traits in one column and beside each trait a scale (or box) which the rater marks to indicate the extent to which the rated employee demonstrates the trait. An example of a graphic rating scale appears in Figure 10-1.

2. *Ranking techniques* are similar to graphic-rating scales in that they are also based on traits. However, they require the rater to rank-order each employee on each of the listed traits. While they overcome one fault of graphic-rating scales, the tendency of raters to rate all employees high on all characteristics, it is difficult for raters to rank more than ten employees against one another.

3. *Forced-choice techniques* are the most valid trait-rating method. Based on a previous analysis of the position, job analysts have determined which traits or behaviors are most related to successful job performance. Several positive traits or behaviors are given in the form of multiple-choice questions, and the rater is asked to indicate the one that corresponds most closely with the ratee's job performance or personality. Because supervisors are unsure which item is the "best" response according to the person who designed the test, forced-choice techniques reduce supervisory bias. Naturally, they are disliked by supervisors, who want to know how they are rating their employees. An example of the forced-choice format appears in Figure 10-2.

4. The fourth appraisal technique, the *essay*, is among the oldest and

Person Evaluated_____

Position _____

Organization Unit_____

Date_____

Instructions: Please place a check on the line to the left of the statement that best describes this employee.

1. This employee
   _____ a. always looks presentable
   _____ b. shows initiative and independence
   _____ c. works well with others in groups
   _____ d. produces work of high quality

2. This employee
   _____ a. completes work promptly and on time
   _____ b. pays much attention to detail
   _____ c. works well under pressure
   _____ d. works well without supervisory guidance

3. This employee
   _____ a. is loyal to his or her supervisor
   _____ b. uses imagination and creativity
   _____ c. is thorough and dependable
   _____ d. accepts responsibility willingly

FIGURE   10-2   Forced-Choice Performance Evaluation Format

most widely used forms of appraisal. The rater simply makes narrative comments about the employee. Since these may relate to personality or performance, the essay method is suitable for person- or performance-oriented systems. However, it has the disadvantages of being time-consuming, biased in favor of employees with supervisors who can write well, and impossible to standardize. It is frequently used in conjunction with graphic-rating or ranking techniques to clarify extremely low or high ratings. But the burden on supervisors is so great that when essay elaboration is required to justify high or low ratings, supervisors have a tendency to rate employees toward the middle of a normal curve.

5. The *objective method* is a measure of work performance—quality, quantity, or timeliness—against previously established standards. It is used most often in private industry by companies with piece-rate pay plans; public sector organizations are adopting a variant of this approach by measuring workload indicators. For example, employment counselors may be evaluated on the number of jobs they fill or on the percentage of placements who remain on the job after three months.

6. The sixth technique has been termed *critical incident* or *work sampling*. It is an objective technique that records representative examples of good (or bad) performance in relation to agreed-upon employee objectives. It has the advantages and disadvantages of performance-oriented systems generally. One cautionary note, however: To the extent that the selected incidents are not representative of employee performance over time, the method is open to distortion and bias. Figure 10–3 presents an example of a critical incident appraisal form.

FIGURE 10-3 Critical Incident Performance Evaluation Format

Person Evaluated_____

Position _____

Organizational Unit_____

Time Period _____ to _____

	Employee Objectives		Examples of Successful or Unsuccessful Performance
1.		a.	
		b.	
		c.	
		d.	
2.		a.	
		b.	
		c.	
		d.	
3.		a.	
		b.	
		c.	
		d.	

TABLE 10-1 Behaviorally Anchored Rating Scales (BARS) Evaluation Format

Student evaluated: _____ Course: _____ Dates: _____ to _____

EVALUATIVE CRITERIA	COURSE GRADE			
	A	B	C	D
1. Term paper (75 percent of course grade)	Meet criteria for a grade of B and in addition: Develop new insights, theories, or solutions	Meet criteria for a grade of C and in addition: Analyze and critically evaluate existing knowledge presented in lectures, discussion, and outside reading	Completed by date scheduled in course outline; repeat existing knowledge from lectures and outside reading Follow proper style (grammar, organization, footnotes, and bibliograpy)	Not completed by date scheduled; not meeting minimum criteria for a grade of C
2. Class participation (25 percent of course grade)	Meet criteria for a grade of B and in addition: 1. Listen to and evaluate the class participation of other students 2. Show ability to analyze and evaluate material presented in lecture and discussion	Meet criteria for a grade of C and in addition: 1. Participate in class discussions 2. Demonstrate correct factual knowledge of concepts and theories from lectures and reading	Attend class as scheduled or notify professor in advance of absences	Not meet criteria for a grade of C

7. The *behaviorally anchored rating scale* (BARS) is a technique that employs objective performance criteria in a standardized appraisal format. The personnel manager who wishes to use BARS develops a range of possible standards for each task and then translates these statements into numerical scores. To be job-related, these performance-oriented statements must be validated by job analysis.

BARS are handy because they make use of objective appraisal criteria and are easy to employ. But they are time-consuming to develop, and they have not lived up to expectations because the distinction between behavior and traits is not as salient as once thought.[3] Table 10-1 presents an example of a behaviorally anchored rating form for student performance in a classroom setting.

So far our discussion has emphasized that the purpose of an employee appraisal system must be clearly stated and that evaluation methods must be suitable to the evaluative criteria chosen. Table 10-2 summarizes these relationships. While Table 10-2 points out the uses of each appraisal method, judicial reviews of discrimination cases involving appraisal instruments will be forcing more uniformity in future appraisal systems. Feild and Holley[4] report that on the basis of their research examining employment discrimination court decisions involving appraisal systems, the following characteristics clearly contributed to verdicts for the defending organizations: A job analysis was used to develop the appraisal system; a behavior-oriented versus person-oriented system was used; evaluators were given specific written instructions on how to use the rating instrument; the appraisal results were reviewed with employees; and the defending organizations tended to be nonindustrial in nature. A recent survey of 3052 firms

TABLE 10-2 Performance Evaluation Systems

PURPOSE	CRITERIA	METHODS
Communication of objectives	Performance-oriented	Critical incident (work sampling), objective measures, BARS
Reward allocation	Person- or performance-oriented	Graphic rating, ranking, forced-choice, BARS
Performance improvement	Performance-oriented	Critical incident (work sampling), objective measures, BARS
Personnel research	Performance-oriented	Essay, work sampling (critical incident), objective measures, BARS

suggested that successful appraisal systems included written goals, supervisory instructions, senior management training, training in objective setting and providing feedback, and integration with the pay system.[5]

RATERS

An employee's performance may be rated by a number of people. The immediate supervisor most commonly assesses the performance of subordinates, and this is the way most employees prefer it.[6] Supervisory assessments reinforce authority relationships in an organization and are frequently seen as the primary function distinguishing a superior from a subordinate. Because the supervisory-subordinate relationship itself is affected by so many factors, supervisory ratings are easily biased. Self-ratings can be employed to promote an honest discussion between superior and subordinate about the subordinate's performance. But self-ratings receive mixed support: some studies find them inflated, others see them deflated in comparison with supervisory ratings.

In a federal employee survey, 67 percent surveyed indicated that they should have a "considerable/great" input into their performance rating.[7] In the same group, 84 percent indicated their supervisor should have "considerable/great" input into their performance rating. Peer ratings, while infrequently utilized, have proved acceptable both in terms of reliability and validity. However, peer ratings are difficult to sell to employers and employees. Fifty-six percent of the federal sample indicated they felt peers should have "little or no" input into their rating. Subordinate ratings are equally rare, and their main function is to provide data to begin discussion of the superior-subordinate relationship in a work group.

One of the challenges these findings on peer ratings pose for human resources management is that future trends in the design and philosophy of work point toward the necessity of peer and self-ratings. Working in teams and seeking quality through an organizational philosophy of continuous improvement suggest less emphasis on methods of human resources management that grow out of current assessment techniques. It would appear difficult to reconcile the goals of continuous self-improvement with hierarchical control and authority. This observation, frequently made in normative statements during the human relations movement of the 1960s and 1970s, is becoming more relevant in the 1990s as technological changes and pressures for quality and productivity challenge traditional methods of organizational command and control.

A significant amount of effort has gone into creating accurate appraisal instruments and in training supervisors to dismiss inappropriate and irrelevant considerations when making formal assessments, and one wonders if technique dominates purpose in this area. The goal is to minimize rater bias without jeopardizing the supervisory discretion necessary in making judgments about employee performance. The difficulty in eliminating rater bias is that people, including supervisors, tend to make global judgments of others.[8] The fact is that supervisors come to conclusions about employees without the help of assessment instruments. Raters tend to use the performance appraisal process to *document* rather than *discover* how well an employee is performing. This probably helps account for Milkovich and Wigdor's observation that "There is no compelling evidence that one appraisal format is significantly better than another. . . . Global ratings do not appear to produce very different results from job-specific ratings."[9] This leads them to assign marginal value to the expenditure of more time and money developing more accurate assessment instruments.[10]

The inevitable global assessments that supervisors make acknowledge the complexities of work, the multiplicity of factors causing different levels of work performance, the difficulty of actually describing the constituent elements of a job without trivializing it, and the critical role that who a person is influences the kind of work a person does, both its quality and its quantity. In addition, supervisors know that each employee creates an environment for the work of other employees, and to separate out individual performance artificially distorts what happens in an office.

AN EFFECTIVE APPRAISAL SYSTEM

Even though different evaluative methods are likely to identify the same employees as high or low performers, we have already seen in Table 10-2 that different appraisal methods are suitable for different evaluative purposes. Several guidelines follow for the effective use of appraisal *systems* by public organizations.

First, it may be wise to utilize separate systems for separate purposes. It seems clear when one looks at the purposes of appraisal systems that two fundamentally different supervisory roles can be detected. If the purpose is allocation of rewards, the supervisor or other rater becomes a judge. If the purpose it to improve employee performance, the supervisor is a counselor, coach, or facilitator. The fact is that supervisors assume both roles in their day-to-day work, but the roles are difficult to integrate successfully. It may well be that different appraisal instruments lend themselves to the different functions, just as different times should be set aside to discuss allocation decisions and developmental issues with employees.

Second, raters should have the opportunity, ability, and desire to rate employees accurately. Since employee understanding and acceptance of evaluative criteria are keys to performance improvement, it follows that employees must participate in the determination of goals. The performance appraisal system must be job-related, must allow the opportunity for interaction and understanding between evaluator and evaluatee, and must serve the performance improvement needs of both individual and organization.

Third, job analysis and performance appraisal need to be more closely related by developing occupation-specific job descriptions that include performance standards as well as duties, responsibilities, and minimum qualifications. Such job descriptions must specify the conditions under which work is to be performed, including such factors as resources, guidelines, and interrelationships. Necessarily, they will be specific to each occupation and perhaps to each organization as well.

Fourth, appraisal must be tied to long-range employee objectives such as promotion and career planning and more generally capture the employee's motivation for self-improvement. Performance appraisal is not an end in itself; nor should it be driven solely by short-term consequences like pay for performance. While performance improvement is administratively separate from promotional assessment and organizational human resource planning, both employees and organizations realize that performance appraisal relates to rewards, promotional consideration, and career planning. Further, connecting pay to performance places a significant burden on performance appraisal systems.

PAY FOR PERFORMANCE SYSTEMS: AN ANALYSIS

In the 1980s skepticism of the government's ability to solve public problems contributed to the public's declining willingness to fund public programs and reintroduced demands that government become more businesslike. Public-sector experiments with performance-based compensation systems grew out of this movement, with the federal government leading the way.

The Civil Service Reform Act of 1978 required the federal government to develop job-related and objective performance appraisal systems that could be used for training, promotion, and disciplinary personnel actions. The act also mandated performance-based compensation systems for senior and middle-level federal managers. According to a recent comprehensive review of these efforts, "The reforms have by most measures fallen short of expectations, despite fairly substantial midcourse corrections. Yet the belief in merit principles remains strong, as does the expectation that performance appraisal and linking compensation to performance can provide incentives for excellence."[11]

Why have performance-based compensation systems resulted in unrealized expectations? Why do employees, managers, legislators, and the public continue to profess faith in them? Exploring these questions requires an understanding of what is meant by a pay for performance system. Figure 10-4 classifies several of these systems without distinguishing between public and private sectors.

Merit plans add to the individual employee's rate of pay in accordance

LEVEL OF PERFORMANCE

CONTRIBUTION TO BASE SALARY		Individual	Group
	Added to base	(a) Merit plans	(d) Small group incentives
	Not added to base	(b) Piece rates Commissions Bonuses	(c) Profit sharing Gainsharing Bonuses

FIGURE 10-4 Pay for Performance Plan Classes
Source: Reprinted with permission from *Pay for Performance,* © 1991 by the National Academy of Sciences. Published by National Academy Press, Washington, DC.

with the employee's performance during a previous period of time. Increases usually are specified according to a schedule or grid and are tied to the rating an employee receives on a performance appraisal. Merit plans are commonly used to connect pay to performance in the public sector and in large private-sector organizations for managers and professionals. It may be surprising to learn that not much research evaluating the effectiveness of these plans has been conducted.[12] Piece rates, commissions, and bonuses are also tied to individual performance, but are not added to the employee's base rate of pay. Applications of these kinds of incentive plans have proved effective where outcomes are easy to calculate and attribute to individual employees, but research shows that they account for only 9 to 16 percent of the variance in individual performance.[13] Small-group incentives are similar to merit plans in that money is added to the employee's base rate of pay, but team performance is rewarded rather than individual accomplishment. There are few examples of these plans. More common is profit sharing, gainsharing, and bonuses distributed to groups, often on a company-wide basis, but not added to the base rate of pay.

Several benefits are associated with pay for performance which accompany the fundamental belief that a person's pay ought to reflect what that individual has contributed to the organization.[14] First, it is argued that pay for performance systems affect a person's decision to join or leave an organization, to perform, and even to come to work. Second, pay for performance is seen as a way of increasing organizational effectiveness. Another benefit comes from the communication between supervisors and subordinates that occurs regarding performance goals and feedback on performance. And last, performance-based compensation systems are seen as more businesslike in our society, and it is believed that organizations employing them are somehow more legitimate in the eyes of internal and external stakeholders. Again, there is little systematic, empirical research comparing the effectiveness of different pay for performance plans in achieving these benefits.

Based on an understanding of equity and expectancy theory, presented in Chapter 8, it is clear that several elements must be present for a pay for performance system to motivate employee performance:

- Employees must know what constitutes work performance that will be rewarded.
- Employees must have the opportunity—the tools, the time—to perform.
- Employees must believe that they have the knowledge, skills, and ability to accomplish the desired performance.
- Employees must value the monetary reward when they calculate the costs and benefits of performing at the desired level.
- Employees must believe that if they perform well, they will be monetarily rewarded.
- Employees must perceive that monetary rewards will be distributed fairly.

In addition to these specific conditions, other factors complicate the effective implementation of performance-based compensation systems. First, not all work lends itself to pay for performance. For example, where goals are difficult to identify or quantify and when discreet individual contributions are hard to distinguish, such plans face severe obstacles. Second, some organizational cultures and structures do not lend themselves to performance-based compensation. For example, organizations that prize themselves on teamwork and cooperation often find the competitive and individualistic norms underlying many pay for performance plans contrary to their organizational culture. Third, external factors like the presence of a union or legal constraints or political forces may block successful implementation.

Given these many preconditions, it is not surprising that existing performance-based compensation systems—whether found in public or in private sectors—do not accomplish very well the several goals set out for them.[15] Milkovich and Wigdor found that less than one-third of the employees in the various surveys they reviewed rated their performance appraisal plan effective in tying pay to performance or communicating organizational expectations about work.[16] In a recent survey of federal employees, 54 percent responded that it was "very" or "somewhat unlikely" that if they performed better they would receive more pay.[17] And in a 1988 survey of federal personnel officers, only 27 percent indicated that the present performance-management system that ties pay to performance had "greatly" or "somewhat improved" organizational effectiveness, while some 35 percent indicated that it had "greatly" or "somewhat impeded" organizational effectiveness.[18]

At the federal level, where pay for performance has been researched thoroughly, it has been found that not enough money is set aside to establish a motivating effect, that performance appraisals are inflated, and that employees suspect the equitable distribution of the monetary rewards. Gabris and Mitchell summarize the pay for performance experience by writing: "So much do we want to think that extrinsic incentives will, under proper conditions, motivate employees, that we somehow refuse to accept the overwhelming evidence suggesting that this theory does not work well in an applied and general sense. The theory may be internally elegant and logical, but not practical."[19]

Given the overwhelming evidence suggesting at best only cautious optimism for performance-based compensation systems other than incentive plans that work under limited conditions, why do they continue to attract advocates, including their critics? Perry suggests that pay for performance systems have become ingrained in the institutional order of our society.[20] They are "part of the ritual and myth that help to retain the legitimacy of the governance system." Bureaucracies are established as rational instruments of public policy, and nothing appears more rational than rewarding employees monetarily on the basis of their performance. Further, the professed link between performance and pay suggests control by politicians, administrators, and the public over bureaucrats and conveys to the public that government is both responsive and efficient. Continuing faith in performance-based compensation systems may be attributed more to these reasons than to an objective assessment that pay for performance contributes to organizational effectiveness, quality of work, and quality of the employee's work experience.

THE HUMAN DYNAMICS OF THE APPRAISAL PROCESS

Despite the attention appraisal techniques have received in the past decade, appraisal systems are "still widely regarded as a nuisance at best and a necessary evil at worst."[21] Considering that feedback is essential to goal accomplishment and productivity takes the limelight in industry and government, why were appraisal systems regarded so lightly prior to judicial scrutiny and the emphasis on pay for performance?

One reason is that not all employees are interested in productivity. When the caseload of an income maintenance worker in a social service agency is increased because of budgetary constraints to the point where the emphasis is on quantity of cases processed, not quality of service rendered, the individual worker begins to value his or her welfare, working conditions, and equity of the workload more than productivity. A second reason is that multiple sources of performance feedback exist in an organization, with the formal appraisal system constituting only the most visible and tangible. People in organizations are constantly receiving and interpreting cues about others, and attributing motives to their behavior. A third reason concerns the human dynamics of the appraisal process as opposed to measurement issues surrounding the reliability and validity of the appraisal instrument itself.

Douglas Cederblom has reviewed literature on the appraisal interview—the formal part of the process where the rater and the person being rated sit down to talk about performance.[22] He found three factors contributing to the success of the appraisal interview. First, goal setting during the interview seemed positively associated with employee satisfaction with both the interview and its utility. Underlying the goal-setting process is the employee's confidence in the rater's technical knowledge about the subordinate's work. Second, the encouragement of subordinate participation in the interview—"welcoming participation," "opportunity to present ideas or feelings," and "boss asked my opinion"—seemed to produce positive subordinate assessments of the interview process. Last, the support of the rater expressed in terms of encouragement, constructive guidance, and sincere, specific praise of the subordinate also results in positive feelings about the interview.

Criticism from superior to subordinate produces mixed results. On the one hand, a certain amount of criticism should lend perceived credibility to the superior's assessment. On the other hand, research rarely shows much lasting change in an employee following a supervisory critique. In part, this is because few raters know how to provide a constructive critique of an employee, and when a trait-rating form is used, employees inevitably interpret criticism in personal rather than behavioral terms. The obvious here warrants mention. Anything in the appraisal interview that produces a defensive employee reaction (regardless of the rater's intent) is likely to detract from the subordinate's satisfaction with the interview and is unlikely to have much success in altering an employee's behavior at work.

Palguta observes that while it may be statistically impossible for all employees to perform better than average, the emotional investment of employees in believing they are better than average is significant.[23] When pay is tied to performance, this investment is magnified because pay tangibly reflects supervisory judgments about employees in ways that employees cannot ignore or easily discount. The goal of feedback on below-average performers is to encourage poor performers to quit or to improve. There is some evidence that poorer performers are more likely to leave the federal government than those who rate higher.[24] But when the results of appraisals are used for allocation decisions like pay, superiors tend to become more lenient in their ratings.[25] While some may leave, most stay, harboring feelings of inequity and discontent. In the federal government less than one percent of employees receive a rating below "fully successful." In fact, the majority receive a rating of better than fully successful, which is 3 on a 5-point scale. A rating of fully successful puts an employee in the bottom 10 to 20 percent of many occupations in federal agencies.[26] The difficulty with inflated ratings is that the emotional investment of workers in their performance leads them to discount "satisfactory" ratings—which carry few economic rewards—and become disgruntled and then blame their discontent on organizational factors like supervision and managerial policies and practices.[27]

In looking for reasons why appraisal systems seem to have little real effect as a managerial tool despite theoretical promise, Nalbandian has turned to expectancy theory for an explanation.[28] He argues that the appraisal tool an organization uses may increase a supervisor's ability to assess employees, but many factors affecting the willingness of supervisors to evaluate employees seem easily overlooked. From an expectancy theory perspective, raters anticipate few positive outcomes from an honest attempt to rate subordinates. Most supervisors generally know who their effective and ineffective employees are even if they cannot always articulate their reasoning to someone else's satisfaction. From the supervisor's perspective, then, the formal appraisal process duplicates an assessment the supervisor has already made. Thus, when the supervisor conducts an appraisal, it is seen as benefitting someone else. Further, research in the federal government has shown that in 1989, according to supervisory reports, in 43 percent of the cases where employees received a less than satisfactory rating no difference resulted in the employee's performance, 34 percent of the supervisors said performance improved, and 20 percent said it made things worse.[29]

In addition, many authors and practitioners have pointed to the emotionally discomforting outcomes, the ones with negative valences, that the rater associates with the appraisal interview. This is where the supervisor's assessment of the employee must be communicated face to face. Behaviorally oriented rating systems are designed to make assessments more objective and thus more acceptable to employees. Unfortunately, bad news is bad news regardless of whether it results from an assessment a supervisor feels is objective. When employees argue; sulk; look distraught, bewildered, or disappointed; or threaten to file a grievance because they disagree with the supervisor's assessment, most supervisors will experience such behavior in negative terms. The supervisor is likely, then, to find ways of behaving in the future that will not stimulate these employee responses. Is it any wonder that supervisors are prone to assess employees similarly, with most employees rated at least satisfactory? In fact, as we have seen already, in many organizations a satisfactory rating is taken by employees as a sign of disapproval, and the majority of ratings exceed satisfactory.

The negative experiences supervisors have when rating subordinates appear unappreciated by others. For example, in a recent survey federal employees were asked if they would prefer to change the existing five-level system to a simple "pass/fail."[30] While only 25 percent favored the change, 42 percent of the second-level supervisors favored it; 35 percent of the first-level supervisors favored it; only 22 percent of nonsupervisory personnel favored it. The more experience supervisors have with performance appraisal, the less complicated they want it to be.

In sum, while a considerable amount of effort goes into the seemingly endless task of producing accurate measurements of performance, the human dynamics of the appraisal process probably remain a greater challenge. Until supervisors experience the appraisal process positively, the underlying motivation to make appraisal systems work will be absent.

PERFORMANCE APPRAISAL AND ALTERNATIVE PERSONNEL SYSTEMS

Much of the discussion in this chapter has focused on civil service systems. Civil service personnel systems often are called merit systems, frequently confusing even government employees. Personnel systems based on merit are those where a variety of personnel decisions are based on knowledge, skills, ability, and performance rather than seniority or politics. *Merit pay* plans are those that attempt to tie compensation to performance. Performance appraisal and civil service systems go hand in hand, and to the extent they can help distinguish and document employee performance, they advance the goals of personnel systems based on merit.

Affirmative action personnel systems also have a significant investment in reliable and valid appraisal systems. This interest parallels a similar interest in the development of selection devices free of inappropriate or irrelevant judgments. This interest has thrust performance appraisal systems into the judicial arena, subjecting them to standards of validity and reliability that they may not be able to meet when preserving the essential subjectivity involved in one person evaluating another's work.

Performance appraisal systems are largely irrelevant to political personnel systems. Political executives rarely remain on the job long enough to benefit or suffer formal appraisals. Their superiors are other political executives, often elected officials whose subjective criteria for effective job performance make formal assessments like those in civil service systems difficult to implement. Further, the higher up in an organizational hierarchy one travels, the more likely that the substance of an individual's job will be determined by that individual, with only limited guidance by superiors or the previous incumbent's job description.

Collective bargaining personnel systems generally oppose pay for individual performance and appraisal plans developed as a part of performance-based compensation. Unions prefer to negotiate wages for their workers and see individual incentive or merit plans as ways of pitting one union member against another and introducing conditions where managers can favor one employee over another.

SUMMARY

This chapter has identified the purposes and methods of assessing employees as well as the legal framework affecting the appraisal process. The benefits and costs of each method were described, along with the observation that while different methods may be more acceptable to subordinates, they do not seem to produce significantly different ratings of employees.

Despite little evidence in public or private sectors that tying pay to performance enhances organizational effectiveness, it is seen as an activity that appears to convey a businesslike orientation to running the government. Merit pay plans appear to be evaluated less for their effect on employee and organizational performance and more on employee perceptions of fairness and workability and the connection between pay and performance.

Performance-based compensation plans necessitate accurate performance measurement. Unfortunately, performance appraisal is an inherently subjective process, and at least according to one comprehensive review of the literature, there is little to be gained by seeking fundamental measurement improvements. At this point, seeking more objectivity in measuring complex jobs may produce trivial measures—concrete in form but failing to capture the essence of the job.

Part of the difficulty in implementing a successful performance appraisal system in government is failure to recognize the lack of rewards for supervisors who actually do try to rate employees honestly. It appears that supervisors find few positively reinforcing experiences in the appraisal process.

Ultimately, in order to produce an effective appraisal system, some groundwork needs to be laid:

1. Promoting to supervisory positions people who, among their other qualifications, want to supervise and will not look upon the appraisal of employees as a necessary evil

2. An appraisal tool that has been developed with employee participation and that focuses more on performance than traits

3. Training programs directed at supervisory use of the appraisal instrument and understanding of the human dynamics surrounding the appraisal process

4. Rewards for supervisors who competently and seriously approach the appraisal function

5. An open discussion and understanding of the superior-subordinate relationship at work

Does the appraisal process actually fulfill its various functions, or does it represent a triumph of technique over purpose? There is no doubt that the formalism of appraisal systems challenges the essentially subjective nature of one person assessing another's work or even one person assessing his or her own performance. However, as long as the distribution of organizational rewards is connected to individual performance, the formalism can be expected to remain. The desire for organizational justice and the protection of individual rights require that employees know how and why rewards are distributed and that employees be given an opportunity to appeal these judgments and question the processes. This promotes formal performance appraisal methods and processes. If the technology and design of work and the philosophy of total quality management successfully transfer the appraisal process from the individual to the work group, the formalism associated with individual performance appraisal may diminish.

KEY TERMS

BARS
critical incident (work sampling)
employee-ranking scale
essay format
forced-choice techniques
graphic-rating scale
merit pay
objective method
pay for performance
performance-based rating system
person-based rating system
ranking techniques

DISCUSSION QUESTIONS

1. Describe four operational functions of a performance appraisal system. Do you think all four can be accomplished with one appraisal method? Are the four functions complementary?
2. Draw up a list of pros and cons for person-based and performance-based rating systems.
3. Identify the four characteristics of an effective rating system. Why are the four so difficult to implement?
4. Pick an organization you are familiar with—preferably a government organization—and describe the pros and cons of developing one or more pay for performance systems for it.
5. Utilize an expectancy theory perspective and analyze the motivation of supervisors to rate the performance of subordinates honestly and accurately.

CASE STUDY

The accompanying exhibits present the appraisal instruments used in two organizations. Review the exhibits and respond to the following questions:

1. Which of the two forms is more job-related? Which type would you rather use to evaluate employees? Which type would you rather your supervisor use to evaluate you?
2. Discuss the two forms with regard to the following criteria:
   * Job-relatedness
   * Cost in developing
   * Ease of completing
   * Use in counseling and developing employees
   * Use in promotion, pay, or other personnel decisions
   * Rater bias
   * Use in providing specific feedback
   * Accuracy in measuring employee performance

NOTES

[1]*New York Times*, June 30, 1983, p. 8.

[2]Gary P. Latham and Kenneth N. Wexley, *Increasing Productivity Through Performance Appraisal* (Reading, MA: Addison-Wesley, 1981), pp. 28–30.

[3]George T. Milkovich and Alexandra K. Wigdor (eds.), *Pay for Performance: Evaluating Performance Appraisal and Merit Pay* (Washington, DC: National Academy Press), p. 143.

EXHIBIT 1 Employee Rating

Date of Rating _____

White—Personnel; Canary—Dept/Div.; Pink—Employee

Rating Period: From _____ To _____

— Probationary
— Annual
— Special
— Final

Soc. Sec. No.	Activity	Class	Obj.	Employee Name

INSTRUCTIONS

Evaluate employee's performance and behavior to the degree he or she meets job requirements, taking into consideration all factors in the employee's performance. Individual factors under each trait should be designated, where applicable, as (+) high; (✔) average; (−) low. The overall mark for each trait should be indicated by placing an (x) in the applicable columns labeled Outstanding, Above Average, Average, Below Average, and Unsatisfactory. BEFORE RATING EMPLOYEE, PLEASE REVIEW YOUR RATING MANUAL.

TRAIT		Outstdg.	Above Average	Average	Below Average	Unsat.
Quality of Work	— Accuracy — Completeness — Oral expression — Written expression — Soundness of judgment in decisions — Reliability of work results					
Work Output	— Amount of work performed — Completion of work on schedule — Physical fitness — Learning ability					

(continued)

235

EXHIBIT 1 (Continued)

Work Habits	Organization and planning of assignments — Job interest — Attendance	Compliance with work instructions — Observance of work hours — Conscientious use of work time				
Safety	Care of equipment, property and materials	Personal safety habits				
Personal Relations	Cooperation with fellow employees — Personal appearance and habits	Dealing with the public — Ability to get along with others				
Adaptability	Performance in emergencies — Performance with minimum of instruction	Performance under changing conditions — Self-reliance, initiative & problem solving				
Supervisory Skills	FOR USE IN RATING SUPERVISORS ONLY: — Leadership — Acceptance by others — Decision making — Effectiveness and skill in planning and laying out work	— Fairness & impartiality — Communicating problems to others — Training-Safety				

TRAIT

	Outstdg.	Above Average	Average	Below Average	Unsat.
General Evaluation Indicate by an (x) in the appropriate column your own general evaluation of the employee's rating, taking all the above and other pertinent factors into consideration. A written statement must be made on the reverse side of this form if the rating is OUTSTANDING or UNSATISFACTORY on this item.				*	*#

Signature of
Rater: _____

Title: _____

Signature of
Rater's Supervisor: _____

Title: _____

*An (x) here indicates loss of annual salary increase
#An (x) here indicates employee must be rated again in 90 days
TO EMPLOYEE: Your signature is required; however, it does not imply that you agree with the rating.

Date _____   Employee Signature _____

PROVIDENCE-ST. MARGARET HEALTH CENTER
Kansas City, Kansas

JOB DESCRIPTION

JOB TITLE __Primary Nurse__   Department __Nursing Service__   Date _____

Probationary Review [ ]
Merit Review [ ]   Special [ ]

Job Title of Person _____   Job Code No. _____   Date _____
To Whom Reporting __Head Nurse__   Pay Grade _____   Revised _____

Present Grade _____ Step _____
Name _____

Job Summary: A professional nurse, who has responsibility, authority and accountability for quality nursing care for an assigned group of patients.

Date of Hire _____
Evaluation Due Date _____

RESPONSIBILITIES	PERFORMANCE STANDARDS	ATTAINED? YES/NO	IF NO, HOW CAN SUCH BE ATTAINED?
ASSESSMENT: 1. Complete the admission procedure to include	Within one hour of patient's admission to the unit, introduces self and identifies the primary nurse's role to the patient and/or the family.		
Orientation	Orients patient/family to the unit.		
Assesses the patient needs	Tentative assessment and nursing judgment, based on the patient's immediate needs at the time of admission to the unit, will be reflected in the initial notation on the nurse's progress notes and/or the nursing history summary.		

	Performs assessment within 24 hours of admission to the unit. Assessment is based on subjective and objective data which may include records, consultations and test data.
	Physical:
	    breath and bowel sounds
	    peripheral pulses
	    level of consciousness
	    general skin condition and color
	    physical abnormalities

Completes a nursing history	Completes nursing history within 24 hours of admission to the unit and enters notation on Patient Care Guide.
PLANNING: 1. Initiates a patient care guide	Assures that a 24 hour patient care guide is completed within 24 hours of patient admission to the unit. This will define patient/family problems and formulate plan of care that attempts to modify or eliminate each nursing problem.
2. Includes the patient and family in the planning of the patient's care.	Includes the patient and the family in the planning of the patient's care both initially and throughout the hospitalization and reflects this action via documentation on the patient care guide and verbal feedback from the patient and/or family.

(continued)

EXHIBIT 2 (Continued)

RESPONSIBILITIES	PERFORMANCE STANDARDS	ATAINED? YES/NO	IF NO, HOW CAN SUCH BE ATAINED?
3. Initiates discharge planning	Describe short and long term goals, as identified by the patient and/or family, beginning at time of admission.		
INTERVENTION: 1. Performs all independent nursing functions and performs dependent nursing functions as ordered by the physician and *documents* all nursing assessment, plans and interventions.	Within the framework of the health center policies and procedures and documents accordingly on the patient chart.		
2. Communicates patient's status to other health members.	Communicates daily with patient and/or family regarding events of the day and current status. Provides time for questions. Communicates to personnel on her tour of duty verbal and written assignments with deadlines for completion. Communicates patient data to oncoming shift via organized, pertinent, factual walking report and updates Kardex accordingly. Attends doctors' rounds, and communicates with physicians.		
3. Utilizes social service department and resources in order to promote, restore, and maintain optimal health care for patient/family.	Initiates utilization of community health resources with the cooperation of the physician and communicates these actions.		

4. Utilizes team members appropriately, according to their abilities and position description.

Establishes priorities of nursing care based on assessment of patient needs, reflected on the daily primary nursing assignment worksheet. Assures that delegated assignments have been completed before the end of the shift. Schedules break and meal times for team members.

5. Coordinates patient/family teaching, based upon assessment of patient readiness.

Patient/family teaching will be reflected in the chart at the time of discharge.

JOB SPECIFICATIONS:

Comments on Work Habits: _____

Supervisor _____ Date _____ Department Head _____ Date _____

My supervisor has reviewed my Job Description and Performance Evaluation with me. My signature does not necessarily mean that I agree.

Comments: _____

Signature: _____ Date: _____

[4]Hubert S. Feild and William H. Holley, "The Relationship of Performance Appraisal System Characteristics to Verdicts in Selected Employment Discrimination Cases," *Academy of Management Journal 25* (1982), 397.

[5]The Wyatt Communicator: Results of the 1989 Wyatt Performance Management Survey, Fourth Quarter, 1989 (Chicago: The Wyatt Company), pp. 7–8. Reported in George T. Milkovich and Alexandra K. Wigdor (eds.), *Pay for Performance*.

[6]United States Merit Systems Protection Board, *Working for America: A Federal Employee Survey* (Washington, DC: Merit Systems Protection Board, June 1990), p. 17.

[7]*Ibid.*

[8]Milkovich and Wigdor, *Pay for Performance*, p. 50.

[9]Ibid., p. 149.

[10]Ibid., p. 3.

[11]Ibid., p. 135.

[12]Ibid., p. 77.

[13]Ibid., p. 82.

[14]Ibid., p. 136.

[15]Gerald T. Gabris and Kenneth Mitchell, "The Impact of Merit Raise Scores on Employee Attitudes: The Matthew Effect of Performance Appraisal," *Public Personnel Management 17*, 4 (Winter 1988), 369–86; Milkovich and Wigdor, *Pay for Performance*; United States Merit Systems Protection Board, *Federal Personnel Management Since Civil Service Reform* (Washington, DC: Merit Systems Protection Board, November 1989); United States Merit Systems Protection Board, *Working for America*.

[16]Milkovich and Wigdor, *Pay for Performance*, p. 106.

[17]United States Merit Systems Protection Board, *Working for America*, p. 18.

[18]United States Merit Systems Protection Board, *Federal Personnel Management Since Civil Service Reform*, p. 11.

[19]Gabris and Mitchell, "The Impact of Merit Raise Scores on Employee Attitudes," p. 375.

[20]James L. Perry, "Linking Pay to Performance: The Controversy Continues," in Carolyn Ban and Norma M. Riccucci (eds.), *Public Personnel Management: Current Concerns—Future Challenges* (New York: Longman, 1991), p. 80.

[21]R.I. Lazer and W.S. Wikstrom, *Appraising Managerial Performance: Current Practices and Future Directions* (New York: The Conference Board, 1977).

[22]Douglas Cederblom, "The Performance Appraisal Interview: A Review, Implications, and Suggestions," *Academy of Management Review 7* (1982), 219–27.

[23]John Palguta, "Performance Management and Pay for Performance." A presentation before the Pay-for-Performance Labor-Management Committee and the Performance Management and Recognition System Review Committee, United States Merit Systems Protection Board, Washington, DC, May 6, 1991.

[24] United States Merit Systems Protection Board, *Toward Effective Performance Management in Government* (Washington, DC: Merit Systems Protection Board, July 1988), p. 6.

[25]Milkovich and Wigdor, *Pay for Performance*, p. 72.

[26]Palguta, "Performance Management and Pay for Performance."

[27]Gabris and Mitchell, "The Impact of Merit Raise Scores on Employee Attitudes."

[28]John Nalbandian, "Performance Appraisal: If Only People Were Not Involved," *Public Administration Review 41* (1981), 392–96.

[29]United States Merit Systems Protection Board, *Working for America*, p. 20.

[30] Ibid., p. 17.

DRUGS, AIDS, AND OTHER
HEALTH AND SAFETY ISSUES

The health and safety of public employees are important to public agency personnel managers for two reasons. First, health and safety are a sanction-related issue. In other words, these topics have become a significant concern of the employee-employer relationship. The regulations of the Occupational Safety and Health Act (OSHA), which protect employees against agency violations of health or safety standards, apply to public agencies as well as private companies. Second, this topic is a development-related issue because there is increasing evidence that healthier employees are more productive (and happier) than unhealthy ones. If the public service is indeed a national human resource, then preventive maintenance is necessary to reduce the cost of unscheduled downtime—not just in lost productivity, but also in health care and disability retirement costs. Third, because of the increasing cost of health care for employers, health and safety are an allocation issue for the employer. Healthy employees use less sick leave and have lower worker's compensation benefit costs.

Employees are not machines. Particularly under civil service systems, they have the right to constitutional protections against violations of privacy in their personal lives. Yet the high cost of employee illness and premature death makes it imperative that management create conditions which support the maintenance and rehabilitation of employees as human resources.

Some illustrations will provide evidence of the impact of employee health and safety on personnel systems and values. First, consider smoking, especially the conflict between efficiency and individual rights. Research has shown that firefighters who smoke are much more likely than their nonsmoking co-workers to develop heart and lung disorders that generate disability retirement and compensation claims. This has led to the development of programs for smoking cessation as a cost-effective "employee wellness" technique. Are employers also justified in prohibiting smoking in the workplace, or for rejecting applicants who smoke for firefighter positions? Second, consider drug testing. Employee abuse of alcohol and other drugs results in productivity losses and increased health-care costs and liability risks for employers. Is this sufficient justification for testing all employees for use of illegal drugs or alcohol abuse? If so, what should the employer do about employees who test positive?

By the end of this chapter, you will be able to:

1. Discuss the relationship between employee health and productivity, especially for employees in the primary labor market.
2. Discuss the sanctions applied to public employers through the Occupational Safety and Health Act (OSHA)
3. Explain what personnel directors can do to improve workplace health and safety.
4. Describe how smoking, alcoholism, drug abuse, and other treatable health concerns reduce productivity and increase health-care costs.
5. Evaluate the role of workplace substance abuse testing policies and programs.
6. Discuss the emergence of AIDS as a workplace health issue.
7. Discuss the role of the personnel manager in developing and supporting employee assistance programs as a way of responding to health issues.
8. Discuss the dilemmas personnel directors face in designing selection, development, and disciplinary action policies and procedures that balance agency concern for productivity with employee concerns for privacy.

EMPLOYEE HEALTH, SAFETY, AND PRODUCTIVITY

Dual labor markets imply different approaches toward productivity measurement and improvement. The primary labor market tends to regard employees as a capital asset whose value (measured in expected long-term productivity) can be enhanced or diminished by workplace policies and practices. Employers assume that employees hired through this market will be more productive if they are given autonomy or shared responsibility for performing a variety of tasks they can meaningfully relate to a significant outcome.[1] In both the public and the private sectors, personnel practices that derive from this model emphasize employee enrichment, involvement, commitment, flexibility, and teamwork.[2]

Employers who hire from the secondary labor market tend to define productivity as short-term efficiency. They regard employees as a production cost, and treat them as disposable commodities to be hired and fired as needed. Here the focus of productivity improvement is to reduce personnel costs by automation, to make jobs simple and routine so they can be done by employees with minimal skills and abilities, and to subcontract work out at lower wages.[3]

Although the secondary labor market has emerged because the work systems and personnel practices associated with it do reduce the employer's payroll costs and liability risks, their effect on employee productivity is not conclusive. For example, in the private sector IBM has adopted a high-skill employee empowerment approach as part of its full-employment, no layoffs policy. When managers at its Austin (Texas) plant estimated they could save $60 million by buying circuit boards elsewhere rather than manufacturing them, IBM management had other ideas. They cut costs by upgrading worker skills, organized workers into teams, and gave teams responsibility for quality control, repairs, and materials ordering. Skill requirements for manufacturing jobs were increased, and education and training costs increased to 5 percent of payroll. The bottom line result was that productivity increased over 200 percent, quality was up 500 percent, and inventory was cut 40 percent. The plant employs more people than ever before.[4]

In the public sector, Metro-Dade County Transit recently conducted an experiment under which some bus routes, and maintenance of the bus fleet assigned to them, were turned over to a private contractor. Comparable routes and maintenance activities were operated by the public transit system and its unionized workforce. Despite higher salaries for bus drivers and maintenance mechanics, the public system achieved lower operating and maintenance costs over a two-year period than did the private contractor.[5] And when the laid-off employees of the private transit company applied for work with the public transit system, many of them were found to be ineligible for employment due to invalid driver's licenses, accident records, or inability to pass drug tests.

Employees working under contracts, and especially those hired on a part-time, temporary, or seasonal basis, are likely to lack the career status and health and life insurance benefits that lead management to treat them as a human resource. They are likely to be hired when needed, and fired when they are no longer needed, or when they show signs of health problems that will reduce their productivity or increase their health-care costs. Employees hired within the political system lack career status, but they have also been able in many cases to use their collective political power to gain health insurance and pension benefits equal to or greater than those held by civil service employees. For example, under Florida state law, the groups receiving the highest state pension benefits relative to their contributions are members of high-risk civil service positions (state police)—and state judges and legislators!

But it is clear from these observations that employees, at least those working in civil service systems, are assets. The cost to an organization of employees' premature death, disability retirement, illness, and sick leave is tremendous. Given that healthy employees are more satisfied and productive, what can the personnel manager do to improve employee health and safety? Most experts agree that it is necessary to address this issue in two ways—systemic and individual. Systemic treatment addresses the employer's responsibilities for maintaining a safe and healthy workplace (under federal occupational safety and health legislation). Individual treatment focuses on the detection and treatment of dysfunctional, preventable employee practices. Naturally, it is easier to separate these categories analytically than in reality. Unsafe or unhealthy working conditions increase employee stress, and dysfunctional adaptations such as alcohol or drug abuse.

OCCUPATIONAL SAFETY AND HEALTH ACT (OSHA)

The prevention of work-related accidents is of primary concern to public personnel managers. In addition to the personal pain and suffering caused by these incidents, they are also significant because of associated organizational costs. These include not only the direct cost of reduced productivity, but the hidden costs of sick leave, employer insurance payments (for disability and worker's compensation policies), and the costs of processing or contesting disability retirement and worker's compensation claims. These costs represent billions of dollars annually. Moreover, some government employees (police officers and firefighters) receive occupational injuries and disability retirements at more than three times the rate of employees in other jobs.

The cost of work-related injuries and illnesses, and their social consequences, led the federal government to pass legislation regulating private and public employers. The Occupational Safety and Health Act (OSHA) was passed in 1970 to ensure that working conditions for all Americans meet minimum health and safety standards. Under the provisions of this act, the Occupational Safety and Health Administration (OSHA) in the Department of Labor was charged with setting health and safety standards, inspecting public agencies, and levying citations and penalties to enforce compliance.

While most of the OSHA regulations apply to industrial plants and private industry, many regulations apply to government agencies as well. Typical regulations for office buildings include standards for number and size of entrances, lighting, ventilation, fire protection, and first-aid facilities. OSHA field office employees inspect agencies routinely, and act upon reported violations or injuries. If the workplace does not meet standards, inspectors report violations and the field office director may impose financial penalties. While public agencies operating under civil service or political personnel systems are generally not subject to fines, they are subject to administrative sanctions like letters of reprimand.

For agencies operating under other personnel systems, OSHA compliance is accomplished through the contract negotiation and administration process. For services performed under contract, OSHA compliance is routinely required by contract provisions and enforced administratively through the contract compliance process. Under collective bargaining, unions will identify unsafe working conditions, bring them to the attention of state or federal OSHA officials, and monitor agency compliance. Lack of compliance will cause union officials to file grievances, or to apply direct political pressure on agency managers through elected officials. Some recent examples are the pressures exerted by postal workers, schoolteachers, and administrators to remove or contain the asbestos insulation used in many older buildings.

Both employers and employees have rights and responsibilities under OSHA. These are summarized in Table 11-1.

The Occupational Safety and Health Act does not establish standards for state and municipal agencies. Instead, it gives states the option of complying with established federal standards or of establishing standards at least as strict as the federal standards and enforcing them through a designated state agency. Most states have chosen the option of designating a state agency to administer the plan. If this second option is chosen, the state must develop standards at least as effective as those promulgated by the Occupational Health and Safety Administration under federal regulations; must staff the agency with qualified employees; and must submit required reports on agency compliance to the Department of Labor.

Table 11-1 indicates the effect of OSHA in sanctioning employers for unsafe working conditions and providing for employee rights in correcting these conditions. Both employer and employee responsibilities relate to the sanctions process. That is, they prescribe behavior and outline sanctions for noncompliance. Employer and employee rights relate to due process concerns for both parties. For example, the employee has the right not to be harassed for reporting a violation; the employer has the right to contest a

TABLE 11-1   Employer and Employee Rights and Responsibilities under OSHA

EMPLOYER RESPONSIBILITIES	EMPLOYEE RESPONSIBILITIES
1. Provide a hazard-free workplace and comply with OSHA rules, regulations, and standards	1. Read the OSHA poster at the job site
2. Inform all employees about OSHA and make copies of standards available for them to review upon request	2. Comply with all applicable OSHA standards
3. Furnish employees with safe tools and equipment	3. Follow all employer safety and health rules and regulations, and wear or use prescribed protective equipment while working
4. Establish, update, and communicate operating procedures to promote health and safety	4. Report hazardous conditions to the supervisor
5. Report fatal accidents to the nearest OSHA office within 48 hours	5. Report any job-related injury or illness to the employer and seek treatment promptly
6. Keep OSHA-required records of work-related injuries and illnesses, and post summary figures each February	6. Cooperate with the OSHA compliance officer conducting an inspection if he or she inquires about safety and health conditions in your work place
7. Cooperate with the OSHA compliance officer by providing names of authorized employee representatives for inspectors to accompany or consult with during inspections	7. Exercise your rights under the Act in a responsible manner
8. Not discriminate against employees who properly exercise their rights under OSHA	
9. Post OSHA citations of apparent violations and abate cited violations within the prescribed time period	

EMPLOYER RIGHTS	EMPLOYEE RIGHTS
1. Seek advice and off-site consultation by writing, calling, or visiting the nearest OSHA office (OSHA will not inspect merely because an employer requests help)	1. Review copies of any of the OSHA standards, rules, regulations, and requirements that the employer should have available at the work place
2. Be advised by an OSHA compliance officer of the reasons for an inspection	2. Request information from your employer on safety and health hazards, precautions that may be taken and procedures to be followed if involved in an accident
3. Have an opening and a closing conference with the inspection officer	3. Request (in writing) an OSHA inspection if you believe hazardous conditions exist
4. File a Notice of Contest with the nearest OSHA area director within 15 working days of receipt of a notice of citation and proposed penalty	

(continued)

TABLE 11-1 (*Continued*)

EMPLOYER RIGHTS	EMPLOYEE RIGHTS
5. Apply to OSHA for a temporary variance from a standard if you can furnish proof that chosen facilities or method of operation provide employee protection that is at least as effective as that required by the standard.	4. Have your name withheld from your employer, upon request to OSHA, if you file a written and signed complaint
6. Influence the development of job safety and health standards through participation in OSHA Standards Advisory Committees	5. Be advised of OSHA actions regarding your complaint and have informal review, if requested, of any decision not to make an inspection or not to issue a citation
	6. File a complaint to OSHA within 30 days if you believe you have been discriminated against because of asserting a right under the act, and be notified by OSHA of its determination within 90 days of filing
	7. Have an authorized employee representative accompany the OSHA compliance officer during the inspection tour
	8. Respond to questions from the OSHA compliance officer, particularly if there is no authorized employee representative accompanying the compliance officer
	9. Observe any monitoring or measuring of hazardous materials, and have the right of access to records on those materials
	10. Submit a written request to the National Institute for Occupational Safety and Health for information on whether any substance in your work place has potential toxic effects in the concentrations being used, and have your name withheld from your employer if you so wish
	11. Object to the abatement period set in the citation issued to your employer
	12. Be notified by your employer if he or she applies for a variance from an OSHA standard, testify at a variance hearing, and appeal the final decision if you disagree with it
	13. Submit information or comment to OSHA on the issuance, modification, or revocation of OSHA standards, and request a public hearing

Source: U.S. Department of Labor, *All About OSHA* (Washington, DC: U.S. Government Printing Office, April 1976).

violation notice. Both rights and responsibilities are part of the sanctions process.

IMPROVING WORKPLACE HEALTH AND SAFETY

Public personnel managers can exert great influence on several aspects of an organization that affect occupational health and safety. These include workplace conditions, selection criteria, employee orientation procedures, reward systems, training, and job design.

They can improve workplace conditions by aiding facilities managers and safety engineers to correct unsafe working conditions reported by employees or supervisors. If other managers object to the cost and inconvenience of safety regulations, the personnel director can provide them with information on the costs of noncompliance in terms of job-related injuries, worker's compensation insurance rates, disability retirement, and grievances.

They can investigate jobs that have a high rate of job-related injuries to determine if the incidence of accidents or injuries is less among certain groups of employees than others. If patterns emerge, they can use these data to develop valid selection criteria. But because such practices can act to exclude high-risk groups from consideration for positions, they must carefully document the relationship between the selection criterion and the reduction of health and safety risks, and compare this reduction to the impact on the employment rights of affected employees or applicants.

Preemployment physicals are routinely used to exclude applicants whose medical history places them at risk. But the Supreme Court also recently (1991) overturned selection standards under which chemical companies refused to employ females of childbearing age in positions in which there was risk of exposure to chemical toxins that could cause birth defects in unborn children. In the first example, courts have held that the risk to the employer outweighs the right of the individual applicant to be considered for jobs for which they are interested and qualified. In the second example, the Supreme Court has ruled that the risk of birth defects and subsequent lawsuits is relatively slight compared to the employment rights of the affected individuals.

Employee orientation programs should contain information on work safety, potentially hazardous conditions that may be encountered on the job, emergency evacuation procedures, the location of fire extinguishers and alarms, and procedures for reporting job-related injuries or illnesses. This will reinforce the importance of health and safety for supervisors and employees. It will also minimize the employer's financial and legal liability for workplace injuries and accidents. If employees have read and signed policies for reporting accidents, they will be ineligible for disability benefits based on claims of accidents or injuries that were not reported at the time. This is the basis of requirements in many police and fire departments, where some slight chance of blood-to-blood contact exists during the performance of job duties, that police officers or firefighters who suspect they may have contracted AIDS through job-related contact be given an AIDS antibody test immediately. If the test is positive, the employer can claim immunity because the lengthy incubation period for the virus (at least 6 months) guarantees that it was not contracted on the job. If the test is negative, and remains negative when the employee is retested in six months, the incident can be dismissed as unrelated to any disability or illness. Only in those cases where the employee initially tests negative and subsequently tests positive (and there are no demonstrable lifestyle choices that can be claimed as causal factors) will the employer be liable for damages.

The growth of training and orientation programs as a means of increasing employee health and safety are definitely an outgrowth of risk management—the organization's ability to compare the cost of a program with the cost of a problem, and to determine that in many cases prevention is cheaper than treatment or litigation. However, neither feedback nor training will be effective at inducing compliance unless employees and supervisors are rewarded for safety. Since most local governments are self-insured, it makes sense to pass on some of the savings from safety to responsible employees through incentive programs. For example, some cities award savings bonds to employees whose job duties require the use of a city car, and who drive for a year or more without any chargeable accidents (those attributable to traffic violations).

It is important not only to reward employees for safe work habits, but also to reward their supervisors for recognizing, evaluating, and controlling occupational health and safety hazards. This means publicizing the agency's record of time lost through work-related accidents or injuries, comparing this with other work units or over time, and using compensation and disability payouts as one measure of the supervisor's performance evaluation. Granted, supervisors cannot control all the unsafe conditions inherent in a job. But they can work with employees on safer ways of handling jobs, and with top management on ways of designing work so that it can be performed with less risk to employees.

In many cases, high accident rates are caused by faulty job design. A job that is alternately boring and stressful, or a job that requires the use of dangerous equipment, increases the risk to the employee. Perhaps the personnel department can redesign the work procedure to reduce these factors. For example, many nurses are physically unable to lift and move heavy patients, so hospitals have assigned this duty to male nurses' aides or orderlies. Yet hospitals are frequently understaffed, particularly on the night shift, so nurses often end up doing this themselves. The result can be a disabling back injury. This situation could be prevented by greater recognition of the costs of not filling nurses' aide positions, or by redesigning the nurse's job not to include lifting heavy patients.

THE EFFECTS OF ALCOHOL AND DRUG ABUSE

There is ample evidence that preventable risk factors (such as smoking, alcoholism, and drug abuse) are major workplace health issues because of lost productivity, increased liability risks, and increased health care costs.

Smoking

Many municipal fire departments are refusing to hire smokers as firefighters because smoking increases the likelihood that firefighters will subsequently be eligible for workers' compensation or disability retirement due to heart and lung disease, and because courts and disability claims examiners have routinely held these conditions to be job-related. Even for general employees, research has shown that smoking is linked to increased risk of cancer, heart attacks, and strokes. Smoking costs employers $25.8 billion in productivity each year, including costs for medical care, absenteeism, premature retirement and early death.[6] According to a 1982 study, excess insurance costs for each smoker average $247–$347 annually.[7]

As a result of these escalating costs, 16 states and more than 340 localities require at least some smoking restrictions in private businesses; 32 states regulate smoking by public employees in the workplace.[8] Agencies usually implement smoking policies in response to complaints by nonsmokers about the effects of co-workers' smoke, or to reflect management's overall interest in employee health. Usually, an exploratory survey by the personnel department to assess employee attitudes toward smoking will show that relatively few people smoke, and that many who do are willing to limit their use of tobacco on the job. A 1985 Gallup poll found that 80 percent of smokers, 92 percent of non-smokers, and 89 percent of former smokers feel company policies should designate specific non-smoking and smoking areas or ban smoking altogether.

Employee cooperation with smoking policies can best be achieved by managerial compliance with the policies, union involvement, the availability of smoking cessation programs offered by the employer, and passing some of the savings along to nonsmoking employees in the form of lower health insurance premiums or health benefit costs. In cases where consensus and voluntary compliance are ineffective, it is sometimes necessary for the agency to discipline employees who violate no-smoking policies, or to defend its no-smoking policies in court (as an example of its responsibility to provide employees with a healthy and safe workplace).

Alcohol Abuse

A joke made the rounds among personnel directors twenty years ago when many of them were grappling for the first time with affirmative action reporting requirements. Late one night, a weary personnel director was completing an EEOC form requiring him to specify the number of employees in each work unit, "broken down by sex." Puzzled, he wrote the following response in the margin: "None. Our problem seems to be alcohol."

Productivity losses from employee alcohol abuse include those resulting from impaired performance, absenteeism, injuries, and fatalities.[9] One Fortune 500 company released profiles of the typical drug abuser indicating that, in comparison with the typical employee, this person functions at about 67 percent of potential, is 3.6 times as likely to be involved in an accident, receives three times the average level of health-care benefits, is five times as likely to file a compensation claim and more likely to file grievances, and misses more that ten times as many work days![10]

It is estimated that between 12 and 15 percent of any given workforce will be substance abusers at any one time.[11] And this does not include the 35 percent of the work force whose use of tobacco also raises health and productivity concerns. Experts estimate that employees who are substance abusers produce 30 to 35 percent less than other employees.[12] Beyond direct productivity impacts, studies have shown that employees do not like to work with others who are substance abusers because this tends to reduce their own morale and productivity. These costs add up—most knowledgeable observers say the annual toll in lost productivity is at least $100 billion. The National Institute of Drug Abuse (NIDA) estimates $42 billion annually is lost in production and higher medical bills.[13] The U.S. Chamber of Commerce claims $60–$100 billion annually is lost in productivity alone.[14] In data which are dated but still indicative of the extent of the problem, the Research Triangle Institute reported in 1986 that the cost of reduced productivity from alcohol abuse alone in 1980 was $50.6 billion, with an additional $25.7 billion for other drugs.[15] The National Institute on Alcohol Abuse and Alcoholism concluded that alcoholism accounts for about 105,000 deaths each year, and would cost the nation an estimated $136 billion in lost employment, reduced productivity, and health-care costs in 1990.[16] In 1983, from alcohol alone, there were 10 million injuries (2 million of which were disabling), and 18,000 fatalities.[17]

While it is difficult to separate the effects of substance abuse from other causes of increased health-care costs (such as changes in technology, the aging population, and the practice of defensive medicine), many observers claim that substance abuse results in higher health-care costs for employers. According to one estimate, it increased the cost of health insurance as much as 170 percent in three years for several major plans.[18]

Last, substance abuse increases liability risks for employers because of the increased chance of performance impairments that will affect customers, co-workers, or the public.[19] These can include injuries or deaths resulting from assaults or accidents with vehicles and equipment. One major private corporation recently paid millions of dollars to the victims and survivors of an auto accident caused by one of its employees. The circumstances? The employee had shown up for work intoxicated, and had been immediately ordered to go home by the supervisor. The court ruled that even though the employee was primarily responsible for the accident, the employer was also responsible because the employee had been involved in the accident while following a supervisory order. (A better supervisory response might have been to call a cab and put the employee in it!)

SUBSTANCE ABUSE TESTING POLICIES AND PROGRAMS

Major private- and public-sector employers throughout the United States have responded to the problem of substance abuse by agreeing that a substance-abuse-free workplace is desirable. Most employers have moved to create this situation by testing all job applicants, and also employees under some conditions.

Because random testing of all employees raises profound issues concerning employees' legal rights, testing in public agencies was initiated by the federal government for military personnel (whose constitutional protections against due process and invasion of privacy are already circumscribed by the Uniform Code of Military Justice). Testing first occurred in 1981, followed by testing of civilian employees within the Department of Defense in 1985.[20] In September 1986, President Reagan expanded substance abuse testing of federal employees by issuing Executive Order 12564 (Drug Free Federal Work Place). This order provided for mandatory drug testing for federal employees occupying sensitive positions—those with access to classified data, or those considered to affect public health and safety.

State and local governments followed. Because of the number and variety of local governments, it is difficult to develop a comprehensive view of drug testing policies and practices. However, some general trends are clear.[21] Most large cities and counties have policies on drug and alcohol abuse, or are in the process of adopting them. Most of these policies provide for the mandatory testing of applicants, primarily police officers, firefighters, and transit drivers. In almost all cases, those who test positive are not offered employment (though in many cases applicants may reapply after six months or a year).

In many cases, the policies adopted by local and state governments also call for the testing of employees. This is a more troublesome issue because civil service employees generally have greater rights under constitutional law and collective bargaining agreements than do applicants. If employees are tested, it is usually on the basis of performance incidents or upon the supervisor's reasonable suspicion. Employees who test positive are referred to an employee assistance program for counseling rehabilitation; refusal to enter the program, or positive drug tests after completion of rehabilitation, are usually considered grounds for continued disciplinary action.

THE EMERGENCE OF AIDS AS A WORKPLACE HEALTH ISSUE

AIDS was first reported in the United States in 1981. Since that time, the U.S. Public Health Service has received reports that almost 100,000 persons have contracted AIDS, and over half of them have died of the disease.[22] It is currently estimated that 1.5 million people have the virus, of whom any number between 30 and 99 percent can be expected to contract full-blown AIDS.

AIDS is a progressive disease. Although there are drugs that will slow its advance or prevent those carrying the virus from developing symptoms of the disease itself, the disease is invariably fatal once the victim's immune system has been destroyed. Although there is an increasing rate of heterosexual transmission, AIDS has been transmitted primarily by unsafe homosexual practices, needle sharing by intravenous drug addicts, and transfusions of blood from infected donors.

The health-care costs of AIDS are enormous. Early studies estimated a cost of $61,000–$94,000 per person from onset to death, but these figures were based on a brief life span from onset to death (1 to 3 years), and extensive use of volunteer patient care providers from within the gay community. As AIDS is detected earlier, and patients survive longer, life span estimates have now increased to 7 to 10 years. And the magnitude of the AIDS epidemic has increased far beyond the abilities of volunteer social service agencies to provide treatment. This means that health-care providers must be increasingly used, at a far greater cost.[23]

AIDS is beginning to be a workplace problem for two distinct groups of employees. The group that runs the greatest risk of contracting AIDS are the health-care workers (doctors, dentists, nurses, dental hygienists, laboratory technicians, paramedics) whose jobs involve working with the body fluids of AIDS patients. There is a very slight chance that one of these workers can become infected through an accidental needle stick from a syringe containing blood from an infected person, or by blood from an infected person entering the employee's bloodstream through a cut.

Although patients may have a strong reaction to being treated by a health-care worker who has AIDS, there is no possibility that AIDS can be transmitted if the employee is following the safety precautions required by hospitals and other agencies to prevent the spread of blood-borne diseases. However, there is a possibility that other opportunistic infections to which the AIDS victim is susceptible may be transmitted from employees to patients through workplace contact, especially to patients whose immune systems may be weakened by the conditions for which they are hospitalized.

The second group is composed of those who have AIDS victims among their co-workers. While these employees are in absolutely no danger of contracting AIDS from a co-worker under normal working conditions, the fear and denial that AIDS generates among employees and their families can cause the issue to give rise to serious personnel problems. For example, employees (or their union representatives) might demand that employees with the AIDS virus be identified and isolated or discharged to prevent them from infecting others, even if there is no chance of the infection being transmitted in the ordinary course of job duties. Employees with the AIDS virus might demand confidentiality and the right not to be discriminated against in personnel actions on the basis of a handicap, as long as they can continue to do their jobs.

Thus, AIDS generates increased concern among employers about liability risks and employee productivity. But these are relatively simple issues to address, at least in theory. Liability risks for contracting AIDS can be minimized or eliminated (for that small group of employees whose jobs require it) by developing protective policies to eliminate the risk of exchanging body fluids. Liability issues for other positions can be dealt with by educating employees about the impossibility of contracting AIDS in the workplace. Concerns for productivity can be met by developing clear policies designed to determine whether an AIDS carrier can perform the duties of the position. The desired outcome is a balanced approach reflecting the employer's desire to make reasonable accommodation to the AIDS victim while this person is still healthy enough to perform the primary duties of the position, and to clarify policies with respect to sick leave, disability retirement, and dependent benefits once the person is forced by failing health to leave the workforce.

But tremendous pressure is being exerted on employers by the health insurance industry. Obviously, it is in their best interest to identify carriers of the AIDS virus prior to employment, and to have AIDS or AIDS-related diseases excluded from coverage as preexisting conditions. Similarly, it is in the employer's best interest to do this if the agency is self-insured. Some employers who want to treat AIDS as an exclusionary precondition may also discriminate against homosexuals in hiring on the basis that they are members of a high-risk group. These pressures cause a fundamental conflict between the values of individual rights (for AIDS victims, homosexuals, and their co-workers) and efficiency (defined as reduced health-care costs and employee productivity).

The traditional response of employers to this dilemma has been identical to the response of individuals and public policy makers—first denial, then panic, and last the development of clear and reasonable policies. And health and life insurance companies are taking the lead in spurring their corporate and agency clients to move quickly from denial to policy making in this area.[24]

As a workplace issue, AIDS is beginning to become critically important because of its implications for productivity and liability. Most of all, the potentially huge losses it threatens for health insurance carriers or self-insured employers means that it brings two fundamental values into open conflict. Under penalty of lawsuit for violation of handicap protection laws (such as Section 504 of the Vocational Rehabilitation Act, or the Americans with Disabilities Act), applicants and employees who carry the AIDS virus have the right to a job as long as they can perform its primary duties with reasonable modifications by the employer.[25] But no employer or health insurance carrier would make a voluntary, rational decision to employ an applicant knowing that this person would only live a few more years, and would cost the employer $100,000–$250,000 in health care from onset until death.

Employers are only now beginning to address this dilemma. They are being urged to do so by insurance companies, which are confronted by this dilemma right now. The result, one hopes, will be the development of AIDS policies by employers, and increased education of employees and managers.[26] What is not being addressed now is the related issue of discrimination in employment based on sexual orientation. While it may be rational not to employ someone who has AIDS, it is not rational or fair to refuse to hire homosexuals—AIDS is spread by high-risk behaviors rather than by high-risk groups. If insurance companies and employers cannot discriminate against African-Americans who are at greater risk of hypertension than Anglos, what justification can be given for allowing them to discriminate against homosexuals based on sexual orientation? As a society, under what conditions are we willing to create a "protected class" (as we have done with minorities, handicapped persons and women through civil rights legislation)?

EMPLOYEE ASSISTANCE PROGRAM (EAPS) AND EMPLOYEE HEALTH

Consistent with the view of employees as human resources is the value of health promotion programs as preventive maintenance. This is done primarily through Employee Assistance Programs (EAPs), whose purpose is to diagnose, treat, and rehabilitate employees whose personal problems are interfering with work performance. Usually, employers contract with a private group to provide preventive, diagnostic, and treatment programs. In this way, the personnel function in an agency is expanded without directly increasing the size of the personnel department itself. From the employee's viewpoint, the objective is to treat personal problems before they have an irreparable effect on job status.[27] From the employer's viewpoint, the objective is to rehabilitate employees whose personal problems are a threat to productivity, health-care costs, or legal liability; and to lay the groundwork for possible disciplinary action and discharge (if the employee cannot be rehabilitated) before these threats become a reality.)[28]

Over time, both the functions of the EAP and the role of the supervisor have changed substantially and rapidly. First, while the traditional EAP was charged almost exclusively with confronting the problem of alcohol abuse, the contemporary EAP also addresses drug abuse, AIDS education, and a range of other personal problems that may affect job performance (family problems, emotional and psychiatric problems, legal counseling, financial counseling).[29]

This increase in the range of functions performed by the EAP has meant that responsibility for the diagnosis and treatment of personal problems is no longer a supervisory responsibility, if indeed it ever was. Today the supervisor is expected to observe and record changes in employee behavior and job performance. This is the documentation that can be used to discipline employees, and to refer them to the EAP for professional diagnosis and treatment.

And while EAP proponents may take heart from statistics chronicling the growth in the number of EAPs or the range of functions they perform, other observers might reasonably wonder whether focusing attention on whether or not employees are covered by an EAP only serves to deflect attention from how effective they are. By focusing attention on the number of EAPs, or the number of employees covered by them, researchers tend to ignore more critical substantive issues: Have employers endorsed the concept of the EAP for its value in rehabilitation and productivity, or as a sort of legal insurance policy against employee grievances and lawsuits arising out of disciplinary action?[30]

EAPs are important in AIDS prevention and treatment from two perspectives. First, they are responsible for counseling employees and families of AIDS victims concerning their employment rights and health benefits. Second, they are responsible for developing and presenting educational programs to reduce employees' irrational fear of catching AIDS in the workplace. In the case of health-care employers, the EAP must develop educational programs to train employees how to eliminate the risk of catching AIDS in the workplace while continuing to provide compassionate and professional health care to patients who have the disease.

BALANCING ORGANIZATIONAL EFFECTIVENESS AND EMPLOYEE RIGHTS

The issues discussed in this chapter pose tough dilemmas for human resource managers because they underscore the conflict between two legitimate and fundamental values—organizational efficiency and employee rights. This dilemma raises many practical and legal issues with respect to several types of personnel decisions: substance abuse policies, AIDS policies, and the general use of medical screening factors to exclude high-risk applicants from the workplace.

Substance Abuse

With respect to drug testing, the primary practical issue for personnel directors is whether rejecting applicants and disciplining employees who test positive is a useful way of stopping employee drug abuse. The primary legal issue is whether personnel policies or practices should distinguish between legal drugs (alcohol and prescription drugs) and illegal ones.[31] Ethically sensitive personnel directors may also wonder if substance abuse has a greater effect on employee job performance than employees' personalities, family problems, debts, mental illness, or other issues. Once managers admit that some employees have a substance abuse problem, the agency is legally and politically bound to do something about it (though the economic costs of treatment and the legal risks of liability may make an "ostrich" approach more attractive to management).

Agencies that test current employees do so primarily based upon incidents or reasonable suspicion, as defined by the supervisor. But because the use of drugs is not clearly and directly related to work performance, it does not seem reasonable to expect that supervisors can identify or refer employees suspected of substance abuse skillfully and equitably, particularly in the face of union opposition and due process protections. Instead, in the absence of clear guidelines and rewards, they are more likely to avoid these risks by declining to identify suspected substance abusers or to refer them for testing and treatment. If substance-abuse testing is to work, we must face the issue of how to sell it to supervisors.

Most employers report that they have employee assistance programs (EAPs), and that these help employees with abuse problems. These are commendable responses. But do we really solve a problem by creating an organizational unit (such as affirmative action, collective bargaining, risk management), and then assigning troublesome problems to it? Given the uncertain adequacy of their location, mission, budget, and objectives, can EAPs provide the quality of testing and rehabilitative services needed to meet this crisis, at a price agencies and their employees can afford?

AIDS

AIDS is at present less of a workplace problem than is substance abuse. But it is a more frightening issue to employees, and raises fundamental questions about protecting the rights of victims, while at the same time educating the workforce to prevent panicky reactions. On the risk-management side, it means treating AIDS like any other life-threatening illness, while recognizing that insurance carriers will have a vested interest in excluding AIDS carriers from the workplace. But in reality, the lengthy incubation period for AIDS means that even screening applicants (which is illegal in public agencies) is not an effective technique for preventing them from entering the workforce.

Exclusion of High-Risk Applicants

Whenever possible, given the limits of available technology and the applicability of handicap laws protecting applicant rights,[32] employers have sought to reduce benefit costs by excluding high-risk applicants (including drug abusers and AIDS carriers) from "permanent" employment in the primary labor market.[33] The ability to predict long-term health risks by evaluating employee health profiles was originally developed as a component of employee wellness programs to prevent the occurrence of serious health problems among current employees. But because "permanent" employees incur high benefit costs,[34] and because these costs correlate with health indicators, medical health indicators are also being used as selection criteria.[35] In selecting applicants for positions filled through the primary labor market, employers are moving from narrowly focused screening methods (such as the use of back X rays to determine whether laborers are physically able to lift or carry) to more generalized health indicators which may indicate that the applicant is a long-term health risk because his or her general health indicators are outside normal limits.[36] Examples: abnormal weight to height, abnormal electrocardiogram, abnormal blood chemistry (such as cholesterol levels), history of heavy drinking (as determined by liver enzyme activity), history of substance abuse (as determined by urinalysis), or likelihood of developing AIDS (as determined by AIDS antibody tests).[37]

SUMMARY

At least in civil service systems, employees are considered an asset rather than a production cost. This means that employee health and safety are important from the viewpoint of maintaining human resources as an asset and reducing the health-care costs and liability risks generated by unsafe or unhealthy workplace conditions. Personnel directors have a critical role to play in assessing and eliminating systemic practices and individual lifestyle choices that are unproductive for the agency. This includes occupational safety and health, smoking, drug and alcohol abuse, and AIDS.

Many public personnel directors justifiably view controversial topics such as AIDS education or substance abuse policy as risks because these issues confront them with unavoidable conflicts among key human resource management values—responsiveness to elected officials, administrative efficiency, and protection of employee rights. But these issues also present personnel directors with opportunities to play a critical role in the resolution of emergent public policy. The significance the personnel director attaches to these issues correlates highly with whether the agency has developed policies in this area. The professionalism of the public personnel director, and the personnel director's view of himself or herself within the agency, is a key factor in the extent to which innovative employee wellness policies and programs are adopted.[38]

KEY TERMS

ADA (Americans with Disabilities Act)
AIDS
drug testing
Employee Assistance Program (EAP)
lifestyle choices
medical risk factors
Occupational Safety and Health Act (OSHA)
Occupational Safety and Health Administration (OSHA)
smoking cessation program
substance abuse
substance abuse testing
wellness program

DISCUSSION QUESTIONS

1. What is the relationship between employee health and productivity?
2. What is the Occupational Safety and Health Act (OSHA)? What does it require of employers?
3. What can personnel directors do to improve workplace health and safety?
4. How does employee substance abuse affect productivity, liability, and risk management?

5. What policies and programs have employers adopted to combat work-place substance abuse?
6. Why is AIDS a workplace health issue for public agencies? For health care employers?
7. What are Employee Assistance Programs (EAPs)? What is their role with respect to workplace substance abuse and AIDS?
8. What dilemmas do public personnel directors face in designing selection, development, and disciplinary action policies and procedures that balance agency concerns for productivity with employee concerns for privacy and individual rights? How should they resolve these dilemmas?

CASE STUDY: DEVELOPING A WORKPLACE AIDS POLICY

You are the personnel director of a state government agency. Top management and employees have both been putting pressure on you to develop a comprehensive agency policy for AIDS and other life-threatening diseases. Because the agency does not provide health-care services, there is no risk of blood-to-blood contact in the course of employees' job duties.

Questions:

1. What would be the major components of your policy?
2. How would you "sell" it to employees and management?
3. What would be the role of the employee assistance program? How would you evaluate the effectiveness of its services?

NOTES

[1]J. Hackman and G. Oldham, *Work Redesign* (Reading, MA: Addison-Wesley, 1980), p. 90.

[2]V. Kafka, "A New Look at Motivation-for-Productivity," *Supervisory Management 31* (April 1988), 19.

[3]S. Yoder, "Putting It All Together," *Workplace of the Future, The Wall Street Journal Reports*, June 4, 1990, pp. R24–R26.

[4]A. Karr, "Workplace Panel Is Urging Changes in Schools, On Job," *The Wall Street Journal*, June 19, 1990, p. C-15.

[5]E. Talley, "Public-Transit Privatization is a Failure," *The Miami Herald*, October 8, 1990, p. 10A.

[6]Syd Teague, "Smoke Gets in Your Eyes: The Hazard of Second-hand Smoke," *Heart Corps*, January-February 1990, p. 60.

[7]D. Kent and L. Cenci, "Smoking and the Workplace," *Journal of Medicine*, June 1982, p. 470.

[8]Barbara Trenk, "Clearing the Air about Smoking Policies," *Management Review*, April 1989, p. 32.

[9]J. Lodge, "Drugs: Abuse is an Economic Issue, *Credit 13* (1987), 28–29.

[10]E. Greenberg, "To Test or Not to Test: Drugs and the Workplace," *Management Review* 12 (March 1987), 24.

[11]T. J. Delaney, Jr., "The EAP Part of the Personnel Function," *Public Personnel Management 16* (1987), p. 359.

[12]T. Nutile, "Business Battles Enemy That Costs $71 billion," *Boston Herald*, February 1, 1988, p. 2.

[13]P. V. Lyons, "EAPs the Only Real Cure," *Management Review 12* (March 1987), 38.

[14]Theodore Rosen, "Identification of Substance Abusers in the Workplace, *Public Personnel Management 16* (1987), p. 200.

[15]Rosen, *Ibid.*, p. 198.

[16]S. Nazario, "Alcohol Is Linked to a Gene," *The Wall Street Journal*, April 18, 1990, p. B1.

[17]Rosen, p. 198.

[18]R. Donkin, "New Hope for Diagnosing Alcoholism," *Business & Health*, April 1989, pp. 20–23.

[19]Donald Klingner, "The Personal Liability of State and Local Personnel Directors: Legal, Organizational, and Ethical Implications," *Public Personnel Management 17*, 1 (1988), 125–133.

[20]Department of Defense Directive 1010.9 as cited in *National Federation of Government Employees* v. *Weinberger*, 640 F. Supp. 642 (D.C. Cir. 1986), rev'd and remanded, 919 f.2nd 935 (D.C. Cir. 1987).

[21]Donald Klingner, Nancy O'Neill, and Mohamed Sabet, "Drug Testing in Public Agencies: Are Public Personnel Directors Doing Things Right?" *Public Personnel Management 19*, 4 (Winter 1990), 391–97.

[22]H. Makadon, F. Seage III, K. Thorpe, and H. Fineberg, "Paying the Medical Cost of the HIV Epidemic: A Review of Policy Options," *Journal of Acquired Immune Deficiency Syndromes 3* (1990), 123–33.

[23]*Ibid.*

[24]C. Woolsey, "AIDS Effort Praised: Life Insurer Called Leader in Workplace Education," *Business Insurance*, January 8, 1990, pp. 2, 4.

[25]*School Board of Nassau County Fla* v. *Arline*, 107 S. Ct. 1123 (1987); and *Shuttleworth* v. *Broward County*, 639 F. Supp. (S.D. Fla. 1986).

[26]Makadon, Seage, Thorpe, and Fineberg, "Paying the Medical Cost of the HIV Epidemic."

[27]R. Sloan and J. Gruman, "Participation in Workplace Health Promotion Programs: The Contribution of Health and Organizational Factors," *Health Education Quarterly 15*, 3 (Fall, 1988), 269–288.

[28]M. Bowers, D. DeCenzo, C. Walton, and W. Grazer, "What Do Employers See as the Benefits of Assistance Programs?" *Risk Management 36*, 10 (October 1989), 46–50.

[29]C. Brumback, "EAPs: Bringing Health and Productivity to the Workplace" *Business 37* (April-June 1987), 42–45.

[30]A. Starr and G. Byram, "Cost/Benefit Analysis for Employee Assistance Programs," *Personnel Administrator 30*, 8 (August, 1985), 55–60.

[31]William Staudenmeier, Jr., "Content and Variation in Employer Policies on Alcohol," *The Journal of Drug Issues 17*, 5 (1987), 255–71.

[32]J. Jenks, "Protecting Privacy Rights," *Personnel Journal 66* (September 1987), 123–26.

[33]Donald Klingner, Nancy O'Neill and Mohamed Sabet, "Drug Testing in Public Agencies;" and Dale Masi, "Company Response to Drug Abuse from the AMA's National Survey," *Personnel 63* (March 1987), 40–46.

[34]R. Holton, "AIDS in the Workplace: Underwriting Update," *Best's Review, Property-*

Casualty Edition, September 1988, pp. 96–98; and A. Solovy, "Insurers, HMOs and BC-BS Plans Talk About AIDS," *Hospitals 63* (January 20, 1989), 24.

[35]M. Rowe, M. Russell-Einhorn, and J. Weinstein, "New Issues in Testing the Work Force: Genetic Diseases," *Labor Law Journal 38* (August 1987), 518–23.

[36]L. Uzych, "HIV Testing: The Legal Balance Between Individual and Societal Rights," *Southern Medical Journal 83*, 3 (March 1990), 303–7.

[37]K. Slater, "Likely Methuselahs Get More Life-Insurance Breaks," *The Wall Street Journal*, June 7, 1990, pp. C1, C8.

[38]The Clearinghouse is currently conducting additional research on the relationship to substance abuse testing of other variables such as agency structure, functions of the personnel department, and the professionalism of public personnel directors.

CHAPTER

12

ORGANIZATIONAL JUSTICE

In 1981 Ardith McPherson was a clerk in the sheriff's office in Harris County, Texas. While at work she was talking to her boyfriend about President Reagan's social policies when it was announced over the radio that the president had been shot. Not knowing anyone else was in the room, she was overheard saying to her boyfriend, "If they go for him again, I hope they get him." The sheriff fired her, claiming she was not a suitable law enforcement employee. McPherson claimed her constitutional right to express herself had been violated by the dismissal. The case went all the way to the Supreme Court.[1] Does McPherson have a constitutional right to speak out in this way? Has she been treated unfairly? If McPherson had been employed by a private security agency and her boss had fired her under the same circumstances, would she have been able to make a claim that her right to free speech had been violated? In this case, the Supreme Court sided with McPherson, 5–4.

By the end of this chapter you will be able to:

1. Identify the ways an organization establishes and maintains the terms of the employment relationship between employee and employer and discuss the concept of organizational justice.

2. Describe the rights of employees who have been sexually harassed or who are considered whistleblowers.

3. Discuss the balance the Court examines when deciding whether a public employer has violated an employee's First Amendment right to free speech and when a drug testing program violates an employee's Fourth Amendment rights.

4. Describe the role of property rights and due process in establishing and maintaining the terms of the employment relationship.

5. Discuss how discipline and grievance procedures are connected to the sanction function.

6. Diagram a typical disciplinary procedure and describe various steps in a grievance procedure.

7. Describe the ways different personnel systems view the sanction function.

8. Describe the relationship between disciplinary action and other personnel activities.

THE SANCTION FUNCTION

Every organization, public or private, must establish and maintain *terms of the relationship between employee and employer*. This is called the sanction function, and it is the last of the four core functions. The terms of the employment relationship are captured in expectations employees have of their employer and contributions employees are willing to make in order to have their expectations fulfilled. Similarly, employers have expectations of employees and make contributions to employees in order to have those expectations fulfilled. The heart of the sanction function involves the interplay of these various expectations and contributions or obligations.

The terms in an employment relationship commonly include wages and working conditions. These generally are tangible factors that can be established precisely in writing. But the expectations that employees and employers have of one another go beyond the tangible. Employees often expect that their employer will provide "interesting work," "opportunities for advancement," and "recognition." Employers often expect "an honest day's work," "loyalty and commitment," "cooperation and harmony."

Establishing Expectations

There are several formal mechanisms by which these tangible terms, and sometimes the intangible ones as well, are established. The first is the personnel manual, which contains the policies, rules, regulations, procedures and practices that constitute a particular personnel system. For example, there may be a policy giving priority to promoting from within. There may be rules limiting political activity of employees while on the job. There may be a policy about bonuses or pay for performance. These policies and rules constitute some of the terms of the employment relationship.

Second, in some jurisdictions, the terms of the employment relationship are established through collective bargaining between employer and union. These terms are contained in working rules mutually agreed upon by employer and union membership. Third, various local, state, and federal laws establish expectations and obligations of employees and employer. For example, legislatures establish pay rates for public employees; the Fair Labor Standards Act describes required compensation policies; the Civil Rights Act of 1964 proscribes various forms of discrimination in employment; The Hatch Act and its counterparts in state and local governments proscribe political activity by employees. These and other laws contain provisions that affect the expectations and obligations employees and employers have of one another.

Last, the sanction function in public employment differs fundamentally from private employment because public employees have certain rights conferred upon them by the U. S. Constitution. Citizens are protected from government action by the Bill of Rights, including the Fourteenth amendment. When citizens become employees of the government, they give up some of those rights, but they still have substantially more protection in speech, association, privacy, and equal treatment than do employees of private employers. We will discuss these protections later in the chapter.

Maintaining Expectations

Various processes maintain and enforce the terms established through these four mechanisms. Commonly, we think of employees suing their employer for violating some employee right. But more commonly, it is an organization's discipline and grievance procedure that maintains the terms of the employment relationship or contract. Most disagreements are handled informally between supervisor and employee, but when informal channels are inadequate formal discipline and grievance procedures are invoked. Sometimes, if those prove ineffective in resolving differences, the employee takes judicial action or complains directly to political leaders.

An employee is disciplined when the employer believes the employee is not living up to the terms of the employment contract. Usually, this means that the employee is not contributing to the organization in the way the employer expects. On the other hand, when the employee believes the employer has violated its obligations, the employee "grieves" the employer's action, setting in motion some review. In large measure, the quality of the grievance processes due an employee subject to discipline determines whether employees believe they have been treated with equity and dignity. (We will discuss discipline and grievance procedures in more detail later in the chapter.)

ORGANIZATIONAL JUSTICE: COMPETING PERCEPTIONS OF FAIRNESS

Organizational justice concerns the degree of fairness in the employment relationship. In the simplest terms, fairness can be measured in the confidence employees have that they will be treated equitably and with dignity. More formally, organizational justice centers on the fairness employees associate with their own and the organization's expectations and obligations—their substance and how they are established and maintained. But even this formal description does not describe the concept because it suggests that fairness is derived only from the employee's perspective. The concept of justice in organizations is complicated because individual rights are expressed in an environment where demands for administrative efficiency, political responsiveness, and social equity compete for the attention of various stakeholders. It is probably more accurate to suggest that organizational justice involves the perceptions of organizational stakeholders—a much broader term than employees alone—about the fairest balance between various organizational values and individual rights. In this sense, we can see how in the same organization different perceptions of justice may exist because different people weigh the values differently. Further, we might suggest that the more agreement between stakeholders, especially employees and managers, on the appropriate balance between the values, the more likely the organization will be perceived as being just.

An example of the tension between individual rights and administrative efficiency is captured by Justice Marshall in his dissent in *Skinner v. Railway Labor Executives' Association* (1989). In this important drug testing case he writes: "The majority ignores the text and doctrinal history of the Fourth Amendment, which require that highly intrusive searches of this type be based on probable cause, not on the evanescent cost-benefit calculations of agencies or judges."[2] At its core, administrative efficiency is captured in the concept of cost-benefit analysis and pursuing the greatest good for the greatest number. Yet individuals clearly are protected from illegal search and seizure by the Fourth Amendment to the Constitution. This is a right, and public employees enjoy it, even if employees of private firms do not. Yet this right conflicts with the safety concerns (efficiency/effectiveness) of running railroads, and justice requires a balance. The notion that organizational justice is derived from balancing values suggests that the processes which establish and maintain expectations and obligations are as important as what those expectations and obligations actually are—their substance.

SUBSTANTIVE RIGHTS

In this section we are going to describe some of the major rights that public employees have based on federal statutes and constitutional protections. The discussion includes rights regarding sexual harassment, whistleblowing, speech, belief or patronage, drug testing, and disabilities. These are not the only areas of public employee rights. For example, protection from discrimination based on race was discussed in Chapter 6, and Table 6-1 describes a number of relevant employment discrimination laws. In addition, employee rights are enumerated in state and local statutes and in the organization's personnel manual and working rules.

Sexual Harassment

What is sexual harassment? The United States Equal Employment Opportunity Commission, responsible for enforcing the Civil Rights Act of 1964, as amended, and various other employment discrimination laws, has issued the following guidelines:

> Unwelcomed sexual advances, requests for sexual favors, and other verbal or physical conduct of a sexual nature constitute sexual harassment when (1) submission to such conduct is made either explicitly or implicitly a term or condition of an individual's employment, (2) submission to or rejection of such conduct by an individual is used as the basis for employment decisions affecting such individual, or (3) such conduct has the purpose or effect of unreasonably interfering with an individual's work performance or creating an intimidating, hostile, or offensive working environment.[3]

In simple terms, sexual harassment is not romance. It is the coercive and hostile behavior of one person toward another based on gender. Evidently, it occurs quite frequently at work. Dresang and Stuiber's literature review cites a Bureau of National Affairs study showing 40 percent of the female respondents having experienced sexual harassment; the United States Merit Systems Review Board studies in 1981 and 1987 of federal employees showed 42 percent of the respondents reporting sexual harassment.[4] In their literature review, Robison, Kirk, and Powell[5] cite a Cornell study showing 92 percent of the 155 respondents believing sexual harassment was a serious problem and 70 percent who had experienced it themselves. Their own research shows that 71 percent of the business and professional women they surveyed reported being sexual harassed, with only 33 percent actually reporting the harassment.

The consequences of sexual discrimination appear to be significant both to victims and to the organization. Most women deal with sexual harassment privately, in many cases by simply leaving the organization. The psychological effects of sexual harassment may be traumatic. According to Dresang and Stuiber, "In addition to shame and guilt, women frequently experience feelings of helplessness, of being trapped, and of undirected fear. One of the most prevalent phenomena reported is a loss of self-esteem."[6] Costs to employers are significant as well: the cost of replacing employees; paying sick leave benefits to victims seeking to avoid sexual harassment; paying medical insurance claims for psychological help in dealing with harassment; and reduced worker productivity.

While sexual harassment ultimately must be dealt with in the workplace, conflicts involving claims of harassment frequently find their way into the court system as interested parties seek justice through the law. In *Meritor Savings Bank v. Vinson*[7] (1986), the Supreme court established several significant legal guidelines in its interpretation of the Civil Rights Act of 1964, as amended. Mechelle Vinson, who was employed by the bank in 1974, rose through the ranks to assistant branch manager on her merits when in 1978 she was discharged for excessive use of sick leave. Ms. Vinson claimed that during her four years with the bank she had been constantly subjected to sexual harassment. She estimated that over the four-year period she had sexual intercourse with Sidney Taylor, the branch manager, some 40 or 50 times. "In addition, [she] testified that Taylor fondled her in front of other employees, followed her into the women's restroom when she went there alone, exposed himself to her, and even forcibly raped her on several occasions (p. 55)." Vinson testified that she was afraid to report the harassment to Taylor's superiors. Taylor denied her charges completely, contending that they resulted from a business dispute.

Even though the conflicting testimony was never resolved, the Supreme Court made several significant legal points in its 9–0 judgment. First, it concluded that an adverse personnel action need not be taken in order to prove that sexual harassment has occurred. It affirmed lower court findings and the EEOC's guidelines that "Title VII affords employees the right to work in an environment free from discriminatory intimidation, ridicule and insult (p. 59)." Further, it affirmed that "a plaintiff may establish a violation of Title VII by proving that discrimination based on sex has created a hostile or abusive work environment (p. 59)." However, it tempered its stance somewhat by saying that in order for a legal violation to occur, the sexual harassment must be "sufficiently severe or pervasive 'to alter the conditions of the [victim's] employment and create an abusive working environment (p. 60)'" [internal cite omitted].

Second, the Court found that when trying to determine the nature of

the relationship, "The correct inquiry is whether respondent by her conduct indicated that the alleged sexual advances were *unwelcome,* not
whether her actual participation in sexual intercourse was *voluntary* [em-
phasis added] (p. 60)." However, the Court added that evidence regarding
sexually provocative speech or dress is not necessarily irrelevant in determining whether the advances are unwelcomed.

Last, contrary to its findings in race discrimination cases, the Court
found that an employer is not automatically accountable for sexual harassment by one of its supervisors. At the same time, the presence of a sexual
harassment policy does not automatically protect an employer from liability. The Court does suggest that an employer's defense would be
strengthened with evidence of a procedure that encourages victims of harassment to come forward.

Despite *Vinson,* Dresang and Stuiber observe that sexual harassment is
not easy to eliminate or even to minimize: "In part, the difficulties of taking
corrective action relate to organizational power and societal sex-role stereotypes, forces beyond the easy reach of reformers."[8] Evidence shows clearly
that discrimination at work originates with the powerful. Most victims of
discrimination and harassment are women and subordinates.

But the problem of sexual harassment involves more than issues of
power, stereotypes, and litigation. It would be naive to claim that productivity in organizations is disconnected from personal attraction and cooperation. Productivity is often enhanced by close, affectionate working relationships that develop within an organizational culture that encourages respect,
dignity, and tolerance. But the proper relationship between sexuality, productivity, and fair treatment is difficult to realize in any organizational
context because of divergent and unspoken expectations and perceptions.
The relationship between sexuality, productivity, and equity promises to
become more complicated in the 1990s with increasing ethnic diversity in
the workplace.

Americans with Disabilities Act of 1990[9]

This act is probably the most significant piece of civil rights legislation
since Congress passed the Civil Rights Act of 1964. Its purpose is to eliminate discrimination against individuals with disabilities or against those
perceived to have a disability. Individuals recovering from drug or alcohol
abuse are considered disabled, and those who are HIV infected are covered
as well.

According to the act, some 43 million Americans suffer from a physical or mental disability. The act states: "Individuals with disabilities are a
discrete and insular minority who have been faced with restrictions and
limitations, subjected to a history of purposeful unequal treatment, and
relegated to a position of political powerlessness in our society, based on
characteristics that are beyond the control of such individuals and resulting

from stereotypic assumptions not truly indicative of the individual ability of such individuals to participate in, and contribute to, society."[10]

The act, which covers both private and public employers, prohibits discrimination in employment against otherwise qualified applicants and employees and requires that reasonable accommodations in employment conditions and facilities be made for otherwise qualified disabled applicants and employees. According to an article in *USA Today*, reasonable accommodations might require installing ramps, widening doorways, repositioning telephones, making Braille menus available, and rearranging furniture and office layouts. The requirement that employers make reasonable accommodations for the disabled may be mitigated if the employer can show an undue financial hardship would be incurred. It is, of course, not yet clear without litigation what an undue financial burden might be.

The act also requires public entities to make reasonable modifications to government facilities and programs to make them accessible to the disabled. The act is far-reaching as well in the areas of transportation and telecommunications, and in its requirement to make public accommodations like supermarkets, retail establishments, movie houses, restaurants, and day care centers accessible to the disabled except where an undue financial hardship can be demonstrated by the owner. Under the Civil Rights Act of 1991, those discriminated against may sue successfully for damages if the discrimination is shown to be intentional.

Whistleblowing

The tendency of public organizations and administrators to withhold self-incriminating information from the public is counterbalanced theoretically by whistleblowing. This form of dissent focuses public attention on behavior the whistleblower considers illegal or unethical. It is this moral imperative, accompanied by the whistleblower's knowledge that his or her charges will be scrutinized and possibly met with reprisal, that distinguishes the whistleblower's actions from a simple act of insubordination for private purposes.

Whistleblowing is a well-publicized phenomenon because it plays upon the public's desire to expose corruption and increase responsiveness or efficiency in government agencies. The Civil Service Reform Act of 1978, which applies to federal employees, includes as a merit principle: "Employees should be protected against reprisal for the lawful disclosure of information which the employees reasonably believe evidences: a) a violation of any law, rule, or regulation, or b) mismanagement, a gross waste of funds, an abuse of authority, or a substantial and specific danger to pubic health or safety."

Despite these protections and similar ones in several state and local governments, employees usually blow the whistle on their employer only as a last resort, when the conflict between their ethical standards and their perception of their agency's behavior is so great as to leave them no choice. In other terms, whistleblowing results from a perceived gross breach in the employment contract—in this case, the expectations an employee has of his or her employer or co-workers. Whistleblowers often exhaust organizational channels for dissent before they "go public" with charges and information.

The U.S. Merit Systems Protection Board surveyed federal personnel specialists in 1980 and again in 1988 regarding the occurrence of prohibited personnel practices. In the 1988 survey, 19 percent of the respondents said they had observed at least one instance of retaliation for whistleblowing during the previous 12 months. Only half of those surveyed in 1988 believed that protections for persons attempting to expose prohibited personnel practices were adequate—down slightly from 1980.[11]

How should whistleblowing be evaluated? On the one hand, it divides the agency and undercuts its management, and causes serious organizational harm—sometimes for the self-serving purposes of a disgruntled employee. On the other hand, it may prevent managers from hiding information harmful to the agency or its managers, using specious reasons such as security and efficiency. Whistleblowing represents a classic conflict between individual rights, possibly under the rubric of the First Amendment, and the desire of managers to control the flow of information out of the agency in order to preserve individual careers, administrative efficiency or maintain political support.

Constitutional Protections

Citizens who work for a government are covered by various amendments to the Constitution. The Bill of Rights protects citizens from arbitrary action against them by the government, and when citizens become employees of a government, they are similarly protected. The balance among values we discussed earlier in the section on organizational justice is particularly relevant here, because as an employer the government cannot simply dismiss the values of administrative efficiency in favor of employee rights. Thus, as we see in the following sections, various government employers argue that the constitutional protections public employees claim often disadvantage the government's ability to operate efficiently and responsively. In this section we try to share some of the discussion the Supreme Court engages in to give some sense of how the balance is discussed and how solutions are reached.

Speech The First Amendment to the constitution states that "Congress shall make no law respecting an establishment of religion, or prohibiting the free exercise thereof; or abridging the freedom of speech, or of the press; or the right of the people peaceably to assemble, and to petition the Government for a redress of grievances." This amendment protects citizens from government's intrusions on the free exercise of speech, political beliefs, and political association. Citing passages from many of the Court's precedents, Justice Brennan in *New York Times v. Sullivan* (1964)[12] indicates the importance of the First Amendment in our form of government. The constitutional safeguard "was fashioned to assure unfettered interchange of ideas for the bringing about of political and social changes desired by the people." The First Amendment "presupposes that right conclusions are more likely to be gathered out of a multitude of tongues, than through any kind of authoritative selection. . . . To many this is, and always will be folly; but we have staked upon it our all." Justice Brennan himself writes: "We consider this case against the background of a profound national commitment to the principle that debate on public issues should be uninhibited, robust, and wide-open, and that it may well include vehement, caustic, and sometimes unpleasantly sharp attacks on government and public officials"(p. 701).

Commonly, we think that the purpose of the First Amendment is to protect a speaker's right to expression—as an end in itself. Actually, as Cooper observes from his review of judicial opinions, the free flow of information is vital to the *listener's* ability to come to conclusions about government affairs, and this is what justifies the "untrammeled communication of ideas."[13]

While citizens often endorse the First Amendment uncritically, the Court faces a difficult task when applying it to public employment situations. The First Amendment provides the vehicle for classic confrontations between advocates of administrative efficiency and the individual rights of public employees. On the one hand, government has a duty to conduct its business efficiently, which means requiring respect for hierarchy and organizational loyalty. On the other hand, no one knows better how taxes are being spent than civil servants; and if they feel their jobs will be jeopardized if they speak out, is the public being deprived of information vital to its understanding of government?

The way the Court decides free speech cases is first to ask whether the employee has expressed him or herself on a *matter of public concern*. If the answer is "yes," the Court looks to see how much the administrative efficiency of the agency has been disrupted. It then tries to balance the two considerations, asking if the disruption is sufficient enough to outweigh the employee's right to free speech.[14] The more clearly the matter addresses a significant public concern, the more difficult the employer's defense becomes.

In many ways, the balance the Court tries to draw among the values of administrative efficiency and individual rights depends on the extent to which the Justices believe that public employees should give up the constitutional rights they have as citizens when they go to work for a public employer; on the extent to which they feel that what goes on *inside* a public agency is a matter of public concern; and on the extent to which they feel the judiciary should be involved in public personnel management at all.

The contemporary Supreme Court, compared to its recent predecessors, appears to tip the balance in favor of administrative efficiency over individual rights. For example, in *Rust v. Sullivan* (1991), the Court upheld administrative regulations prohibiting the discussion of abortion by Title X grant recipients of the Public Health Service Act against a First Amendment challenge. Those recipients argued that the regulations precluded health-care workers from disseminating a full range of information to patients on a matter of public concern—one of "'the most divisive and contentious issues that our Nation has faced in years.'" Writing for a 5–4 Court, Chief Justice Rehnquist argued in part: "The employees' freedom of expression is limited during the time that they actually work for the project; but this limitation is a consequence of their decision to accept employment in a project, the scope of which is permissibly restricted by the funding authority."[15] In his dissent, Justice Blackmun counters: "It is beyond question 'that a government may not require an individual to relinquish rights guaranteed him by the First Amendment as a condition of public employment'" (p. 268; internal citations omitted).

In *Connick v. Myers* (1983)[16] a 5–4 Court decided that Sheila Myers was appropriately discharged for insubordination when she refused a transfer and then distributed a questionnaire to colleagues regarding the way Harry Connick, the elected district attorney in New Orleans, ran his office. The Court's deference to administrative efficiency is seen in two ways in this case. First, the Court tempered its decision on whether Ms. Myers was speaking out on a matter of public concern by noting that she was a disgruntled employee. In other words, her aims and motives were considered, as well as the content of the information she was providing with the questionnaire results. Further, the majority dismissed the importance of most of the information itself, suggesting that matters of internal agency operations are not a matter of public importance in judging the performance of the district attorney.

Because the Court acknowledged that a few of Myers' questions addressed matters of public concern, they turned to the government's argument on why she should be dismissed. The Court concluded: "The limited First Amendment interest involved here does not require that Connick tolerate action which he reasonably believed would disrupt the office, undermine his authority, and destroy close working relationships" (p. 724). Here the Court retreated from previous judgments, where *evidence* of disruption would have been required before the employer could have justly considered terminating the employee.

Patronage   Governments have struggled since the early 1800s to draw a balance between a responsive and an efficient government. Advocates of responsiveness have generally favored more political control over public bureaucracies; advocates of administrative efficiency have fought to keep politics out of administration. Political personnel systems fight for the allocation of public jobs on the basis of political loyalty as a reward for service to a political party and as a way of ensuring that newly elected officials can appoint people committed to their goals. For years, limitations on the political activity of employees as well as constraints on political influence over them have been dealt with in legislatures and executive branches of government.

The courts stepped into this battle in the mid-1970s by limiting the patronage practice of discharging public employees on the basis of political affiliation. The Court argued that patronage dismissals violated a public employee's First Amendment right to freedom of belief and association— to belong to a political party of choice and maintain one's own political beliefs. In *Rutan v. Republican Party of Illinois* (1990), a 5–4 Court extended its ruling to hiring, promotion, transfer, and recall decisions.[17]

In 1980 Governor James Thompson, Republican of Illinois, declared a hiring freeze for every agency under the governor's control. Only the governor's office could grant exceptions, of which there were some 5,000 a year. Evidently, agencies were screening applicants under the state's civil service procedures and then forwarding eligible names to the governor's Office of Personnel for approval or disapproval. The governor's office determined whether the candidate had voted in Republican primaries and had supported the Republican party. Cynthia Rutan, who had been a state employee since 1974, claimed that since 1981 she had been "repeatedly denied promotions to supervisory positions for which she was qualified because she had not worked for or supported the Republican Party" (p. 61).

The Court said the government must show a vital governmental interest before it could condition personnel actions on political belief and association. The majority claimed that preservation of democratic processes was not advantaged by patronage enough to outweigh a public employee's First Amendment rights.

In an earlier case, *Branti v. Finkel* (1980), the Court decided 6–3 that in trying to determine what positions were exempt from restrictions on patronage dismissals, "The ultimate inquiry is not whether the label 'policymaker' or 'confidential' fits a particular position; rather, the question is whether the hiring authority can demonstrate that party affiliation is an appropriate requirement for the effective performance of the public office involved."[18] In light of *Rutan*, this restriction on patronage dismissals would seem to apply to hiring as well.

Advocates of civil service systems and administrative efficiency may take heart in *Rutan*. But Justice Scalia's dissent, joined by three other conservative justices, may anticipate a reversal of *Rutan* and restrictions on the constitutional rights of public employees more generally. In his dissent, he argues like the majority in *Rust v. Sullivan* (1991) that the government's relationship with its employees is different from its relationship in private matters with citizens. In other words, the government should be able to regulate the lives of its employees more easily than it may regulate the lives of private citizens. The government may treat those who work for it as employees first and citizens second. This issue, of course, is at the heart of determining the extent to which public employee rights in the future will be protected through the Constitution or through legislation, civil service regulations, and collective bargaining agreements.

The Court always has shown some reluctance to enter personnel management in public agencies, but Justice Scalia's dissent in *Rutan* may anticipate increasing deference to legislative and administrative discretion in place of judicial venues.[19] In dissent, Justice Scalia wrote: "The whole point of my dissent is that the desirability of patronage is a policy question to be decided by the people's representatives" (p. 85). The Court's 5–4 majority in *Connick v. Myers* expressed similar reluctance to enter the realm of public personnel management when Justice White wrote: "When employee expression cannot be fairly considered as relating to any matter of political, social, or other concern to the community, government officials should enjoy wide latitude in managing their offices without intrusive oversight by the judiciary in the name of the First Amendment. Perhaps the government employer's dismissal of the worker may not be fair, but ordinary dismissals from government service which violate no fixed tenure or applicable statute or regulation are not subject to judicial review even if the reasons for the dismissal are alleged to be mistaken or unreasonable."[20]

To summarize this discussion of the public employee's rights under the First Amendment: It appears that recent Court decisions suggest a balance shifting toward the value of administrative efficiency and away from the protection of constitutionally guaranteed individual rights. There are some indications that citizens may have to relinquish some constitutional rights when they become public employees; that the standard a public employer must meet in order to discipline an employee claiming a First Amendment interest has diminished; that what constitutes a "matter of public concern" has become more restrictive; and that the Court may be showing more of a predilection than its recent predecessors to distance the judiciary from public personnel management.

Drug testing and the Fourth Amendment   The rights of employees with regard to a public employer's use of drug and alcohol tests points out that no constitutional right is absolute. In this case, the Fourth Amendment would seem clearly to prohibit drug and alcohol testing without a search warrant by the government, but the Supreme Court has ruled that this is not the case with regard to public employees. A public employee's constitutional protection from unwarranted search and seizure by a public employer can be outweighed by the government's interest in ensuring the safety and security of the public.

The Fourth Amendment to the Constitution states: "The right of the people to be secure in their persons, houses, papers, and effects, against unreasonable searches and seizures, shall not be violated, and no Warrants shall issue, but upon probable cause, supported by Oath or affirmation, and particularly describing the place to be searched, and the persons or things to be seized." In other words, in order for a government search to be reasonable, the government must have good reason to believe that the individual being searched has violated the law. The government's reasoning must be tested prior to the search by securing a warrant which only a judge can issue after determining that yes, indeed, the government does have probable cause to believe this particular individual has violated the law.

In 1985 the Federal Railroad Administration promulgated rules to curb alcohol and drug abuse by railway employees. Among other provisions, the rules called for drug and alcohol testing for certain railway employees following a major train accident. The Railway Labor Executives' Association, acting on behalf of several unions, charged that the regulations violated the employees' Fourth Amendment rights against unreasonable search and seizure. They claimed a violation because the rules called for the testing of all employees covered by the regulations, regardless of any evidence leading to suspicion that they had broken the law.

In *Skinner v. Railway Labor Executives' Association* (1989),[21] the Supreme Court ruled 7–2 that where "special needs" go beyond normal law enforcement and make impractical securing of a warrant and establishing probable cause, the Court must balance the government's interest against the privacy interests of the individual in order to determine if the Fourth Amendment has been violated. According to the Court in *Skinner*, regulating the conduct of railroad employees to ensure safe transportation constitutes a compelling government interest, especially because the railroad industry had a history of alcohol and drug abuse by its employees. Further, the Court ruled that the drug testing constituted a minimal intrusion into the privacy of the railroad workers since they knew in advance who would be tested, and when and under what conditions the testing would take place.

The Court's reasoning in its drug testing cases has implications generally for the relationship between the courts and public employers. In *National Treasury Employees Union v. Von Raab* (1989), the Court said that the intrusion of privacy by United States Customs Service drug testing procedures was minimized by the administrative regulations themselves: "These procedures significantly minimize the program's intrusion on privacy interests."[22] In other words, the Customs Service developed a set of procedures on drug testing that successfully anticipated a constitutional challenge. Those procedures where aimed not only at promoting political responsiveness and administrative efficiency, but also at recognizing the individual rights of the employees—at least according to the Court. In other words, the impact of the Court on public personnel administration is evident in these drug testing cases not only in the specific decisions it has rendered, but in the Court's power to encourage administrative agencies to think like a judge as they develop administrative rules and procedures.

Liability of Public Employees

In the 1970s the Court enlarged the scope of its constitutional inquiry, granting more rights to public employees, clients or beneficiaries of the government, prisoners, and citizens who otherwise might come in contact with government officials. It is one thing for the courts to grant new rights; it is another to enforce recognition of and respect for them. One mechanism to advance these ends is the threat that a public official might be held personally liable for violating a citizen's constitutional rights. Traditionally, administrators came to share the same immunity from civil suits arising out of actions connected with their official functions as had formerly belonged only to legislators and judges and other special classes of public employees. But in order to balance the need to protect the rights of citizens with the need to protect public officials who are required to exercise discretion that affects citizens, the doctrine of *sovereign immunity* gave way to a more limited form of immunity for administrative officials. The revised doctrine, captured clearly now in *Harlow v. Fitzgerald* (1982) states that "government officials performing discretionary functions generally are shielded from liability for civil damages insofar as their conduct does not violate clearly established statutory or Constitutional rights of which a reasonable person would have known."[23]

The concept of *qualified immunity* outlined in *Harlow* suggests that in order to perform their job effectively and with only minor fear of being sued, public officials must become aware of the constitutional law that impinges upon their work and the work of their agency. Moreover, the threat of liability for a public official is directly related to the scope of constitutional rights the Court is willing to grant public employees and citizens. The broader the rights, the greater the threat of liability; the narrower the interpretation of rights, the less the threat, because it takes a strong case for a plaintiff to substantiate a claim that a right has been violated. A more liberal Court might have found that Harry Connick violated the First Amendment rights of Sheila Myers. If it had, the threat of liability would have hung more threateningly over the heads of future public officials contemplating adverse personnel actions against public employees who speak out against them and disrupt the workplace. But it did not, and the threat to public officials in the 1990s seems less ominous. Whether or not the public benefits is less clear.

PROCEDURAL RIGHTS

Earlier, we suggested that the sanction function is concerned with both the substance of employee and employer expectations and obligations and the processes by which these expectations and obligations are established and maintained.

Property Rights and Due Process

The process side of this concern is found in two concepts—property rights and due process. It has become popular to assert that civil service rules "hamstring" management by making it impossible to discharge or discipline employees protected by civil service systems. In one respect, this statement is correct. Public employees have rights to their jobs that exceed those of their private sector counterparts. Yet this statement is also incorrect, for these rights ultimately are derived from the constitutional requirement of due process, rather than civil service regulations. Constitutional protections accorded *public* employees are an extension of the government's responsibility to guarantee certain freedoms to its citizens. The key here is that the *government* is bound by the Constitution, whether in its dealings with citizens simply as individuals or citizens as employees.

The Fifth and Fourteenth amendments to the Constitution require that a government may deprive an individual of life, liberty or property only after due process of law. Over the years, the courts have come to conclude that public employees have a property interest in their jobs if they have been led to expect that they will hold their jobs permanently as long as they perform satisfactorily. In other words, a job can be considered a public employee's property, and once that is established, the government—the public employer—can take the property/job only after due process.

What is due process? Minimal due process requires that an employer notify an employee of the employee's violation and give the employee a chance to state his or her side of the story. Due process comes in degrees, where the amount depends on the scope of the discipline contemplated. The critical step in linking due process with fairness comes when the person or board hearing the employee appeal or grievance is not in the employee's normal chain of command. This conveys the message that the employee will be heard impartially—by an investigator, board, or arbitrator.

A simple written reprimand might appropriately call for minimal due process, but a contemplated firing that would deprive a public employee of the economic means of supporting him or herself and possibly create difficulty for the employee when seeking another job (infringe on the employee's liberty to seek employment), would require a pretermination hearing.[24]

Discipline and Grievance Procedures

A disciplinary action is an employer-imposed reduction in organizational rewards for cause. It is the employer's formal mechanism to inform an employee that he or she has not lived up to the terms of the relationship from the employer's perspective. With disciplinary action, the employer is telling the employee that he or she is not living up to implied or explicit obligations. Disciplinary actions include oral and written reprimands, suspensions, reductions in rank or pay, and dismissal. They do not include temporary layoffs or workforce reductions that arise from budget cuts or lack of work. Rather, they are caused by specific behaviors by the employee that result in low productivity or violations of agency rules and regulations.

Grievances are complaints by employees concerning unfair treatment in the distribution of organizational rewards or punishments. A grievance is the employee's mechanism for letting the employer know that from the employee's perspective the employer is not living up to the terms of the employment relationship. Employees may allege that they are not being treated equitably with respect to their contributions to the organization, or with respect to other employees. They may also use the grievance system to appeal what they consider as unfair disciplinary action instituted by the organization.

Discipline and counseling the unproductive employee   Disciplinary action is the last step—never the first—in dealing with an employee whose performance is substandard. It assumes that a number of other questions have already been asked regarding job design, selection, orientation, performance appraisal, training, and compensation:

Job design	Are the tasks, conditions, and performance standards of the position reasonable and equitable?
Selection	Does the employee meet the minimum qualifications established for the position?
Orientation	Were organizational rules and regulations, and position requirements clearly communicated to the new employee?
Performance appraisal	Was the employee's performance adequately documented, and was the employee provided informal and formal feedback on the quality of his or her performance?
Training	Does the employee have adequate skills to perform the required tasks at the expected level of competence?

Compensation   Is good performance rewarded, or are
                                there factors in the work environment that
                                make it impossible or punishing to perform
                                well?

Disciplinary action, therefore, theoretically represents the last step in supervising employees because it symbolizes a failure to adjust the expectations/obligations of the employment relationship by less intrusive means. It is primarily a supervisory responsibility, since most performance problems are handled informally within the work unit with minimal involvement by the personnel department.

If the performance problem cannot be resolved informally by the supervisor and other employees within the unit, the supervisor may request that formal disciplinary action be taken by the personnel department. If this occurs, it is the personnel manager's responsibility to ensure that all other causes of the performance problem have been considered. Figure 12-1 shows the sequence of personnel activities that occur prior to disciplinary action. It is the primary responsibility of the employee's immediate supervisor to ensure that each of these steps is followed. Together, they represent the counseling and disciplinary action process.

The personnel manager has three important responsibilities with respect to disciplinary action. Initially, the personnel department is responsible for establishing the process. Once it has been established as part of the agency's personnel rules and regulations, the personnel director is frequently responsible for counseling unproductive employees and for assisting the supervisor in implementing evaluation and training procedures to improve performance or institute disciplinary action. Last, the personnel director is responsible for making sure the system is applied equitably. Figure 12-2, a memorandum from the personnel director in Kansas City, Missouri, to department heads, shows that the personnel director has both a facilitating and a policing role in the disciplinary process.

It is often necessary to confront an unproductive employee in order to bring the person's poor job performance out into the open. This is done through a counseling session. The personnel manager should prepare for this session by reviewing its objectives—namely, behavioral change in the direction of increased productivity. Its purpose is not to attack the employee's personality, habits, or attitudes; nor is it intended to intimidate the employee or drive him or her out of the organization.

If an employee has violated agency regulations or has not responded to previous counseling or performance deficiencies, an interview informing the employee of disciplinary action would be in order. However, where a performance problem has not been previously discussed with the employee or where the employee shows evidence of a gradual deterioration in productivity or work habits, a nondirective interview may be in order.

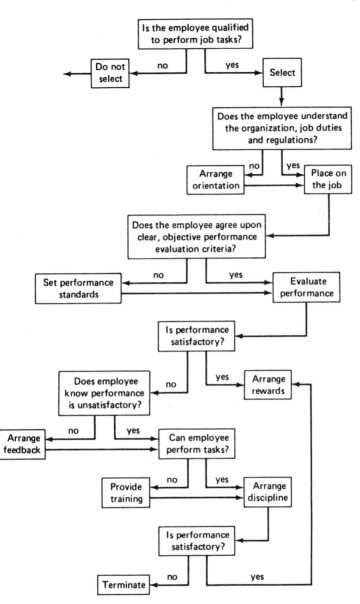

FIGURE 12-1 Disciplinary Action and Other Personnel Activities

During the nondirective interview it is the supervisor's responsibility to advise the employee of the supervisor's concern and to try to determine what factors are influencing the employee's behavior and if the supervisor is in a position to be of assistance. If, after ensuring that the employee knows not only what the problem is but what the supervisor considers

FIGURE 12-2 Memorandum from Personnel Director to Department Heads in Kansas City, Missouri

---

INTERDEPARTMENTAL COMMUNICATION

Date: April 7, 1986
To: All Department Heads
From: Tom F. Lewinsohn, Director of Personnel
Subject: Employee Rights and Obligations

In today's world of work we hear much about employee rights but seldom hear about employee obligations. With our departmental budgets becoming tighter those employee obligations deserve even more critical attention. For their paychecks, which is only one of their rights, employees can be expected to fulfill obligations such as showing up for work regularly and punctually, taking directions from supervisors, doing their jobs correctly, and following rules.

Too often supervisors do not act soon enough in trying to correct employees not living up to their job obligations. Employees failing to show up for work regularly and/or punctually may be accommodated by giving them status as part-time employees which more accurately reflects their availability for work. Some employees not living up to their job obligations are tolerated until their supervisors can no longer bear it. Then, by taking disciplinary action, the supervisors may have overreacted to one offense with no back-up data to support their action. Supervisors must be able to justify their disciplinary actions which may be more often justified and upheld when they acted after having considered the following:

1.   Did the employee know that his or her behavior could result in disciplinary action?
2.   Was the rule being enforced fairly, and was it applied consistently?
3.   Was there an objective investigation of the offense?
4.   Does the severity of the discipline reflect the seriousness of the offense and, when possible, take into consideration the employee's service record?

Most of the employees' rights and obligations, listed in the Personnel Rules and Regulations, are sometimes expanded upon by departmental regulations. However, departmental regulations must not conflict with the Personnel Rules and Regulations. Even though departments may become legally bound by their departmental regulations, in cases of appeal of disciplinary action, the departments may lose their enforcement of that disciplinary action if the disciplining supervisor failed to follow departmental regulations.

Employee rights and obligations will become, if they have not already become, a crucial part of managing better with less in the coming austere budget year. It is perhaps the time to rejuvenate the work ethic, "a fair day's pay for a fair day's work," which includes fair and equitable treatment. Also, it may be time for a reminder that no one has a right to a job, only a right to compete for a job and to retain a job with its rights as a result of fulfilling job obligations.

TFL:njc

desirable employee performance, after a reasonable period of time discipline may be in order.

The supervisor and the personnel department play mutually supporting roles for the disciplinary system to work effectively. The personnel manager must help establish a clear and equitable system; the supervisor must provide adequate supervision of employees and enforce work rules fairly. If discipline is required, it is a good idea for it to be handed out by the personnel department on the basis of information provided by the supervisor. This will provide equitable treatment for employees throughout the organization.

Grievance procedures Every day, in thousands of instances, employees—public and private—claim they have been treated unjustly. In a very provocative statement, David Ewing, a well-known authority on employee rights, recently observed: "It appears that very few [nonunion] companies in this country—possibly as few as thirty to fifty—have had effective grievance procedures in place for several years or more."[25] This will come as a surprise to most public employees and their employers, who have had grievance procedures for years as an integral part of merit systems.

It is important that discipline and grievance systems and procedures provide for protection of the employee's substantive and procedural rights. An employee's appeal of a disciplinary action will usually follow the same channels as a grievance initiated by an employee. In the case of discipline, documentation showing that an employee's performance is contrary to expectations the employer holds of all employees must be provided. The employee must be given ample opportunity to respond to these charges. Figure 12-3 provides a diagram of typical disciplinary action and grievance procedures. Note that if the employee is a member of a minority group, the affirmative action officer may be involved in the process.

Management should establish with employees grievance procedures

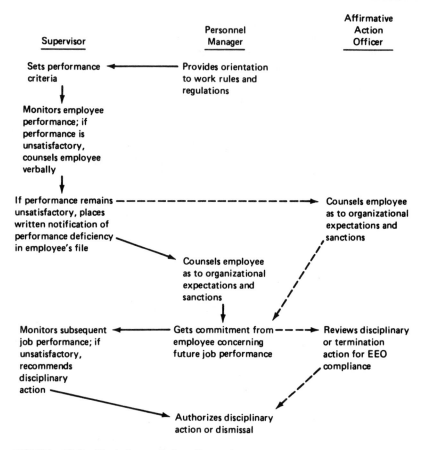

FIGURE 12-3 Disciplinary Action Procedures

that clearly establish the employee's right to file written complaints concerning alleged unfair management practices, and procedures for hearing these complaints in the agency. The specific items that might arise and be subject to a grievance complaint could be defined in personnel rules and regulations. If a collective bargaining agreement exists, the grievance procedure will be defined in the contract. Usually, grievances will be limited to topics in the working rules that an employee believes management has violated. Topics such as the following will probably be included as issues contained in a negotiated contract or in personnel rules enforced by a civil service board. Under each possible area of grievance we have given an example drawn from the exit interview files of a state agency in Kansas.

Work assignments   Employees may feel that work assignments are made subjectively.

I don't know how other sections are, but in our section conditions were very bad. There is too much favoritism by the supervisors. Not all employees are treated equal; some are picked on. Blacks are favored only because they are afraid of them, and that they will yell "discrimination" when whites are really the ones discriminated against. There is also a lot of unfairness as to who does what work.

Promotion   An employee may feel that the promotional criteria established for a position were not valid or not utilized, or that promotional procedures were improper.

The chances for advancement, unless you knew the correct people, were very poor. There were some cases I knew for sure that people who were most qualified for the job were passed over in favor of a friend, relative, or friend of a friend. There was one case in particular I remember. A person started out at a Clerk I position, took the test for Clerk-Typist I, failed the test, but still secured a Clerk-Typist II position elsewhere in the department.

Poor supervision   Employees may feel that supervision is inadequate, and that supervisors are biased or incompetent.

The people I worked beside were nice, for the most part. There was a supervisor in the position above me who was only 19 years old and lacked the knowledge of how to handle the situation. I brought this up to her supervisor and was told that it could be made very hard for me if I "caused waves," so I gave up my job.

Political interference   Conflict arises between elected and appointed officials, or among supervisors.

Also, the department should back up their own policies. I found several cases during my five years of employment when I received a memo dictating what my actions should be in certain circumstances, which I followed to the letter. However, if someone complained to the department heads stationed in the capital, they changed the rules on the spot and left me looking like I didn't know my own job. In general, I feel that the state should quit playing politics with civil service employment. Then they could get a little efficiency back into the system.

Sexual discrimination

It is a little unfortunate that the chiefs are allowed to carry on, then customers make comments to the effect: "Are he and missy still playing doctor or hanky panky in the halls or in the observation booth?" The same chief allows some of his girls to do whatever they want and only a few have to toe the line anytime the others crack the whip. It's also a shame the same man is capable of destroying your future.

In any of these instances, it is important that the agency have an established informal and formal grievance procedure that would allow employees to bring their charges to the notice of higher ups and get a fair hearing. The following steps might constitute a typical grievance process:

1. *Informal counseling.* The aggrieved employee should meet and discuss the situation with his or her supervisor or the next higher up if the complaint is about the employee's immediate supervisor. The success of this step depends on an organizational environment that encourages employees to speak openly about their concerns.
2. *Formal grievance.* If informal counseling is unsuccessful, the aggrieved employee should have the opportunity to file a formal grievance in writing stating the problem and what the employee thinks ought to be done to correct the situation. If asked by the employee, the personnel department can help the employee prepare the necessary document.
3. *Consultation between supervisor and personnel director.* After the grievance is filed, the personnel department should consult with the employee to verify the situation and then work with the parties to see if an agreement can be reached.
4. *Investigation/adjudication/arbitration.* A number of steps can follow the attempt by the personnel department to work out a solution between the parties. These might include assigning an impartial person—often from the personnel department—to investigate and make a decision; convening a panel to hear the complaint and make a decision; and securing an outside arbitrator to hear the complaint and render a decision.

Employees can seek redress of grievances by following agency procedures. The more due process afforded the employee internally, the less likely it is that an employee will seek an external channel to air a grievance.[26] In fact, some legal proceedings will require that internal grievance procedures be followed before undertaking judicial avenues. In other cases, the external investigating agency or court will incorporate the proceedings of an internal process as part of its own review.

THE SANCTION FUNCTION IN ALTERNATE PERSONNEL SYSTEMS

We have talked in general about organizational justice, the mechanisms for establishing the terms of the employment relationship, and various processes for maintaining or enforcing those terms. But there truly are significant differences in the sanction function, depending upon which personnel system the employee is part of. This is because with the sanction function, the rules of the personnel game are established and maintained. This is where the expectations and obligations of employee and employer are determined and enforced. Every so often, one group or another will test its power to influence the rules. This is what inevitably happens with a strike. Regardless of the outcomes on wages, a strike gives the adversaries the opportunity to see where they stand with regard to setting expectations and obligations of employee and employer. Taking a case to court or arbitration can serve the same purpose. Battles between the legislature and executive branches of government are often fought over who has the discretion to set the personnel rules.

The reason why unions were so successful in early years of this century was because they held out the promise of organizational justice for employees. One of the first objectives of a union is to negotiate a grievance procedure that includes a third-party decision-making process—one that takes the employee's grievance outside the managerial chain of command. Civil service systems similarly value individual rights as a way of protecting employees from partisan political pressure. The first objective of civil service reform in the late nineteenth century was to legislate the elimination of politics from administration through the creation of systems in which employees could be dismissed only for performance deficiencies, not because they belonged to the wrong party or failed to pay voluntary dues. With regard to the sanction function, however, civil service systems differ from collective bargaining, because civil service systems are founded on dual values—individual rights and efficiency. Thus, even though we often see elaborate due process protections for public employees, we also hear complaints from managers, themselves covered by the same civil service protections, about the red tape and due process that hardly makes it worth the effort, in their eyes, to discipline employees.

Affirmative action personnel systems are driven by the value of social equity and, depending upon the context, individual rights. The expectation in affirmative action systems is that each person will be treated on his or her own merits and performance. But the benign use of racial classifications benefitting minorities at the expense of the individual rights of nonminorities are rarely rejected by affirmative action advocates. Affirmative action personnel systems strongly advocate due process as a way of ensuring fair treatment in organizational systems suspected of bias.

When it comes to political personnel systems and also to contracting out, the value of individual rights diminishes in favor of responsiveness and efficiency, respectively. Due process may not be highly valued. Political executives who serve at the pleasure of elected leaders enjoy virtually no employee rights. Their positions do not fall under merit system provisions, and they are hired, moved, and dismissed largely based on a calculation of the political value they bring to an administration. Consequently, they may be less respectful of the rights of others, and see them as impediments to political and administrative action.

Contracting out is often seen as a way of circumventing personnel systems where individual rights have become entrenched at the expense of efficiency and responsiveness. Once a service is contracted out to a private employer, employees will find themselves operating under a new personnel system, usually with fewer employee rights. The constitutional protections that employees enjoy under a public personnel system no longer apply, and the due process public employees generally enjoy may be sacrificed to the goal of administrative efficiency and profit.

ORGANIZATIONAL JUSTICE, PRODUCTIVITY AND WORKFORCE DIVERSITY

It seems clear that over the years the expectations employees have of their employers have risen. Employees expect job security, a decent wage, health benefits, a sound retirement system, safe working conditions, an environment free of unfair discrimination, participation in decisions that affect them, and in some cases, childcare and parental leave. At the same time, demands on public employers for productivity have resulted in layoffs, declining health benefits, and reduced rights. These contrasting forces place considerable strain on the sanction function and complicate perceptions of organizational justice.

But the sanction function is not driven simply by demands for individual rights versus productivity or administrative efficiency. Added to this contentious set of factors is the demographic trend toward increasing ethnic diversity in the workforce. Ethnic diversity will complicate employee expectations and what employers can expect from employees. This heterogeneity in expectations and obligations can be expected to place additional strain on the organizational processes aimed at matching them.

It appears that one of the issues that will dominate human resources management in the 1990s is how organizations can effectively manage the relationship between workforce diversity, organizational justice, and productivity. The relationship between any two of these factors might be predictable, but inserting the third adds a dimension of significant uncertainty.

SUMMARY

In some ways, the sanction function is the most important of the four core functions. Activities designed to fulfill this function aim to establish and maintain the terms of the relationship between employee and employer. These terms consist of expectations and obligations employee and employer have of each other, and they constitute the rules of the game. Expectations and obligations arise from a number of sources. Of these, only public employees enjoy rights stemming from the Constitution. However, practically, these rights are balanced against the duty a public employer has to operate efficiently. In this balance we can see the inevitable conflict between administrative efficiency and individual rights and resultant perceptions about organizational justice.

Recent rulings suggest that the contemporary Supreme Court has tipped the balance in favor of administrative efficiency over individual rights. With the judicial avenue narrowing, the rights of employees are likely to result from new legislation and administrative policy, rules and regulations rather than appeals to constitutional protections.

Internal disciplinary and grievance procedures are mechanisms to enforce the terms of the employment relationship. Increasing diversity of the workforce will bring a broader array of employee expectations and obligations to the workplace. Relatively objective disciplinary guidelines and impartial grievance procedures might be expected to ameliorate the negative impact of these differences and provide a foundation of respect necessary to channel the differences into creativity and productivity.

KEY TERMS

Branti v. Finkel (1980)
Connick v. Myers (1983)
discipline
due process
grievance procedure
Harlow v. Fitzgerald (1982)
Meritor Savings Bank v. Vinson (1986)
National Treasury Employees Union v. Von Raab (1989)
New York Times v. Sullivan (1964)
organizational justice
procedural rights
property rights

Rust v. Sullivan (1991)
Rutan v. Republican Party of Illinois (1990)
sanction function
sexual harassment
Skinner v. Railway Labor Executives' Association (1989)
sovereign versus qualified immunity
substantive rights
terms of the employment relationship
whistleblowing

DISCUSSION QUESTIONS

1. Define the sanction function and identify the ways an organization establishes and maintains the terms of the employment relationship between employee and employer.

2. Public employees are granted more rights generally than private-sector employees. Why is this so? Do you think public employees should give up their rights as citizens in their capacity as employees? Do you think public-sector employees should have fewer rights? Do you think that private-sector employees should have more rights?

3. Describe the rights of employees who have been sexually harassed or who are considered whistleblowers.

4. Discuss the balance the Supreme Court examines when deciding whether a public employer has violated an employee's First Amendment right to free speech.

5. Do you agree with the provisions of the Fourth Amendment? Do you agree that public employers ought to be able to conduct drug screens of their employees? If you answer "yes" to both questions, how do you reconcile the tension between your positions? How does the Court reconcile the tension?

6. Why do you think the Supreme Court considers a person's job their property? Describe the role of property rights and due process in establishing and maintaining the terms of the employment relationship.

7. Discuss how discipline and grievance procedures are connected to the sanction function.

8. Diagram a typical disciplinary procedure.

9. Are the interests of employee and employer the same in establishing a grievance procedure? Construct a model grievance procedure from the employee's standpoint. Construct it now from the employer's standpoint. Do you have any differences? As an employer, what process would you use to construct a grievance procedure?

10. How does the sanction function differ in alternate personnel systems?

11. What relationship do you see between organizational justice, productivity, and workforce diversity?

CASE STUDY: JUAN HERNANDEZ V. LOS ANGELES COUNTY

Introduction

Metropolitan Los Angeles County is the largest local government in California. County government is divided into about 50 operating departments and employs about 20,000 people. Among the departments is the Office of Data Processing Center (DPC).

Juan Hernandez, a Hispanic male, was employed by the DPC on July 15, 1972, as a data processing trainee. On May 10, 1973, he was promoted to the position of Computer Operator I and attained permanent status in that position six months later. He remained in that position until his termination on March 9, 1982.

This case study will examine the circumstances leading to his dismissal, his role as a union steward for Local 121 of the American Federation of State, County and Municipal Employees (AFSCME), and the various steps involved in his termination. It will reach conclusions relating to the disciplinary action and grievance process in public agencies in general.

Employment History

From his initial employment until April 1977, Juan Hernandez's record reflected satisfactory and dependable service. On April 25, 1977, however, he received a written reprimand for loading 25,000 United Fund cards into a computer punch backwards, thus rendering them useless (Exhibit A).

Mr. Hernandez reacted to the reprimand by a letter of rebuttal which indicated that he disagreed sharply with management's allegations of his lack of general competence (Exhibit B).

EXHIBIT A Reprimand Re United Fund Cards (April 25, 1977)

April 25, 1977

To:　Juan Hernandez
From:　Richard White
　　　　Computer Supervisor I
　　　　Subj:　Reprimand

On April 13, 1977 you were assigned to read United Fund Cards into the card punch. The next day it was found that all 25,000 cards were punched incorrectly because they were fed into the machine backwards. Because United Fund had no more cards on hand, this required that new cards be printed at considerable cost and waste of time.

This situation caused a great deal of consternation on the part of top officials in DPC. As a senior computer operator, you should know enough to feed cards into the card punch correctly, or to ask for instructions if you are unsure of what you are doing.

Unless your performance improves, an unsatisfactory performance evaluation may result, or other forms of disciplinary action may occur. As always, I stand ready to help you with any advice and assistance you consider necessary.

I have read this letter and have been given a copy. My signature hereupon does not signify agreement or disagreement with its contents

_____ Juan Hernandez

In October 1977, he received an evaluation summarizing his performance as "in need of attention." His scheduled merit increase was deferred for three months. Although the overall tone of the evaluation was encouraging, it implied an incompetence in his ability to grasp the concepts of a large computer system. Mr. Hernandez appealed the evaluation, but withdrew the appeal when he received a satisfactory evaluation along with his merit increase three months later.

In January 1978, the Director of Operations for the DPC brought about a reorganization that resulted in Mr. Hernandez being switched from the day to night shift. Despite his objections to this change, Mr. Her-

EXHIBIT B Rebuttal from Mr. Hernandez (April 25, 1977)

April 30, 1977

To: Mr. Otto Gesellschaft, Director, DPC
      Mr. Richard White, Supervisor
From: Juan Hernandez
        Computer Operator I
Subj: Answer to Reprimand

Mr. Richard White has forced me to sign a letter of reprimand which I totally disagree with. The purpose of this letter is to demand that you review the facts of the case and vindicate my reputation.

While it is true that the punch cards were fed into the machine backwards, two other operators as well as myself were assigned to this job. Yet none of these people received reprimands. Mr. White said that the United Fund people had to have someone to blame, and that because the other two employees were trainees they were not responsible, but I don't think this is fair.

There have been other incidents where employees have improperly set up machines and never received reprimands. For example, Stephen Hays caused improper printing of over 200 time sheets last year.

This reprimand is injurious to my character, my reputation, and my future. I demand that it be withdrawn as prejudicial.

---

nandez's employment continued satisfactorily for the next 18 months, until he suffered a severe on-the-job injury on July 26, 1979. A portion of the raised computer floor collapsed while he was on it carrying a box of computer paper. His resultant knee and leg injuries caused Mr. Hernandez to be absent from work for 425 hours.

Upon his return to work on October 27, 1979, he was presented with a formal record of counseling dated July 29, 1979, just three days after his injury had occurred. This record, which was prepared by his supervisor as a summary of the informal counseling that had occurred with him, cited a number of infractions (Exhibit C).

On June 29, 1981, Mr. Hernandez was given a formal record of counseling citing his involvement in a technical failure that occurred in the computer room at the main console (Exhibit D).

EXHIBIT C Record of counseling (July 29, 1979)

RECORD OF COUNSELING

Employee Name: Juan Hernandez
Classification: Computer Operator I
Department: DPC
Date: July 29, 1979
Date of Hire: July 5, 1972
Employee Status: Permanent

Several incidents underscore a pattern of behavior that is of concern to me. You show increasing disregard to operational and personal conduct and have failed to take responsibility for your actions. I am bringing these items to your attention in an attempt to make you realize that your attitude is detrimental to your performance.

On Tuesday, May 20, 1979, at approximately 0900 hours, you approached Mr. White to ask to be allowed to leave at 1500 hours to go to the Credit Union. You stated that you would make up the time by not taking your lunch hour. Mr. White told you not to do that; to take the usual lunch hour, then to write a leave slip for one hour. You agreed and Mr. White had the impression that it was settled.

When you were asked by the time clerk to produce a leave slip for your absence, you presented a 15-minute leave-without-pay slip and indicated that Mr. Manny Ramirez had asked you to watch a job until it was finished and that this prevented you from having your lunch hour at the usual time; and that you had taken lunch and break at 1500 hours, thus the remaining 15 minutes represented your actual absence. I have checked with Mr. Ramirez and all members of his group and have found that neither he nor his staff had asked you for any special assistance.

On a previous occasion, a similar event took place and you were absent from the Computer Room without authorization.

The incident involving a box of forms improperly mounted was also brought to your attention; you denied having done it although a number of people actually saw you putting the forms on the printer.

I expect that you will give this matter prompt attention and proper consideration and will make every effort to avoid creating similar situations. I consider this very important and feel that counseling you at this time may help us avoid having to resort to stronger disciplinary action. I am also offering you an opportunity to discuss with me your plans to improve your attitude and your overall performance. I am willing to help you.

EXHIBIT D   Record of Counseling (June 29, 1981)

RECORD OF COUNSELING

Employee Name: Juan Hernandez
Classification: Computer Operator
Department: DPC, Computer Room
Date: June 29, 1981
Date of Hire: July 15, 1972
Employee Status: Permanent

This formal counseling is a result of an incident which occurred on 6/9/81 involving potential damage to the System 3000 data base. This incident was witnessed by the following people: Mr. Ronald White, EDP Operations Supervisor; Mr. John Pardo, DPC Assistant Director; Mr. Donald Jenkins, Systems Programmer; and Ms. Maria Melendez, Teleprocessing Coordinator.

When program CICS (S337) would not run, the need to reload System 3000 Data Base became evident. Mr. Hernandez was the senior person on the console at this time. This process should require about ten minutes system outage if procedures are exercised normally. In this case, the total outage was in excess of 35 minutes because:

1. Mr. Hernandez failed to assume senior operator responsibility when the problem became evident. It was necessary for Mr. Pardo and Mr. White to intervene and demand Mr. Hernandez to assume responsibility.

2. Mr. Hernandez was unfamiliar with procedures required to terminate and restart System 3000. These procedures should be familiar to a Senior Computer Operator I since they have remained unchanged for over three months.

3. Mr. Hernandez responded "GO" to a CICS startup message he was instructed not to respond to, resulting in a requirement to cancel CICS again and reload to avoid data base damage.

The essence of this counseling is to inform Mr. Hernandez that he must be more willing to assume responsibility in the absence of a Computer Operator II. Also, he must familiarize himself with existing procedures within the computer room.

These errors must be corrected immediately. Additional errors regarding these or other operational procedures may result in progressive discipline to include formal reprimand, suspension and/or termination.

_____   _____
Supervisor/Date   Employee/Date

Shop Steward

On July 27, 1981, Mr. Hernandez was elected to the position of shop steward representing the DPC employees with AFSCME Local 121. During his term as shop steward, he aided several employees who were contemplating filing grievances against the DPC on the grounds that the agency was illegally testing computer operators prior to giving them permanent appointments.

Termination

On January 9, 1982, Juan Hernandez was himself given an "unsatisfactory" performance evaluation based on his failure to complete certain training courses. He refused to sign this evaluation (Exhibit E).

On January 23, 1982, he was charged one day without pay for calling in sick the day before the start of his scheduled one-week vacation. Upon returning to work, he submitted a doctor's statement excusing him for the absence. This doctor's statement, coupled with other evidence, would later prove the grounds for his termination.

Mr. Robert Hess, an administrative officer for the DPC, began to compile evidence that Mr. Hernandez had falsified doctors' statements that excused several of his absences. He had observed that the handwriting of doctors' excuses dated June 15, 1981, and January 23, 1982, did not match the handwriting of other excuses obtained from the same doctor for the injuries suffered in his 1979 accident. In addition, the excuses in question were written on Pacific Hospital of Los Angeles forms, while the others were not.

Interviews were conducted with the physician, Dr. Herman Wilbanks, and with Mr. Vincent Pico, administrative resident at Pacific Hospital. Dr. Wilbanks denied writing the excuses; and Mr. Pico confirmed that Mr. Hernandez had not been a patient at the hospital on the dates in question.

EXHIBIT E Employee Evaluation (January 9, 1982)

INTERIM PERFORMANCE EVALUATION

This interim performance evaluation on Mr. Juan Hernandez is brought about by Data Processing's concern for Mr. Hernandez' technical abilities and our continued desire to assist him to further his own knowledge and skills.

Since the relocation of this Computer Center to the Regional Data Processing Center facility, massive hardware and software changes have occurred. Coupled with these changes, Data Processing has also offered to all of its employees a massive educational and training program. In an environment such as ours, changes mandate a continual update to each employee's knowledges and skills. Nowhere is this more essential than to those actually involved in the understanding, manipulation, and daily operation of the computer itself. It is necessary that each Computer Operator understand his duties and responsibilities to the Center, the Community, and fellow Computer Operators.

It is for this reason that you are receiving this Performance Evaluation.

1. In June 1981, you received a formal written counseling pertaining to your inability to function while at the console.
2. In October 1981, your Performance Evaluation indicates a "needs improvement" in the achievement of objectives and use of tools and equipment. A recommended action is clearly outlined to assist furthering your technical expertise by attending courses offered within the Center.
3. During the months of October and November 1981, two classes on the Payroll System and the operation of the OMICROM system were offered. You were the only operator to fail both courses.
4. You are currently enrolled in the OPS-JES2 course. This course takes an average of 6 to 10 hours to complete. You started on November 1, 1981, and the last computer "logon" for you was December 12, 1981, which reflects only 3.5 hours.
5. You still have not signed up to take required training courses in BFD or MVS.

We recognize that it is sometimes difficult to leave your work station to attend classes; however, this has not been the problem. In the schedule listed below, we will allow you as much time from now until January 23, 1982 to complete or retake the following courses:

1. Complete OPS-JES2, approximately 6.5 hours remaining.
2. Initiate and complete the OMEGAMON course, approximately 5 hours.
3. Initiate and complete the MVS course, approximately 15 hours.
4. Retake the examinations on the Payroll system and OMICROM courses, approximately 2 hours.

It is expected that you, as a senior Computer Operator I with over 10 years experience in Computer Operations, will sustain a passing grade in all of the above mentioned courses. You must be prepared to respond to either a written or oral quiz upon completion of each course.

If you cannot elicit a passing grade for each of the above courses, the Data Processing Center has no recourse but to consider demotion and/or suspension. This Department will offer you as much assistance as is possible to help you attain the knowledge and skills necessary to function in your position.

Mr. Hernandez then altered his story by stating that the excuse that he had submitted for the January 23 absence was a copy of the original. He claimed that his daughter, a pre-med student at Long Beach State University, had copied the original one "as practice for her classes," and he had mistakenly submitted the copy. However, the Los Angeles County Crime Laboratory Bureau confirmed that the handwriting was the same on both forms (Exhibit F).

On March 10, 1982, Mr. Hernandez attended a scheduled disciplinary action meeting in the office of the Deputy Director of the DPC. He was represented by the union. At this meeting, he was given a termination letter and a disciplinary action report effecting his dismissal. He signed the form at the union representative's advice.

Appeal Hearing

An appeal hearing was held on May 10, 1982. Mr. Hernandez was represented by AFSCME Local 121; Los Angeles County was represented by the County Attorney's Office.

EXHIBIT F Crime Laboratory Bureau Report

County of Los Angeles
Public Safety Department
Crime Laboratory Bureau

LABORATORY ANALYSIS REPORT

DATE: March 5, 1982
LACPSD Case #101374
Victim:
Defendant: Juan Hernandez

To: Robert Hess
      Administrative Officer
      Data Processing Center
      County of Los Angeles

The evidence listed below was submitted to this laboratory on March 5, 1982 by Robert Hess:

—Exhibit A: Questioned Pacific Hospital Prescription Form dated 6/15/81
—Exhibit B: Questioned Pacific Hospital Prescription Form dated 1/23/82

Findings, Opinions: The two questioned hospital prescription forms were written by the same author. The author's handwriting is identical to that of the defendant.

Respectfully submitted,

Silas Smith

Silas Smith, Criminalist
Questioned Documents Examiner
Crime Laboratory Bureau

The impartial hearing examiner concluded that violations 1 through 4 were not substantiated, but that the charge of a false claim of leave was substantiated. Mr. Hernandez's termination was sustained (Exhibit G).

EXHIBIT   G   Hearing Examiner's Report

Monk, Murphy, Tannenbaum, and Endicott
Attorneys at Law

Hearing Examiner's Report

Date: June 20, 1982
To: The Honorable Samuel Shapiro
County Attorney
County of Los Angeles

The Honorable Jeremy Irving
Attorney at Law
AFSCME Local 121

On May 10, 1982, the Hearing Examiner heard testimony and considered evidence relative to the termination of Mr. Juan Hernandez from the County of Los Angeles, Data Processing Center. The following charges were advanced to support termination:

1.   alleged violation of time and leave regulations, as described in the formal record of counseling that Mr. Hernandez received on July 29, 1979

2.   alleged willful negligence in the performance of Mr. Hernandez's job duties in the improper printing of forms, as described in the formal record of counseling which he received on July 29, 1979

3.   alleged willful negligence in the performance of Mr. Hernandez's job duties in the failure to properly load programs CICS (S337) so as to prevent damage to the System 3000 Data Base on June 9, 1981, as described in the formal record of counseling which he received on June 29, 1981

4.   alleged failure to complete required training courses (MVS, Payroll system, OMICROM, OMEGAMON, and OPS-JES2) by January 23, 1982, as required by his performance evaluation of January 9, 1982

5.   alleged falsification of physician's excuses for sick leave for June 15, 1981 and January 23, 1982, as described in the Laboratory Analysis Report dated March 5, 1982, LACPSD Case #101374)

Having evaluated all evidence and testimony presented relative to these charges, the Hearing Examiner finds that insufficient evidence exists to document discharge on grounds 1, 2, 3, or 4. However, under the terms of the collective bargaining agreement between AFSCME Local 121 and the Board of Supervisors of the County of Los Angeles, dated October 27, 1981, sufficient evidence has been presented to document discharge on ground 5.

Discharge is hereby affirmed.

Conclusion

Both collective bargaining agreements and disciplinary action procedures provide for progressive discipline of employees for poor performance, and they protect employees against unfair harassment or unsubstantiated allegations.

In the case of Juan Hernandez, the pattern and timing of management's disciplinary action against him are both suspect. A casual review of his record of disciplinary action indicates that it followed on-the-job injuries and his election as shop steward.

On the other hand, it is also clear that Mr. Hernandez's work performance was frequently careless or incompetent. Moreover, his falsification of medical excuses was flagrantly dishonest. Management's efforts to substantiate this required the spending of much time, money, and effort. It was also aided by the fact that the DPC, as a computer-oriented agency, was able to establish objective performance standards (in terms of quantity, quality, and timeliness of production). By monitoring these incidents, it was able to document irregular performance incidents.

Yet despite management's advantages, the only incident of willful misconduct that was upheld was the falsification of medical statements, an infraction relating to personnel rules rather than productivity. The lesson to be learned from this is that management, in the final analysis, when attempting to terminate an employee who is backed by union and legal representation in front of an impartial examiner, must have documentation that unquestionably proves guilt on the part of the employee charged with the violation of a concise, tangible regulation.

Questions:

After finishing the case study and studying the exhibits carefully, be prepared to discuss the following questions in a small group, and to defend your answers in subsequent class discussion.

1. Did the employer (the Data Processing Center) provide Mr. Hernandez with clear performance standards from the time of his employment to the time of his termination?
2. Did the DPC provide Mr. Hernandez with adequate informal counseling concerning his performance discrepancies prior to initiating formal counseling and disciplinary action?
3. Did the employer adequately document Mr. Hernandez's alleged violation of clear performance standards?
4. Who, if anyone, benefitted from the outcome of this case study?

NOTES

[1]*Rankin v. McPherson*, 97 *L Ed 2d* 315 (1987).

[2]*Skinner v. Railway Labor Executives' Association*, 103 *L Ed 2d*, 639 (1989) at 672.

[3]United States Equal Employment Opportunity Commission, "Guidelines on Discrimination Because of Sex," 29 *Code of Federal Regulations* 1604.11, 1985.

[4]Dennis L. Dresang and Paul J. Stuiber, "Sexual Harassment: Challenges for the Future," in Carolyn Ban and Norma M. Riccucci, (eds.), *Public Personnel Management: Current Concerns—Future Challenges* (New York: Longman, 1991), pp. 114–26.

[5]Robert K. Robinson, Delaney J. Kirk, and James D. Powell, "Sexual Harassment: New Approaches for a Changed Environment," in John Matzer, Jr. (ed.), *Personnel Practices for the '90s* (Washington, DC: International City Management Association), 1988, pp. 202–08.

[6]Dresang and Stuiber, "Sexual Harassment," p. 115.

[7]*Meritor Savings Bank v. Vinson*, 91 *L Ed 2d* 49 (1986).

[8]Dresang and Stuiber, "Sexual Harassment," p. 123.

[9]Americans with Disabilities Act of 1990, Public Law 101-336, July 26, 1990.

[10]Ibid., Section 2, Paragraph 7.

[11]U.S. Merit Systems Protection Board, *Federal Personnel Management Since Civil Service Reform* (Washington, DC: MSPB, 1989), pp. 3–8.

[12]*New York Times v. Sullivan*, 11 *L Ed 2d* 686, 700 (1964).

[13]Phillip J. Cooper, "The Supreme Court, the First Amendment, and Freedom of Information," *Public Administration Review 46* (November–December 1986), pp. 622–28.

[14]*Pickering v. Board of Education of Township High School*, 20 *L Ed 2d* 811, 817 (1968).

[15]*Rust v. Sullivan*, 114 *L Ed 2d* 233 (1991) at 259.

[16]*Connick v. Myers*, 75 *L Ed 2d* 708 (1983).

[17]*Rutan v. Republican Party of Illinois*, 111 *L Ed 2d* 52 (1990).

[18]*Branti v. Finkel*, 445 *U.S.* 507 (1980) at 518.

[19]*Rutan v. Republican Party of Illinois*, 111 *L Ed 2d* 52 (1990).

[20]*Connick v. Myers*, 75 *L Ed 2d* 708, 719–720 (1983).

[21]*Skinner v. Railway Labor Executives' Association*, 103 *L Ed 2d* 639 (1989).

[22]*National Treasury Employees' Union v. Von Raab*, 103 *L Ed 2d* 685 (1989) at fn 2.

[23]*Harlow v. Fitzgerald*, 73 *L Ed 2d* 396, 410 (1982).

[24]*Cleveland v. Loudermill*, 470 *U.S.* 532 (1985).

[25]David E. Ewing, *Justice on the Job: Resolving Grievances in the Nonunion Workplace* (Boston: Harvard Business School, 1989), p. vii.

[26]Ibid.

CHAPTER

13

COLLECTIVE BARGAINING

Collective bargaining is the process by which agency managers negotiate terms and conditions of employment with the recognized representative of public employees. It is an alternative personnel system based on the primacy of the value of individual employee rights achieved through the collective voice and power of employees. Collective bargaining is a primary example of the sanction function, in that through collective bargaining the conditions and terms of the employment relationship between employee and employer are determined and maintained. The context for bargaining and resolution of disputes is determined by law and state and federal compliance agencies. Collective bargaining is a set of techniques under which employees are represented in the negotiation and administration of the terms and conditions of their employment. Because collective bargaining can conflict with other personnel systems (primarily civil service, privatization, and affirmative action), it is also an arena which focuses conflict over a number of public policy issues. These include employment quotas versus seniority, drug testing versus employee rights, adversarial dispute resolution versus alternative dispute resolution techniques, and win-lose bargaining versus TQM (total quality management).

By the end of this chapter, you will be able to:

1. Discuss the history of collective bargaining in the public and private sectors.
2. Explain why collective bargaining has a unique role in the public sector because of the close connection between the legal obligation of public agencies to protect employees' constitutional rights, and the focus of unions on the value of the individual rights of their members as employees.
3. Describe the primary practices involved in collective bargaining: unit determination, recognition and certification, contract negotiation, and contract administration.
4. Describe the nature and outcomes of the conflict between collective bargaining and other public personnel systems.
5. Evaluate the role of collective bargaining in influencing the outcome of such public policy conflicts as employment quotas versus seniority, drug testing versus employee rights, adversarial dispute resolution versus alternative dispute resolution techniques, and win-lose bargaining versus TQM (total quality management).

THE HISTORY OF COLLECTIVE BARGAINING

The Private Sector

In the private sector, collective bargaining began in the late 1800s with the rise of industrial unions (The Congress of Industrial Organization) and craft unions (The American Federation of Labor). In the face of bitter opposition by management, aided in many cases by the federal court system, these unions gained political power and legal protection. The New Deal brought about the passage of the Wagner Act (1935), which union leaders hailed as the "Magna Carta of organized labor." This law recognized the right of all private employees to join unions for the purpose of collective bargaining, and it required that management recognize and bargain collectively with these unions. It prohibited the use of many previously common labor practices by management: blacklisting union members, signing "sweetheart contracts" with company unions, and so on. It established a federal agency—the National Labor Relations Board (NLRB)—with the responsibility of certifying unions as appropriate bargaining representatives, supervising negotiations to ensure "good faith" bargaining, and adjudicating deadlocks (impasses) that might arise during contract negotiations. This law was counterbalanced (from management's point of view, at least), by the Taft-Hartley Act (1947), which prohibited labor unions from engaging in unfair labor practices and which allowed states to pass "right to work" laws (statutes forbidding unions from requiring that employees be union members in order to apply for employment).

With the change in economic focus from manufacturing to service that began during the 1960s, the percentage of employees operating under collective bargaining agreements has declined steadily from a high point of about 35 percent in 1957 to a low of about 12 percent today. And with current economic trends (including out-sourcing, job export, automation, tiered wage systems, and continued growth of service jobs in the secondary labor market), it can be expected that labor unions will decline still further. In many cases, their focus on win-lose bargaining over economic issues, and the adversarial approach taken by many negotiators, has made them seem an outmoded method of insuring equitable treatment of employees in an economy where the demand for union-protected jobs has declined substantially.[1]

The Public Sector—Federal

The history of collective bargaining in the public sector has been different. With the exception of a minor provision of the Taft-Hartley Act prohibiting strikes by public employees, and the Postal Service Reorganization Act (1970), which provides for supervision of the U.S. Postal Service collective bargaining by the NLRB, neither the Wagner Act, the Taft-Hartley Act, nor the NLRB is involved at all in public-sector collective bargaining. Rather, collective bargaining in the public sector is regulated by a complex of laws that apply differentially to federal, state, and local governments.

Collective bargaining developed differently in the public sector for two fundamental philosophical reasons. First, in the private sector, the unitary nature of company management makes it possible for a single union to negotiate bilaterally with a single employer. In the public sector, agency managers are accountable to the chief executive, to the legislature, and ultimately to the taxpayers. Thus it is impossible to negotiate binding contracts at the negotiating table (especially on economic issues) without their being subject to further negotiation and ultimate ratification elsewhere within the political arena. Second, the strike, as an ultimate weapon for exercising collective employee power by withholding services, is more difficult to justify and apply in the public sector because its direct impact is on the public, rather than on corporate directors or stockholders.

Within the federal government, the development of collective bargaining lagged behind the private sector because the types of jobs were different, treatment of employees by employers was better, and federal agencies were relatively small compared to the large industrial firms organized during the 1930s in the private sector. Civil service employees were largely incorporated into the merit system that arose between 1923 and 1945. At the same time, politicians began to lose interest in protecting civil service employees because their jobs were no longer subject to favoritism. Between 1961 and 1975, a number of executive orders were issued which gradually granted federal employees the right to join unions and to bargain collectively. Public employees' unions were recognized as legitimate bargaining agents in 1961. Binding grievance arbitration with management was permitted (though not required) in 1969, and the scope of bargaining was broadened in 1975.

In 1978, Congress passed the Civil Service Reform Act, Title VII of which incorporated these executive orders into legislation, and it created a regulatory agency (the Federal Labor Relations Authority) formally authorized to mediate disputes between unions and agency managers. Though this law has clarified such issues as unit determination, scope of bargaining and impasse resolution procedures, federal agency employees still may not strike or bargain collectively over wages and benefits, both of which are set by Congress. The most significant variation from this practice is the U.S. Postal Service. Collective bargaining for this agency, an independent government corporation, is supervised by the NLRB rather than the FLRA.

The Public Sector—State and Local

It is more difficult to comprehend and summarize the status of collective bargaining in state and local governments. This is primarily due to federalism, which means that the authorization and regulation of collective bargaining for state and local governments is a state responsibility. Many federal laws (such as affirmative action requirements and the wage and hour provisions of the Fair Labor Standards Act) regulate personnel practices in state and local government. But without violating federal law, each state is responsible for developing and administering its own laws to regulate collective bargaining by state agencies, and for all local governments within the state as well.

State governments have often gone beyond the federal government in enacting laws to clarify collective bargaining for their employees and for employees of local governments within their jurisdiction. Forty-three states presently have enacted laws affording at least some public employees the right to "meet and confer" or negotiate on wages and working conditions. Public employees in six states are not covered by any labor relations laws, with the possible exception of no-strike provisions applicable to public employees.

In our federal system of government, both the national and state governments have sovereign powers. Local governments are created and regulated by state governments, so they have no sovereignty. With respect to collective bargaining, this has meant that they cannot enter into collective bargaining agreements with employee organizations unless the state has passed legislation authorizing them to do so. Home rule powers make it possible in some cases for a local government to opt out of the state law if state law makes it optional, or to create its own "meet and confer" ordinances. Typically, this has meant that pressure for public sector bargaining first arose among teachers, police, or firefighters in big cities and spread to other areas of a state once it was authorized by state statutes or constitutional revisions. In the forty-three states allowing some form of collective bargaining, over 14,000 governments were conferring or negotiating with over 33,000 bargaining units by 1980. In 1985, 62 percent of all federal employees (1,266,000) were unionized, compared with 40 percent (1,163,000) of state employees and 52 percent (3,868,000) of local government employees.[2] The most heavily unionized groups are mail carriers (90%), school teachers (64%), and firefighters (67%).[3]

The conditions imposed on public-sector collective bargaining make the extent of unionization and the growth of collective bargaining understandable. First, the inability of employees to negotiate bilaterally with management has meant that public-sector unions have developed primarily as interest groups whose objective is to influence the decisions of the legislatures (Congress, state legislatures, city councils, and school boards) that will have the ultimate authority to ratify or reject negotiated agreements, or to set pay and benefits if these are outside the scope of bargaining. This has meant the focus of union organizing activity has been on gaining certification by the state collective bargaining regulatory agency as the designated employee representative and on persuading as many employees within the bargaining unit to become members as soon as possible so that their dues are contributed to the union. Because the Taft-Hartley Act forbids states from enacting "closed shop" provisions applicable to public agencies, public employees are not required to join a union as a condition of employment in a public agency, even though these employees will also be covered by the provisions of the collective bargaining agreement negotiated between the union and agency management. These "free riders" benefit from the gains won by the union for its members, but are able to avoid paying dues if they so choose by declining to join the union.

As a public personnel system with the authority to allocate jobs, collective bargaining reached its zenith between 1970 and 1980. Since then, the relative power of pubic employee unions has declined because of adverse economic and political conditions. There was an overall decline in total public union membership of 7 percent between 1976 and 1982—11 percent among federal employees, 2 percent in state and local government, and 8 percent in education.[4] The reasons are not hard to understand: a declining growth rate in new public-sector employment, increasing voter bias toward economic efficiency (privatization and management rights) and away from the values underlying collective bargaining, and the general movement of population toward the Sun Belt (southern and western states lacking a strong history of private-sector industrial unions and public-sector collective bargaining).[5]

In spite of their recent decline, unions have been successful in gaining support from state and local government employees for many reasons. Unions are not only a powerful interest group, but a source of social and economic benefits outside the scope of a collective bargaining agreement (such as social events, cheaper life and health insurance, consumer co-ops). Also, unions offer their members an additional means of protecting their interest in jobs beyond the protections available through the civil service system.

COLLECTIVE BARGAINING, INDIVIDUAL RIGHTS, AND THE CONSTITUTION

Collective bargaining plays a unique role in the public sector because of its close and interactive relationship with the constitutional rights afforded public employees within civil service systems, and because of the union's role in protecting the individual rights of public employees as a dominant value.

In the private sector, there are only two dominant values competing in the context of collective bargaining—administrative efficiency and employee rights. And management's only legitimate interest is the "bottom line"—protecting profits by keeping production costs (including wages and benefits) low. In the absence of collective bargaining or employment contracts, most employees are hired and fired "at will" (meaning they may be discharged for any reason, or for no reason at all). Similarly, pay and benefits are often negotiated on an individual basis, without general awareness by other employees in the company. Employees are more mobile, often moving from company to company in a quest for higher salaries and benefits. At the same time, companies seek to lower production costs by eliminating jobs, and by moving jobs to regions (or countries) where labor costs are lower (or where environmental health and workplace safety laws are less onerous for employers).

In the public sector, government agencies are required to protect the individual rights of employees. This goal originated in the desire of civil service reformers at the turn of the century to protect public employees from partisan political pressure and to promote efficiency rather than favoritism in public service delivery. In the last few decades, federal courts have recognized that agencies which are constitutionally required to protect the rights of citizens in general cannot violate the constitutional rights of citizens as public employees. But the cumbersome nature of civil service laws regulating disciplinary action, and the need of public managers to maintain efficiency along with other values, has meant that elected officials and public managers continue to exert pressures challenging the individual rights of employees. These include contracting out, privatization, political appointments, and affirmative action (where the rigidities of civil service or collective bargaining systems based on seniority have had an adverse impact on minorities).

In responding to these pressures, public-sector unions have three advantages over their private-sector counterparts. First, public agencies are required to provide services to residents of a particular geographic area. This means that with some exceptions (primarily contracting out or out-sourcing), the employer is required to remain in a fixed geographic area. Second, union members are not just employees, they are voters as well. Given the key role of legislative action in ratifying negotiated collective bargaining agreements in the public sector, the strength of union members as political action arms and voting blocks is important in understanding their political strength. Third, unions in the public sector have been able to obtain court opinions enforcing the value of individual rights as it is defined and protected by seniority systems. This means that not everyone's individual rights are equally protected, only those of union members (which frequently conflict with the rights of protected groups under affirmative action, or of applicants for employment).

Thus, understanding the unique role of collective bargaining in public agencies means understanding the relationship among union power and individual rights, constitutional protection, and political action.

COLLECTIVE BARGAINING PRACTICES

In accordance with the enabling legislation and administrative regulations enacted by federal and state governments, collective bargaining has evolved into a formal and technical process. It is an administrative ritual that involves a number of prescribed concepts: unit determination, recognition and certification, scope of bargaining, contract negotiation, impasse resolution, ratification, contract administration, and unfair labor practices. In this section we discuss their meaning and general application to public-sector collective bargaining.

Unit Determination

Before collective bargaining can occur, a primary responsibility of the federal or state collective bargaining agency is to determine appropriate criteria for the formation of unions.[6] The two most commonly used criteria are to divide employees by agency or by occupation. Agency bargaining units establish each state or local government agency as a separate bargaining unit. While this offers the advantages of working within existing management structure, it can cause a proliferation of bargaining units and inequities among agency contracts.

An alternative is to group employees into general occupational classes, usually on the basis of the state or local government's job classification system. This will result in the establishment of bargaining units such as health, public safety, teachers, general civil service employees, state university system employees, and so on. This method has the advantage of limiting the number of bargaining units and automatically including employees of new agencies in preestablished units. It also clarifies, on a systemwide basis, which employees are excluded from participation in bargaining units because their jobs are managerial or of a policy-making nature.

Both agency-based and occupation-based methods of unit determination require the creation of coordinating mechanisms to ensure that negotiated contracts treat employees in different agencies or occupations equitably. Some public organizations—New York City, for example—have opted to establish a multilevel system of bargaining. Agency-based units bargain over salaries and benefits, while department- and occupation-based units bargain over work rules and grievance procedures.

Both management and labor tend to prefer a relatively small number of bargaining units. From management's viewpoint, it avoids the administrative work created by bargaining with multiple unions and avoids the risk of being "whipsawed" (each union demanding that any changes in pay, benefits, or working conditions recently negotiated for one union apply to all other unions with which management is negotiating). Established unions also prefer fewer bargaining units because they reduce the pressure on union leaders, and increase the economic and political power of large unions. Small and growing unions are more likely to favor proliferation, either because the members consider themselves poorly represented by larger units, or because the leaders wish to gain "a piece of the action" for themselves.

Recognition and Certification

Once appropriate bargaining units have been established by the federal or state labor relations agency, unions are free to organize employees for the purpose of bargaining collectively. While no uniformity among state laws exists, recognition and certification procedures are generally similar in all states, because New York State's Taylor Law was used as a model by many of them.

An employer may voluntarily recognize a union as the exclusive bargaining agent for employees in that bargaining unit without a recognition election if the union can demonstrate that a majority of the employees in the bargaining unit want to be represented by that union. This is done by showing signed authorization cards from the employees.

If voluntary recognition does not occur, the union can win recognition through a representation election. Here, employees are offered the option of approving any union that has been able to show support (through signed authorization cards) from 10 percent of the eligible employees, or declining union representation. Depending upon state law, winning the representation election requires that the union win a majority of the votes cast, or a majority of votes from eligible members of the bargaining unit, regardless of the actual number of votes cast.

Once a union has been voluntarily recognized or has won a representation election, it is formally certified by the labor relations agency as the exclusive agent for that bargaining unit. Certification requires that management recognize this union as the legitimate representative of employees, and that it engage in collective bargaining over all items required or permitted by applicable law.

Scope of Bargaining

The scope of bargaining is simply the range of issues which applicable law requires or permits be negotiated during collective bargaining. If the laws specify which issues are included or excluded, the scope of bargaining is considered *closed*. If no restrictions are placed upon bargainable issues, the scope of bargaining is termed *open*.

Nonetheless, certain issues are usually excluded from the scope of bargaining because they are management prerogatives. Among these are agency structure, agency mission, and work methods or processes. The Civil Service Reform Act (Title VII) prohibits covered federal employees from bargaining over wages and other economic issues such as retirement and health benefits, which are established by Congress. Most state collective bargaining laws allow or require bargaining over wages, benefits, and working conditions. Yet the distinction between issues included in bargaining— or excluded from it—is not always clear. Issues that management considers excluded, such as adding drug testing to selection or promotion criteria, are frequently considered bargainable by unions because they affect member rights or important public policy issues. In such cases, their bargainability must be clarified by the state labor relations agency.

Contract Negotiation and Preparations for Negotiation

Contract negotiation usually begins immediately following recognition and certification, or (if the union has previously been certified) in anticipation of the expiration of an existing contract. The union may be represented by local union officials representing their own membership, or by a professional negotiator who has negotiated similar contracts with other state or local governments. Management is represented by an experienced negotiator supported by a team of experts that will include the personnel manager, the budget officer, a lawyer, and some line managers who understand the impact of contract provisions on agency operations.

In most cases, negotiation occurs "in the sunshine." That is, negotiations are conducted in public because states have an open meetings law that prohibits government officials from determining public policy through back room deals. Prior to the negotiations, it is important that management's negotiators reach a clear understanding with elected officials concerning their preferred contract provisions and their minimally acceptable contract provisions (particularly with respect to economic issues). And it is important that the management team prepare adequately for negotiations by collecting comparative data on other agencies and contract agreements, by preparing spread-sheet analyses of the costs of alternative settlements on economic issues, and by estimating projected revenues available to pay the price tag on economic items. Good negotiation is impossible without good research.

Negotiation itself is concerned with both task-oriented and process-oriented issues. Both sides see it as the opportunity to shape organizational human resource policy and practice. As in any strategic contest, each side attempts to discover the other's strengths and priorities, while keeping its own hidden until the opposition appears most willing to concede on an issue. Good negotiation depends on the negotiators' ability to marshal facts, sense the opposition's strengths and weaknesses, and judge the influence of outside events (such as job actions or media coverage) on the negotiations. "Good faith" bargaining requires negotiators to work for the best deal their side can get, while still remaining receptive to the needs of the other party. Symbolically, negotiation also represents the opportunity for both labor and management to assert their influence over the human resource management policy process within the agency.

Impasse Resolution during Contract Negotiations

There are two types of collective bargaining impasses. The first are disagreements over the substance of negotiations (such factors as pay or benefits). The second are disagreements over the interpretation of contract provisions that have previously been negotiated and approved. The first of these will be discussed below, and the second in the section on contract administration.

If management and union are unable to resolve differences through two-party contract negotiations, there remain three procedures involving intervention by a third party: mediation, fact-finding, and arbitration. The order in which these are employed, and whether they are used at all, will depend on the provisions of the state's collective bargaining law (or federal law, if the negotiation involves a federal agency).

Mediation is the intervention of a neutral third party in an attempt to persuade the bargaining parties to reach an agreement. This may be an independent individual, or one from a group designated by an agency such as the American Arbitration Association or the Federal Mediation and

Conciliation Service. It is in the interest of both parties to make a good-faith effort to reach a voluntary mediated settlement, since this is the last stage at which they will have full control over contract provisions.

If mediation is not successful, negotiations may progress to the second step—*fact-finding*. A fact-finder appointed by the federal or state collective bargaining agency will conduct a hearing at which both sides present data in support of their positions. After these hearings, the fact-finder releases a report to both parties, and to the public, that outlines what he or she considers a reasonable settlement. Although this advisory opinion is not binding, the threat of unfavorable publicity may make either side more willing to reach a negotiated settlement.

If fact-finding is unsuccessful, the final stage may be *arbitration*. Essentially the same procedures are followed as in fact-finding. However, the arbitrator's formal report contains contract provisions that both parties have agreed in advance will be binding. In an effort to avoid having to "split the difference" between extreme positions, the arbitrator may decide in advance to take the "last, best final offer" presented by either side, on the basis of either the entire contract or on an issue-by issue basis. Arbitration of substantive items at impasse during contract negotiation is termed *interest arbitration*, to distinguish it from subsequent arbitration over the meaning of previously ratified contract provisions (*grievance arbitration*) during the contract administration process.

The cost of third-party dispute resolution during negotiations is usually borne equally by both parties.

Contract Ratification

Once a contract has been negotiated by representatives of labor and management, it must be ratified by both the appropriate legislative body and the union's membership before becoming law. For the union, ratification requires support of the negotiated contract by a majority of those voting. For management, it requires that the legislature (state, county, school district) appropriate the funds required to fund the economic provisions of the contract. Because all states have laws or constitutional provisions prohibiting deficit financing of operating expenses, revenue estimates impose an absolute ceiling on the pay and benefits that may be negotiated through collective bargaining. Nor is it considered bad-faith bargaining for a legislature to refuse to ratify a negotiated contract on the grounds that projected revenues will not meet projected expenses. This is why connecting contract negotiations to the budgeting process is so important to effective fiscal management in government.

The requirement that a negotiated contract be ratified by the legislature is a key difference between private- and public-sector negotiations. It is also a sore point for union advocates because it limits the application of binding interest arbitration to public- sector contract negotiations, because courts have uniformly held that the legislature cannot delegate its responsibility for keeping expenditures within revenues. Although union advocates frequently (and justifiably) protest that the legislature is biased toward management, state laws require that the state or local legislature take all interests into account—including those of the union and its members—in deciding whether to ratify a negotiated contract.

Contract Administration

Once a contract has been negotiated and ratified, both union and management are responsible for administering its provisions. Key actors in implementation include the union steward, a union member who will interpret the contract for the employees and serve as their advocate and representative to management; supervisors, who will be implementing contract provisions relating to everyday employee-employer relations; and the personnel manager, who is management's expert on how the contract affects human resource policy and practice.

Conflicts are bound to arise during contract administration because reaching compromises during negotiations often requires agreement on what will later turn out to be ambiguous contract language. For example, labor and management may agree during contract negotiations that the shop steward "may spend a reasonable amount of time not to exceed two hours per week on union activities." Subsequently, differences may arise over such issues as whether the steward is in fact spending a "reasonable" amount of time on union business, or whether management has the right to approve when this time can be taken. Negotiations will then be needed to determine whether the shop steward's or the supervisor's actions constitute a violation of the contract's provisions.

Part of the contract will therefore outline the process for resolving grievances that occur during contract implementation. The process may begin very informally with discussion between union and management representatives. If the issue is not satisfactorily resolved informally, it is written up as a formal grievance and appealed through channels up to a neutral third party outside the agency. Binding grievance is the norm (in contrast to the lack of binding interest arbitration over contract negotiation impasses).

Management should view the grievance process as one more potentially beneficial effort by employees to make the organization more effective by calling attention to inefficient or inequitable supervisory practices. It can serve as an internal evaluation device, a means of instituting planned change, and a method of redressing inequitable organizational practices. It is recommended that supervisors and public personnel managers know the contract, maintain open lines of communication with employees, meet and deal informally with union representatives over potential grievances, exhibit uniform and adequate documentation for all personnel actions, and keep the record open to unions and employees.

Unfair Labor Practices

Federal and state collective bargaining laws all include lists of personnel practices forbidden to labor and management. In this regard, it is most important that management remember that employees have an *absolute* right to organize and bargain collectively in federal agencies, and in those states where enabling collective bargaining legislation exists. Management has no corresponding right to prevent employees from doing so. This means that management cannot seek to influence the outcome of a representation election by coercing, threatening, or intimidating employees. It can present information on the comparative advantages and disadvantages of union membership; and it can restrict union organizing to public locations (lunchrooms, bulletin boards) that do not interfere with the work of the agency and do not occur on company time.

During negotiations, each party is bound to bargain in "good faith." This means that each party will listen to the other side and will negotiate. A failure to show up for scheduled negotiations, or a "take it or leave it" approach to the negotiations themselves, will likely lead to a formal charge of unfair labor practices being filed with the labor relations regulatory agency. Findings against the agency can result in fines, administrative sanctions, or the invalidation of negotiated settlements or representation elections.

Whether or not public employees should have the right to strike is a hotly contested issue in public agencies because it pits fundamental rights against each other. On the one hand, public employees are guaranteed constitutional protections of association and expression. In addition, there is strong justification for extending to employees the same right to withhold their services as a bargaining weapon that private employees enjoy. On the other hand, the importance of services to the public, and the monopolistic nature of most public agencies, strengthens the argument that public-sector strikes are less tolerable or politically acceptable than those in the private sector.

In practice, the outcome of strikes by public employees seems to depend on a variety of fairly predictable factors, among them applicable laws, historical practice, and the relative control of the union over the job market. In the federal government and most states, all strikes by public employees are illegal. In some cases (such as the ill-fated strike of the 10,000 member Professional Air Traffic Controllers Organization in 1981), employees who strike are fired, the union is de-certified, and union officers are fined and jailed. Yet in fields where strikes are the norm (such as education), and where there are no available qualified substitutes for union members (such as law enforcement) strikes often occur with impunity. Or they occur under a different guise, such as "sickouts," "job actions," and "blue flu" (where employees are absent or unproductive in concert, without a strike formally being called).

In reality, increasing economic pressures have both increased and diminished the likelihood of strikes by public employees. Most employees have lost real purchasing power over the past two decades, and see themselves as making sacrifices in order to maintain a high level of public service without tax increases, under conditions of inflation. However, the willingness of management to use alternative instruments (such as contracting out or privatization) to provide public services frequently reminds public employees (or threatens them, depending on your perspective) that they are likely to have better job security, pay, and benefits within civil service systems and collective bargaining than they would ever get under contracting out or privatization.

COLLECTIVE BARGAINING AND OTHER PERSONNEL SYSTEMS

Collective bargaining is one method by which terms and conditions of employment are determined. But while collective bargaining contracts demonstrate employee influence on some personnel functions (primarily pay, benefits, promotion, and disciplinary action), it is not a complete personnel system. That is, it has no impact on selection (applicants are not eligible for union membership until they are hired and pass their probationary period) and no control over other personnel systems (like affirmative action). Both agency managers and unions are required to comply with affirmative action laws. In this sense, both unions and management have been affected by affirmative action much more than collective bargaining has influenced the selection and promotion process. Although bona fide seniority systems are protected under affirmative action law, systems developed after 1964 that discriminate against particular groups are illegal. Redress may require that particular applicants or employees be given "fictional seniority" to enable them to compete fairly for promotions or reassignments.

The compensation and benefits granted to public employees have been particularly affected by collective bargaining. Control over these activities has passed from management to the legislature, which now has three roles in the process: to pass enabling legislation governing contract negotiations, to pass appropriations bills funding negotiated collective bargaining agreements, and to pass substantive legislation incorporating noneconomic issues into the jurisdiction's personnel laws and relations. Salaries and benefits are the main reason employees unionize, and there is some evidence that employees who bargain collectively enjoy higher pay and benefits (about 7 percent higher) than their nonunionized counterparts. Yet other factors like urbanization, population, the local economic climate, and the relative demand for employees in the field are more significant determinants of salary. And continued pressure to reduce the cost of government has lessened the impact of collective bargaining on public employee salaries.[7]

Ultimately, it seems likely that unions will continue to decline in the private sector, especially given the trends toward dual labor markets, outsourcing, and job flight. In the public sector, union survival will be dependent on public perceptions of union members' concern for costs and productivity (rather than just working conditions, pay, and benefits); and elected officials' assessment of the political strength of unions in making decisions about contracting out or privatization of functions that were previously performed by unionized civil service employees.

COLLECTIVE BARGAINING AND PUBLIC POLICY

Collective bargain affects a number of public policy issues. A primary issue, which has already been discussed in the chapter on affirmative action, is the conflict over the use of seniority systems in making personnel decisions. And there are others, notably the controversy over drug testing and employee rights, and the underlying conflict between participative and adversarial dispute resolution procedures between employees and managers.

Drug Testing versus Employee Rights

Most major public- and private-sector employers have by now made a decision routinely to test applicants for substance abuse. Or they will soon make this decision. Michael Walsh, head of behavioral and clinical pharmacology at the National Institute of Drug Abuse, predicts that substance abuse testing will be a standard requirement to get a job with a public agency or major private-sector employer within five years.[8] By this time, employers will have decided that the risks of substance abuse (and the political pressure for drug testing) outweigh the indignities and uncertainties of testing or interpreting test results.[9]

Collective bargaining complicates the process of implementing a substance abuse testing program because it introduces a third party—the union or employee association—into what had previously been a two-party relationship (employer-employee). It does not necessarily make the implementation process more difficult, because the union can be a powerful ally if it is treated with respect and encouraged to participate in the development and implementation of testing policies and programs. It does mean that management should recognize that the union's initial reaction to management's proposing a substance abuse testing program will be suspicion, if not outright hostility.[10]

Here's how to implement substance abuse testing without incurring this reaction:

First, the employer should recognize that increasing awareness of workplace substance abuse places the union in a difficult position. On the one hand, unions recognize that the problems caused by employee substance abuse (low productivity, increased health-care costs, and increased liability risks) are legitimate concerns of both labor and management. On the other hand, the union is obligated to protect its members rights against unfair, unreasonable, and possibly unconstitutional testing procedures. Just as it is unfair for the union to criticize all management attempts to control substance abuse as unwarranted, so it is unfair for management to criticize the union as being inherently and unalterably opposed to all substance abuse programs implemented by management.

With this in mind, the employer should recognize that the first step is to cooperate fully with the union by involving it completely in the development and implementation of any program that is being contemplated. This includes the collection or analysis of data on the extent of the problem, the development of proposals to combat it, the negotiation of those proposals as part of a collective bargaining agreement, and the effective and fair administration of the program once it has become company (or agency) policy.

Initially, the company or agency may wish to start by implementing some of the steps to combat workplace substance abuse without implementing a testing program. This can include increased monitoring of employee productivity, increased education and training for employees on the personal and organizational problems caused by substance abuse, the availability of employee assistance programs outside the employer on a voluntary basis, and the institution of progressive discipline following informal counseling for performance deficiencies, even if substance abuse is suspected as the underlying cause of the problem. All of these programs can be instituted easily and unilaterally by management, provided the union is involved at the outset, because their intent is not only to increase productivity, but to help employees (on a voluntary basis) with personal problems that are beginning to affect productivity. Even the most adversarial union will support these measures, unless past managerial practices give it cause to suspect the employer's intentions.

The employer may also be able unilaterally to initiate mandatory testing of applicants. These people are not union members at the time of application, nor is the union normally interested in protecting their rights until they have been hired, become dues-paying members, and passed their probationary period. Even if the union suspects that the employer intends to eventually implement testing for employees as well, applicant testing is still a legitimate means of gaining information about applicants, learning more about the testing process and employee reactions to it, and reducing the risks of workplace substance abuse for new employees.

If the employer does decide to implement testing of current employees, this should never be done unilaterally.[11] At the very least, it will antagonize the union unnecessarily, in that union leaders will be forced by their members to react strongly against testing if it is presented as a nonnegotiable change in working conditions. The union will file a grievance against testing, or allege that the unilateral imposition of testing for employees is an unfair labor practice. The collective bargaining regulatory agency (such as the National Labor Relations Board in the private sector) or the courts will order that bargaining occur with respect to this issue, and management will be required to negotiate anyway. It would have been simpler, and more constructive, to have discussed the proposal with the union in the first place, either informally or formally during contract negotiations.

An employer who wishes to implement testing for employees should carefully develop a complete policy covering the critical policy issues discussed in Chapter 11. Particular attention should be given to those aspects of the testing policy or procedure that are most likely to be resisted by the union as violative of employee rights, and to those aspects that are potentially most capable of winning union support through their emphasis on rehabilitation and protection of employee rights. Here are some particularly critical areas.

The basis for testing must be clearly established. Unions will generally object to all random or universal testing as a violation of employees' individual rights. An employer who wishes to implement such testing must be prepared to face a court challenge, or be supported by previous court decisions establishing the legitimacy of such testing on the basis of the need for public health and safety, or the sensitive nature of the position. Also, an employer who wishes to test employees on the basis of reasonable suspicion must be prepared to define this operationally and demonstrate that supervisors (or whoever makes this determination) have the skills to refer employees for testing knowledgeably and fairly.

The employer must solicit the union's help to ensure that the testing procedure itself (collection, handling, analysis, and storage of the sample) will be done according to appropriate technical standards so that the possibility of "false positives" is reduced to a minimum. The invasiveness and indignities of the collection process itself must be minimized insofar as possible.

Management should solicit and follow union suggestions designed to protect the confidentiality of the testing process, and the referral of employees who test positive to the employee assistance program.

Management should join with the union in affirming that substance abuse (whether of alcohol, prescription drugs, or illegal drugs) is an illness.

The employer should affirm that the primary objective of substance abuse testing is to provide helpful treatment to employees before their personal problems (including substance abuse) have an irreparable effect on their job performance or employment status.

Management should pledge to involve the union in the development, implementation, and evaluation of the testing program—not only of testing itself, but the effectiveness of the employee assistance program (EAP). The objective of the EAP itself should be rehabilitation. The EAP should be supported, staffed, operated, and evaluated to ensure that it can realistically be expected to meet its objectives. The characteristics of the EAP, the services it provides, and the relative contributions of employees and the employer to the cost of those services are all legitimate items for inclusion within the scope of a collective bargaining agreement.

Employees almost universally believe that the employer's first response to employees with a substance abuse problem should be to help the employee. This is regardless of whether the problem is with a legal drug (such as alcohol) or an illegal one. This means that employers who emphasize that alcohol and drug abuse are health and efficiency issues to be dealt with from a medical perspective (at least until it is evident that medical treatment has been unsuccessful), and who follow through on this policy in their personnel practices, are more likely to be able to "sell" themselves to their employees. By continuing to inform employees that help for addiction problems is available through the employer, and by providing this help to employees who seek it, personnel managers are likely to find that more and more employees will favor substance abuse testing.

The employer should carefully and thoroughly train supervisors to manage for productivity, recognize the indicators of a performance problem, adequately document performance discrepancies, and effectively counsel employees with performance problems.

The employer should freely share information with the union about proposed substance abuse testing policies and procedures. It should solicit union help in implementing the program and selling it to employees.

Adversarial Dispute Resolution versus Alternative Dispute Resolution and Total Quality Management

The greatest disagreement over the actual and potential impact of unions lies in the assessment of their contribution to organizational effectiveness and productivity. Opponents claim that unions increase the adversarial climate of supervision within agencies, making it harder for managers to manage productively, and creating a climate in which disagreements are resolved through quasi-legal mechanisms rather than through more informal (and implicitly more effective) procedures like discussion and consensus. They conclude that unions are dinosaurs, as outmoded as the hierarchical organizational structure and the chain of command. They see unions as suited to an era of industrial technology and adversarial relationships between labor and management, but ill-suited to the contemporary challenges of economic competition, dynamism, and teamwork.

Proponents respond by defending unions. They assert, first, that unions are more necessary today than before because of the increased number of service jobs, and because of management's continual tendency to exploit disadvantaged employees (most of them immigrants, women, and minorities) in service positions. Also, they claim management has not lived up to its responsibility of dealing with unions in good faith. Union leaders point with pride to examples of productivity improvement through union efforts to institute TQM (total quality management) and other innovations, once management has admitted the legitimacy of the union and its role in increasing productivity as well as protecting the interests of its members.

SUMMARY

Collective bargaining is law, process, and ritual. As law, it provides the constitutional and statutory foundation which enables employees collectively to negotiate the terms and conditions of employment with managers (and indirectly, with legislators and the public). Second, it is the standardized procedures by which this collective negotiation takes place. And third, it is a ritual through which employees demonstrate their relative power (through the sanction process) over employment policy and practice. As such, it is an alternative personnel system based on the primacy individual employee rights.

Collective bargaining may conflict with other personnel systems (primarily civil service, affirmative action, and politics) over a number of public policy issues. These include employment quotas versus seniority, drug testing versus employee rights, adversarial dispute resolution versus alternative dispute resolution techniques, and win-lose bargaining versus TQM (total quality management).

KEY TERMS

American Arbitration Association
(binding) arbitration
certification
Civil Service Reform Act (Title VII)
concession bargaining

contract administration
contract negotiation
fact-finding
Federal Labor Relations Authority (FLRA)
Federal Mediation and Conciliation Service (FMCS)
givebacks
grievance
grievance arbitration
interest arbitration
labor relations regulatory agency
mediation
National Labor Relations Act (Wagner Act)
National Labor Relations Board (NLRB)
out-sourcing
Postal Service Reorganization Act
ratification
recognition
scope of bargaining
Taft-Hartley Act
unfair labor practice
unit determination

DISCUSSION QUESTIONS

1. Why is the history of collective bargaining in the public sector different from that in the private sector?
2. Why is the legal structure of collective bargaining more complex and confusing in the public sector than in the private sector?
3. What are the reasons for the recent loss of membership by public-sector unions? For their loss of political strength?
4. Should management's strategy toward collective bargaining be (a) opposition to unions and avoidance of collective bargaining, or (b) acceptance of unions' legitimacy and participation in collective bargaining? What factors will influence which option management chooses to pursue?

CASE STUDY: COSTING-OUT A PROPOSED CONTRACT

The Town of Mangrove Junction, located in southeast Florida, has a population of about 22,000. Its city government employs about 120 people, including 16 public works department employees responsible for operating the town's three garbage trucks.

The public works employees are represented by Local 330 of the American Federation of State, County, and Municipal Employees (AFSCME). The composition of the bargaining unit and the salaries of the positions are shown in the table.

Every spring, the Mangrove Junction city manager and public works director sit down and negotiate a contract with AFSCME Local 330. Economic issues are addressed every year; noneconomic issues every three years, unless both labor and management agree to discuss them more frequently. Only economic issues are being negotiated this year.

The union demands are:

- 50 cents per hour increase in the salary of trash truck operators
- A 50 cents per hour increase in the salary of trash assistants
- An increase in paid holidays from 10 to 12 annually

As the management negotiating team, your first task is to compute the present cost of salaries for these 16 employees. Do so in the space below, using the following formulas:

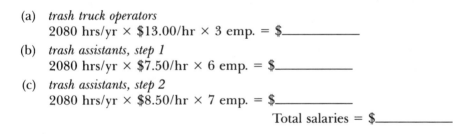

(a) *trash truck operators*
  2080 hrs/yr × $13.00/hr × 3 emp. = $_____

(b) *trash assistants, step 1*
  2080 hrs/yr × $7.50/hr × 6 emp. = $_____

(c) *trash assistants, step 2*
  2080 hrs/yr × $8.50/hr × 7 emp. = $_____

  Total salaries = $_____

Second, compute the total cost of 10 paid holidays per year for each of these groups:

(a) *trash truck operators*
  80 hrs × $13.00/hr × 3 emp. = $_____

(b) *trash assistants, step 1*
  80 hrs × $7.50/hr × 6 emp. = $_____

(c) *trash assistants, step 2*
  80 hrs × $8.50/hr × 7 emp. = $_____

  Total vacations = $_____

Third, compute the additional salary costs involved in paying the salaries requested by the union, and add them to the current salary total:

(a) *trash truck operators*
      2080 hrs × \$14.00/hr × 3 emp. = \$_____

CLASSIFICATION	NUMBER OF EMPLOYEES	SALARY
Trash truck operator	3	\$13.00/hour
Trash assistants		
step 1	6	7.50/hour
step 2	7	8.50/hour
Total	16	

(b) *trash assistants, step 1*
      2080 hrs × \$8.00/hr × 6 emp. = \$_____

(c) *trash assistants, step 2*
      2080 hrs × \$9.00/hr × 7 emp. = \$_____
             Total projected salary = \$_____

Fourth, compute the additional holiday costs involved in increasing the number of paid holidays from 10 to 12, under the new projected salary rate. This increase in vacations combines the increase in vacation benefits (10 days to 12) plus the "roll-up"—the increased value of those vacation days caused by the increase in salary.

(a) *trash truck operators*
      96 hrs × \$14.00/hr × 3 emp. = \$_____

(b) *trash assistants, step 1*
      96 hrs × \$8.50/hr × 6 emp. = \$_____

(c) *trash assistants, step 2*
      96 hrs × \$9.00/hr × 7 emp. = \$_____
             Total projected vacation cost = \$_____

Finally, give the total increase in salary and vacation benefits requested by the union, as both a dollar figure and a percentage of the current benefits. (It should be noted here that other monetary items such as worker's compensation, pension contributions, and sick leave pay will also be affected by changes in pay and benefits.)

$$\frac{\text{new projected salary}}{\text{current salary}} = \text{projected increase} \underline{\quad}\%$$

$$\frac{\text{new projected vacations}}{\text{current vacations}} = \text{projected increase} \underline{\quad}\%$$

$$\frac{\text{total projected salary + vacations}}{\text{current salary + vacations}} = \text{projected increase} \underline{\hspace{1cm}}\%$$

Based on these figures, what economic and other considerations would you advise the Mangrove Junction City manager to study before negotiating a compromise with the union? Consider the rate of inflation, the tax base of the city, the productivity of the trash crews, and any other variables you consider relevant.

NOTES

[1]T. Kochan and H. Katz, *Collective Bargaining and Industrial Relations* (Homewood, Ill: Irwin, 1988).

[2]"Union Recognition in Government," *Government Employee Relations Report 71* (January 18, 1988), 208.

[3]U.S. Department of Commerce, Bureau of the Census, *Labor Relations in State and Local Government 3*, 3 (Washington, DC: U.S. Government Printing Office, 1985).

[4]L. Troy and N. Shiflin, "The Flow and Ebb of U.S. Public Sector Unionism," *Government Union Review 5* (1985), 3–148.

[5]Charles Coleman, *Managing Labor Relations in the Public Sector* (San Francisco: Jossey-Bass, 1990), pp. 74–75.

[6]A good general reference for public-sector unit determination is W. Gershenfeld, "Public Employee Unionization: An Overview." In Association of Labor Relations Agencies, *The Evolving Process: Collective Negotiations in Public Employment* (Ft. Washington, PA: Labor Relations Press, Inc., 1985).

[7]M. Derber, "Management Organization for Collective Bargaining in the Public Sector," in B. Aaron, J. Najita, and J. Stern (eds.), *Public Sector Bargaining*, 2nd ed. (Washington, DC: BNA, 1987).

[8]I. Miners and N. Nykodym, "Put Drug Detection to the Test," *Personnel Journal*, August 1986, p. 10.

[9]T. Sexton and U. Zilz, "On the Wisdom of Mandatory Drug Testing," *Journal of Policy Analysis and Management 7*, 3, 542–64; and L. Gomez-Mejia and D. Balkin, "Dimensions and Characteristics of Personnel Manager Perceptions of Effective Drug-testing Programs," *Personnel Psychology 40* (1987), 745–63.

[10]"Jar Wars: Drug Testing and Your Rights," *Public Employee 51*, 8 (November-December 1986), pp. 6–15.

[11]M. Masters, "The Negotiability of Drug Testing in the Federal Sector: A Political Perspective," *The Journal of Collective Negotiations in the Public Sector 17*, 4 (1988), 309–25; and M. Aron, "Drug Testing: The Employer's Dilemma," *Labor Law Journal*, March 1987, pp. 157–65.

DEVELOPING A STRATEGIC
PUBLIC AGENCY HUMAN
RESOURCE CAPABILITY

Developing a *strategic* human resource capability in a public agency means resolving human resource management and policy issues so as to enhance the agency's ability to accomplish its mission. This is a primary responsibility of political leaders, agency managers, and personnel directors. They will be better able to do this if they understand that (1) human resources are vital to mission accomplishment, (2) the clarity and vision with which human resource management and policy issues are addressed within the agency sends a message to managers and employees inside the agency, and to political leaders outside it; and (3) the success or failure of strategic human resource capabilities within an agency is shaped by underlying realities.

The purpose of this chapter is to condense and analyze the recurrent themes addressed in this book as the emergent issues of public personnel management, and to therefore provide a springboard to research and practice in the field. In so doing, we will explore the underlying realities of public personnel management, and describe how they affect the role of political leaders, agency managers, and personnel directors who wish to develop the agency's strategic human resource capability.

1. THE FOCUS OF HUMAN RESOURCE MANAGEMENT IN PUBLIC AGENCIES HAS CHANGED FUNDAMENTALLY

The 1980s taught public personnel managers that personnel systems must be increasingly responsive to external pressures for productivity, work measurement, and political accountability. Due to a variety of political and economic pressures, the focus of public personnel management changed from management of positions, as was the case under traditional civil service systems, to accomplishment of agency mission.[1]

For public personnel managers accustomed to working primarily within civil service systems, this has meant recognizing the need for increased flexibility and experimentation in many areas (such as rank-in-person personnel systems, broad pay banding, and group performance evaluation and reward systems).[2] Political leaders, agency managers, and personnel managers have often had to lay aside any biases they may have in favor of traditional civil service systems, and objectively evaluate the comparative advantages of alternative personnel systems (such as privatization or contracting out) that may enable them to *manage to budget* and *manage to mission*.[3]

For this objective evaluation to occur, elected officials and agency managers have also had to recognize the ways in which their views have been bounded by traditional views of personnel management. In truth, these officials have been largely responsible for public personnel managers' misplaced concern for position management through their own misplaced focus on political control of agencies (through such devices as line item budgets, personnel ceilings, and average grade level restrictions). Instead, elected officials have now begun to recognize the necessity of granting public executives and personnel managers budget and resource flexibility, and then making these public executives and personnel managers accountable for results.[4]

Once elected officials do this, agency managers and personnel directors need to maximize flexibility of resources by experimenting with a variety of personnel systems and techniques to find those which are most effective at achieving their agency's mission. The managers' and directors' personal development requires that they train themselves to thrive in a contingent environment where objectives are diverse and means-end relationships are uncertain—and that they train and reward subordinates for taking similar risks, and for learning from them. It is only through leadership from the top, leadership that speaks directly to employees' highest aspirations rather than to their fears of political manipulation, that the organizational culture will support self-motivated productivity rather than hierarchy, mistrust and inertia.[5]

2. THE WORKFORCE OF THE FUTURE WILL BE DIVERSE AND HIGHLY TRAINED

The Hudson Institute's report on the changing workforce predicts that the next decade will bring about a change in its composition. Chief among these demographic changes are an older work force, one comprised more of women and minorities, and one requiring technical and professional skills increasingly in short supply because of growing deficiencies in our educational system. This change means that personnel managers, no matter what mix of personnel systems they utilize, will be forced not only to move toward accepting diversity, but embracing it in order to accomplish agency mission. It is important to recognize initially that workforce diversity is not just a variant on civil rights or affirmative action.[6] While the two concepts are related, they differ in three important respects. Workforce diversity is broader and more individualized; it focuses on accomplishment of agency mission rather than compliance with sanctions; and, as a result, its locus of control is internal rather than external.

The objective of affirmative action is the full representation of protected classes of employees within the agency workforce, proportionate to their share of the appropriate labor market. Personnel directors who focus on affirmative action compliance therefore tend to regard employees as members of classes, and use these categories to drive or influence personnel decisions. The focus of affirmative action is therefore on inputs (number and percentage of positions filled by members of particular groups). And the locus of control is external, in that it is based on review of personnel practices by affirmative action compliance agencies.

The concept of workforce diversity implies a broader and more individualized perspective on diversity—not just affirmative action categories, but a range of knowledge, skills, and abilities which managers must recognize and factor into personnel decisions. The importance of this change is accentuated by agency managers' changing focus on work management rather than position management. Once agency managers and personnel directors have changed their focus from position management to work management, they are forced to alter their focus on employees from categorical to individual. Good managers have always done this, of course. They have recognized that the secret of assigning the right employee to the right job means (1) determining the important tasks of the position, (2) specifying the combination of KSAs needed to accomplish these tasks, and (3) picking the employee who has the best combination of requisite KSAs.

To see what this shift in focus means, personnel managers might look at the development of *individual development plans (IDPs)* for employees.

These require a matching, and a conscious assessment of the adequacy of this match, of employee characteristics with mission objectives not just for the present, but as a continual process that takes into account changes in employee KSAs and agency mission. As a second example, personnel directors might look at the individualized matching of jobs and employees with disabilities. It has often been difficult for employers to comply with federal laws—such as the Americans with Disabilities Act—requiring accommodation of what used to be called "handicapped" employees because making "reasonable accommodation" requires flexible, individualized, and insightful matching of employee characteristics and work requirements.

Second, workforce diversity differs from affirmative action in that it focuses on outputs—the combination or balance of KSAs needed to get the work done—rather than inputs—the racial and ethnic composition of the work force. Workforce diversity is therefore linked to a number of other recent trends such as performance management, management by objectives, delegation, and results oriented job descriptions (RODs). All of these focus on work and on mission accomplishment, rather than on position management or process conformity.

Third, workforce diversity differs from affirmative action in that its locus of control is internal rather than external. Agency managers must ask, "Is the agency allocating resources appropriately so as to accomplish its mission?" rather than, "Is our work force sufficiently representative to avoid externally imposed sanctions by affirmative action compliance agencies?" or "Are our personnel policies and procedures adequate to avoid externally imposed sanctions by affirmative action compliance agencies?" Thus, acceptance of workforce diversity goes hand in hand with increased accountability of agency managers for mission accomplishment, and increased focus on employees as resources rather than as positions to be controlled.[7]

The challenge of channeling diversity into productivity is complicated by the breadth of expectations members of diverse cultures bring to their work, both as individuals and as members of those cultures. Differences are not assets without an organizational commitment of respect, tolerance, and dignity. Without these virtues, differences consume organizational resources without positive results. The broader the differences, the more pressure we can expect on organizational processes designed to negotiate and resolve differences in expectations and obligations. The concept of justice and fair play may become as important within organizations marked by diversity as they are in our society generally.

While we can expect to see diversity in the workplace invigorate the goal of organizational justice, the Supreme Court's role in human resources management can be expected to decline. After a brief era when the rights of public employees expanded significantly, we have recently seen a turn away from judicial protection of employee rights in favor of administrative discretion. In part, this reflects a growing acceptance among managers that human resources regulations must respect individual rights. In other ways, the Court simply has shown increasing reluctance to become involved in personnel administration. There is no reason to believe the Court's deference to administrative efficiency will decline in the near future. Gains in organizational justice will have to come from legislative and executive/administrative rather than judicial action.

3. EMPLOYEES AS A CAPITAL ASSET, NOT A PRODUCTION COST

Over the past decade, political and economic considerations have led elected officials to consider privatization and contracting out as alternatives to traditional delivery of public goods and services through civil service systems. As a consequence, much of the growth in public agency employment has been through contract services and a secondary labor market of part-time, temporary and seasonal employees. Chapter 11 concluded that employers (public and private sector) consider this market a valuable strategy for reducing benefit costs and legal liability. And as Chapter 13 noted, the threat of privatization or contracting out is a powerful strategy for breaking unions or gaining give-backs during contract renegotiation. But Chapter 8 also noted examples from the public and private sectors in support of the conclusion that the long-term benefits were less certain, particularly given the relationship between equity and expectancy theories and employee productivity. Clearly, the message for employees hired outside civil service systems through the secondary labor market (on a temporary, part-time, or contract basis without pension or health-care benefits) is, "Our human resource management objective is to reduce costs, not to develop or maintain employees as a human resource asset."

In this era where concern for short-term costs is paramount, it may be well to heed the problems the United States is facing today because of its deteriorating urban infrastructure (public transportation, roads and bridges, and schools). These problems are a direct result of political decisions to reduce short-term costs my postponing scheduled facilities maintenance or replacement. As an example, consider Chicago's postponement of a $10,000 repair project to correct a structural flaw in the underground tunnel system linking buildings throughout the downtown business district. In 1992 the Chicago River broke through the flaw and poured into the tunnel system, paralyzing the business district for weeks and costing businesses an estimated $1 billion daily.

During the 1960s and 1970s, there was increased interest in a concept termed *human resource asset accounting (HRAC)*. This concept applied the capital budgeting principles common in facilities management (buildings and equipment) to proposed personnel programs as well. Programs such as training, retention of key staff, or more effective benefit programs might have high initial operating budget costs; and they would also result in a long-term increase in the value of human resource assets. Other programs such as early retirement or layoffs might considerably reduce operating expenses in the short run, yet result in an eventual greater decrease in the value of the company's human resource assets.[8]

Early retirement programs for university faculty are one example of HRAC in practice. These plans offer universities with declining enrollments the opportunity to reduce short-term pay and benefit costs by offering selected faculty (those who almost meet minimum age and seniority criteria for retirement) a limited "window of opportunity" during which they can retire at close to full benefits. The university maintains productivity by using adjunct or nontenured faculty to teach classes. The asset loss represented by professors who retire early is considered a less significant factor, based on a conscious comparison of short-term operating costs with long-term human resource asset values.

4. PERSONNEL MANAGEMENT IS A STRATEGIC AGENCY CORPORATE ACTIVITY

Public personnel management is the techniques and policy choices related to agency human resource management. Taken together, these techniques and choices send messages to employees, managers, and external stakeholders about the value the agency places on human resources. In an organization with an effective human resource management capability, these messages are clear and positive. For managers and employees within the agency, this is the message: "We need you to achieve our mission." For elected officials outside the agency, the message is: "Employees are a cost and an asset. Personnel management is the functions by which productive agencies reduce costs and maintain assets." And for the personnel director, the message is: "You are the lead member of the management team in developing, implementing and evaluating human resource policies and programs."

5. EFFECTIVE PERSONNEL MANAGEMENT REQUIRES A MANAGEMENT INFORMATION AND EVALUATION SYSTEM

The collection and use of information for program planning, control and evaluation purposes is essential to public management. Yet this collection and use need not be systematic. That is, data can be collected and used on an ad hoc and piecemeal basis, rather than through a management information system whose pieces are related to each other and to the objectives of the agency. For example, a manager can be concerned about a particular problem, such as equipment downtime and low employee productivity. In the absence of a management information system, a manager will probably collect data on this problem by conferring with supervisors and examining existing records (such as equipment repair costs) to determine the extent of the problem. This will result in the development of a solution that seems correct on an intuitive or judgmental basis. For instance, the manager might propose a training program to increase employees' ability to use equipment correctly, or develop an incentive system to increase their desire to do so.

Yet it is also possible to design a management information system that routinely collects information on various factors related to organizational effectiveness, and to present this information to managers in the form of reports they can use to make necessary changes in policies or procedures. A department might routinely produce information on equipment costs, personnel costs, overtime, and productivity. If the method of collecting and compiling information into reports is systematically designed to answer the needs of planners, managers and other evaluators, it is called a *management information system (MIS)*; those elements of the system that concern management of employees are called the *human resource management information system (HRMIS)*.[9]

Let's look at a typical city and see how its human resource management information system (HRMIS) might relate to the four personnel functions introduced in Chapter 1. The relationship between the HRMIS and *planning* occurs during the budget preparation and approval process. Revenue estimates are matched against program proposals. The cost of proposed programs depends upon such factors as the number and type of employees, their pay and benefits, and the training they will need. All these data are collected and stored as part of the budget and payroll system. Affirmative action is the personnel activity that dominates *acquisition* of human resources. The extent to which social equity considerations will influence selection is determined by the extent to which particular groups are underutilized, and the validity of the selection criteria. Both utilization analysis and empirical validation techniques are dependent upon computerized applicant data such as race, sex, age, test scores, and performance evaluations. Employee *development* involves the comparison of performance and productivity data against organizational objectives. Performance appraisal systems and organizational productivity data are routinely computerized. Training needs assessment can be based on a comparison of computerized skill inventories against jobs' required KSAs. The *sanctions* process concerns the involvement of outside organizations such as unions in organizational personnel management. The success of a municipal negotiator, for example, will depend on how well documented the city's wage position is. An outside arbitrator will accept the position as reasonable only if comparative wage data show that the salaries and benefits proposed by the city are comparable with those of employees in similar jobs in similar communities; or that the existing tax structure will not support increased personnel costs. Both require access to a HRMIS, one compatible with the systems in neighboring communities.

Despite widespread recognition that an HRMIS is important, some confusion exists concerning both the criteria that should be used to select such a system and the problems associated with its use. First, public personnel managers need to specify the *data elements* they need to provide the information required to answer questions such as those raised above. Data are the facts on employees and positions needed to assess organizational programs. For example, *position data* might include the salary range, occupational code, and organizational location of each position. *Employee data* might include each employee's age, sex, classification, duty location, seniority, pay, benefits, skill inventory, and affirmative action status.

These data elements are summarized to form *reports*. This is the function most often associated with a HRMIS. Report generation requires that personnel managers ask: "What reports do we need, and how often do we need them, in order to monitor agency inputs, activities, or outputs." In this context, employee skills and tax revenues might be considered inputs; programs are activities; and program results are outputs. Here are some typical reports produced periodically by personnel departments:

- Payroll: total personnel expenditures, by employee, during a pay period
- Human resource planning: number and classification of all filled or vacant organizational positions; turnover rate for selected departments or occupations
- Affirmative action compliance: race and sex of applicants and selections, by organizational unit or type of position
- Collective bargaining: total pay and benefit costs for employees covered by a collective bargaining agreement

Last, program planners use current reports as a means of predicting the future. For example, if health care costs for civil service employees have increased 12 percent annually over the past five years, it is reasonable to assume (barring a reduction in benefits or increased employee contributions) that they will increase 12 percent next year as well. This forecasting combines the use of current or past data with *modeling* (the development of assumptions about the future) to help predict the probable outcomes of alternative policy decisions.

To sum up, an HRMIS is used to collect and store data, to produce reports used to control and evaluate current programs, and to develop simulations to support policy decisions. Therefore, a good HRMIS is one that provides the kind of information needed to the people who need it when they need it. The personnel director must decide what the system needs to do before computer specialists decide how to do it; the HRMIS must be designed to be compatible with the larger organizational management information system (MIS); and computerization should be recognized as a change in work technology that also involves such issues as employee acceptance, job redesign, and training. Because the costs of some applications are high, HRMIS systems designers need to balance them against user expectations and capabilities.

An HRMIS can also provide essential assistance to political leaders and stakeholders who wish an agency's programs to remain responsive to policy pressures originating outside the agency. In these cases, data supportive or critical of an agency's performance are compiled into reports that "drive" the agency's planning, control and evaluation activities. Elected officials, agency managers, or interest groups use these reports to induce changes in organizational policies or procedures (or to compel those changes, if legal sanctions were involved). For example:

- Interest groups or compliance agencies supporting the value of social equity would use utilization data to reinforce their contention that the organization should increase affirmative action efforts.
- Legislators seeking to control or direct the activities of an agency would use resource allocation data (size of budgets, number of positions) to do so. For example, a city commission seeking to restrict the power of an independent police department would do so by limiting the size of its payroll budget, or by refusing to authorize new positions in that agency.
- Managers seeking to increase administrative efficiency would use productivity-related data to recommend changes in work methods. For instance, a city manager concerned about personnel costs in a solid waste department might restrict the use of overtime, investigate possible abuse of sick leave or fraudulent worker's compensation claims, or study the comparative cost effectiveness of privatizing this activity.
- Unions seeking to stop a privatization proposal might compare wages, benefits, and productivity data for a public solid waste agency with similar figures for its private competitors.

A more extensive list of these HRMIS applications is shown in Table 14-1.

TABLE 14-1   HRMIS Applications to Program Evaluation

ACTIVITY	HRMIS APPLICATIONS
Planning	
Human resource planning	Compile inventory of current employees skills; determine whether these meet forecast future needs
Job analysis and classification	How many employees are in different occupations?
Compensation	Determine current pay and benefit costs for all employees; project the cost of alternative proposed pay and benefit packages
Acquisition	
Affirmative action	Compare actual utilization of particular groups with their representation in the labor market; assess organizational affirmative action plan compliance
Recruitment	Compile new hire estimates based on anticipated staffing needs; are current recruitment efforts sufficient to meet them?
Selection	Do an applicant's qualifications meet minimum standards for a given position? Do selected applicants meet performance standards for their positions?
Development	
Productivity	Record performance of organizational units; compare to other units or previous time periods
Performance appraisal	Record employee performance; compare to other employees, performance standards, or previous time periods
Training and development	Summarize training activities and costs; assess training needs by comparing skills; assess OD needs by measuring organizational climate
Employee motivation and job design	Measure employee productivity, turnover, absenteeism, and internal motivation; assess effect of changes in job design on productivity and motivation
Safety	Record injuries, accidents, and illnesses; use these data to change safety regulations, selection criteria, or employee orientation
Sanction	
Labor-management relations	Collect and compare salary and benefit data against that of other positions or jurisdictions; compute the cost of proposed changes in pay and benefits

TABLE 14-1 *(Continued)*

ACTIVITY	HRMIS APPLICATIONS
Discipline and grievances	Compile reports on the number and type of grievances and disciplinary actions; use these data to recommend changes in work rules, employee orientation, or supervisory training
Constitutional rights of employees	Record cases of sexual harassment or civil rights violations; use these to improve affirmative action compliance, employee orientation, or supervisory training
Control and Adaptation	
Evaluation	Collect data through HRMIS to evaluate all public personnel management activities

6. PUBLIC PERSONNEL MANAGEMENT IS CHARACTERIZED BY CONTINUAL CONFLICT AMONG COMPETING SYSTEMS, VALUES, AND STAKEHOLDERS

Public personnel management can be viewed from several perspectives. First, it is the functions (planning, acquisition, allocation, development, and sanction) needed to manage human resources in public agencies. Second, it is the process by which a scarce resource (public jobs) is allocated. Third, it reflects the influence of four competing values (political responsiveness, efficiency, individual rights, and social equity) over how public jobs should be allocated. Fourth, it is the laws, rules and regulations used to express these abstract values—personnel systems (political appointments, civil service, collective bargaining, and affirmative action). Fifth, it reflects the competing stakeholders (managers, employees, clients, and political leaders) that seek to control how public jobs are allocated, as well as how the other personnel functions are performed. The history of public personnel management in the United States, and its history within each government level and agency, can be understood conceptually and operationally as the conflict among competing personnel systems and values.

7. PUBLIC PERSONNEL MANAGEMENT IS DYNAMIC, EVOLVING, AND EMERGENT

Public personnel management may be viewed as static or dynamic. Traditional personnel managers view the field as narrow and static. They picture it as a collection of administrative techniques applied within a structure of rules, policies, and laws that clearly define the limits of acceptable professional behavior. They see themselves as continually acting within a consensus on one system and its underlying values. They tend to define themselves, and to be defined by others, as technical specialists working within a staff agency.

More contemporary public personnel managers view the field as emergent and dynamic. They tend to define themselves, and to be defined by others, as interpreters or mediators among competing systems, stakeholders, and values. They see themselves as professionals whose role involves a blend of technical skills and ethical decision making, and as key players in developing corporate human resource management strategy. The essence of this emergent professional public personnel management role is *synergy*, the exploitation of pressure points where conflicting systems compete and converge, and the reconciliation of conflicting values, changing conditions, competing stakeholders, and a diverse work force into a coherent and dynamic whole.

8. PUBLIC PERSONNEL MANAGERS AND EMPLOYEES HAVE OPPORTUNITIES TO DESIGN FLEXIBLE AND EFFECTIVE HUMAN RESOURCE MANAGEMENT SYSTEMS

The professional public personnel manager is a corporate human resource specialist whose objective is to maximize human resource development and utilization within the agency. Human resources are not a constant, but a variable. Their value can be altered at will by structural and functional changes that enhance or inhibit employees from using their energies and abilities toward the accomplishment of agency mission.

This requires that corporate human resource managers function as organization design and development specialists. They must create and exploit conflict and ambiguity to their organizational advantage.[10] Here are some examples of how this can be done. Within bureaucratic organizations, jobs are usually designed and classified hierarchically on a rank-in-job basis because of the traditional focus on job classification and evaluation. But rank-in-job systems inadequately reflect the impact of individuals on work, the shifting nature of individual contributions to agency mission, and the networking and group activities that must occur for agencies to be successful. One response to this dilemma might be to create a personnel agency comprised of staff specialists classified according to rank-in-person standards, but evaluated and rewarded on a project team basis.

In sum, the conflicting systems, and the conflict they would generate within the organization, would be used to create the possibilities of change and the energy to carry them out.

9. PUBLIC PERSONNEL MANAGERS MUST DEVELOP RESOURCES BY INSTITUTIONALIZING CHANGE

Over the past ten years much research has been conducted concerning organizational innovation. Most of the research, however, has been about technical innovation, not administrative innovation. Yet the strategic design of human resource management systems and structures for the purpose of making agencies more effective is an administrative innovation. This leads to the issue of what causes or enhances administrative innovation in public agencies.

After controlling for external and organizational variables, research studies conclude that the professional role, and the self-perception of that role, is the major factor that leads key agency players to undertake and successfully complete administrative innovations. Those who see themselves as professionals, who recognize the dynamism and conflict inherent in their roles, are more likely to innovate. Both the extent to which they represent a departure from traditional organization policy and practice and the scope of their application (the number of employees they affect) are likely to be greater.[11]

Innovation carries the risk of failure, for it represents experimentation with the unknown. Therefore, those organizations interested (for their own survival's sake) in encouraging innovation must select human resource managers (and other managers) who are experienced and positive risk-takers. Fortunately, the same systems, structures, and rewards the organization uses to exploit dynamism and conflict also create the situations to which public personnel directors must respond. By creating these situations, and by encouraging managers to respond creatively and take some risks, the agency can use dynamism not only to force change and augment human resources, but to develop personnel managers who have leadership ability as well as technical skills.

10. ATTRACTING "THE BEST AND THE BRIGHTEST" TO THE PUBLIC SERVICE

During the New Deal of the 1930s, and again during the 1960s, public service was a desirable profession. It attracted intelligent and motivated people who were idealistic and concerned about the ways in which public agencies could help solve social problems. Now, following a decade of disillusionment with politics (a natural reaction to Watergate) and another decade of amoral selfishness (epitomized by corporate excesses and leveraged buy outs), Americans are understandably less hopeful about the possibilities for social change and the role of government in that process. And although the need for public services (and for a "public service" to perform them) has never been greater, it can only be met if government agencies succeed once again in attracting "the best and the brightest." How do you attract and retain people who are intelligent and humane risk-takers to public service?

By this point, it should be clear that attracting such people is the last step in the equation, not the first. Public service will be attractive if agencies have a clear and worthwhile mission, a demonstrated interest in maintaining and utilizing a diverse workforce, and a clear focus on treating employees as human resource assets rather than as production costs. This means changing the perspectives of political leaders, agency managers, and personnel directors so that the culture of public agencies will change, and then using this cultural "thaw" to tip the internal climate of agencies from the current focus on inertia, caution, and hierarchy (people have learned that to stick your neck out is to risk having your head cut off or being "cut out of the loop") to a new focus on growth, risk, and networking.

It is only when these changes in organizational culture become institutionalized, and when inertia, risk aversion, and hierarchy become the exception rather than the rule, that public agencies will once again be able to attract the best and the brightest.

SUMMARY

The emphasis on a combination of personnel functions, values, and personnel systems has gradually fostered the realization that professionalism in human resources management cannot be limited simply to technical functions. While civil service systems will remain at the forefront of public employment, the "bogey-man" image of political spoils and politicization of the public service does not seem to capture the public interest as it once did. In the future, it seems more likely that civil service systems, like their competitors (affirmative action, collective bargaining, contracting out, and patronage) will be judged more in terms of their contribution to agency mission accomplishment than on their self-evident virtue or moral superiority.

Incorporated into the strategic thinking fostered by advocates of productivity are two related factors affecting tomorrow's organizations: diversity and organizational justice. Diversity results in differences in perceptions of what constitutes a "just" employee-employer relationship. Whether tomorrow's organizations can channel the diversity of the workforce into productivity might very well be the major challenge of the 1990s. Contributing to that challenge will be the role internal organizational mechanisms play in helping to negotiate and resolve differences. As citizens we are much better at articulating our differences than dealing with them; and there is no reason to believe as managers we will act any differently without strong leadership commitments to the virtues of tolerance, respect, and dignity.

The first chapter of this book portrayed public personnel management as representing the fundamental conflict among four opposing values (political responsiveness, efficiency, individual rights, and social equity). It is neither logically inconsistent nor impractical that the last chapter should close by presenting the view that these four values, and the public personnel systems they represent, are fundamentally reconcilable as well as contradictory. Collective bargaining developed out of a need to ensure organizational justice for individuals, affirmative action out of a similar need to ensure organizational justice and acceptance of diversity for historically disadvantaged groups. Both organizational justice and acceptance of diversity are necessary for organizational productivity—the accomplishment of strategic missions through the effective use of human resources. And productivity is the ultimate criterion by which our society measures the political acceptability of alternative public personnel systems.

KEY TERMS

agency mission
capital asset
corporate human resource policy
data elements
demography
employee data
human resource asset accounting (HRAC)
human resource management
human resource management information system (HRMIS)
individual development plan (IDP)
management information system (MIS)
manage to budget
manage to mission
modeling
organizational justice
position data
public policy
public service
reports
strategic human resource capability

synergy
workforce diversity
work management

DISCUSSION QUESTIONS

1. What is the relationship between professionalism in public personnel managers and dynamism and conflict among public personnel systems, values, and stakeholders?

2. Is it possible to change design bureaucratic organizations so that operating divisions, budget officers, and human resource managers can develop and carry out mission-focused resource allocation and program evaluation? If so, how?

3. What is the relationship between the role of the public personnel manager and the future of public service?

4. How do organizational justice and acceptance of workforce diversity affect agency productivity?

5. At heart, is the relationship among alternative public personnel systems characterized by conflict or mutual interdependence?

CASE STUDY

You are the human resource manager within a large federal government agency. The agency's mission is to provide a range of human services to individual clients, and to work with other stake holders to design and implement systems that support this mission. The agency has about 120,000 employees, most of whom work in regional offices around the country.

Personnel activities are performed centrally. The personnel department is divided into four functional areas: the office of human resource programs (which performs personnel activities), management information systems (which designs the data base for operating the personnel system), dispute resolution (which resolves appeals from employees arising through a number of grievance systems), and the office of strategic initiatives, which plans and evaluates human resource policy options for the agency.

Several years ago, the personnel director of the agency established a Center for Management Excellence (CME) within the Office of Human Resource Programs (OHRP). The function of the center is to serve as a matrix organization of project teams within the more bureaucratic structure of the OHRP. CME employees are typically young management interns and professionals who seek assignment with the center because it gives them the opportunity to work flexibly on mission-related assignments they perceive to be career-enhancing.

The CME has a mixed reputation within the OHRP (and the agency in general). It is partly viewed as a creative force for change that makes the agency more effective. And it is partly viewed with suspicion by operating personnel directors, who resent its "meddling" in their systems, and the "arrogance" of those they see as "afraid to get their hands dirty doing real personnel work."

The personnel director has decided to reduce this internal conflict and focus attention by combining the CME and the OHRP.

Task: Break into discussion groups, and focus on these issues:

1. How will employees of both organizational units (OHRP and CME) be likely to react to the proposed reorganization?
2. What steps should the personnel director take to reduce the negative effects of the merger, and to increase the chances that it will positively affect the mission of the agency?
3. What KSAs would you look for in the person chosen to direct the new unit, and how do these relate to the unit's mission?
4. How would you design an HRMIS that would meet the real data needs of personnel staff, case workers, and program evaluators?
5. How do you design human resource management systems that encourage employees to take risks, and to learn from them?
6. How would you design the organization's dispute resolution functions (such as grievances, affirmative action complaints, and sexual harassment prevention programs) to promote organizational justice and acceptance of work force diversity?

NOTES

[1]Public Law 101–576 (Chief Financial Officers Act of 1990), November 15, 1990; and U.S. Office of Personnel Management, *Manage to Budget Programs* (Washington, DC: Office of Systems Innovation and Simplification, Personnel Systems and Oversight Group, PSOG-203), August 1989.

[2]Tom Shoop, "Paying for Performance," *Government Executive*, May 1991, pp. 16–18.

[3]National Academy of Public Administration, *Modernizing Federal Classification: An Opportunity for Excellence* (Washington, DC: NAPA, July 1991).

[4]U.S. Office of Personnel Management, *Strategic Plan for Federal Human Resource Management* (Washington, DC: Office of Systems Innovation and Simplification, November 1990).

[5]U.S. Office of Personnel Management, *Federal Total Quality Management Handbook* (Washington, DC: Federal Quality Institute, May 1991).

[6]William Rodarmor, "The Diversity Project's Troy Duster, *California Monthly, 102,* 1 (September 1991), 40–45.

[7]Gretchen Haight, "Managing Diversity," *Across the Board 27* (March 1990), 22–30; and Julie Solomon, "Firms Address Workers' Cultural Variety: the Differences are Celebrated, Not Suppressed," *The Wall Street Journal,* February 10, 1989, p. B-1.

[8]William C. Pyle, "Monitoring Human Resources—'On Line'", *Michigan Business Review 22,* 4 (July 1970), 19–32; and E. G. Flamholtz, *Human Resource Accounting* (Encino, CA: Dickenson, 1974).

[9]Torrey Whitman and Albert Hyde, "HRIS, Matching the Right Person to the Right Position," *Defense Management Journal,* March 1978, pp. 28–35.

[10]Marshall Sashkin, "Participative Management is an Ethical Imperative," *Organizational Dynamics 12,* 4 (Spring 1984), 5–22.

[11]Mohamed Sabet and Donald Klingner, "Professionalism and Administrative Innovation, *Journal of Public Administration Research and Theory,* pending.

INDEX